Ayu Watanabe

L♥DK

13

L♥DK
Ayu Watanabe
13

c o n t e n t s

#49 An Adult Lovey-Dovey ♡ Cohabitation

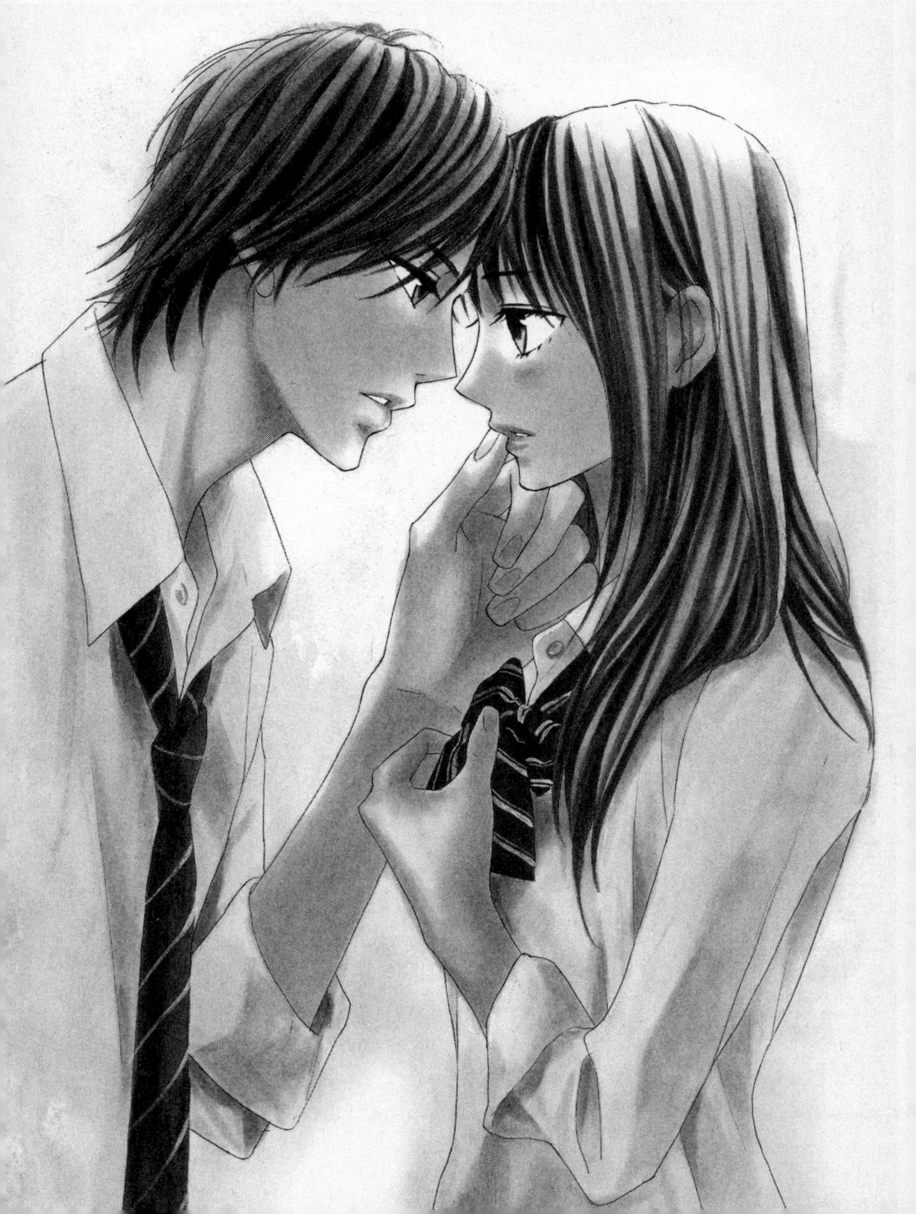

Story So Far

L♥DK

Story

High schooler Aoi lives in a super secret lovey-dovey ♡ living arrangement with Shusei, the boy everyone at school calls "Prince." Then the two start going out. As their feelings for each other grow ever deeper, they still have to uphold their promise to Aoi's father: "All sexual relations prohibited until graduation"!! What will happen now that Shusei's older sister, Eri, has shown up at the apartment of Sanjo, the boy who had had a crush on Aoi?!

Cast

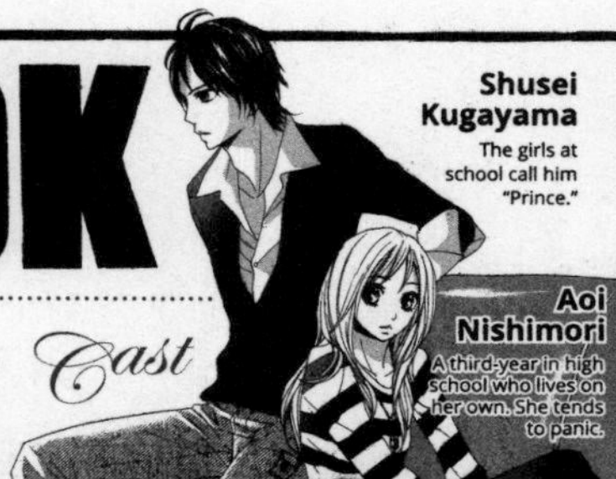

Shusei Kugayama
The girls at school call him "Prince."

Aoi Nishimori
A third-year in high school who lives on her own. She tends to panic.

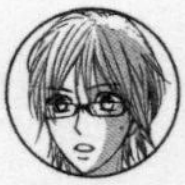

Wataru Sanjo
A neighbor who lives in the same apartment building as our two heroes.

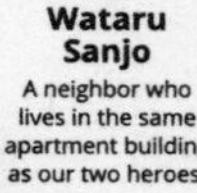

Eri Kugayama
Shusei's older sister.

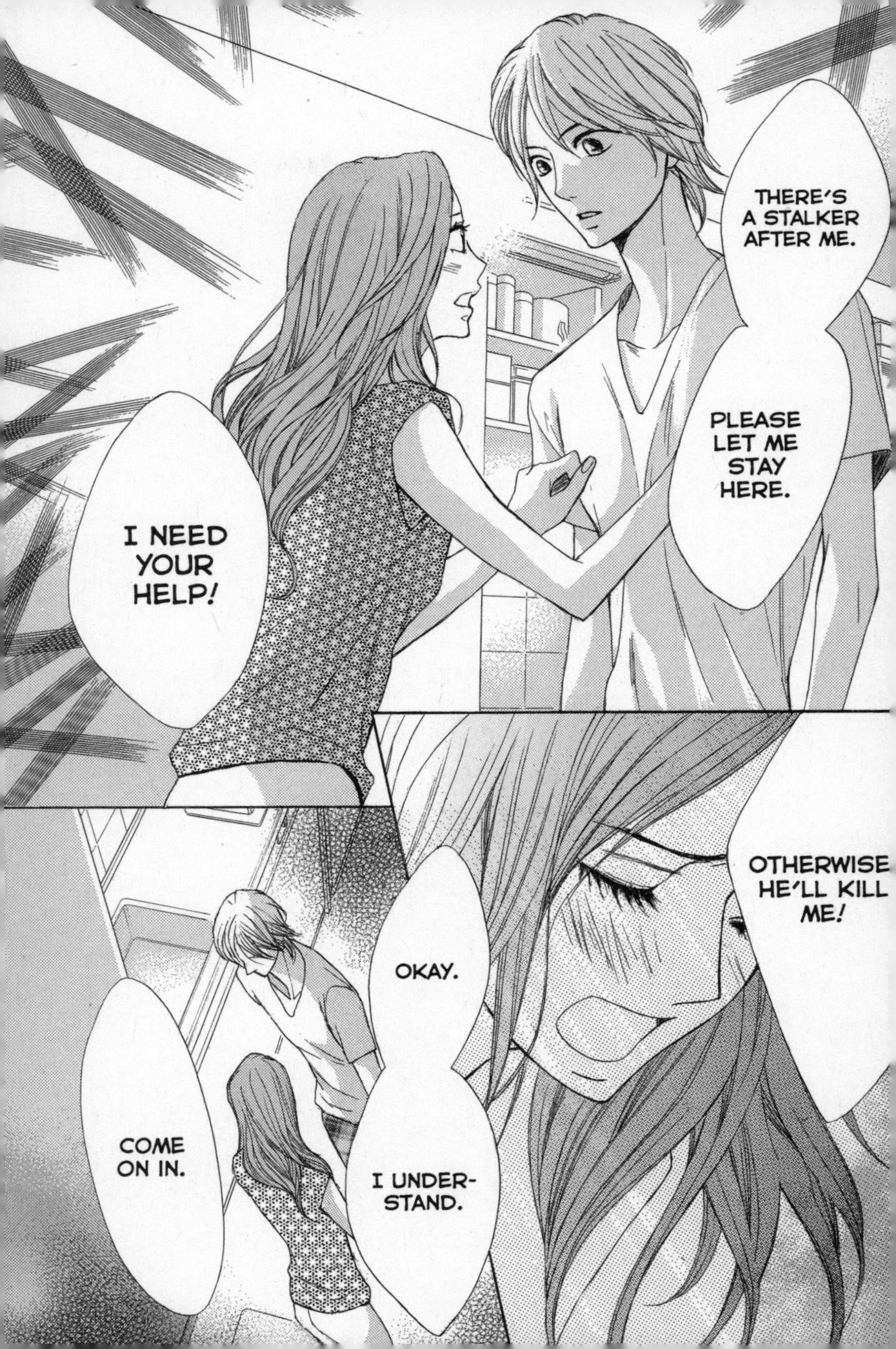
THERE'S A STALKER AFTER ME.
PLEASE LET ME STAY HERE.
I NEED YOUR HELP!
OTHERWISE HE'LL KILL ME!
OKAY.
I UNDER-STAND.
COME ON IN.

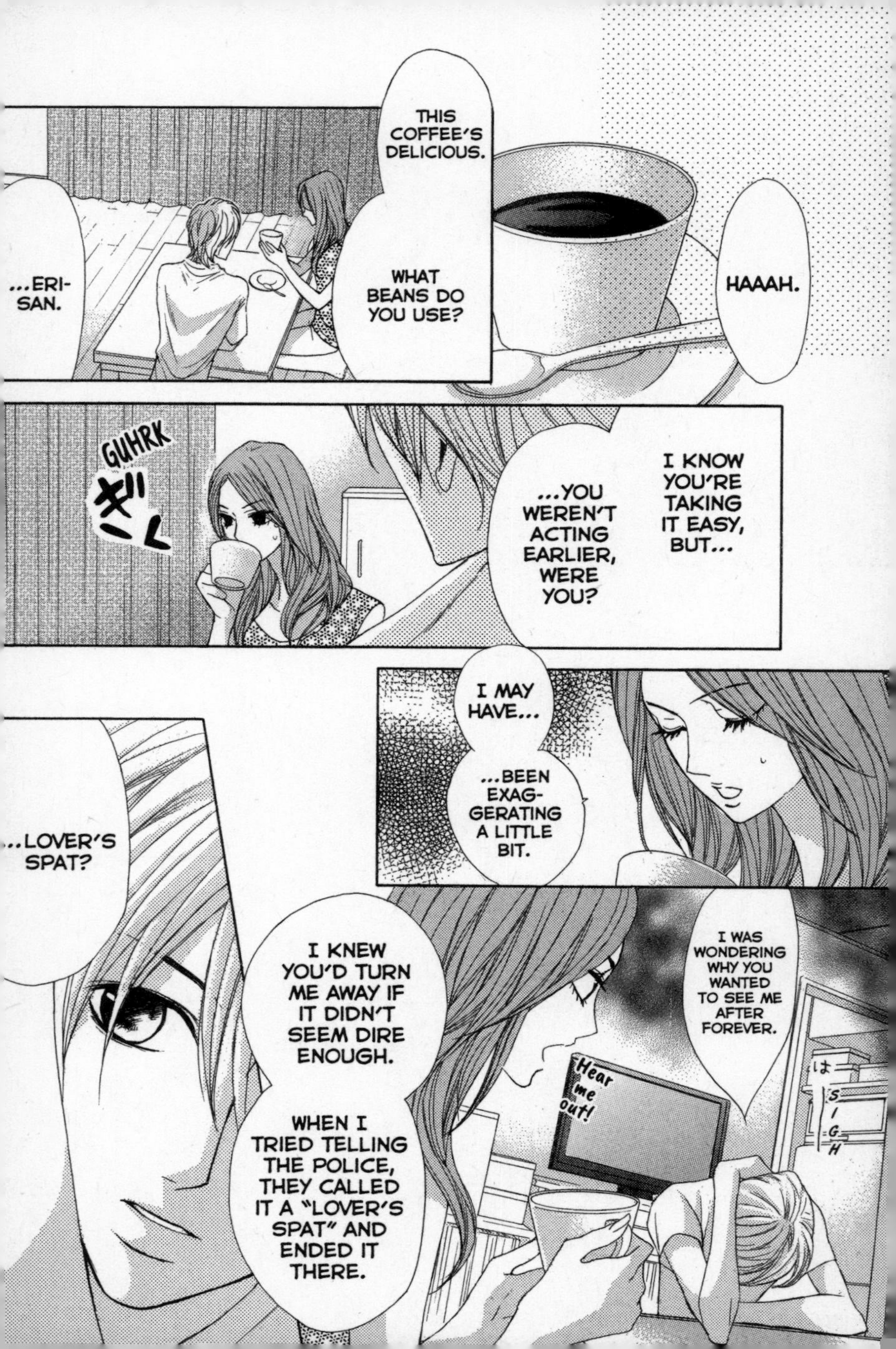
HAAAH.
THIS COFFEE'S DELICIOUS.
WHAT BEANS DO YOU USE?
...ERI-SAN.
I KNOW YOU'RE TAKING IT EASY, BUT...
...YOU WEREN'T ACTING EARLIER, WERE YOU?
GUHRK
ぎくっ
I MAY HAVE...
...BEEN EXAG-GERATING A LITTLE BIT.
...LOVER'S SPAT?
I WAS WONDERING WHY YOU WANTED TO SEE ME AFTER FOREVER.
は
SIGH
Hear me out!
I KNEW YOU'D TURN ME AWAY IF IT DIDN'T SEEM DIRE ENOUGH.
WHEN I TRIED TELLING THE POLICE, THEY CALLED IT A "LOVER'S SPAT" AND ENDED IT THERE.

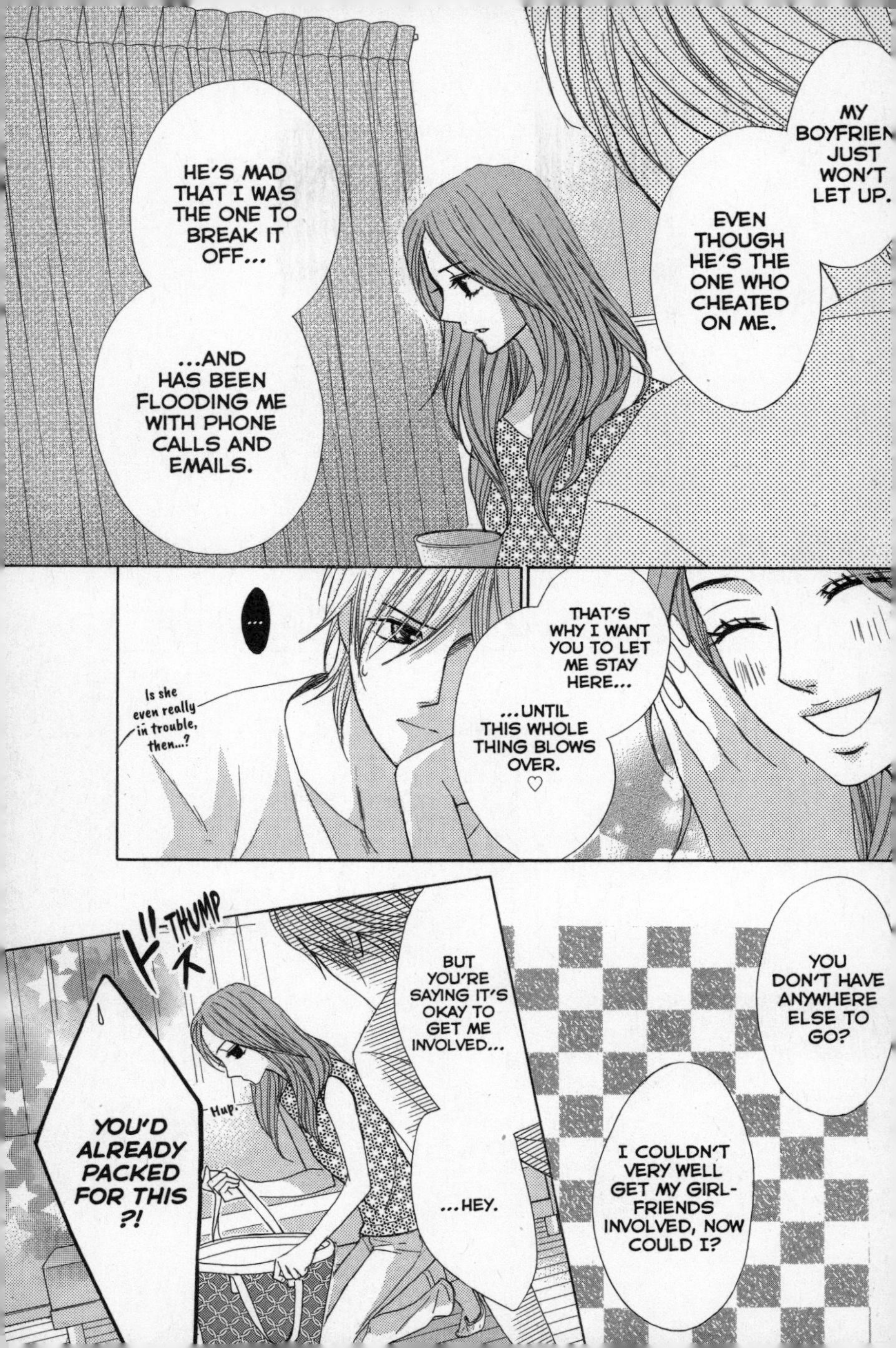
MY BOYFRIEN JUST WON'T LET UP.
EVEN THOUGH HE'S THE ONE WHO CHEATED ON ME.
HE'S MAD THAT I WAS THE ONE TO BREAK IT OFF...
...AND HAS BEEN FLOODING ME WITH PHONE CALLS AND EMAILS.
THAT'S WHY I WANT YOU TO LET ME STAY HERE...
...UNTIL THIS WHOLE THING BLOWS OVER. ♡
...
Is she even really in trouble, then...?
YOU DON'T HAVE ANYWHERE ELSE TO GO?
I COULDN'T VERY WELL GET MY GIRL-FRIENDS INVOLVED, NOW COULD I?
BUT YOU'RE SAYING IT'S OKAY TO GET ME INVOLVED...
...HEY.
ドス-THUMP
Hup.
YOU'D ALREADY PACKED FOR THIS?!

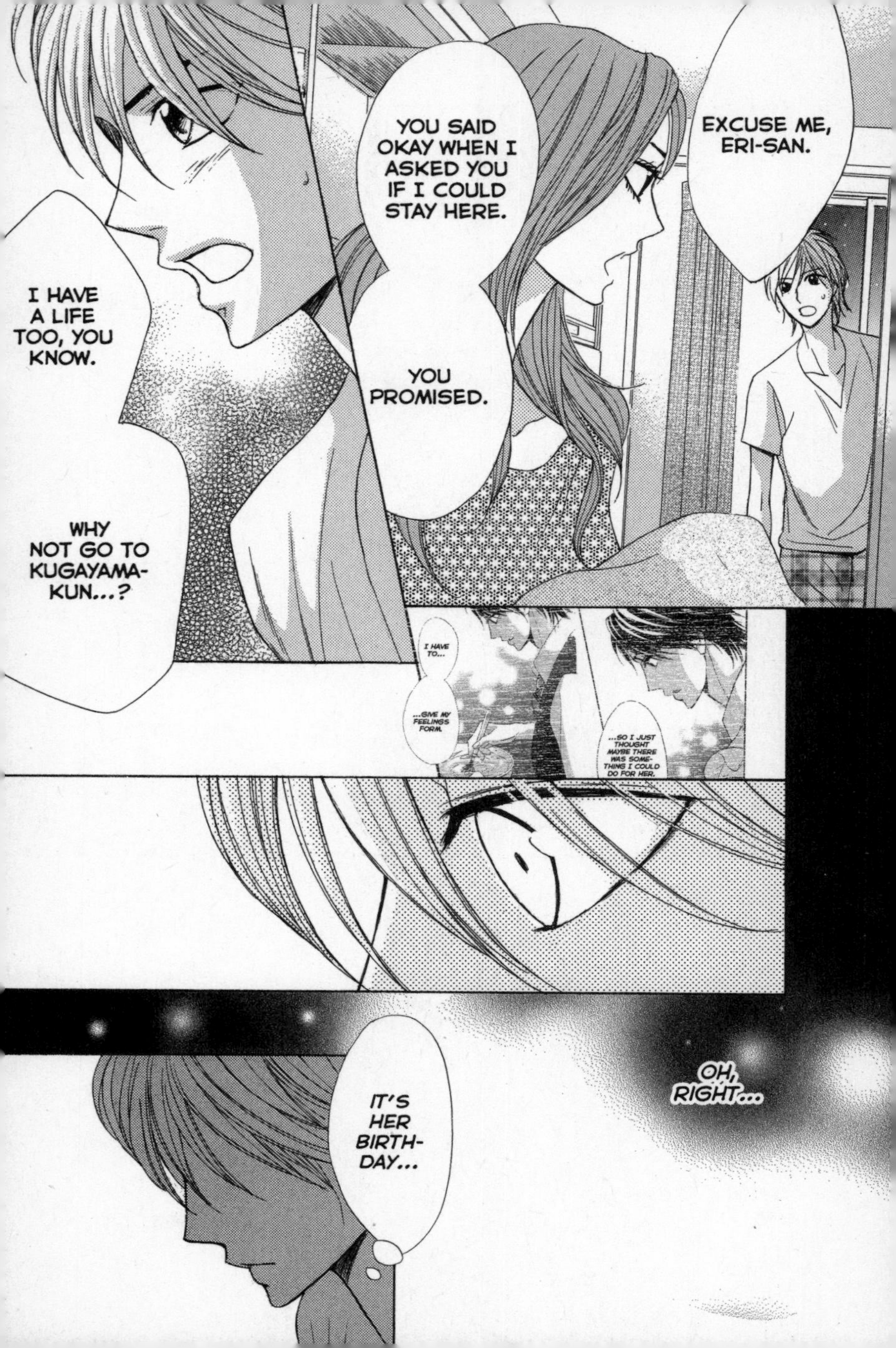
EXCUSE ME, ERI-SAN.
YOU SAID OKAY WHEN I ASKED YOU IF I COULD STAY HERE.
YOU PROMISED.
I HAVE A LIFE TOO, YOU KNOW.
WHY NOT GO TO KUGAYAMA-KUN...?
...SO I JUST THOUGHT MAYBE THERE WAS SOME-THING I COULD DO FOR HER.
I HAVE TO...
...GIVE MY FEELINGS FORM.
OH, RIGHT...
IT'S HER BIRTH-DAY...

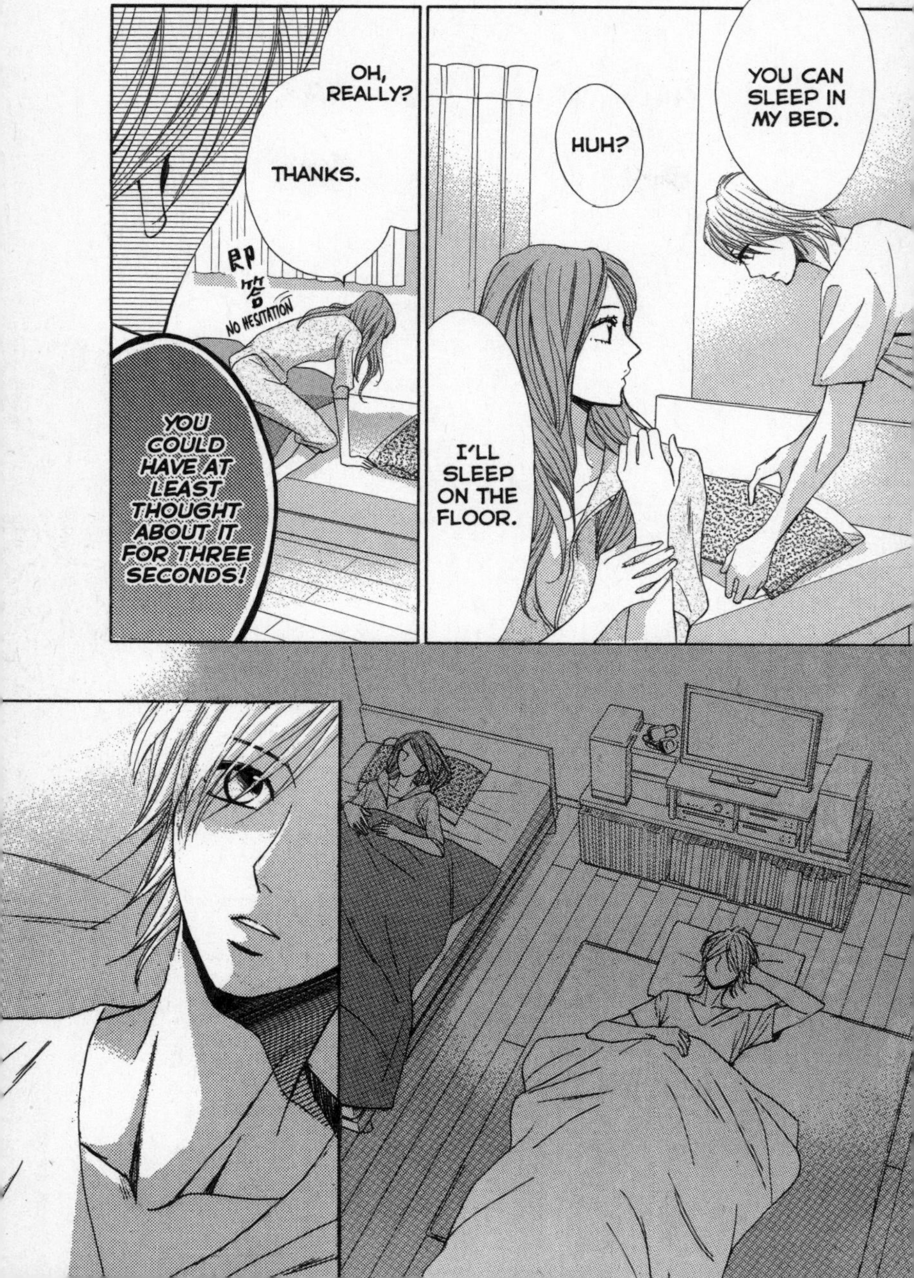
YOU CAN SLEEP IN MY BED.
HUH?
I'LL SLEEP ON THE FLOOR.
OH, REALLY?
THANKS.
即答
NO HESITATION
YOU COULD HAVE AT LEAST THOUGHT ABOUT IT FOR THREE SECONDS!

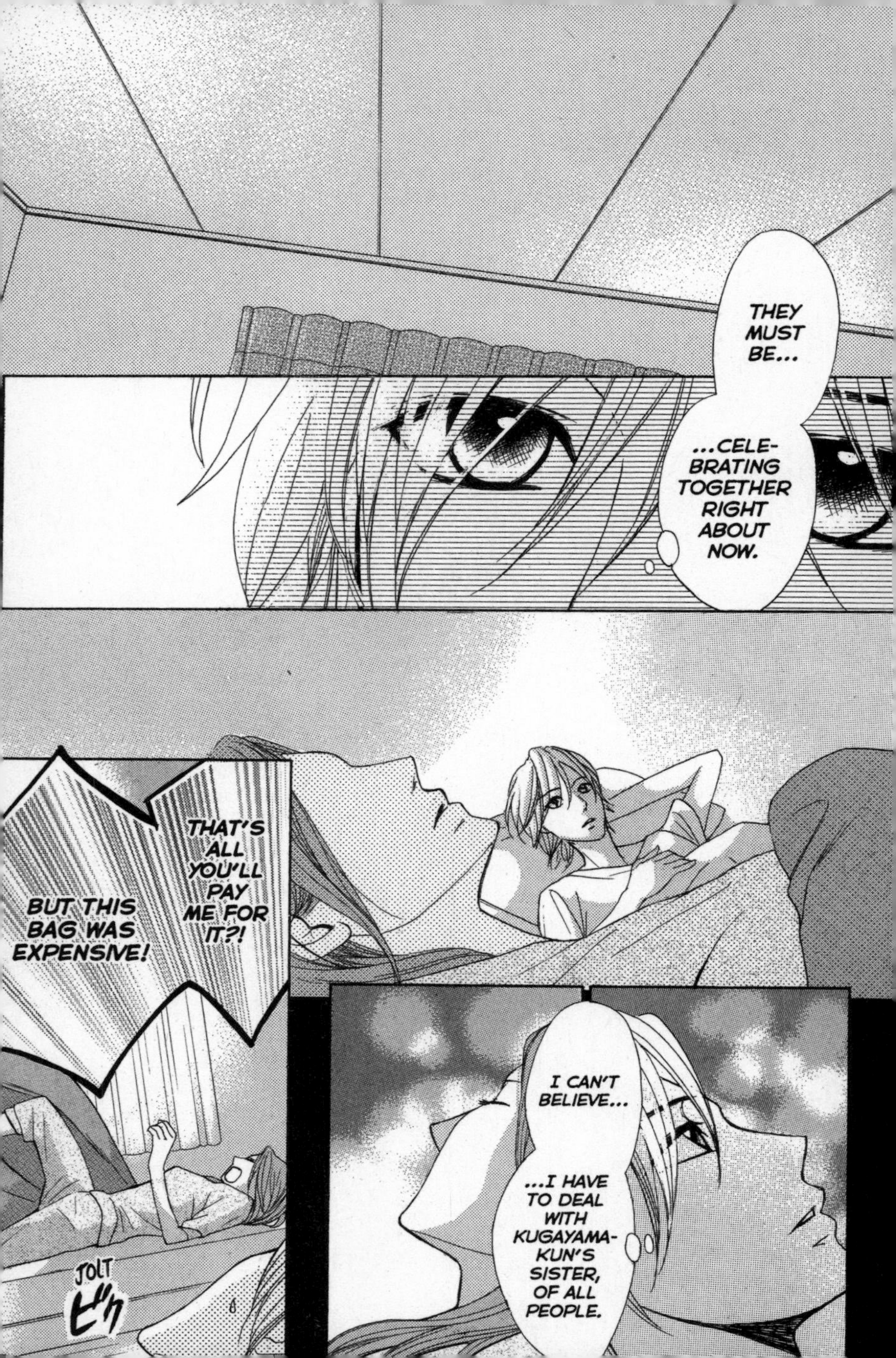
THEY MUST BE...
...CELE-BRATING TOGETHER RIGHT ABOUT NOW.
I CAN'T BELIEVE...
...I HAVE TO DEAL WITH KUGAYAMA-KUN'S SISTER, OF ALL PEOPLE.
THAT'S ALL YOU'LL PAY ME FOR IT?!
BUT THIS BAG WAS EXPENSIVE!
JOLT
ビク

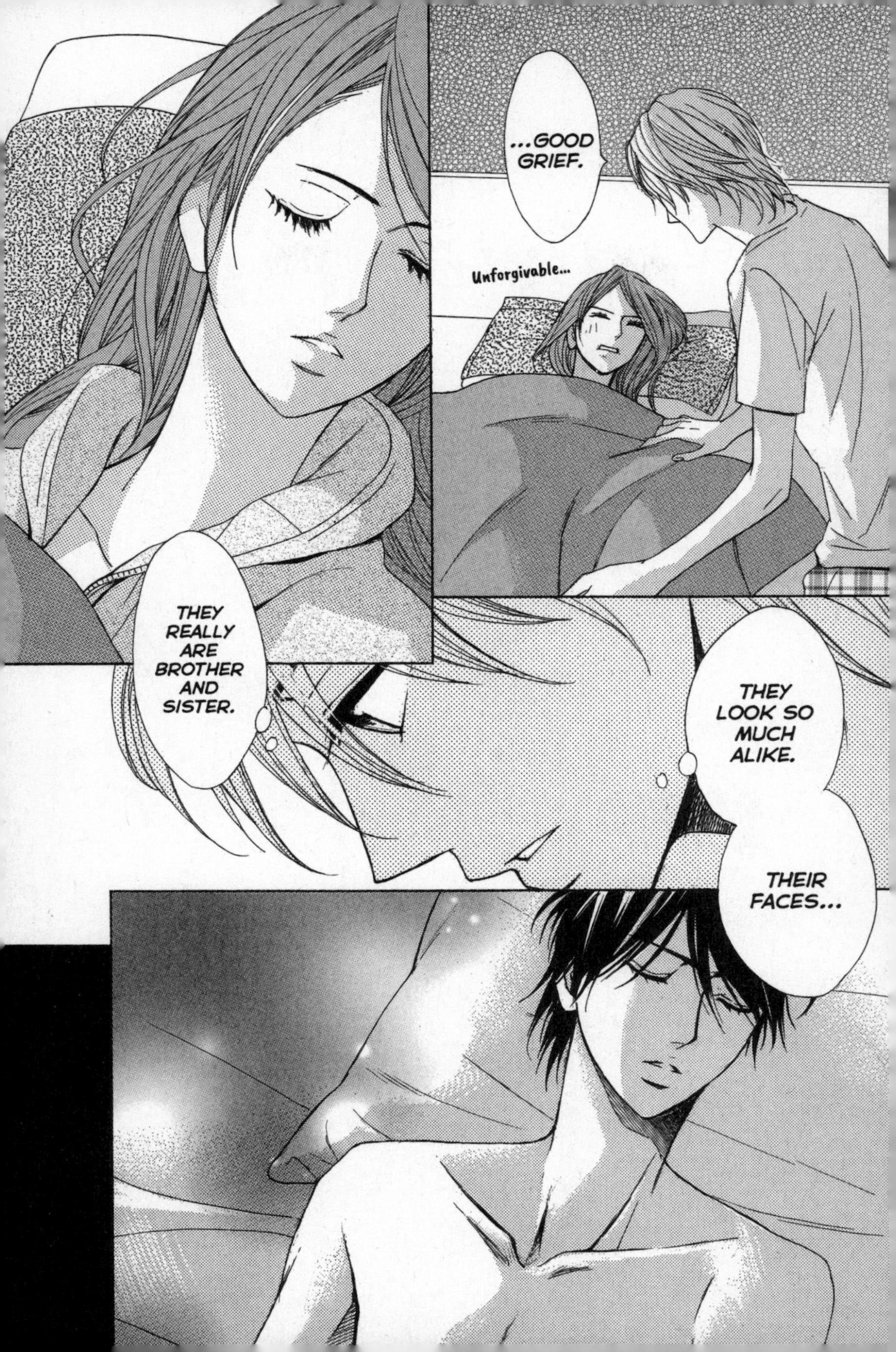
...GOOD GRIEF.
Unforgivable...
THEY LOOK SO MUCH ALIKE.
THEIR FACES...
THEY REALLY ARE BROTHER AND SISTER.

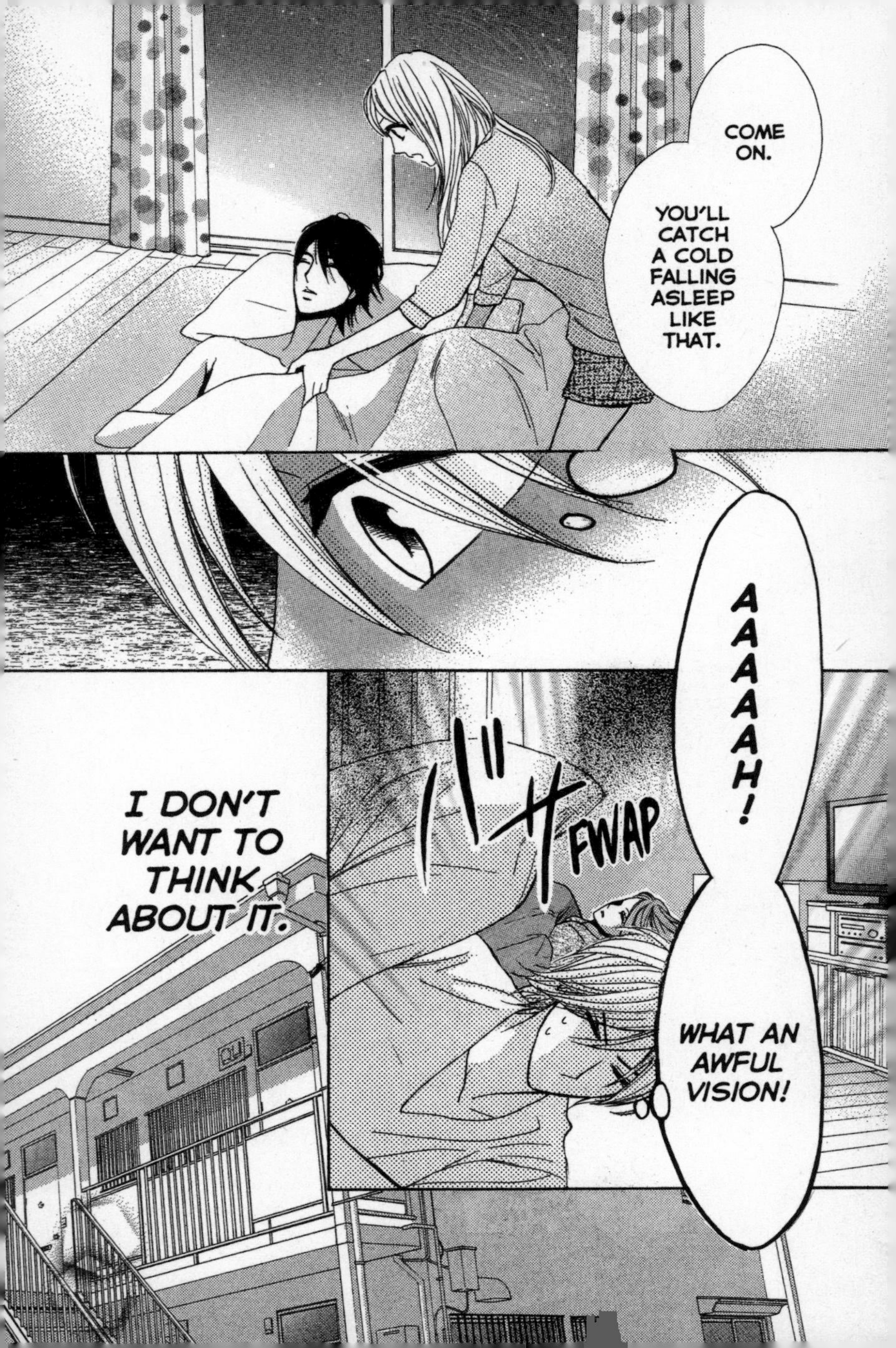
COME ON.
YOU'LL CATCH A COLD FALLING ASLEEP LIKE THAT.
AAAAAAH!
バッ
FWAP
WHAT AN AWFUL VISION!
I DON'T WANT TO THINK ABOUT IT.

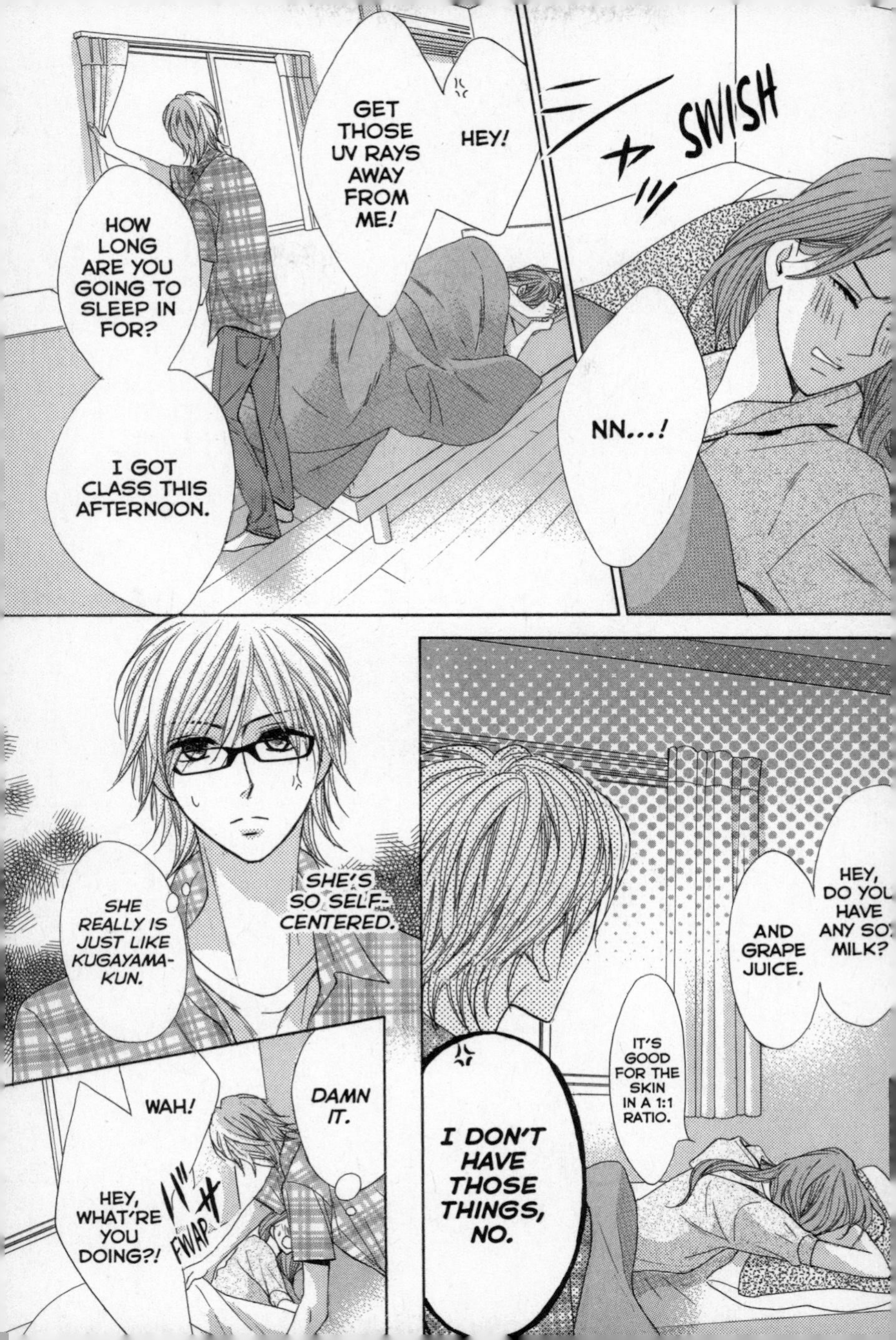
SWISH
NN...!
HEY!
GET THOSE UV RAYS AWAY FROM ME!
HOW LONG ARE YOU GOING TO SLEEP IN FOR?
I GOT CLASS THIS AFTERNOON.
HEY, DO YOU HAVE ANY SO MILK?
AND GRAPE JUICE.
IT'S GOOD FOR THE SKIN IN A 1:1 RATIO.
I DON'T HAVE THOSE THINGS, NO.
SHE'S SO SELF-CENTERED.
SHE REALLY IS JUST LIKE KUGAYAMA-KUN.
DAMN IT.
WAH!
FWAP
HEY, WHAT'RE YOU DOING?!

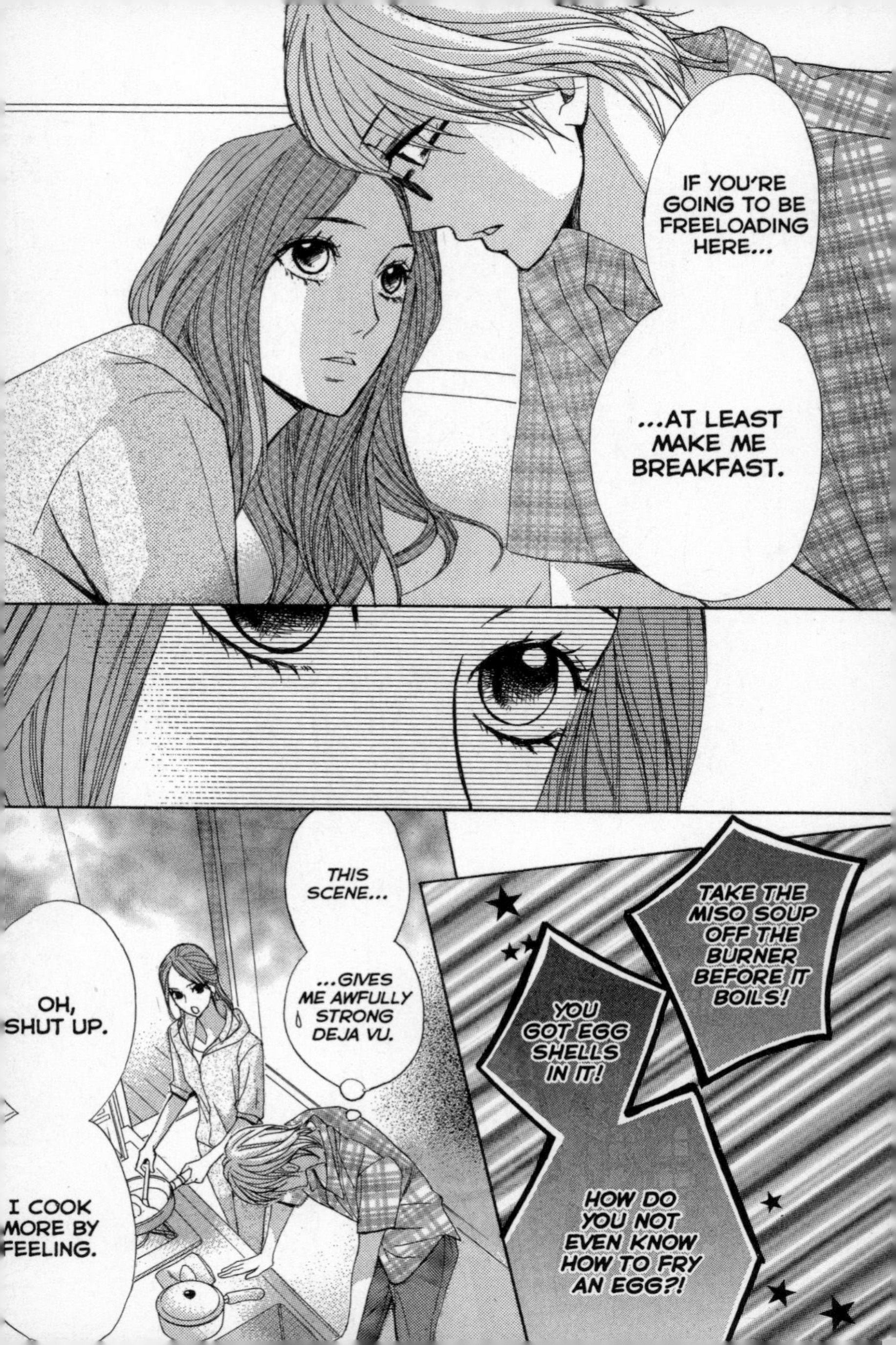
IF YOU'RE GOING TO BE FREELOADING HERE...
...AT LEAST MAKE ME BREAKFAST.
TAKE THE MISO SOUP OFF THE BURNER BEFORE IT BOILS!
YOU GOT EGG SHELLS IN IT!
HOW DO YOU NOT EVEN KNOW HOW TO FRY AN EGG?!
THIS SCENE...
...GIVES ME AWFULLY STRONG DEJA VU.
OH, SHUT UP.
I COOK MORE BY FEELING.

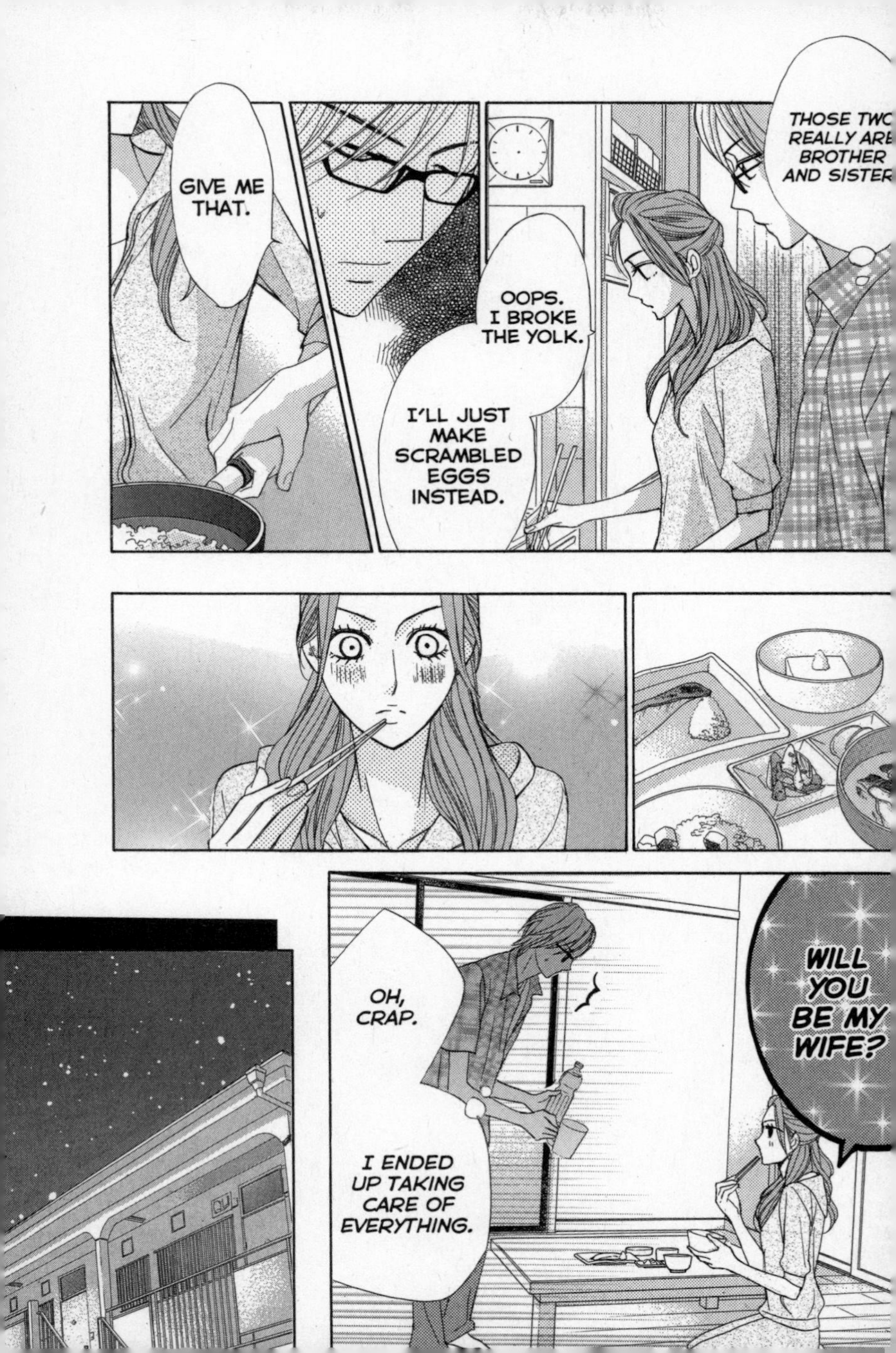
THOSE TWO REALLY ARE BROTHER AND SISTER
OOPS. I BROKE THE YOLK.
I'LL JUST MAKE SCRAMBLED EGGS INSTEAD.
GIVE ME THAT.
WILL YOU BE MY WIFE?
OH, CRAP.
I ENDED UP TAKING CARE OF EVERYTHING.

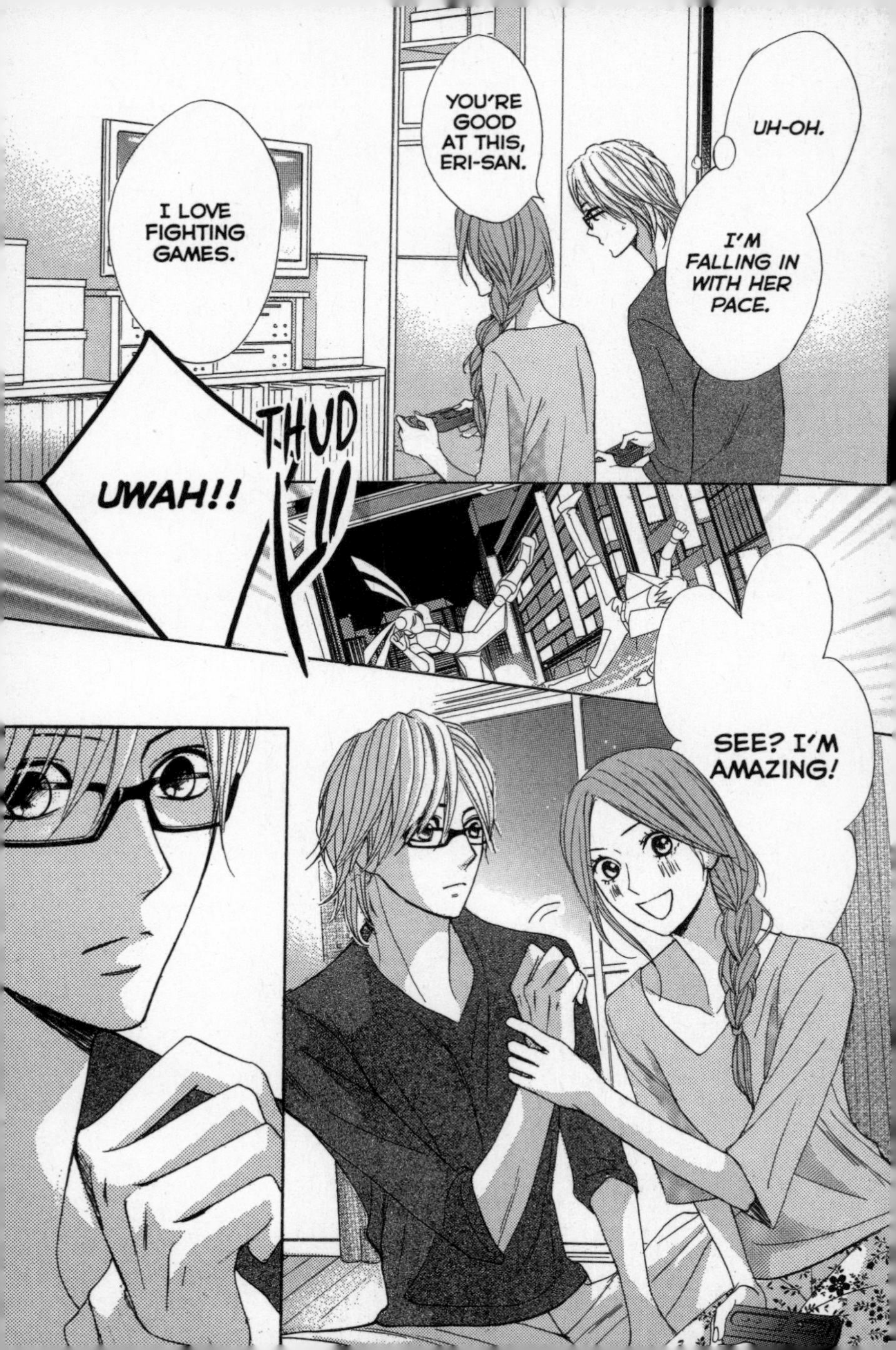
UH-OH.
I'M FALLING IN WITH HER PACE.
YOU'RE GOOD AT THIS, ERI-SAN.
I LOVE FIGHTING GAMES.
THUD
UWAH!!
SEE? I'M AMAZING!

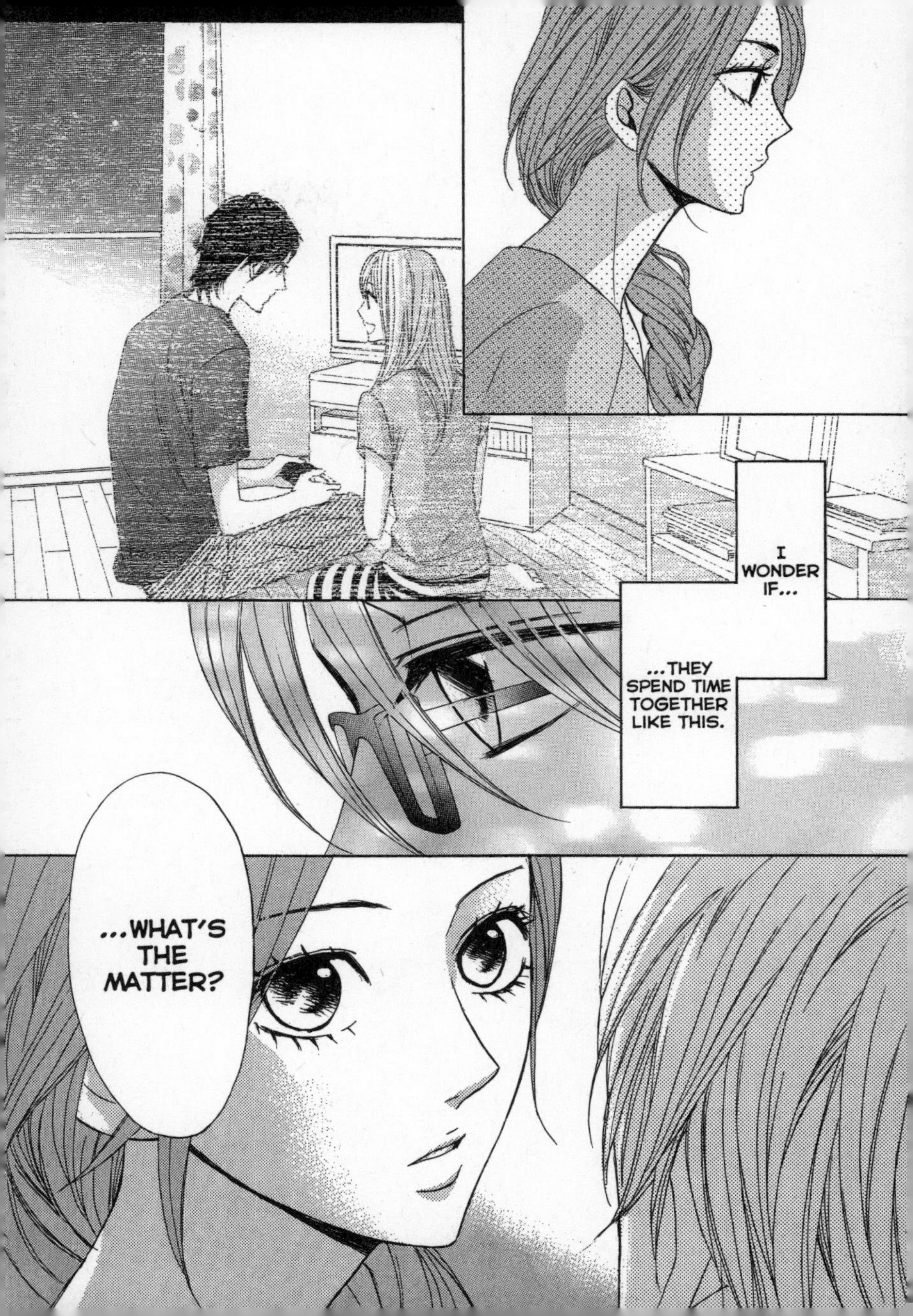
I WONDER IF...
...THEY SPEND TIME TOGETHER LIKE THIS.
...WHAT'S THE MATTER?

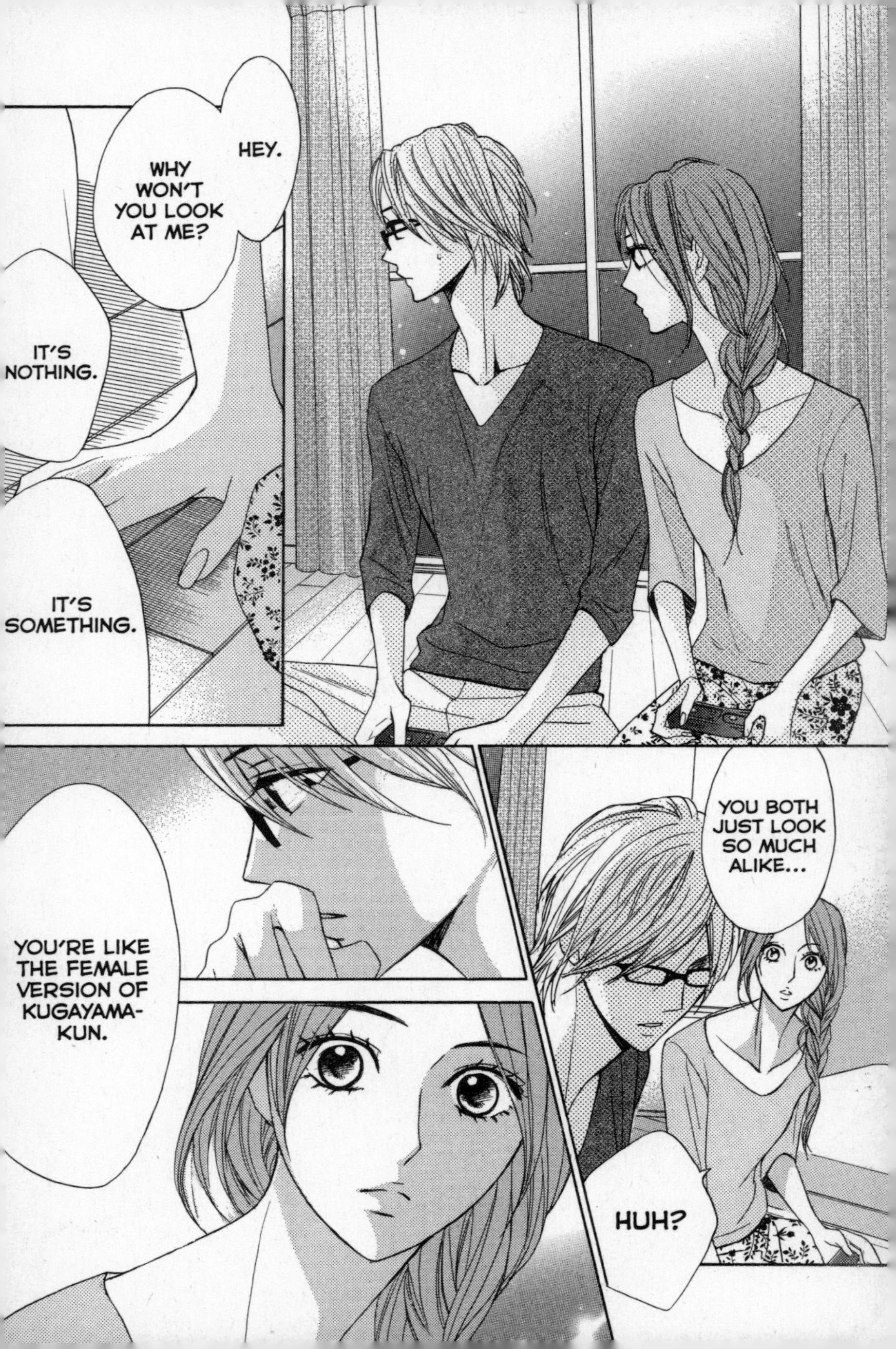
HEY. WHY WON'T YOU LOOK AT ME?
IT'S NOTHING.
IT'S SOMETHING.
YOU BOTH JUST LOOK SO MUCH ALIKE...
HUH?
YOU'RE LIKE THE FEMALE VERSION OF KUGAYAMA-KUN.

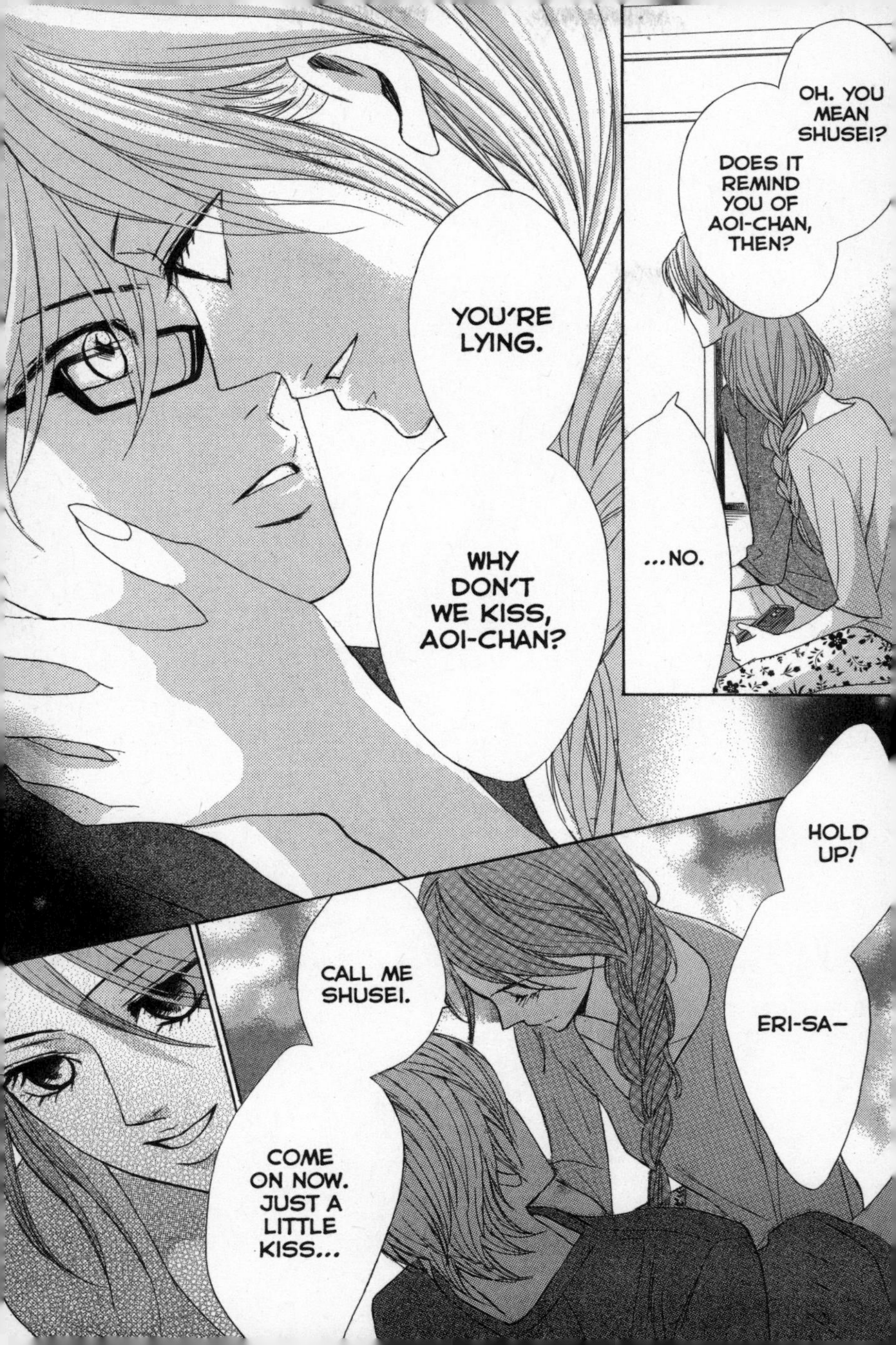
OH. YOU MEAN SHUSEI?
DOES IT REMIND YOU OF AOI-CHAN, THEN?
...NO.
YOU'RE LYING.
WHY DON'T WE KISS, AOI-CHAN?
HOLD UP!
ERI-SA—
CALL ME SHUSEI.
COME ON NOW. JUST A LITTLE KISS...

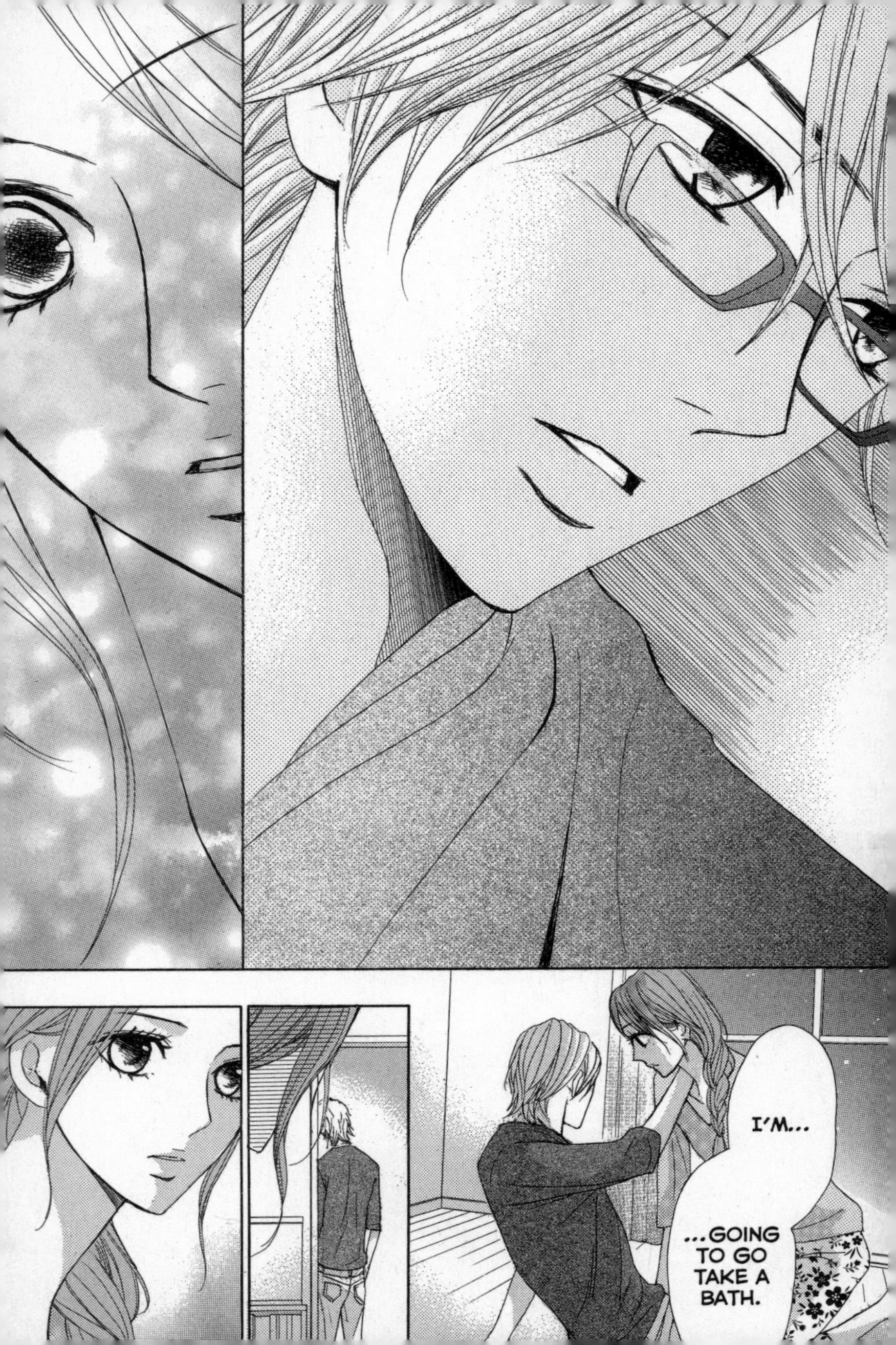
I'M...
...GOING TO GO TAKE A BATH.

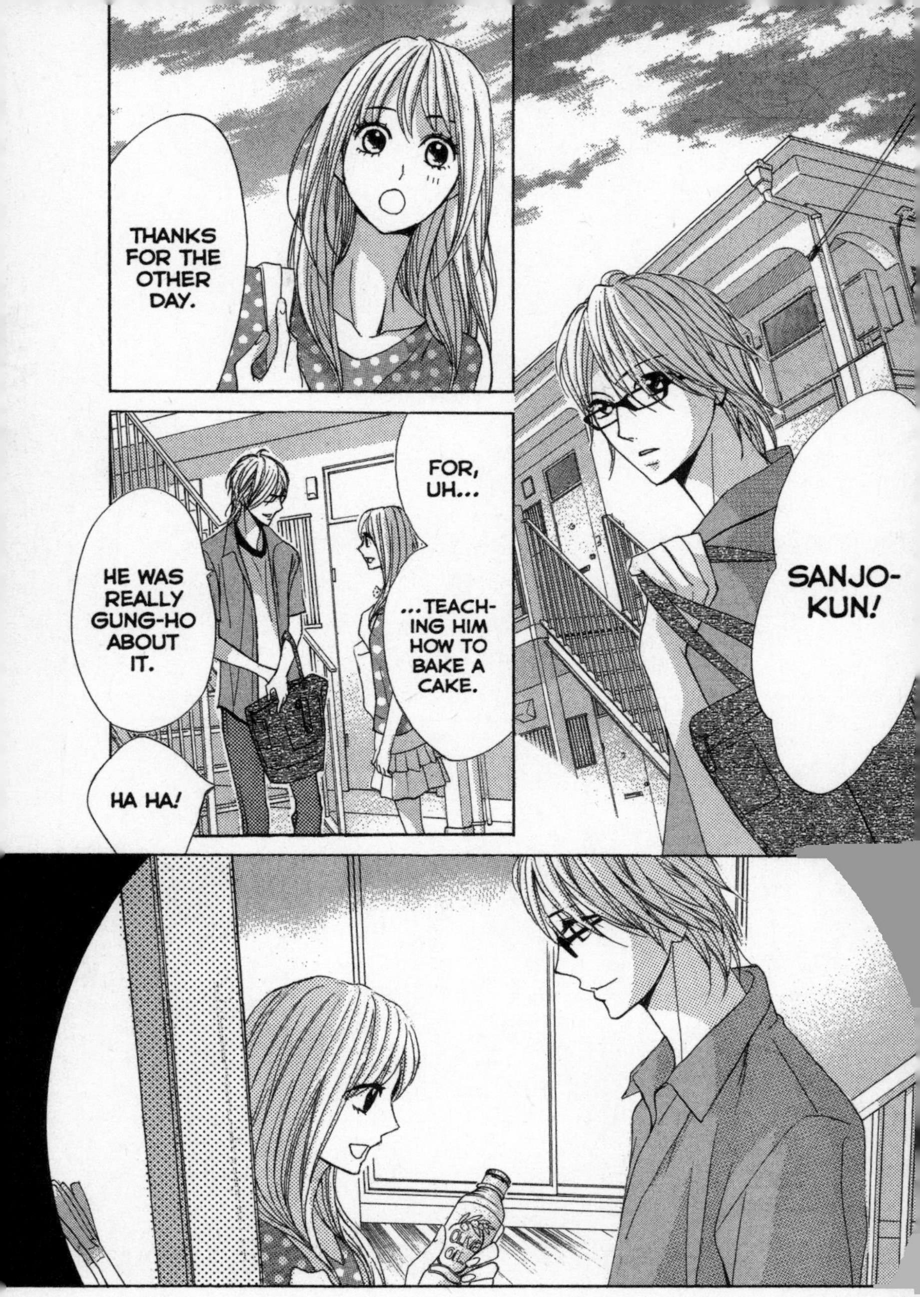
SANJO-KUN!
THANKS FOR THE OTHER DAY.
FOR, UH...
...TEACHING HIM HOW TO BAKE A CAKE.
HE WAS REALLY GUNG-HO ABOUT IT.
HA HA!

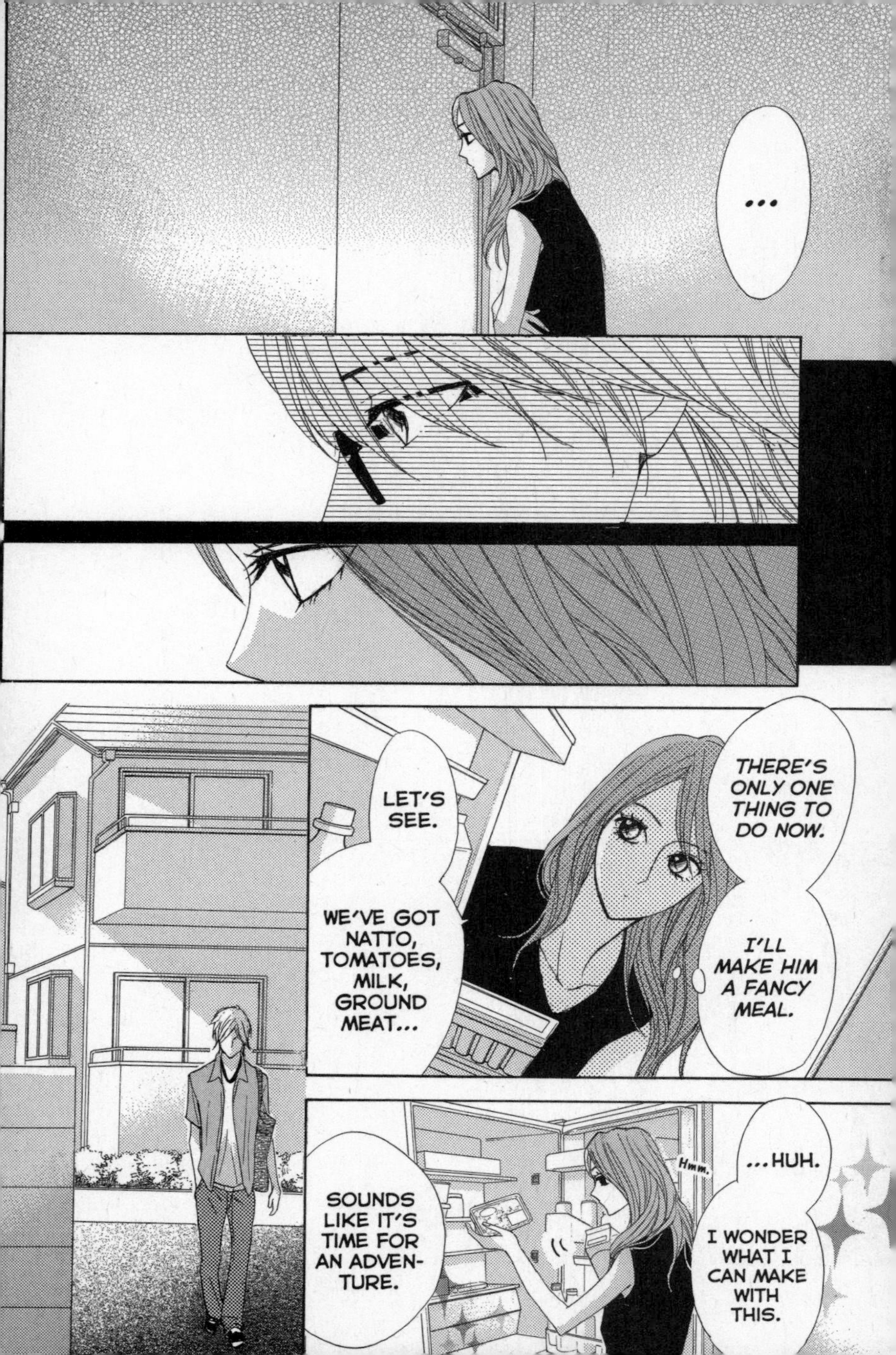
...
THERE'S ONLY ONE THING TO DO NOW.
I'LL MAKE HIM A FANCY MEAL.
LET'S SEE.
WE'VE GOT NATTO, TOMATOES, MILK, GROUND MEAT...
...HUH.
Hmm.
I WONDER WHAT I CAN MAKE WITH THIS.
SOUNDS LIKE IT'S TIME FOR AN ADVEN-TURE.

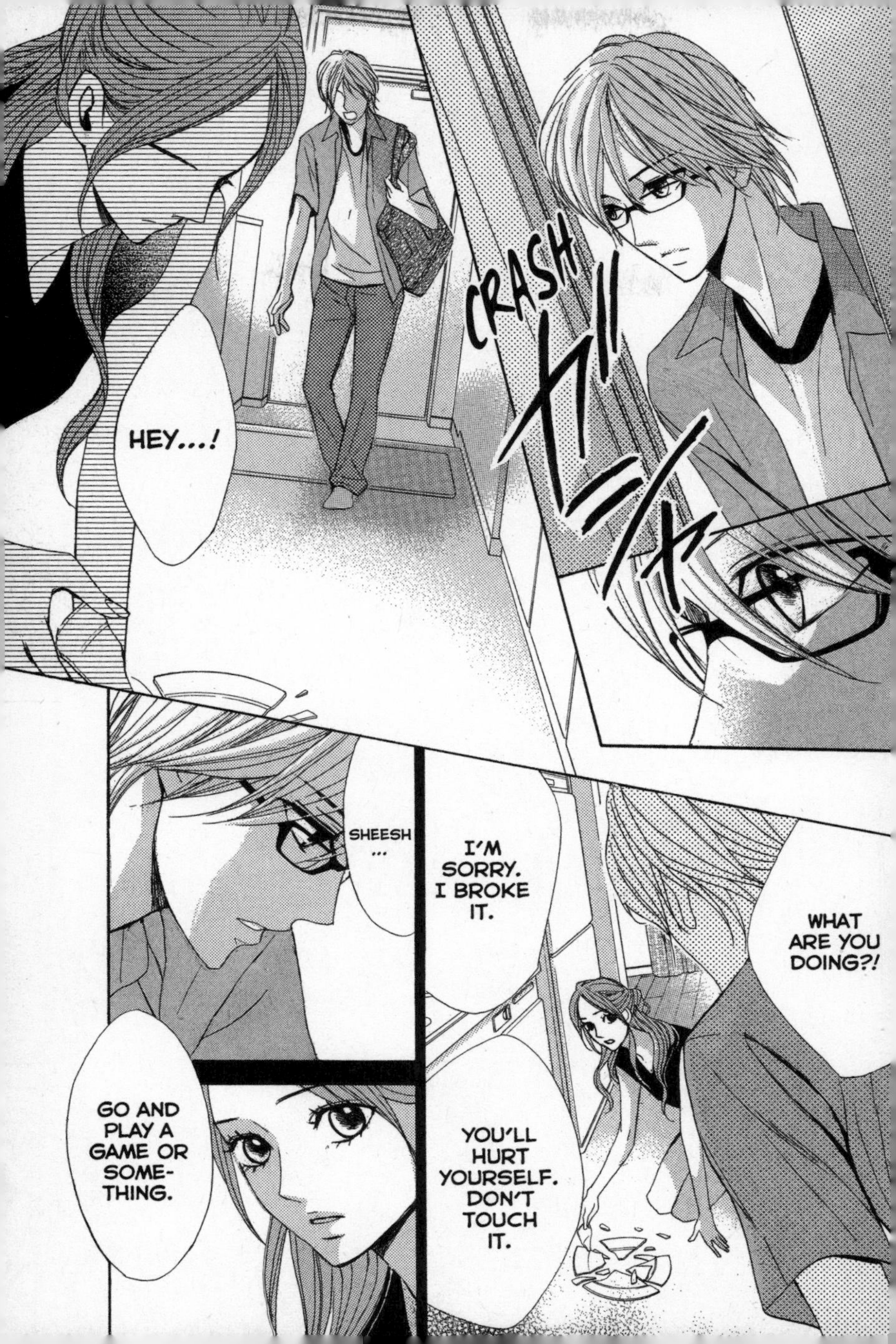
CRASH
HEY...!
WHAT ARE YOU DOING?!
YOU'LL HURT YOURSELF. DON'T TOUCH IT.
I'M SORRY. I BROKE IT.
SHEESH ...
GO AND PLAY A GAME OR SOME-THING.

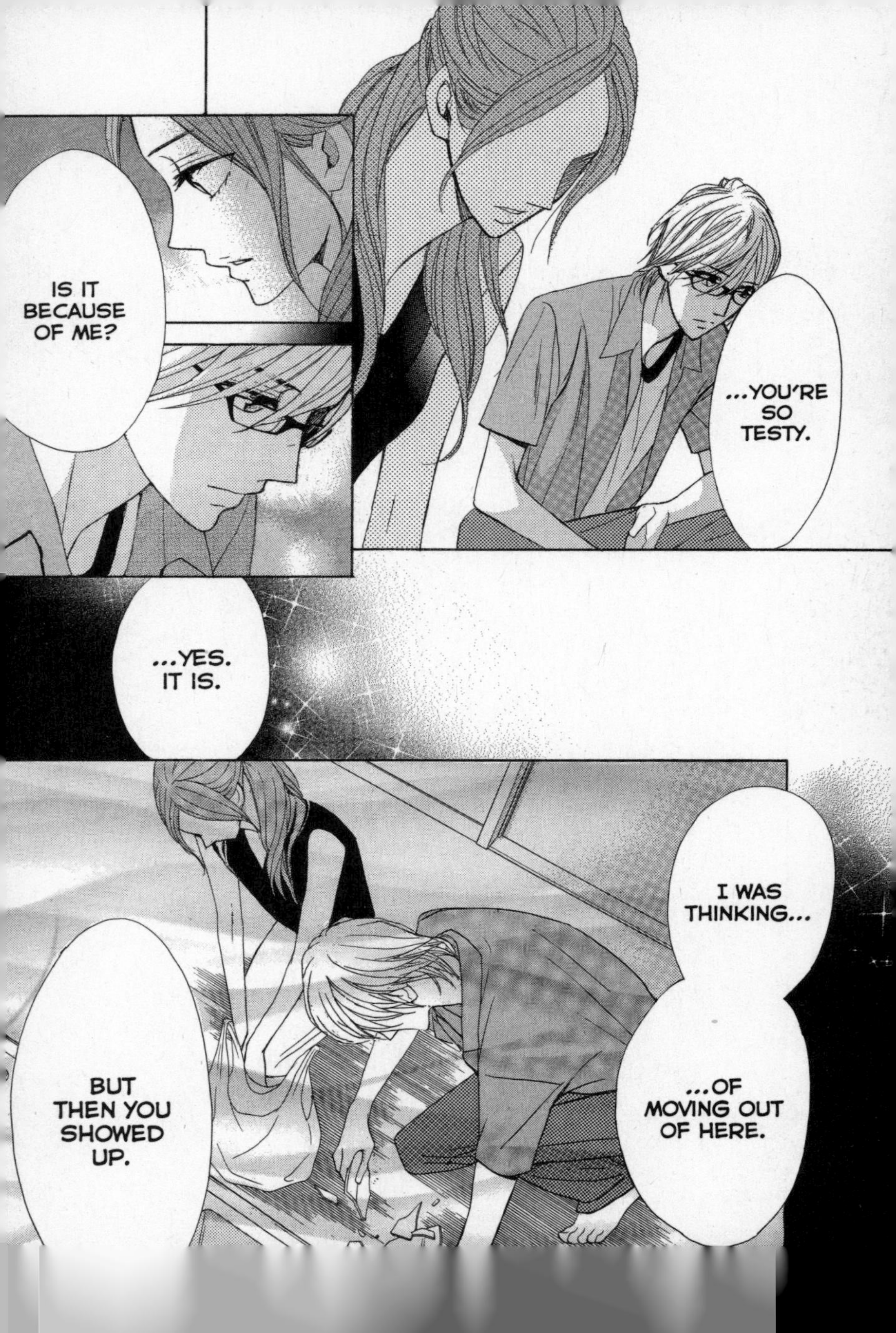
...YOU'RE SO TESTY.
IS IT BECAUSE OF ME?
...YES. IT IS.
I WAS THINKING...
...OF MOVING OUT OF HERE.
BUT THEN YOU SHOWED UP.

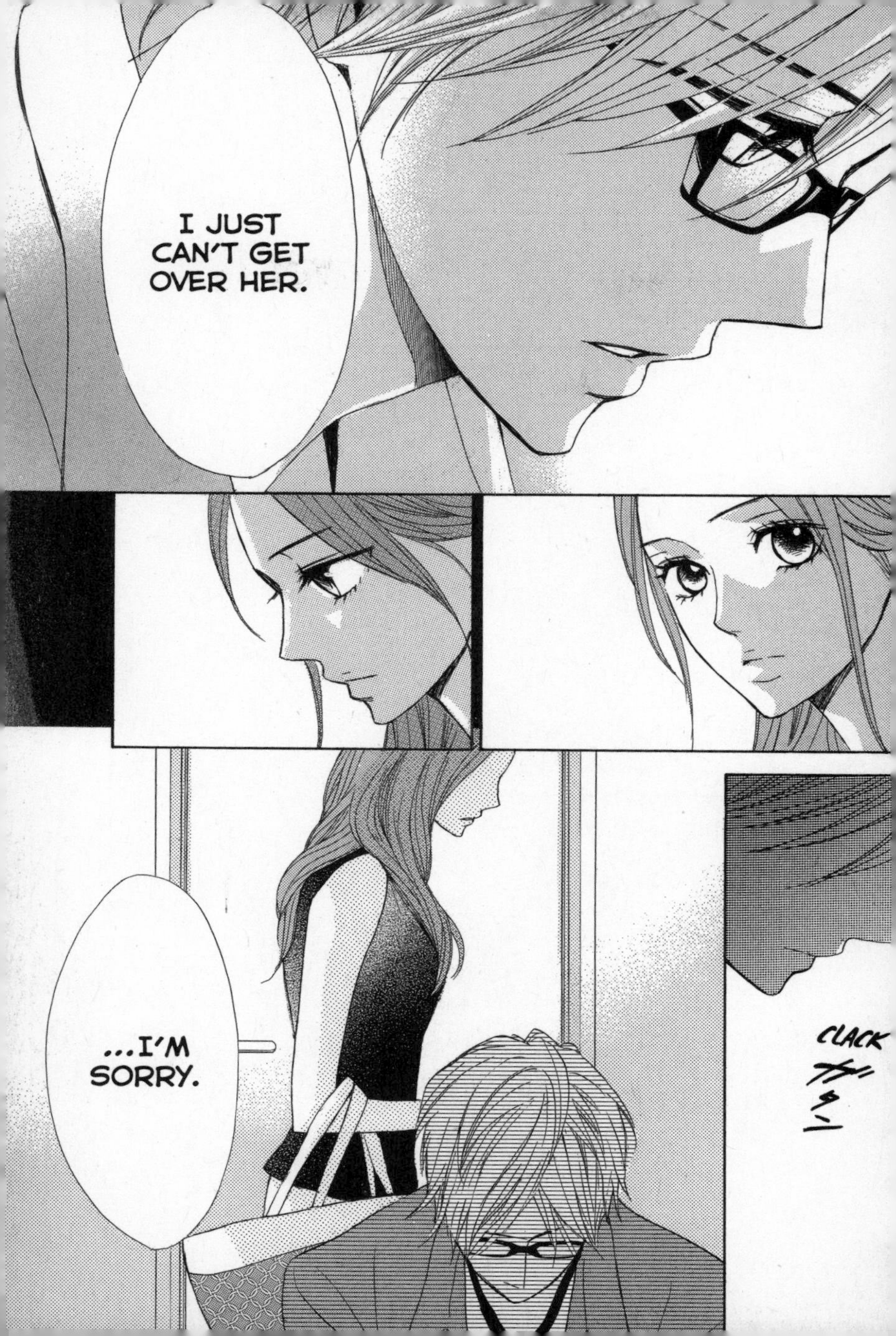
I JUST CAN'T GET OVER HER.
...I'M SORRY.
CLACK

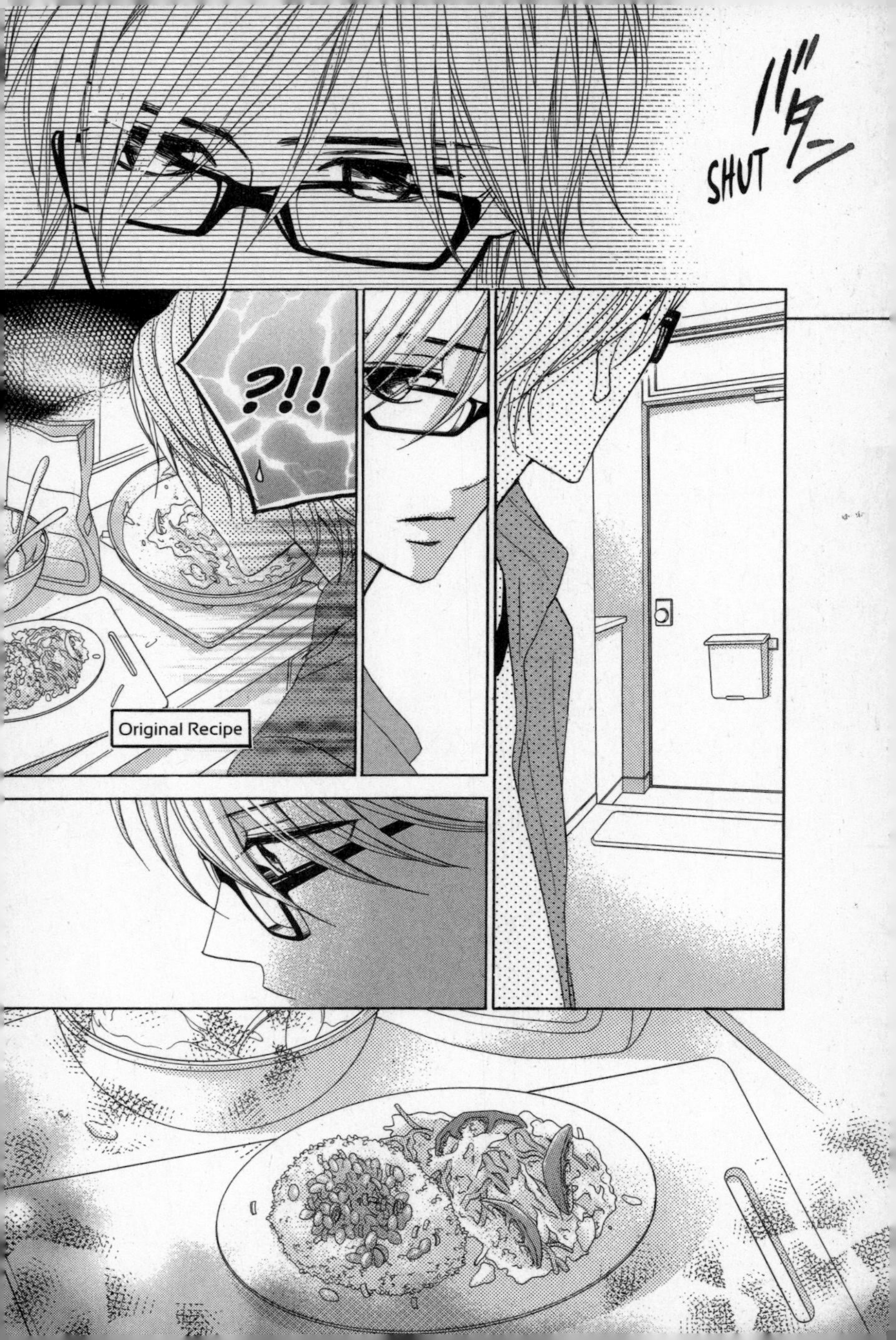

バタン
SHUT
?!!
Original Recipe

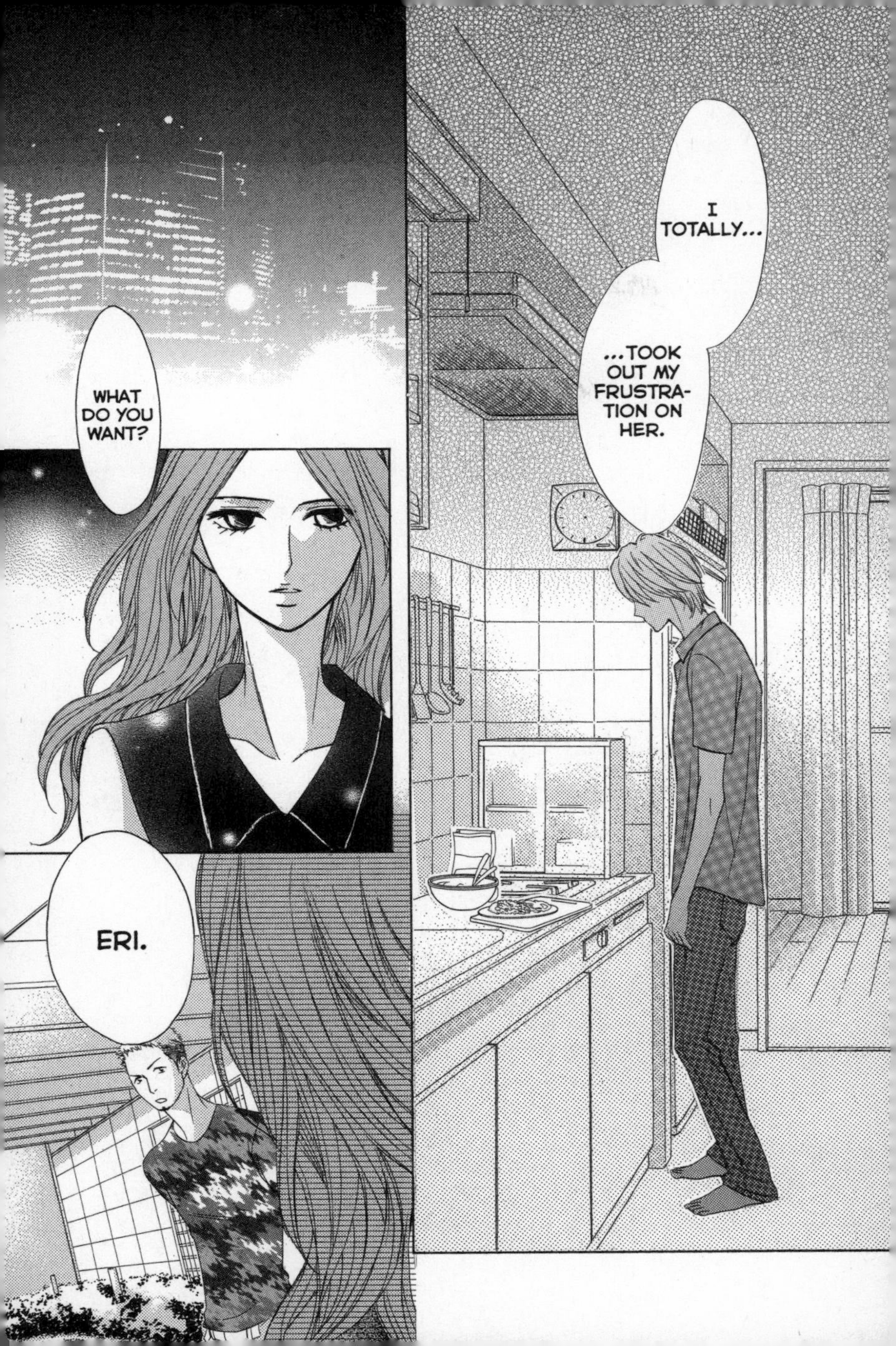
I TOTALLY...
...TOOK OUT MY FRUSTRATION ON HER.
WHAT DO YOU WANT?
ERI.

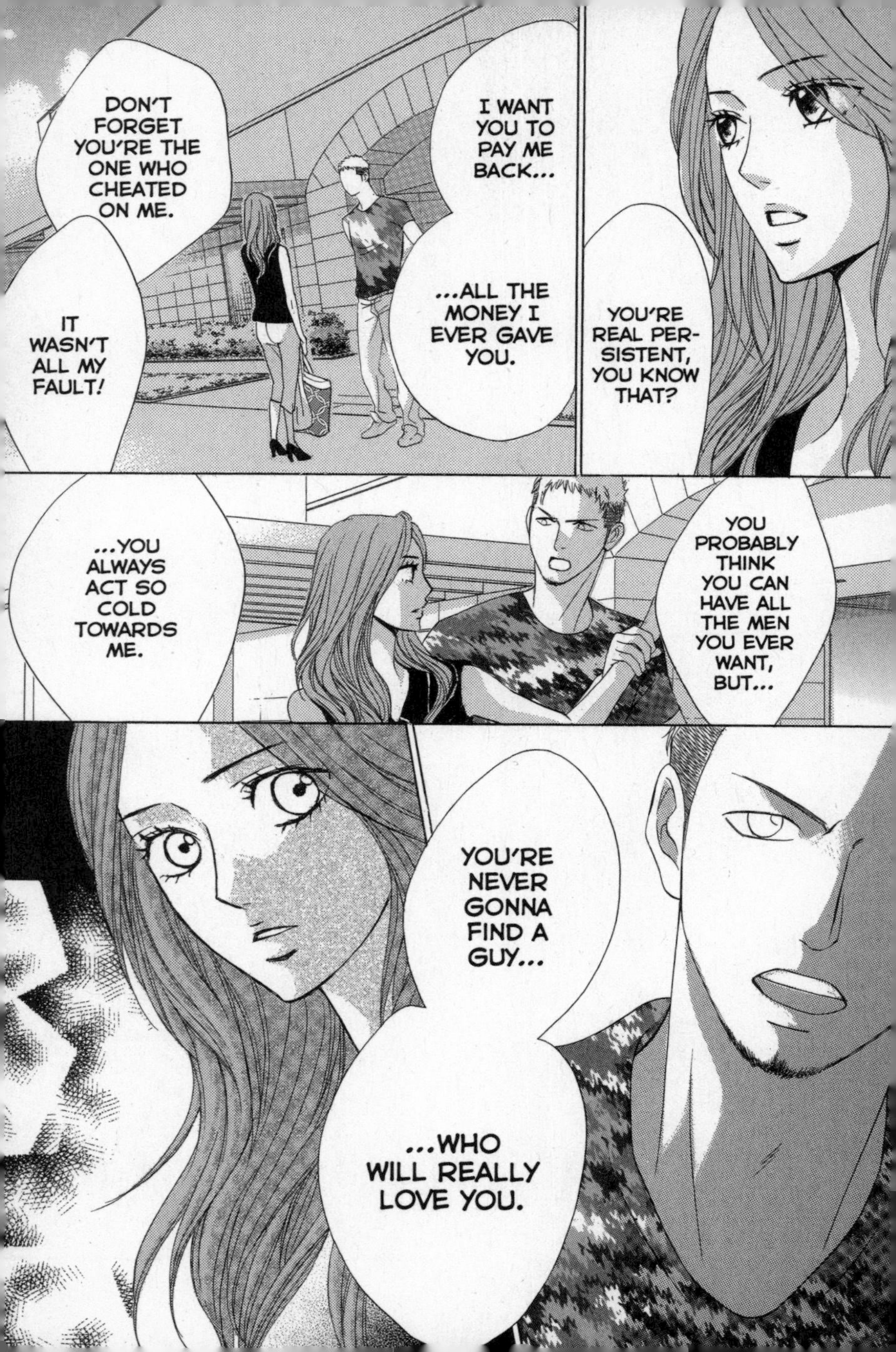
YOU'RE REAL PER-SISTENT, YOU KNOW THAT?
I WANT YOU TO PAY ME BACK...
...ALL THE MONEY I EVER GAVE YOU.
DON'T FORGET YOU'RE THE ONE WHO CHEATED ON ME.
IT WASN'T ALL MY FAULT!
YOU PROBABLY THINK YOU CAN HAVE ALL THE MEN YOU EVER WANT, BUT...
...YOU ALWAYS ACT SO COLD TOWARDS ME.
YOU'RE NEVER GONNA FIND A GUY...
...WHO WILL REALLY LOVE YOU.

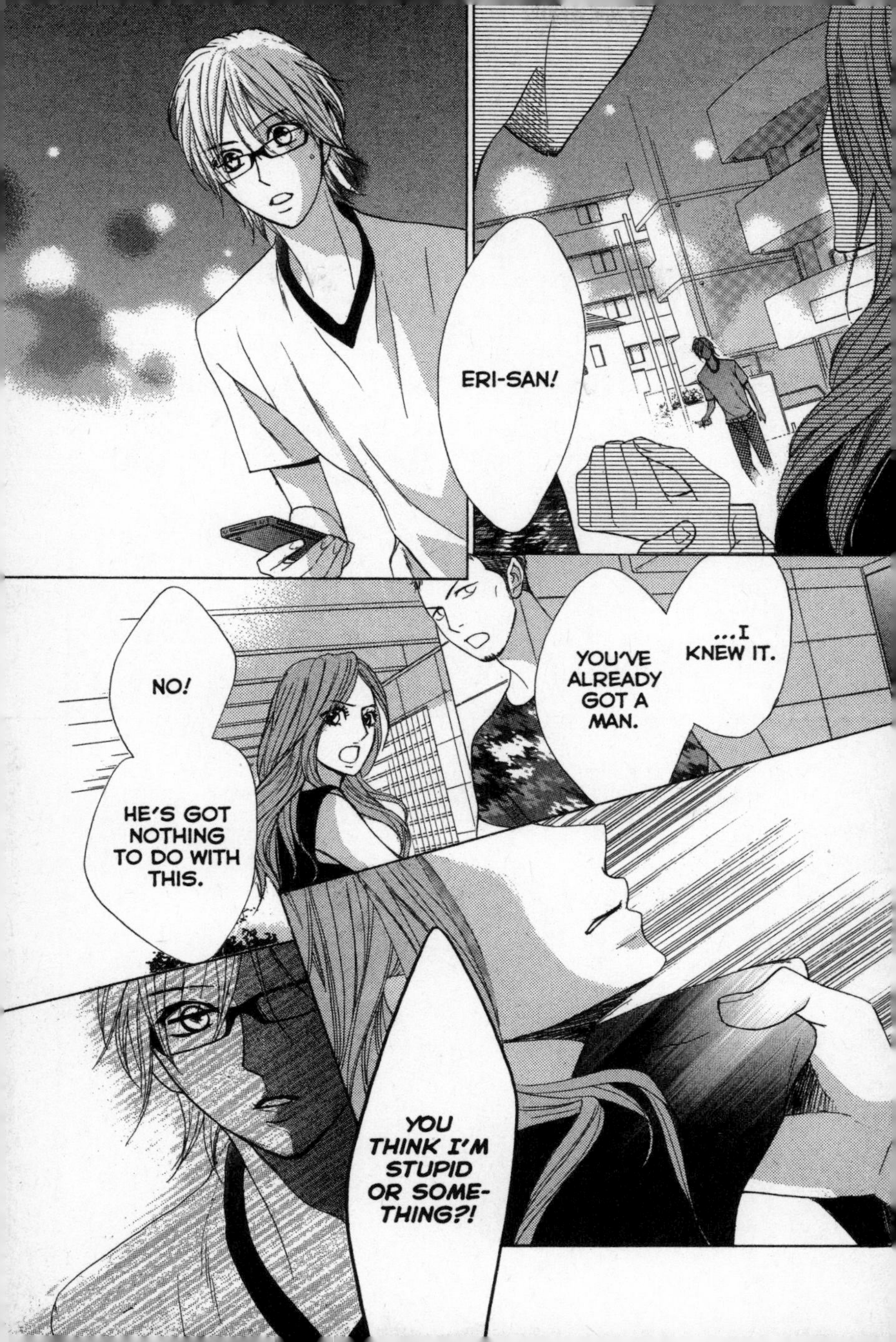
ERI-SAN!
...I KNEW IT.
YOU'VE ALREADY GOT A MAN.
NO!
HE'S GOT NOTHING TO DO WITH THIS.
YOU THINK I'M STUPID OR SOME-THING?!

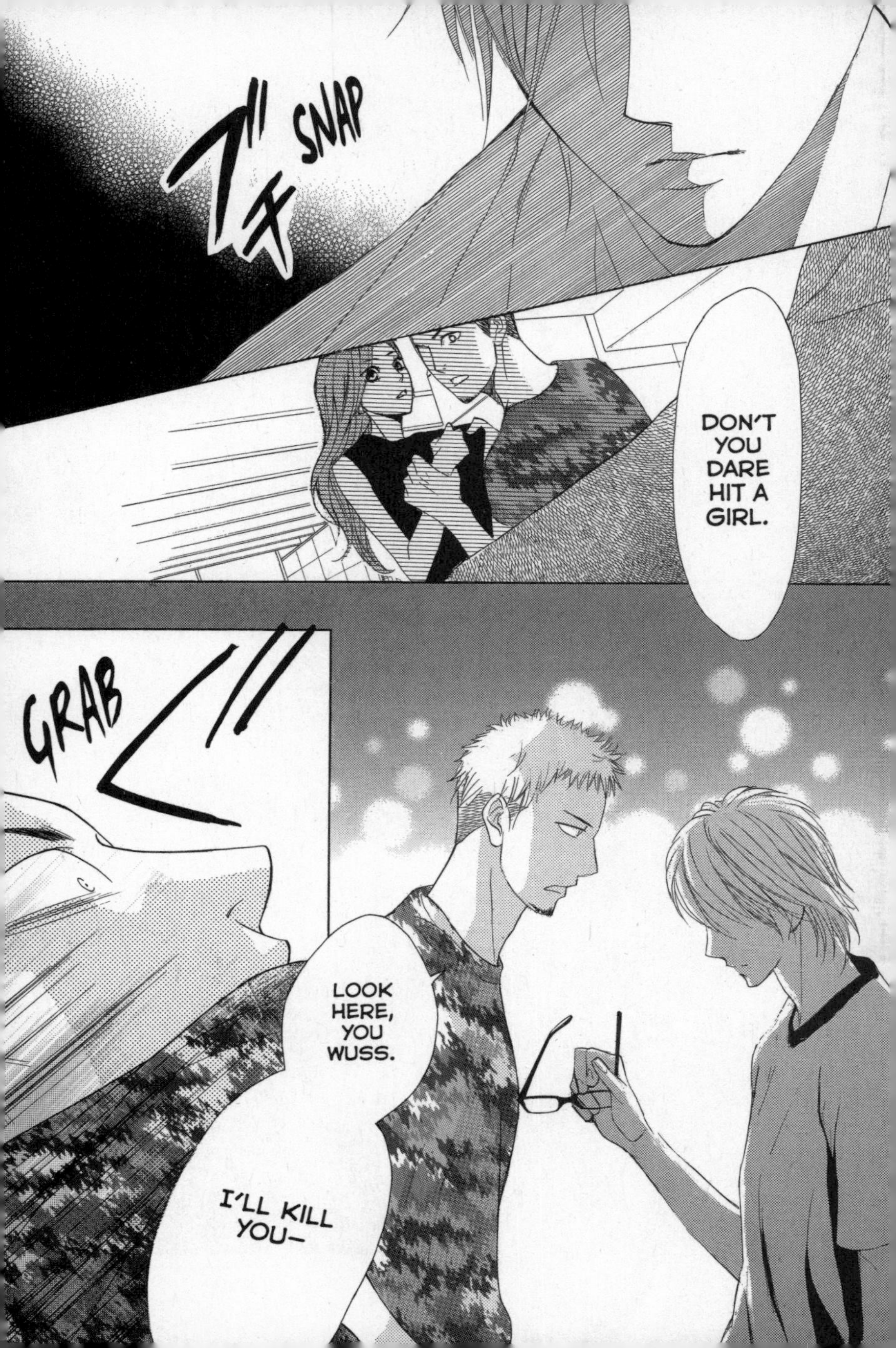
ブチ SNAP
DON'T YOU DARE HIT A GIRL.
GRAB
LOOK HERE, YOU WUSS.
I'LL KILL YOU—

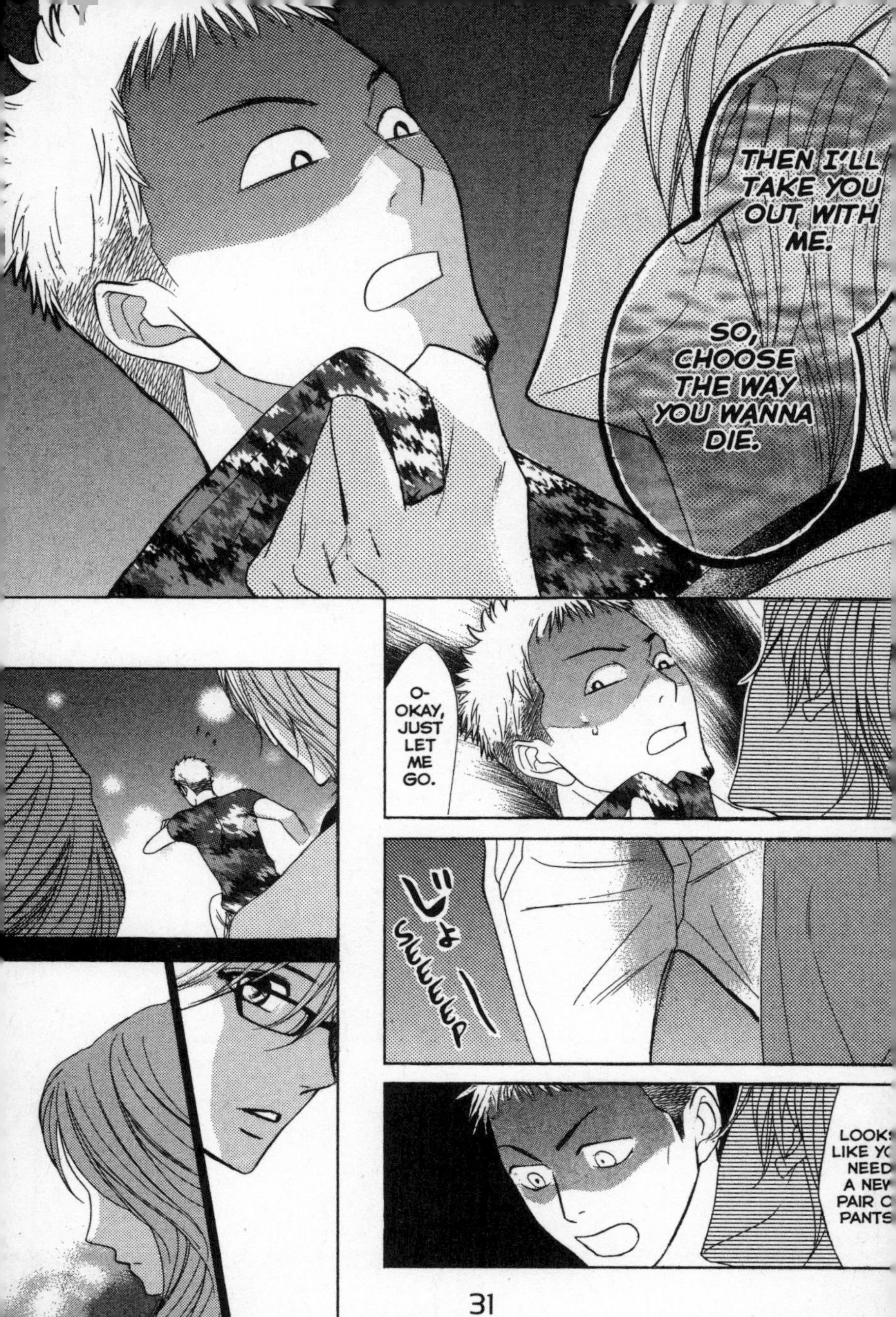
THEN I'LL TAKE YOU OUT WITH ME.
SO, CHOOSE THE WAY YOU WANNA DIE.
O-OKAY, JUST LET ME GO.
じょー
SWEEEEP
LOOKS LIKE YO NEED A NEW PAIR O PANTS

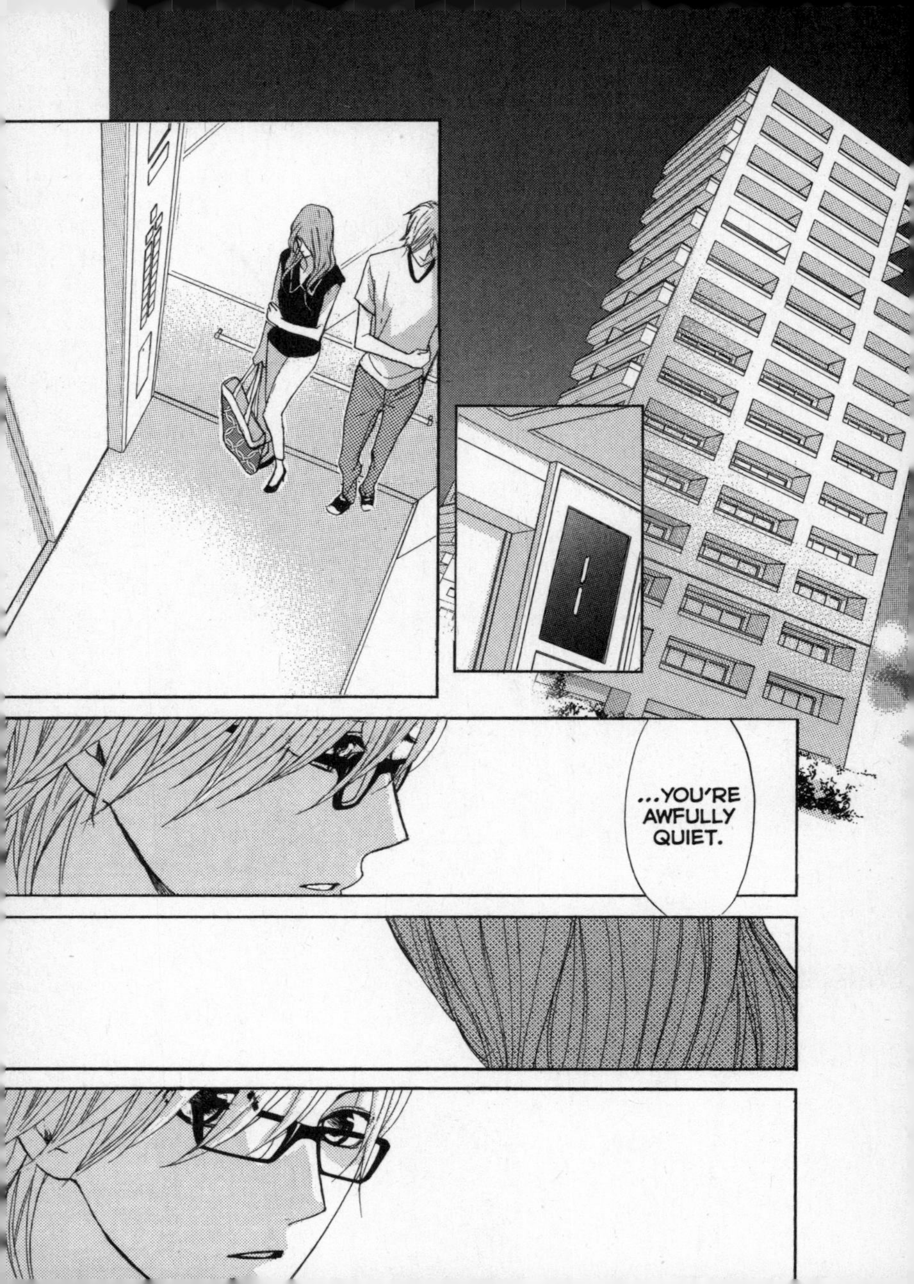
...YOU'RE AWFULLY QUIET.

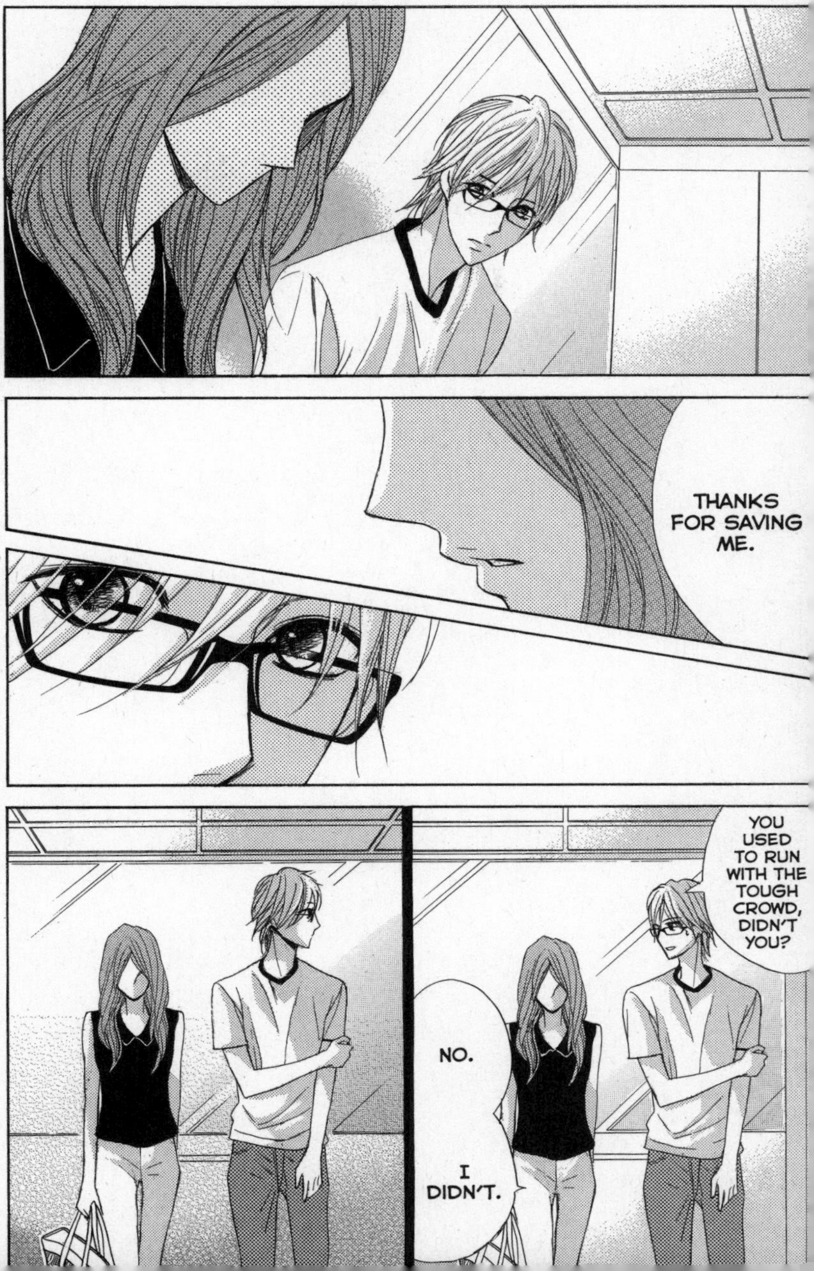
THANKS FOR SAVING ME.
YOU USED TO RUN WITH THE TOUGH CROWD, DIDN'T YOU?
NO.
I DIDN'T.

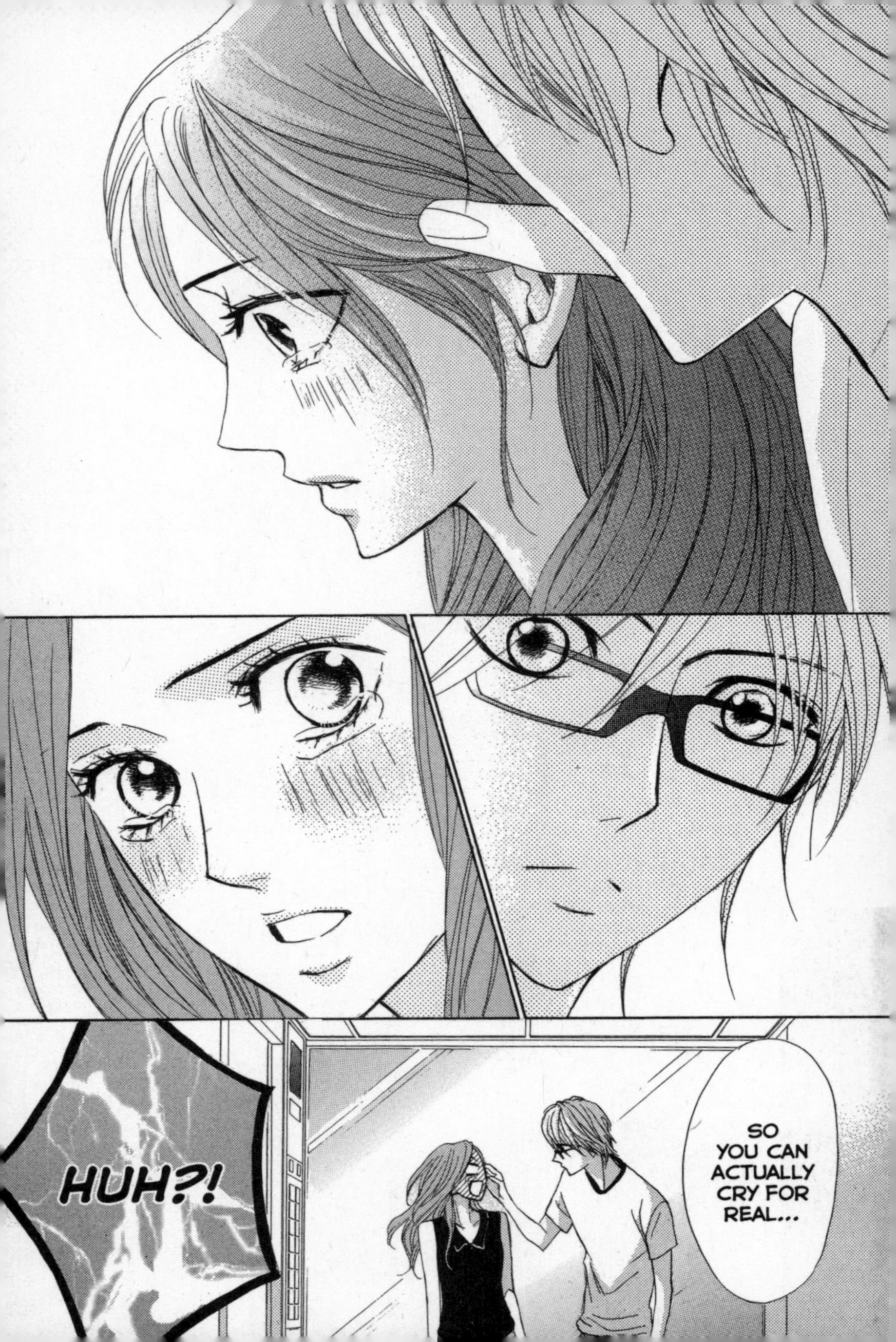
SO YOU CAN ACTUALLY CRY FOR REAL...
HUH?!

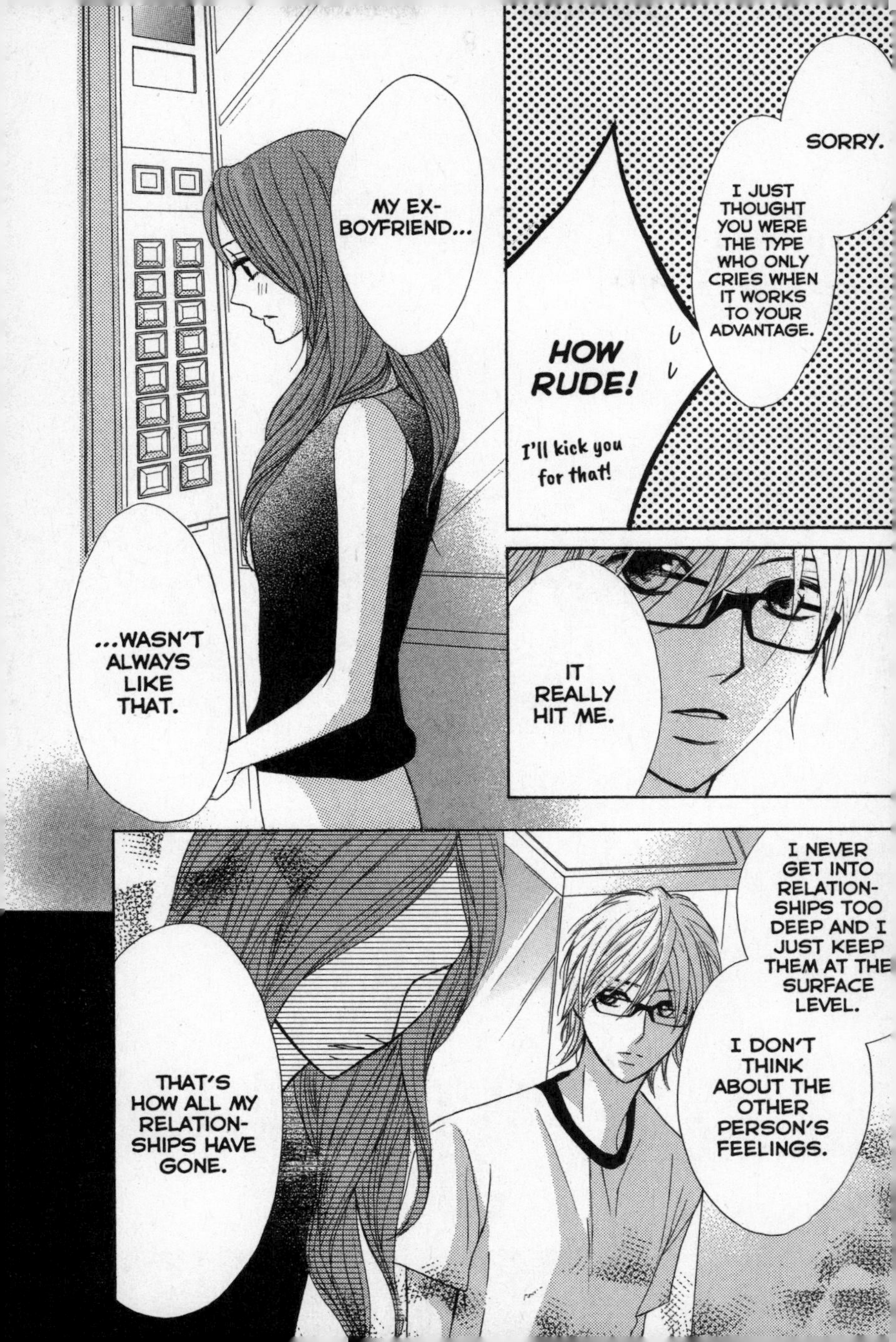
SORRY.
I JUST THOUGHT YOU WERE THE TYPE WHO ONLY CRIES WHEN IT WORKS TO YOUR ADVANTAGE.
HOW RUDE!
I'll kick you for that!
IT REALLY HIT ME.
MY EX-BOYFRIEND...
...WASN'T ALWAYS LIKE THAT.
I NEVER GET INTO RELATIONSHIPS TOO DEEP AND I JUST KEEP THEM AT THE SURFACE LEVEL.
I DON'T THINK ABOUT THE OTHER PERSON'S FEELINGS.
THAT'S HOW ALL MY RELATIONSHIPS HAVE GONE.

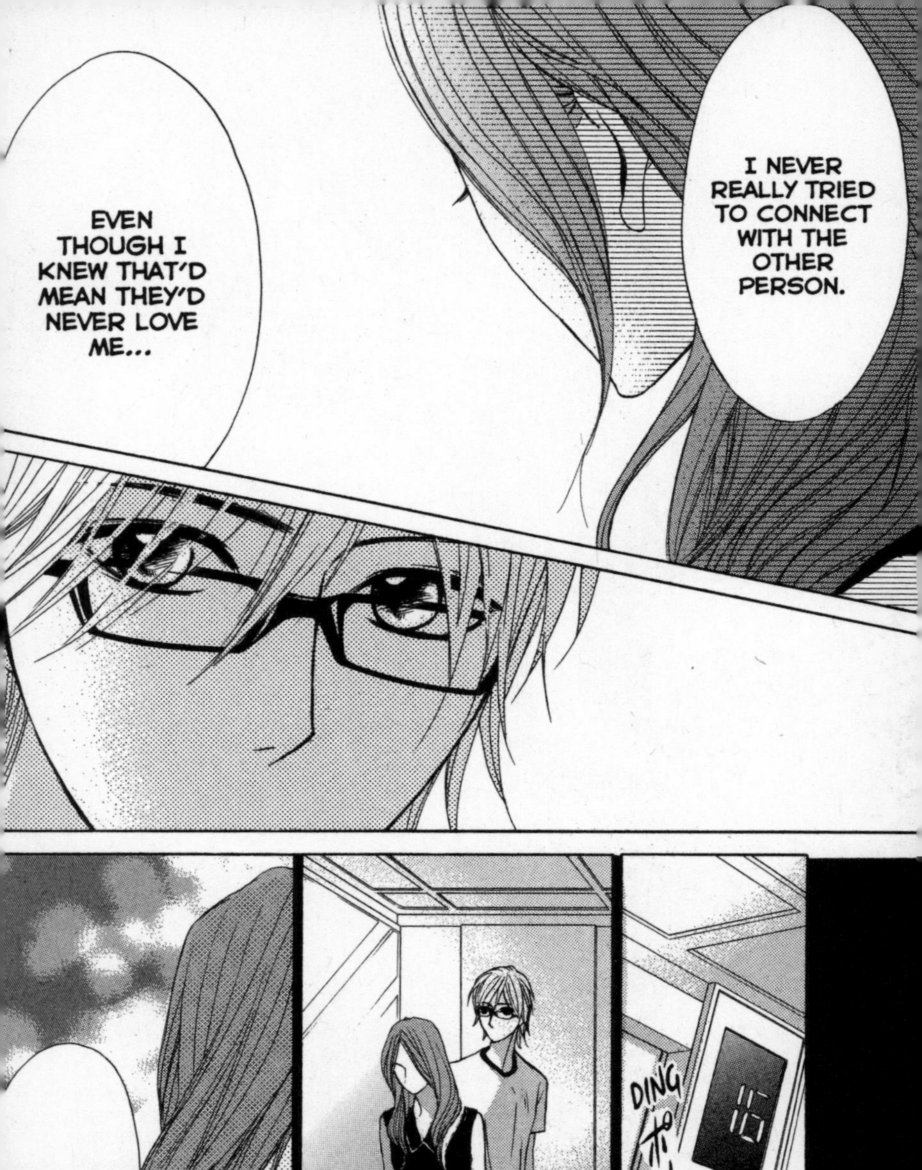
I NEVER REALLY TRIED TO CONNECT WITH THE OTHER PERSON.
EVEN THOUGH I KNEW THAT'D MEAN THEY'D NEVER LOVE ME...
DING
...ERI-SAN.

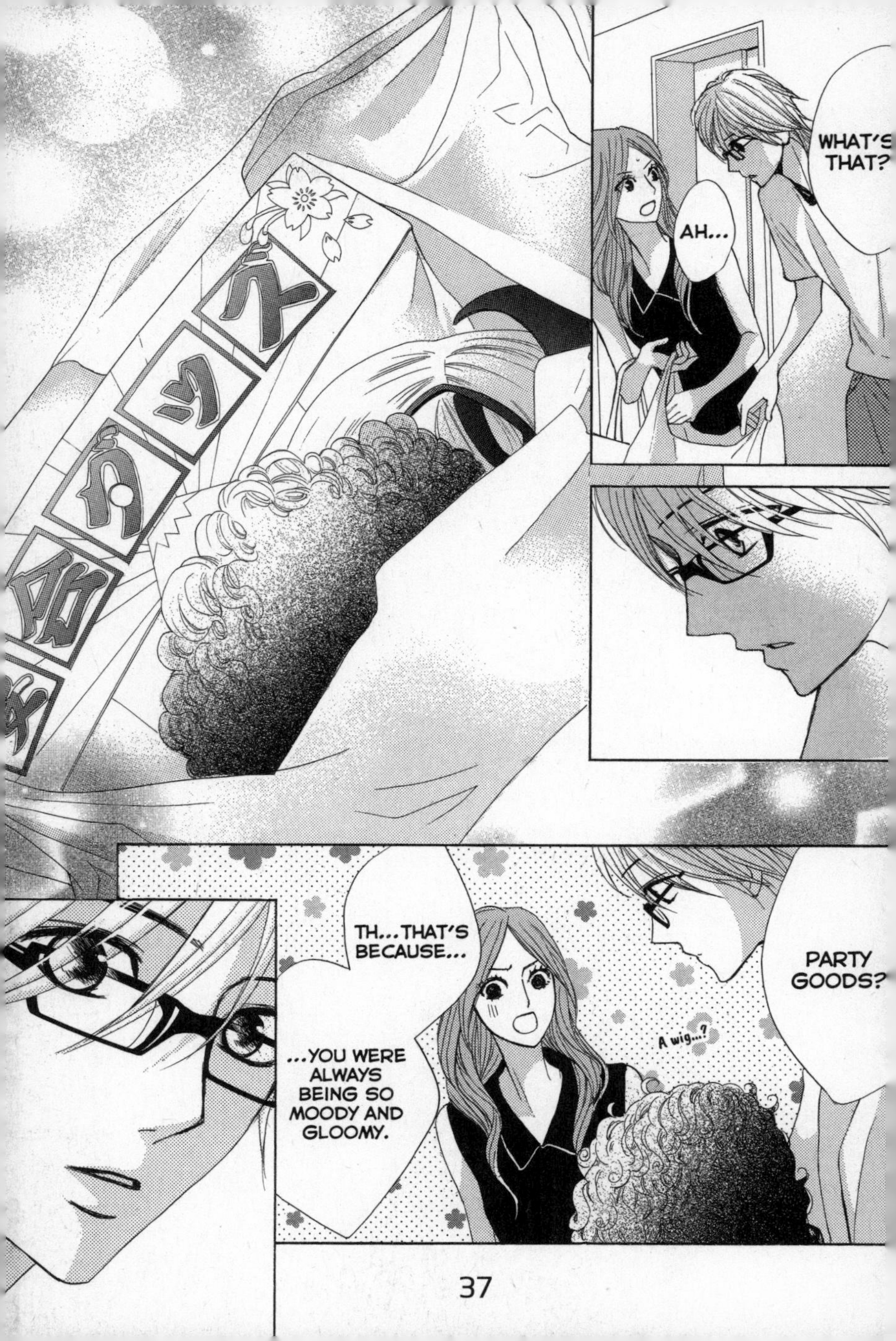
WHAT'S THAT?
AH...
PARTY GOODS?
A wig...?
TH...THAT'S BECAUSE...
...YOU WERE ALWAYS BEING SO MOODY AND GLOOMY.

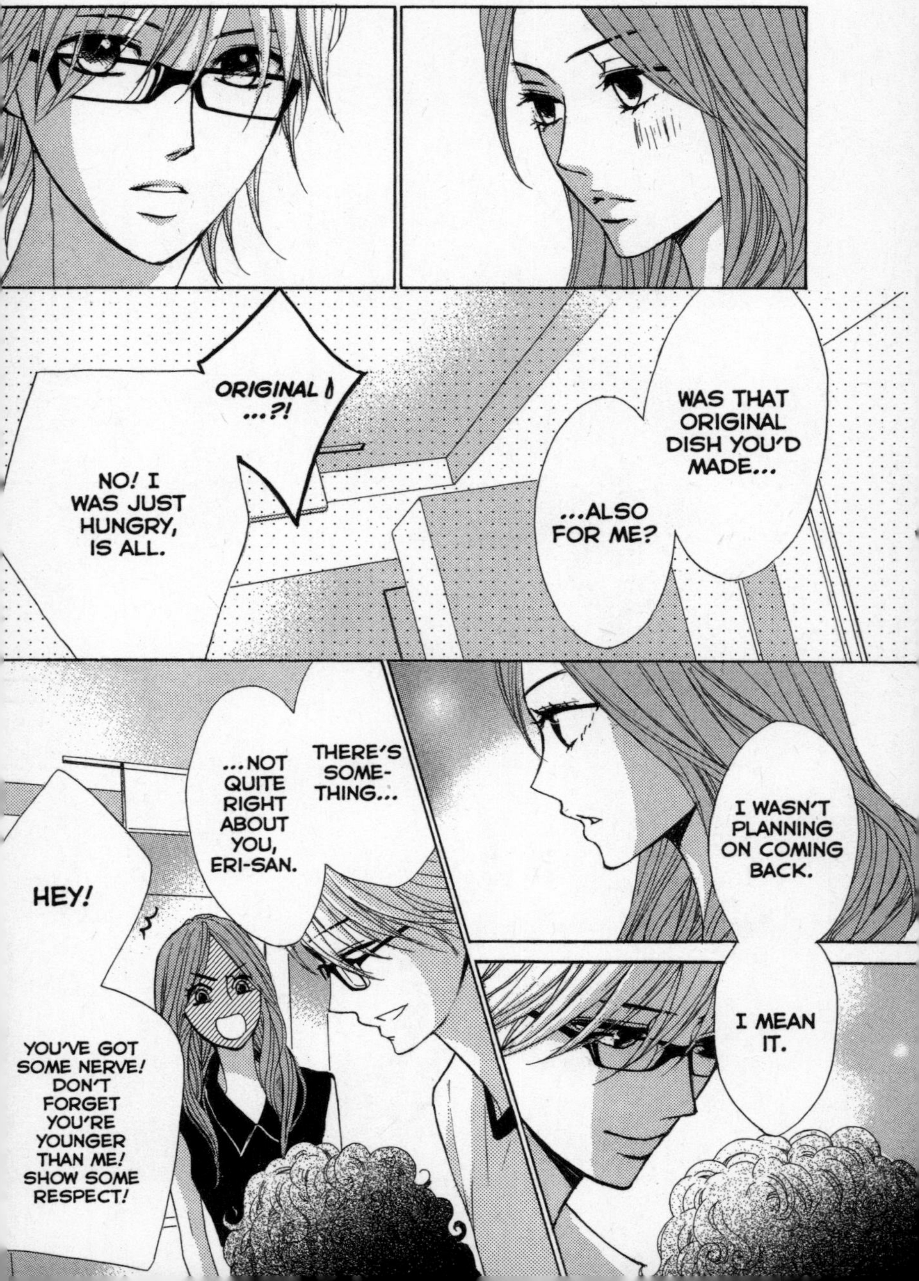
WAS THAT ORIGINAL DISH YOU'D MADE...
...ALSO FOR ME?
ORIGINAL ...?!
NO! I WAS JUST HUNGRY, IS ALL.
I WASN'T PLANNING ON COMING BACK.
I MEAN IT.
THERE'S SOME-THING...
...NOT QUITE RIGHT ABOUT YOU, ERI-SAN.
HEY!
YOU'VE GOT SOME NERVE! DON'T FORGET YOU'RE YOUNGER THAN ME! SHOW SOME RESPECT!

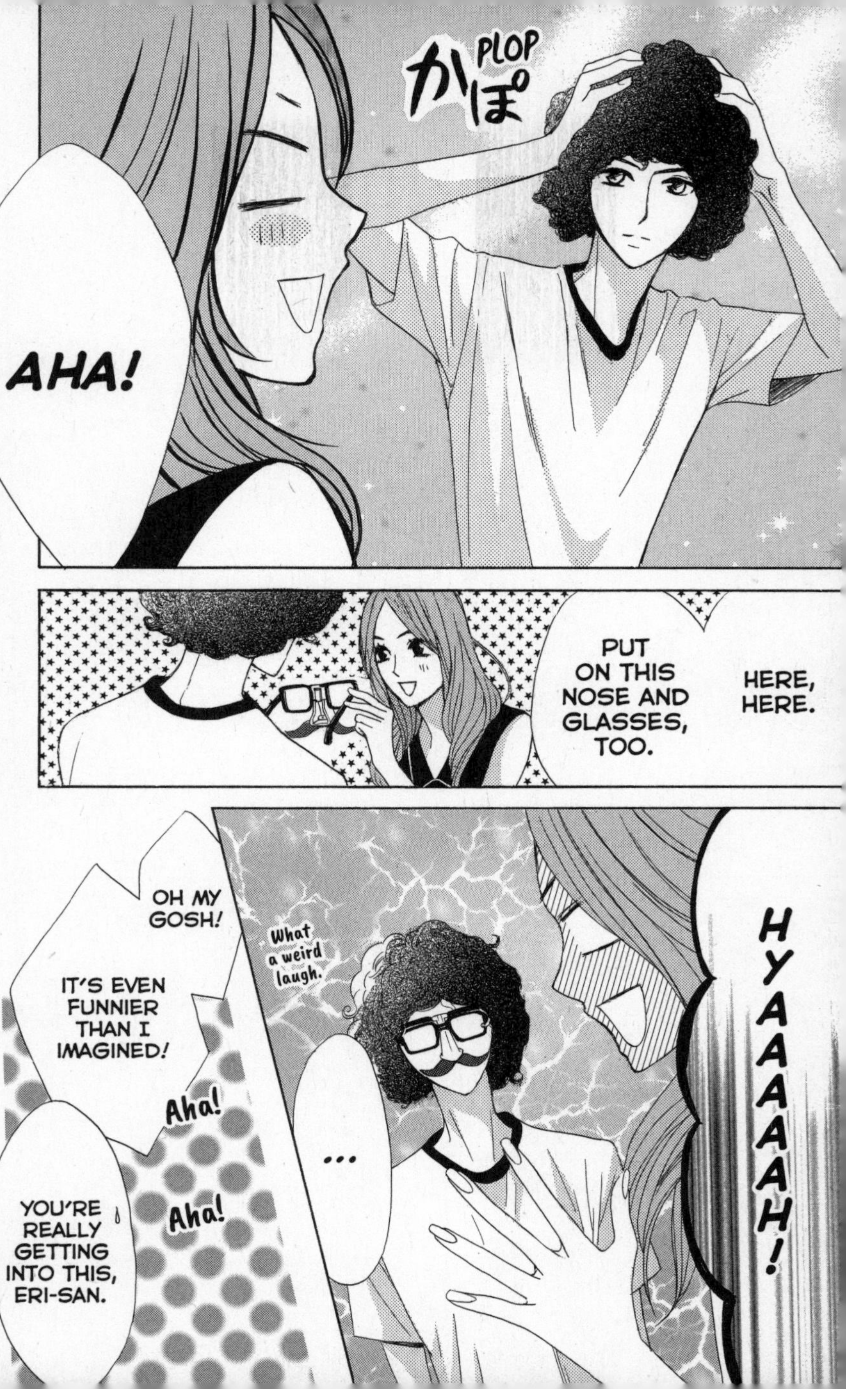
かぽ
PLOP
AHA!
HERE, HERE.
PUT ON THIS NOSE AND GLASSES, TOO.
HYAAAAAH!
What a weird laugh.
...
OH MY GOSH!
IT'S EVEN FUNNIER THAN I IMAGINED!
Aha!
Aha!
YOU'RE REALLY GETTING INTO THIS, ERI-SAN.

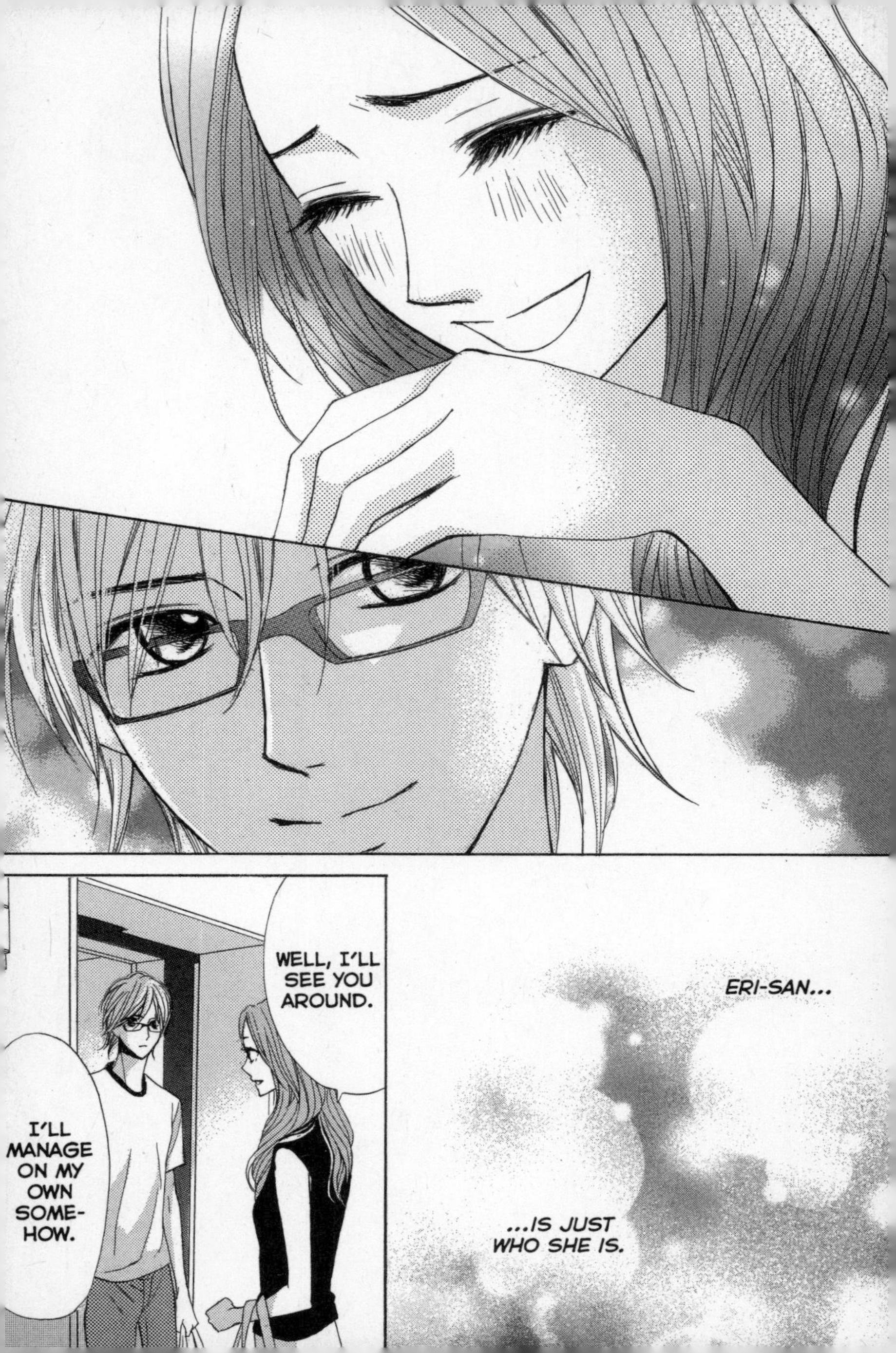
ERI-SAN...
...IS JUST WHO SHE IS.
WELL, I'LL SEE YOU AROUND.
I'LL MANAGE ON MY OWN SOME-HOW.

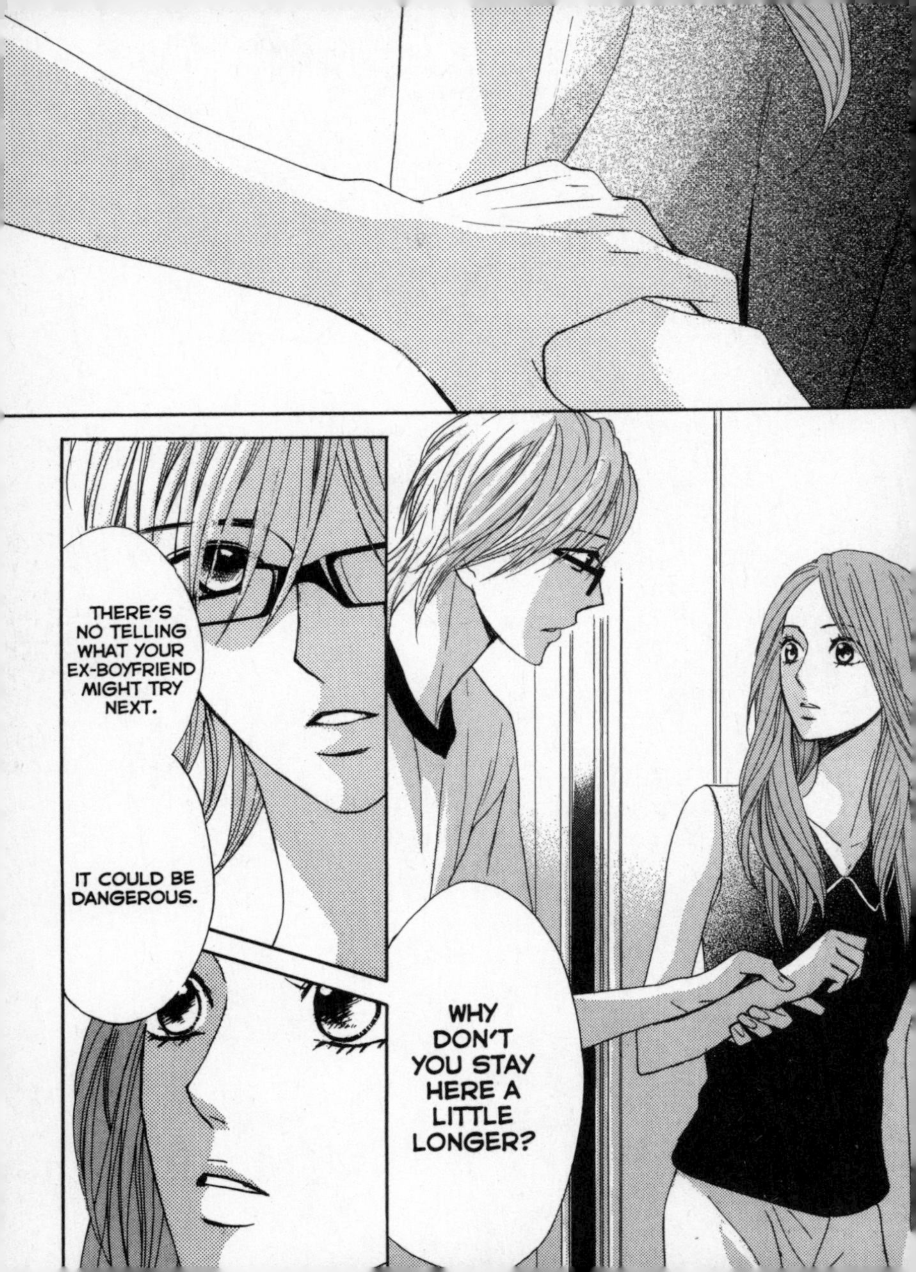
THERE'S NO TELLING WHAT YOUR EX-BOYFRIEND MIGHT TRY NEXT.
IT COULD BE DANGEROUS.
WHY DON'T YOU STAY HERE A LITTLE LONGER?

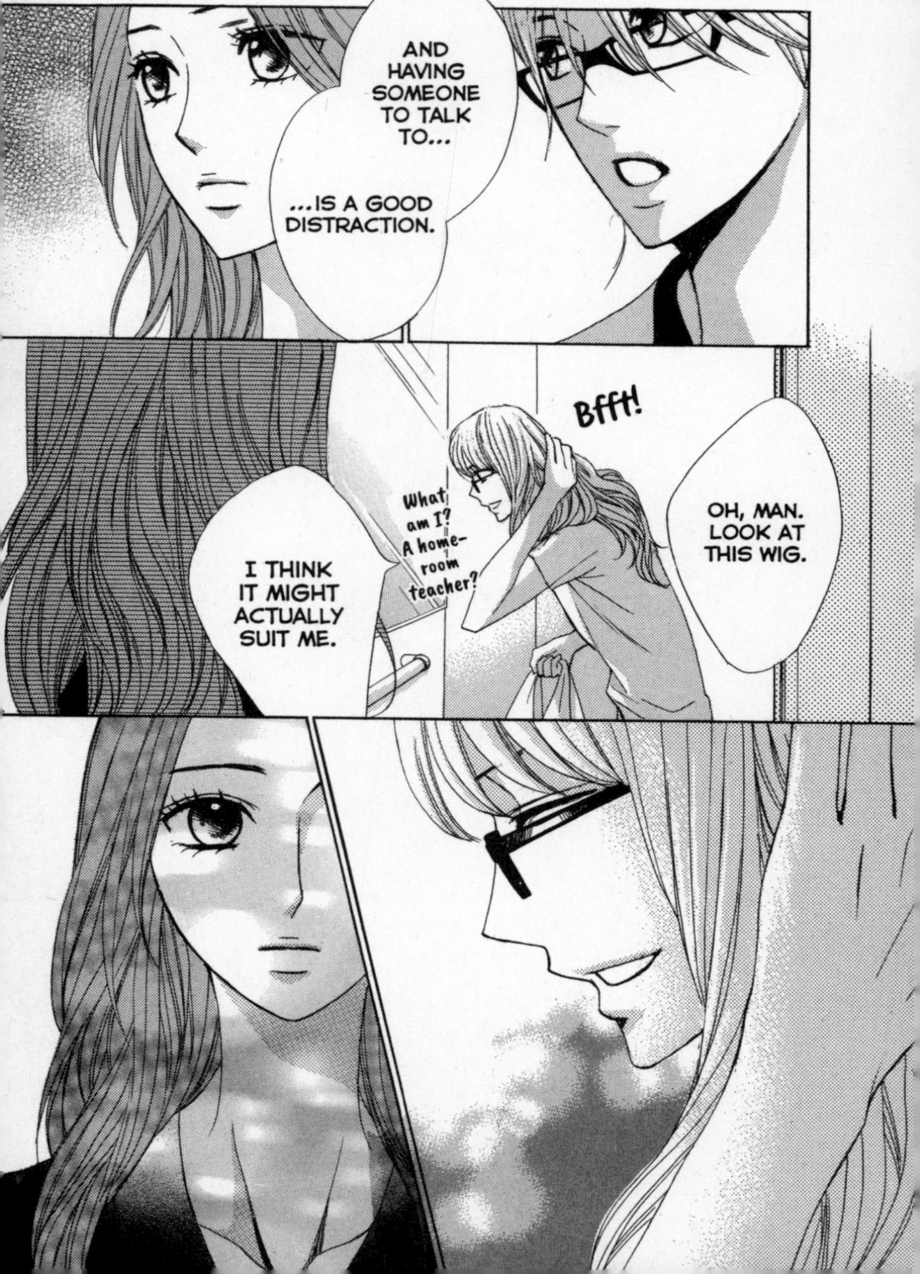
AND HAVING SOMEONE TO TALK TO...
...IS A GOOD DISTRACTION.
Bfft!
OH, MAN. LOOK AT THIS WIG.
What am I? A home-room teacher?
I THINK IT MIGHT ACTUALLY SUIT ME.

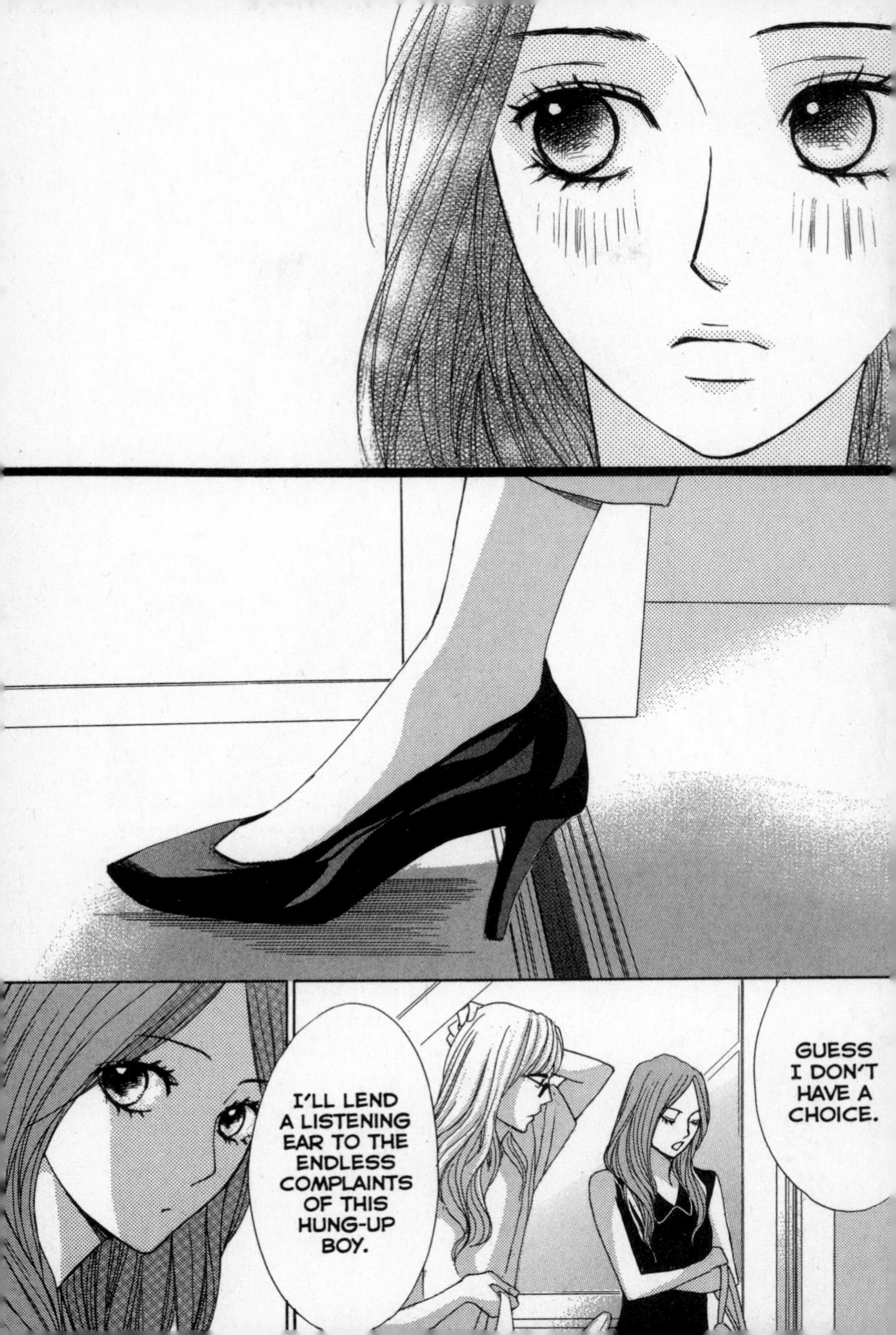
GUESS I DON'T HAVE A CHOICE.
I'LL LEND A LISTENING EAR TO THE ENDLESS COMPLAINTS OF THIS HUNG-UP BOY.

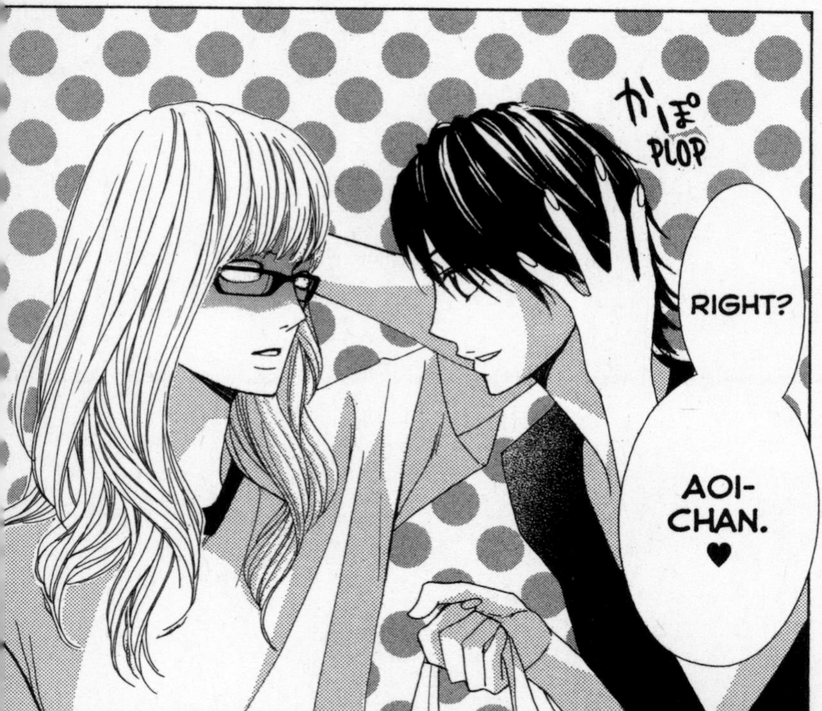
かぽ
PLOP
RIGHT?
AOI-CHAN. ♥

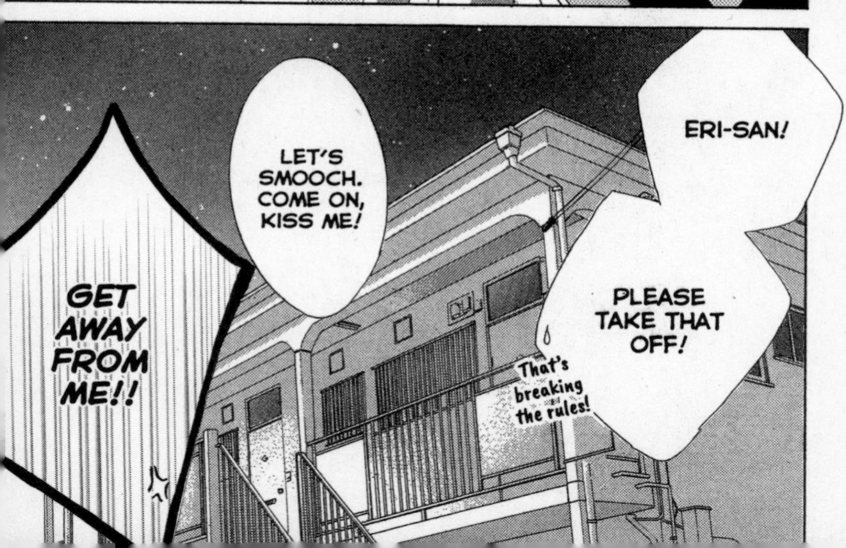
ERI-SAN!
PLEASE TAKE THAT OFF!
That's breaking the rules!
LET'S SMOOCH. COME ON, KISS ME!
GET AWAY FROM ME!!

L♥DK

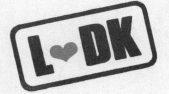

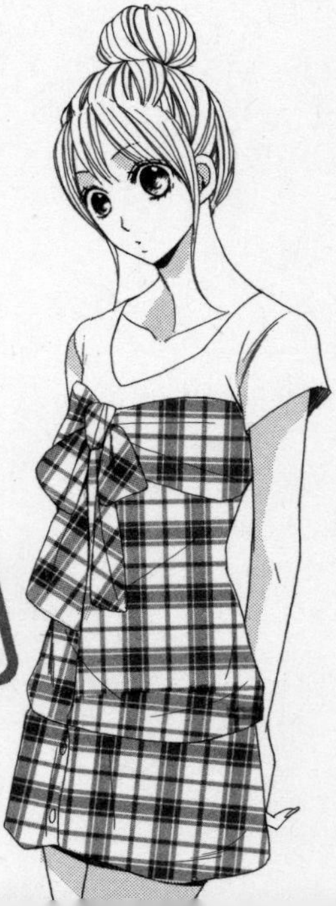

L♥DK

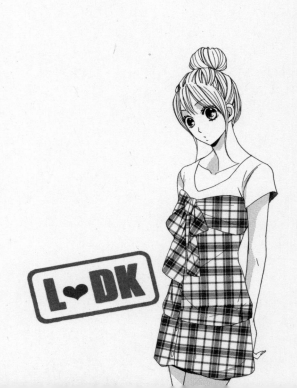

#50 Home Visit

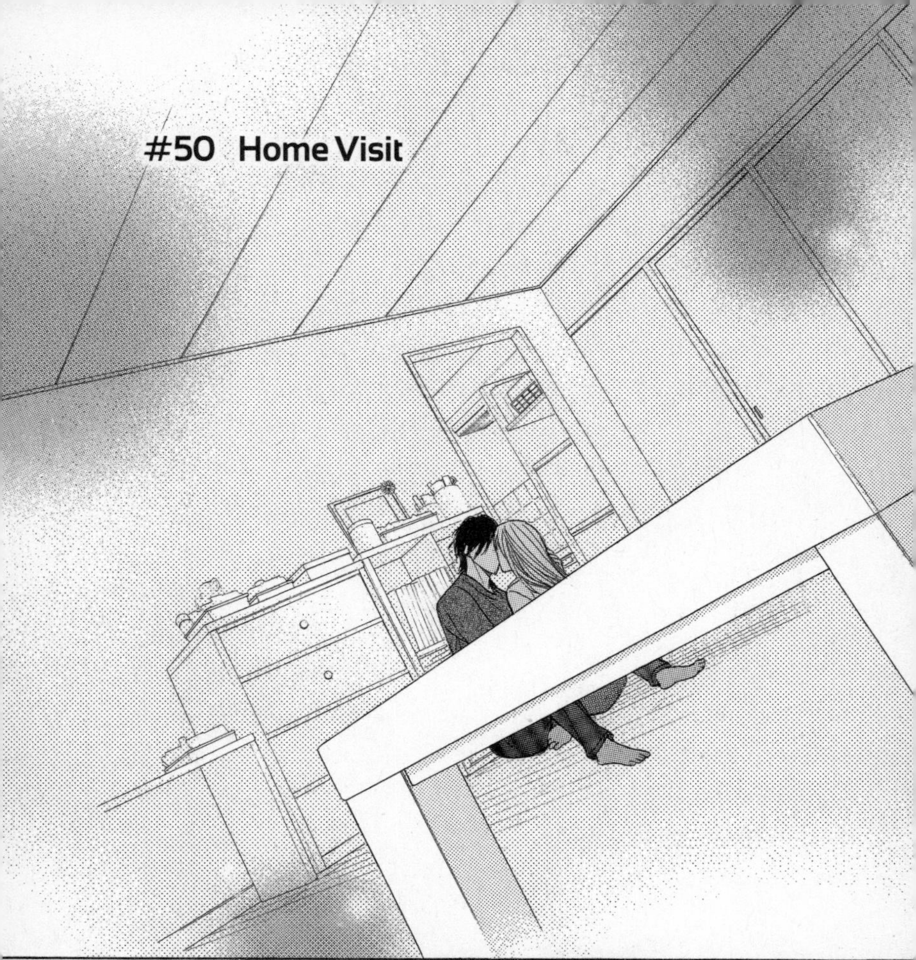

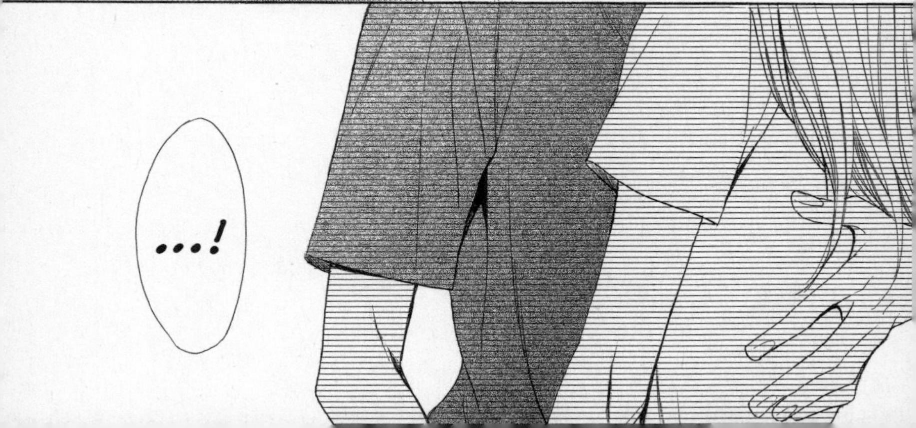
...!

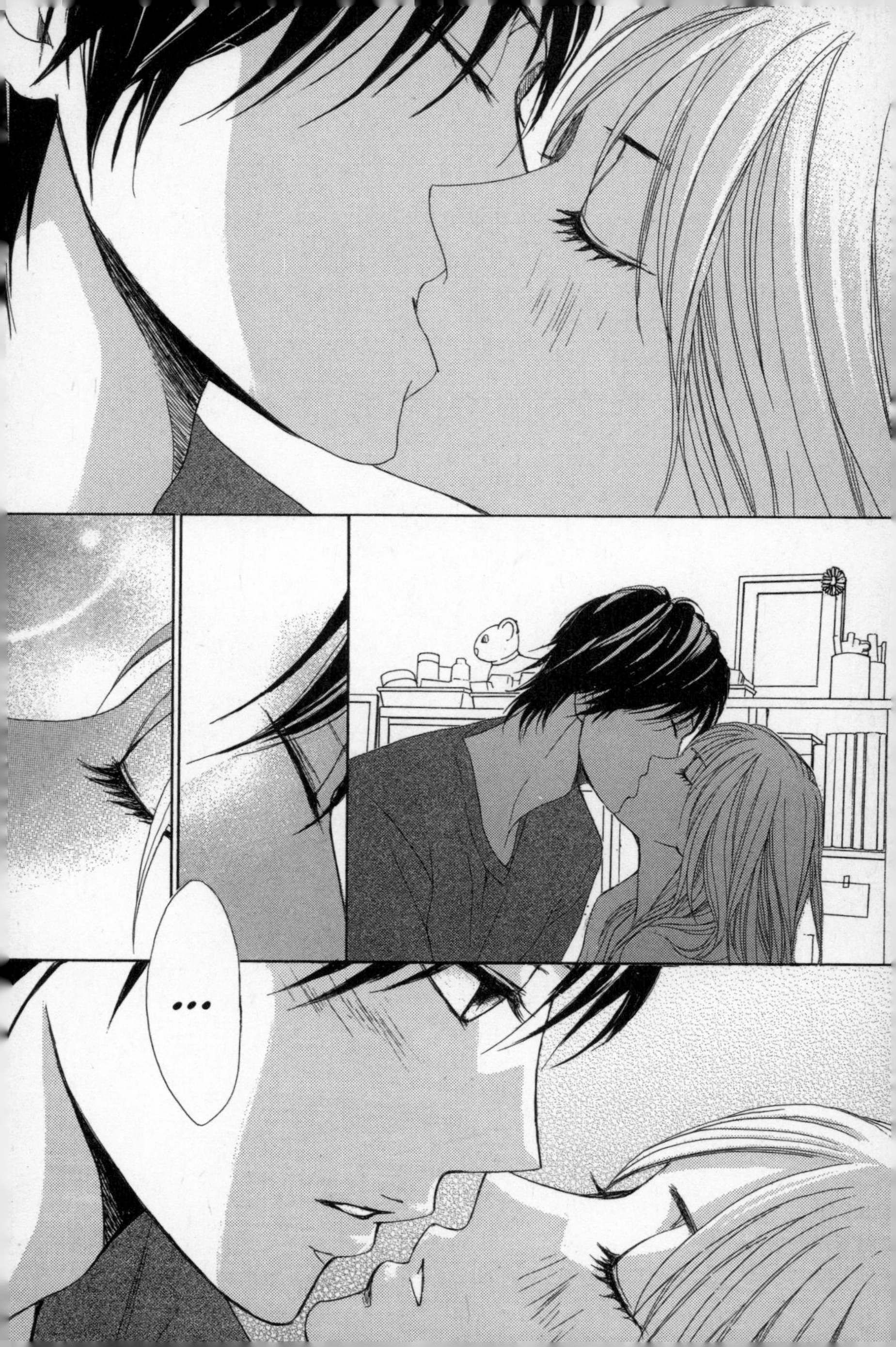
...

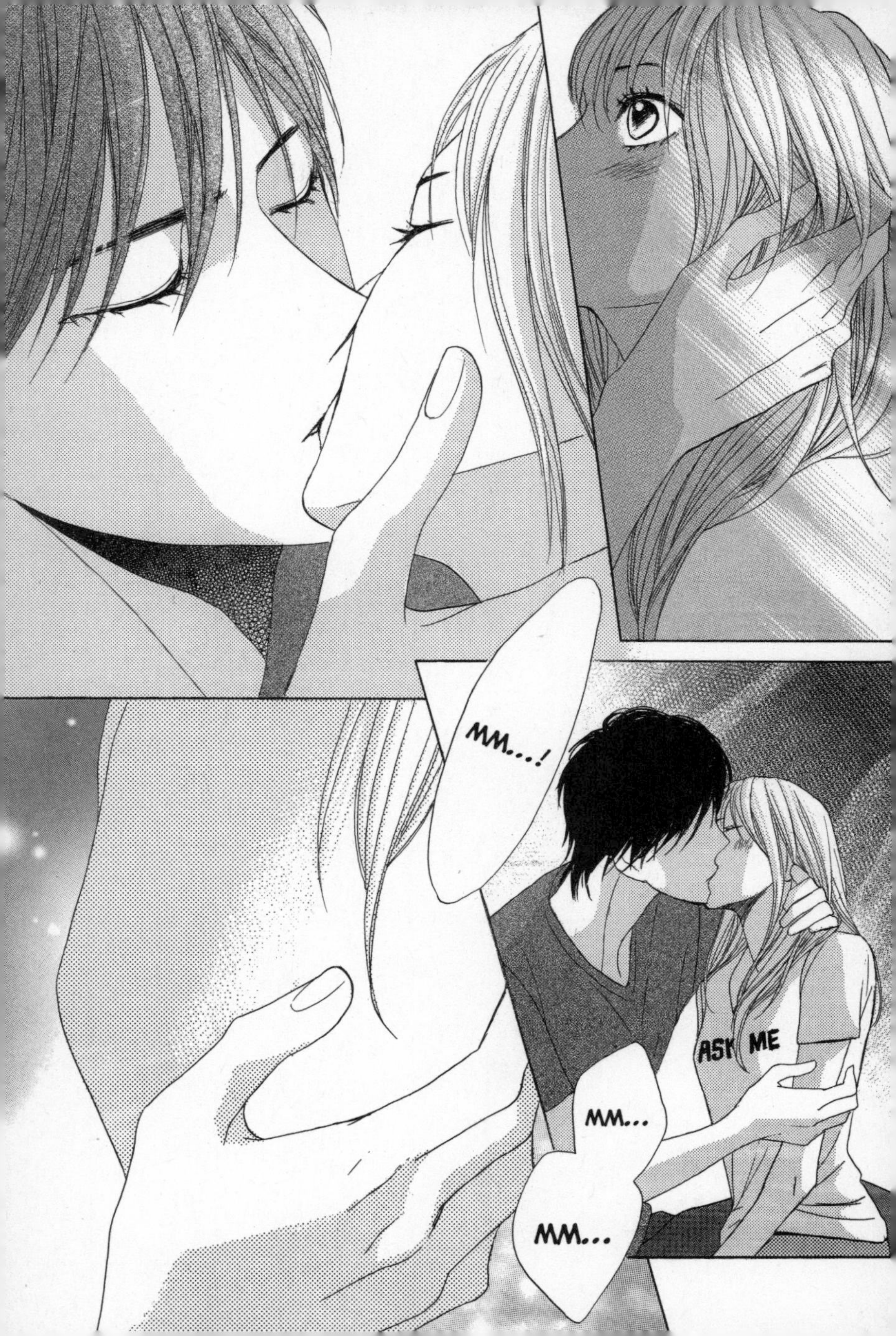
MM...!
ASK ME
MM...
MM...

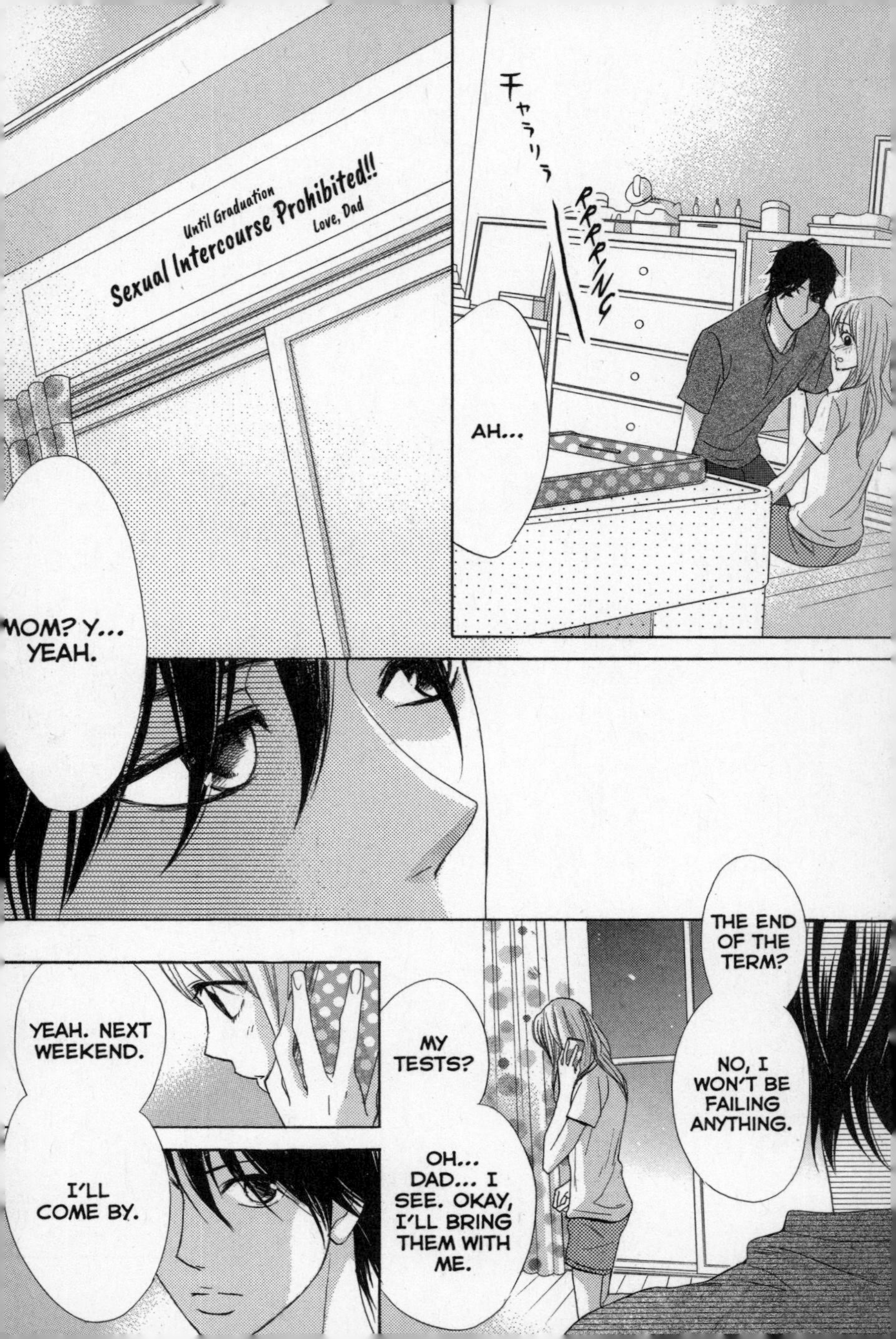
チャラリラ
RRRRING
AH...
Until Graduation
Sexual Intercourse Prohibited!!
Love, Dad
MOM? Y... YEAH.
THE END OF THE TERM?
MY TESTS?
NO, I WON'T BE FAILING ANYTHING.
OH... DAD... I SEE. OKAY, I'LL BRING THEM WITH ME.
YEAH. NEXT WEEKEND.
I'LL COME BY.

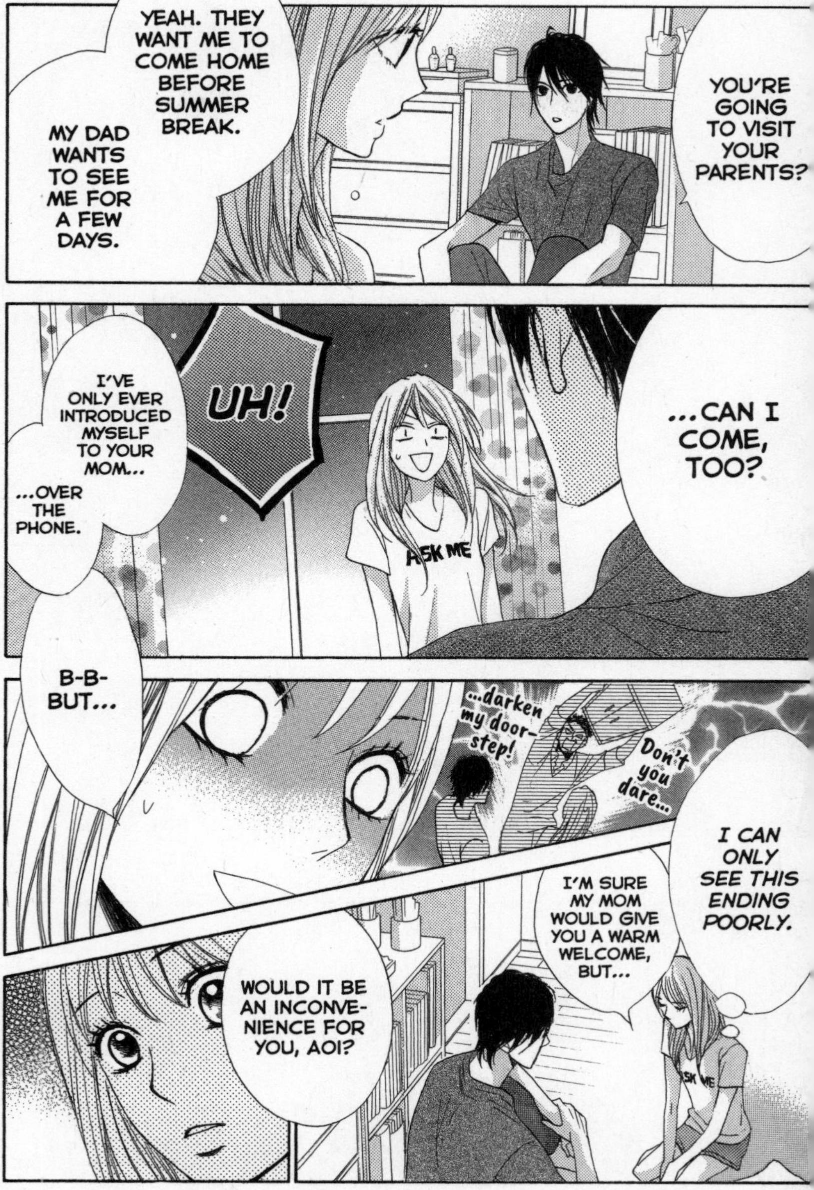
YOU'RE GOING TO VISIT YOUR PARENTS?
YEAH. THEY WANT ME TO COME HOME BEFORE SUMMER BREAK.
MY DAD WANTS TO SEE ME FOR A FEW DAYS.
...CAN I COME, TOO?
UH!
I'VE ONLY EVER INTRODUCED MYSELF TO YOUR MOM...
...OVER THE PHONE.
B-B-BUT...
Don't you dare...
...darken my door-step!
I CAN ONLY SEE THIS ENDING POORLY.
I'M SURE MY MOM WOULD GIVE YOU A WARM WELCOME, BUT...
WOULD IT BE AN INCONVENIENCE FOR YOU, AOI?

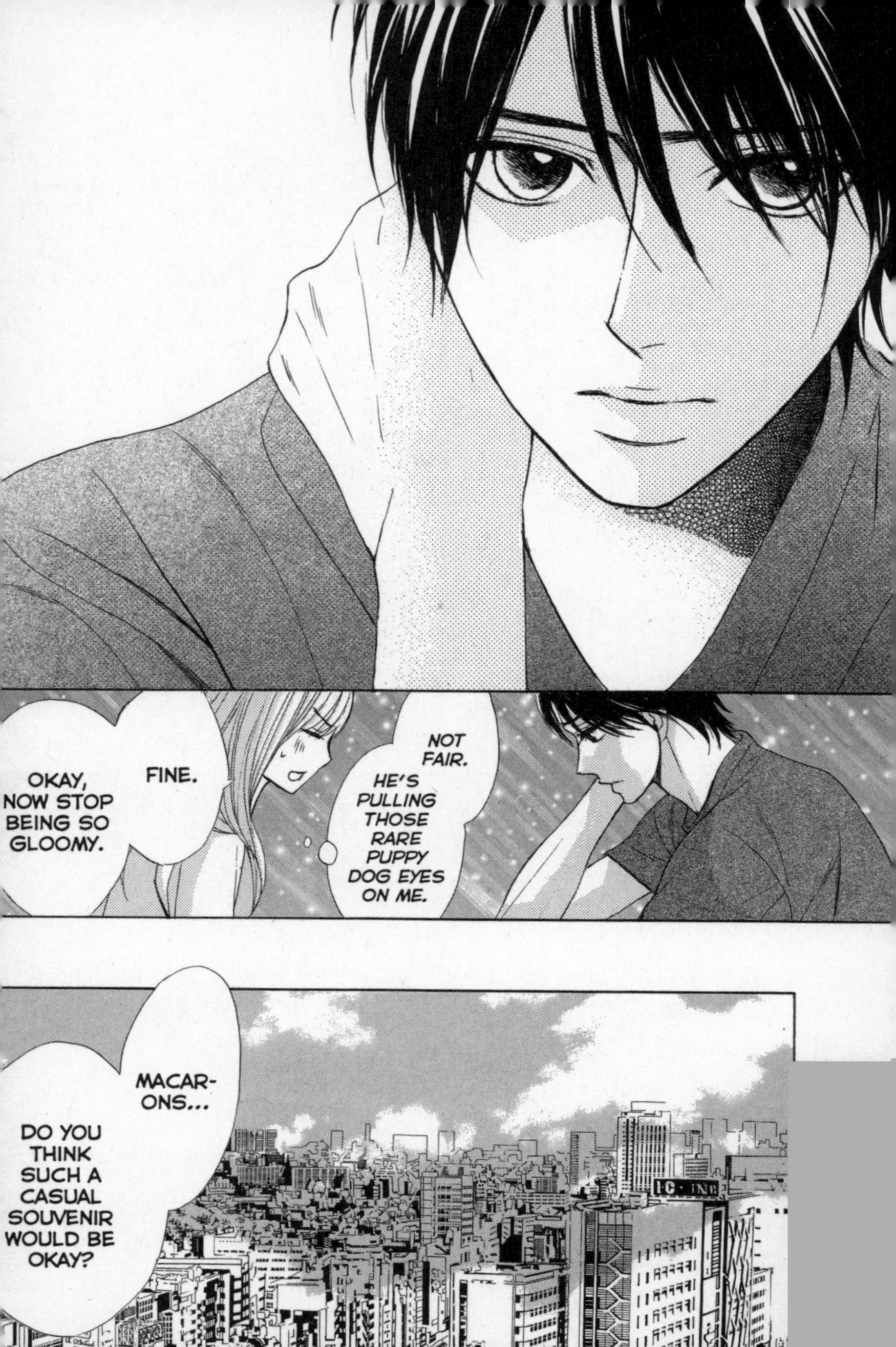
NOT FAIR. HE'S PULLING THOSE RARE PUPPY DOG EYES ON ME.
FINE.
OKAY, NOW STOP BEING SO GLOOMY.
MACAR-ONS...
DO YOU THINK SUCH A CASUAL SOUVENIR WOULD BE OKAY?

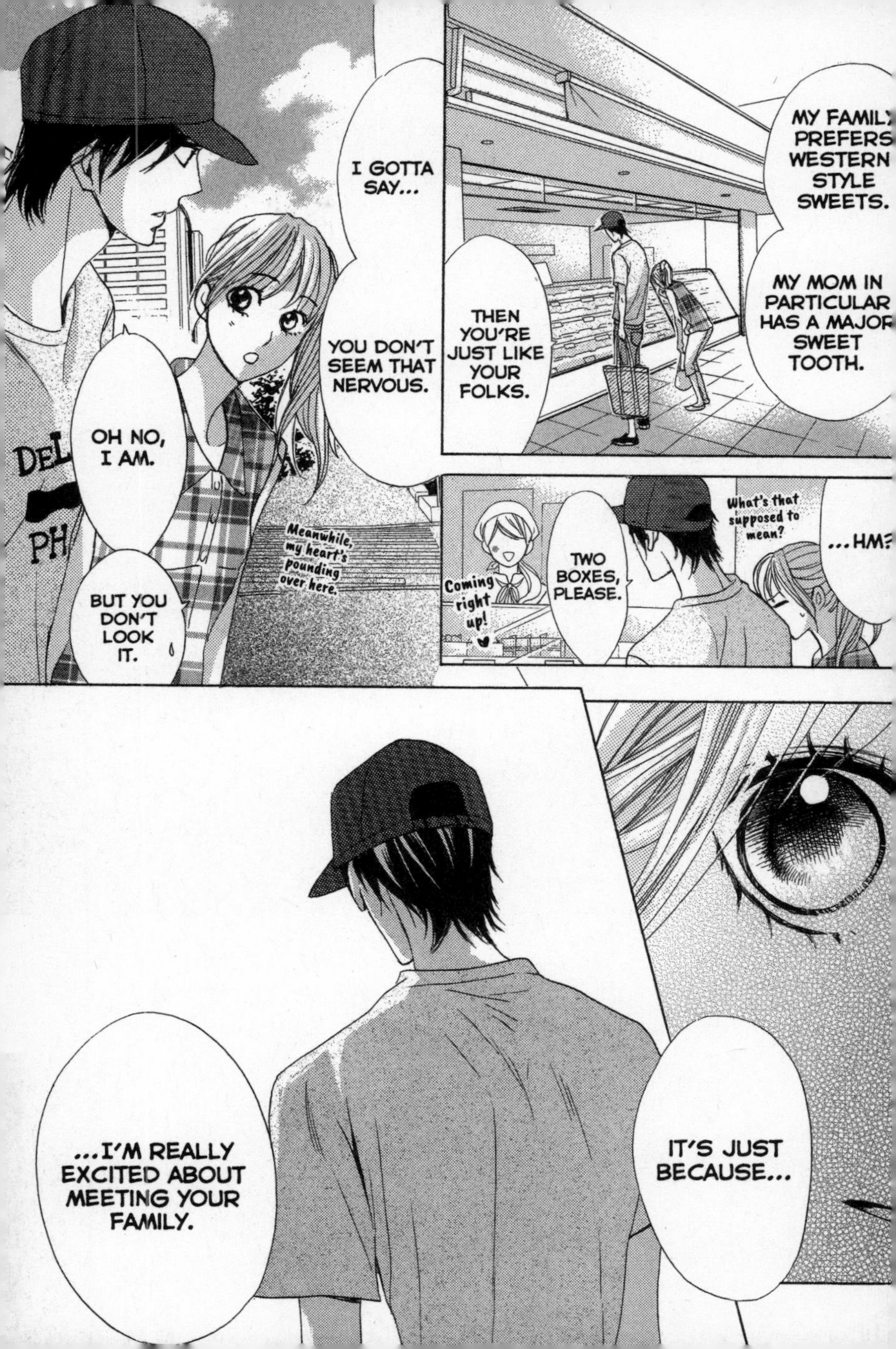

MY FAMILY PREFERS WESTERN STYLE SWEETS.
MY MOM IN PARTICULAR HAS A MAJOR SWEET TOOTH.
THEN YOU'RE JUST LIKE YOUR FOLKS.
...HM?
What's that supposed to mean?
TWO BOXES, PLEASE.
Coming right up!
I GOTTA SAY...
YOU DON'T SEEM THAT NERVOUS.
OH NO, I AM.
BUT YOU DON'T LOOK IT.
Meanwhile, my heart's pounding over here.
IT'S JUST BECAUSE...
...I'M REALLY EXCITED ABOUT MEETING YOUR FAMILY.

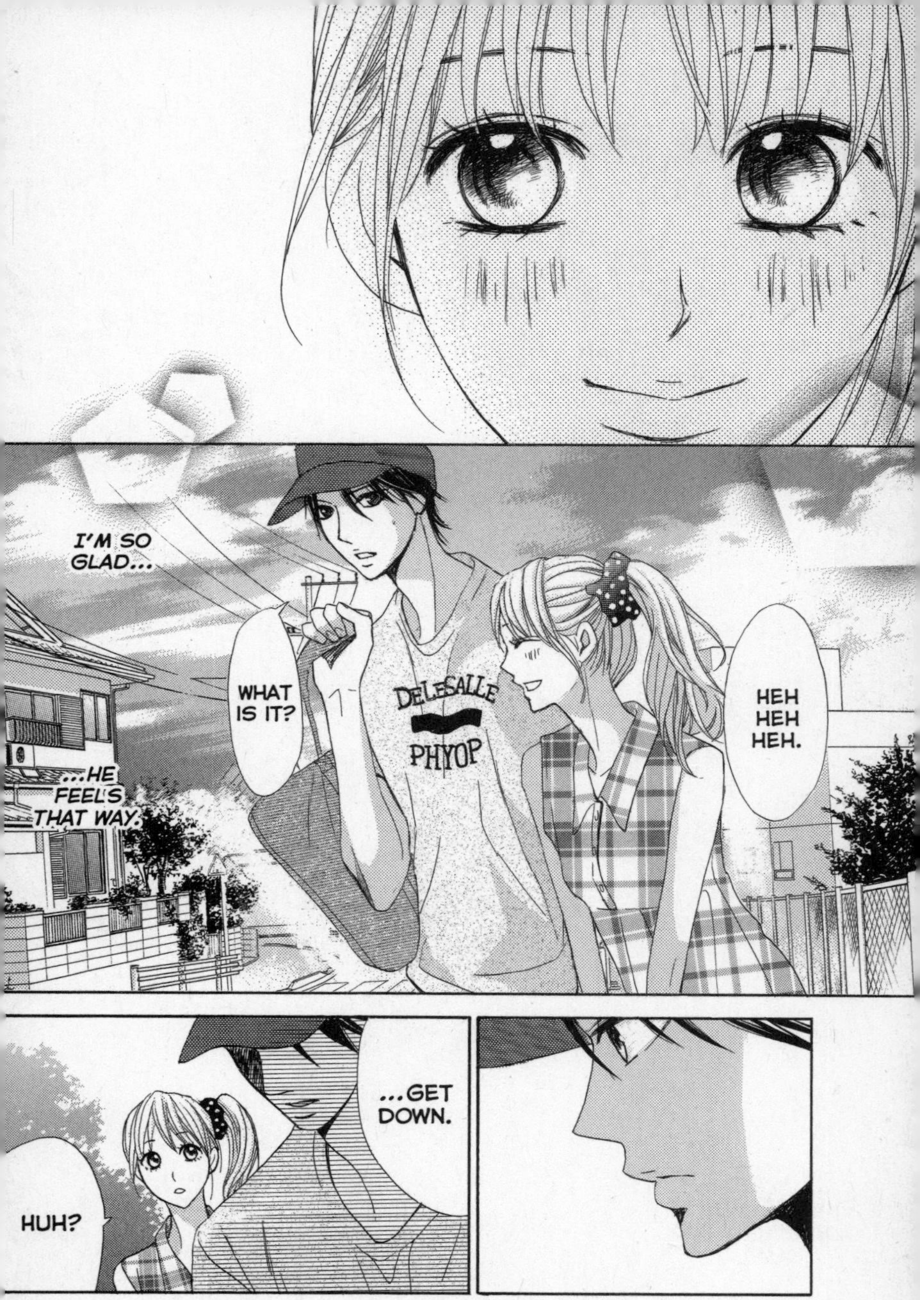
HEH HEH HEH.
WHAT IS IT?
DELESALLE PHYOP
I'M SO GLAD...
...HE FEELS THAT WAY.
...GET DOWN.
HUH?

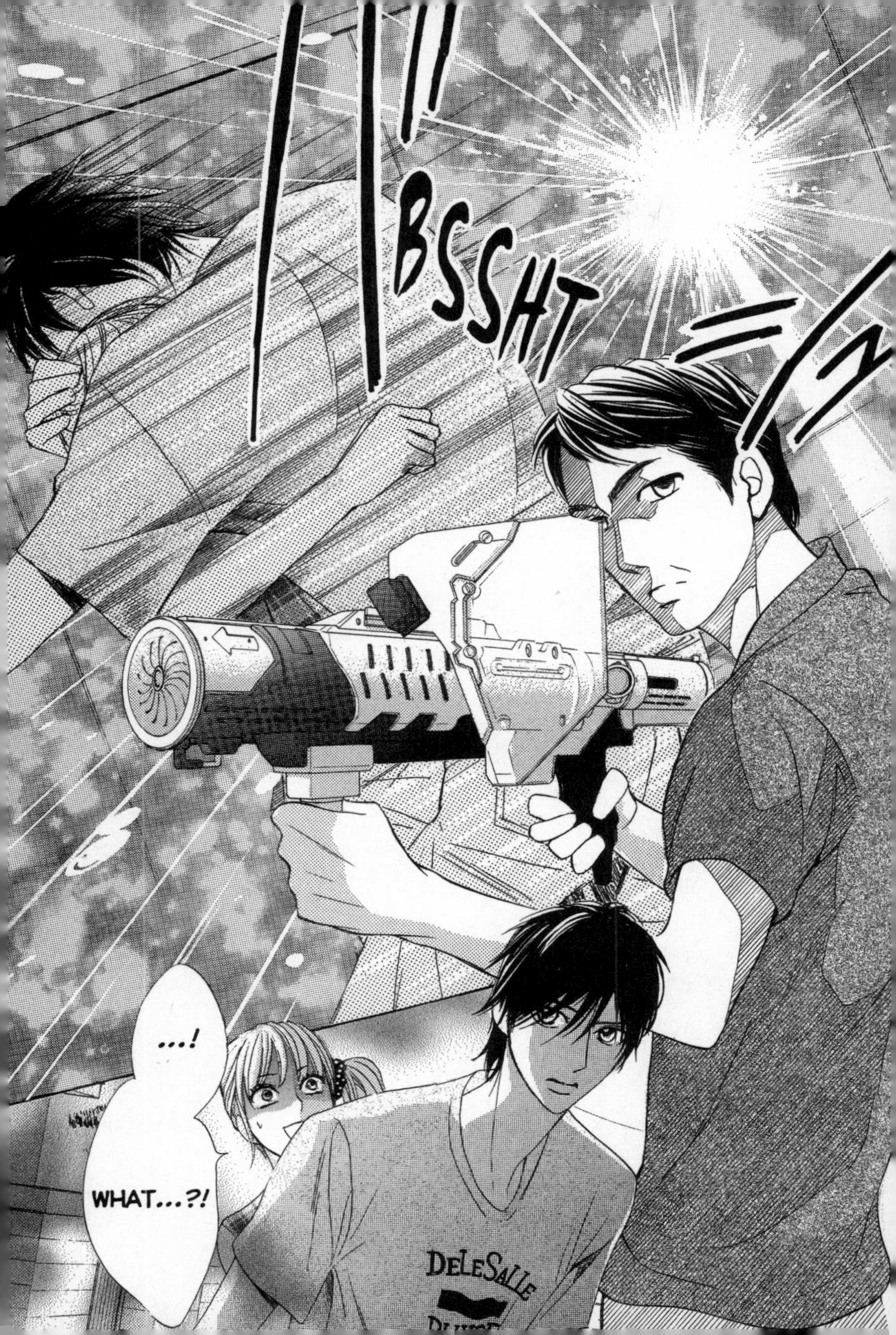
BSSHT
...!
WHAT...?!
DELESALLE

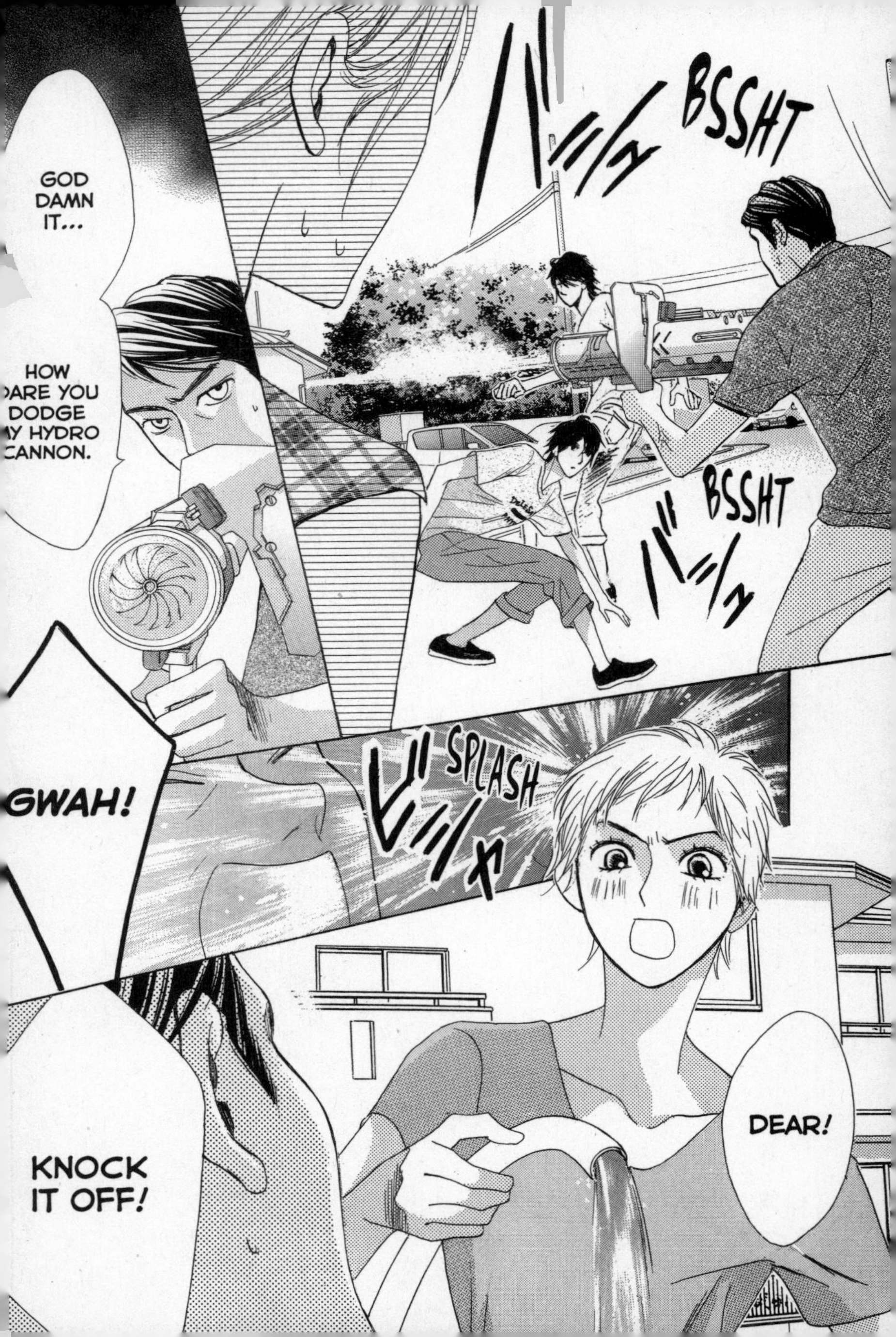
BSSHT
BSSHT
GOD DAMN IT...
HOW DARE YOU DODGE MY HYDRO CANNON.
SPLASH
GWAH!
DEAR!
KNOCK IT OFF!

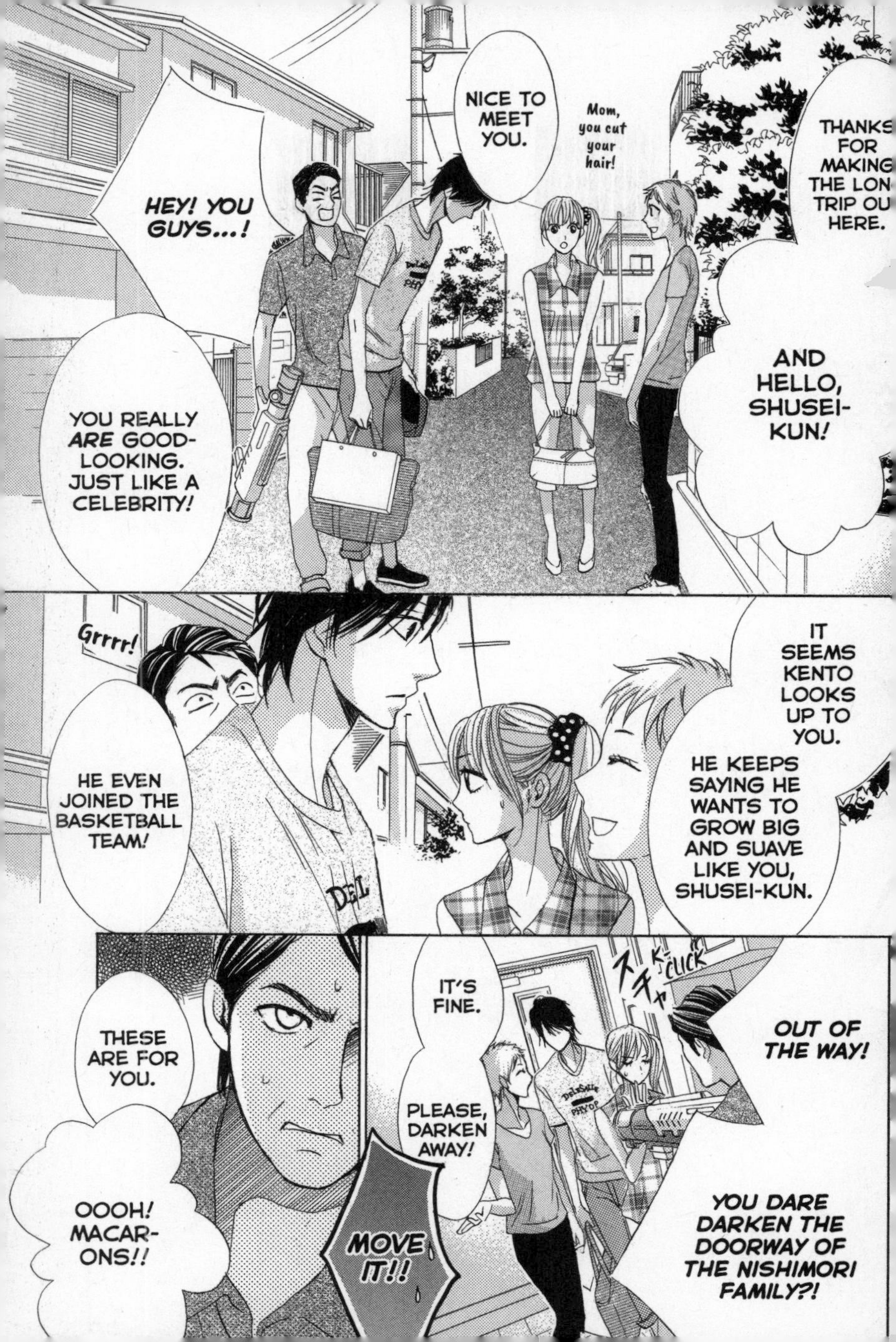
THANKS FOR MAKING THE LON TRIP OU HERE.
AND HELLO, SHUSEI-KUN!
Mom, you cut your hair!
NICE TO MEET YOU.
HEY! YOU GUYS...!
YOU REALLY *ARE* GOOD-LOOKING. JUST LIKE A CELEBRITY!
IT SEEMS KENTO LOOKS UP TO YOU.
HE KEEPS SAYING HE WANTS TO GROW BIG AND SUAVE LIKE YOU, SHUSEI-KUN.
HE EVEN JOINED THE BASKETBALL TEAM!
Grrrr!
OUT OF THE WAY!
YOU DARE DARKEN THE DOORWAY OF THE NISHIMORI FAMILY?!
スチャ K-CLICK
IT'S FINE.
PLEASE, DARKEN AWAY!
THESE ARE FOR YOU.
OOOH! MACARONS!!
MOVE IT!!

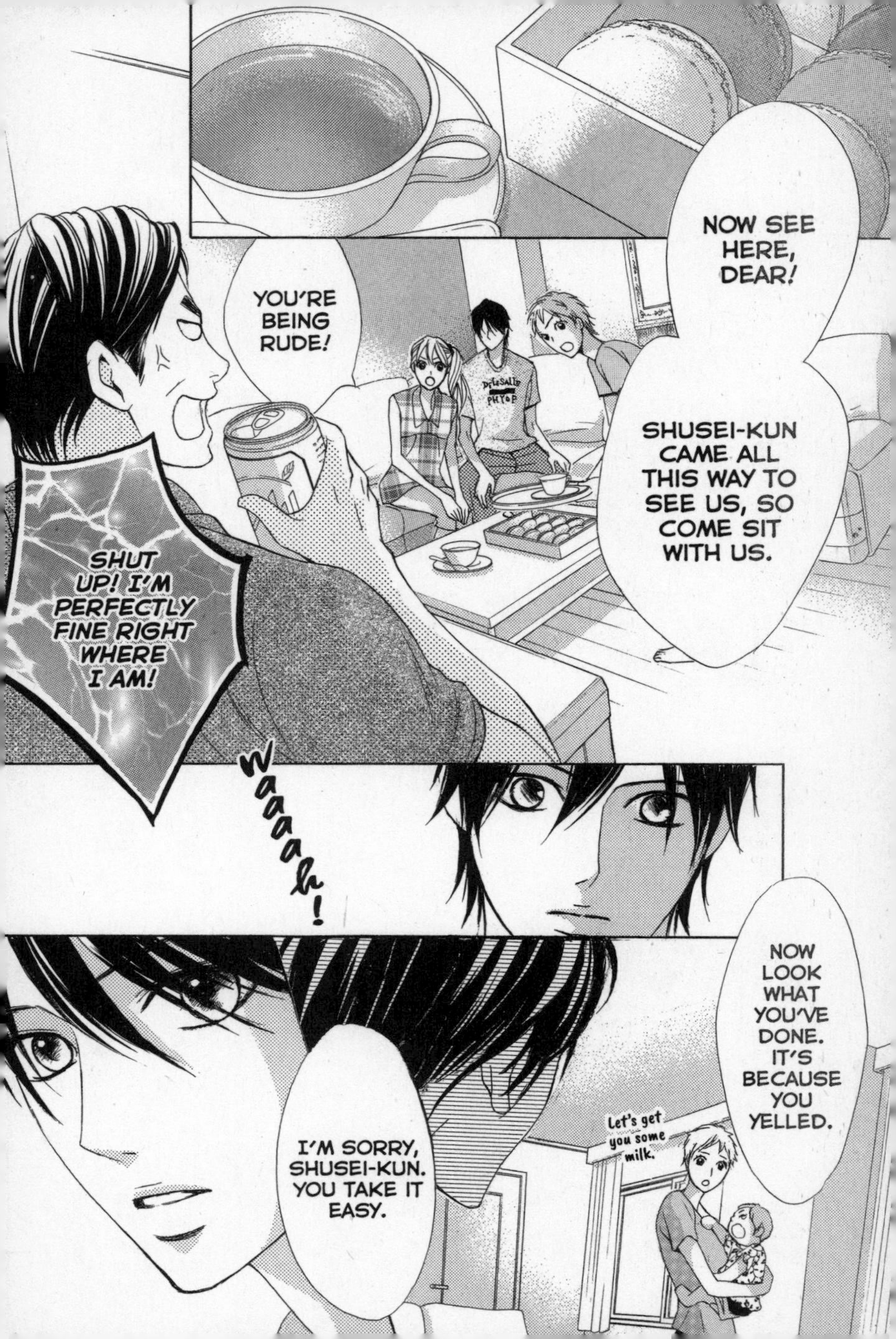
NOW SEE HERE, DEAR!
SHUSEI-KUN CAME ALL THIS WAY TO SEE US, SO COME SIT WITH US.
YOU'RE BEING RUDE!
SHUT UP! I'M PERFECTLY FINE RIGHT WHERE I AM!
Waaaah!
NOW LOOK WHAT YOU'VE DONE. IT'S BECAUSE YOU YELLED.
Let's get you some milk.
I'M SORRY, SHUSEI-KUN. YOU TAKE IT EASY.

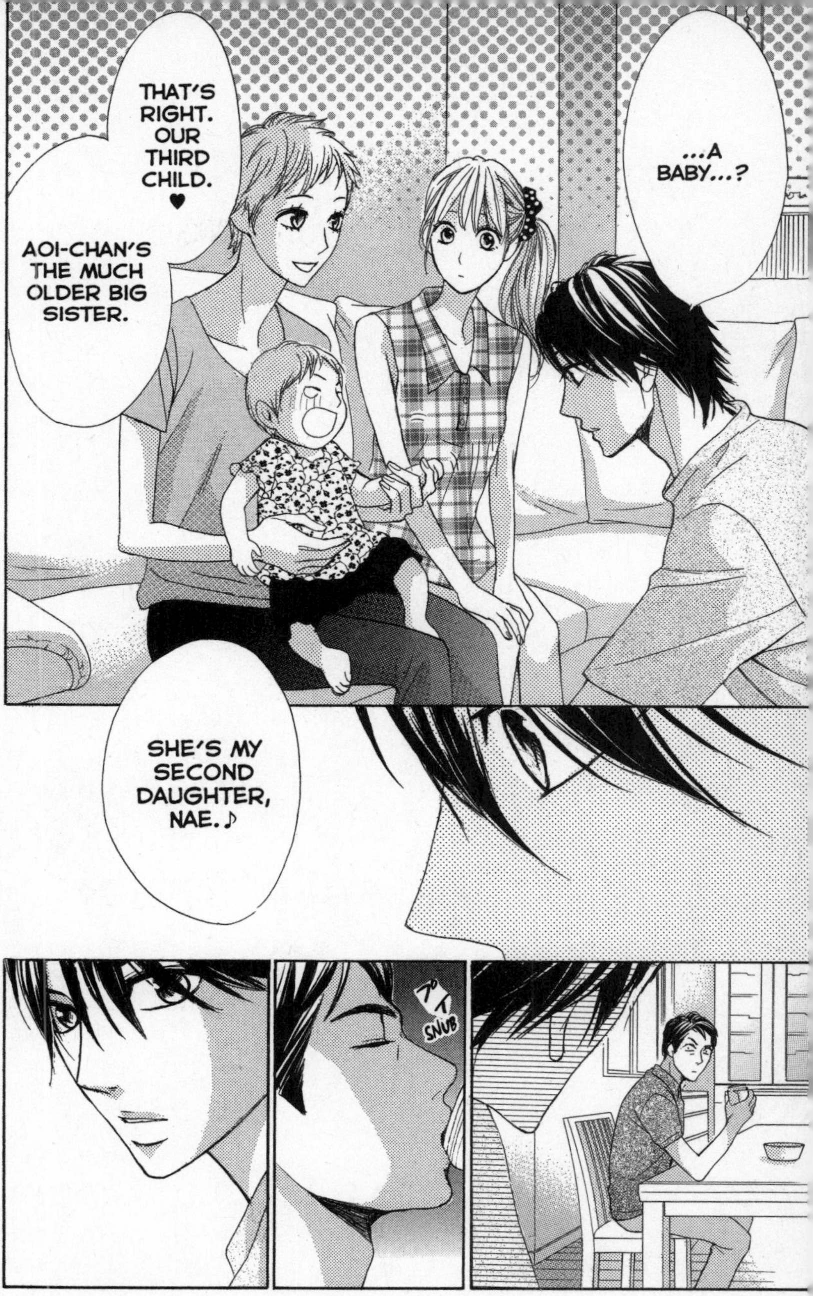
...A BABY...?
THAT'S RIGHT. OUR THIRD CHILD. ♥
AOI-CHAN'S THE MUCH OLDER BIG SISTER.
SHE'S MY SECOND DAUGHTER, NAE. ♪
プイ
SNUB

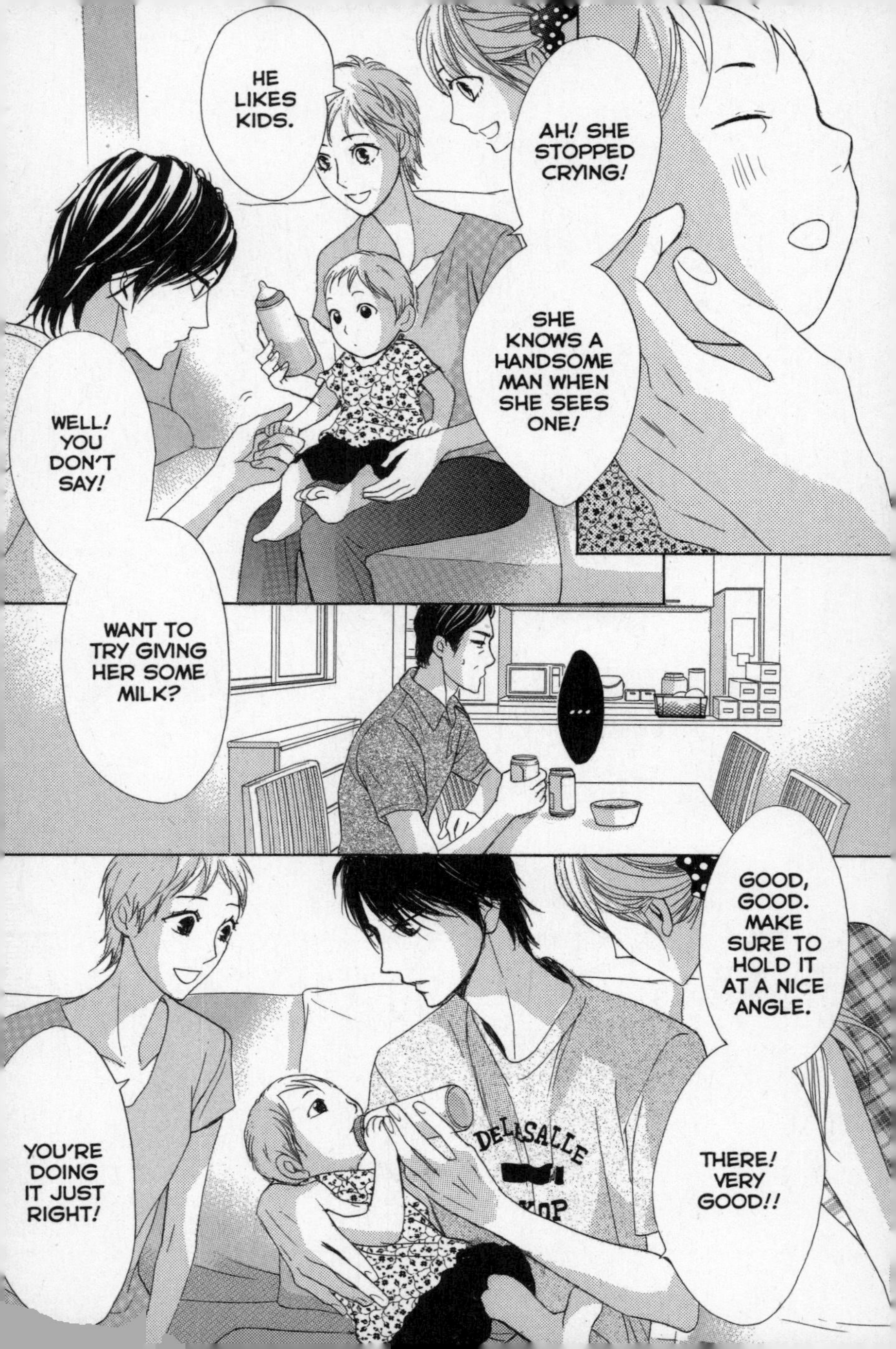
AH! SHE STOPPED CRYING!
HE LIKES KIDS.
SHE KNOWS A HANDSOME MAN WHEN SHE SEES ONE!
WELL! YOU DON'T SAY!
WANT TO TRY GIVING HER SOME MILK?
...
GOOD, GOOD. MAKE SURE TO HOLD IT AT A NICE ANGLE.
THERE! VERY GOOD!!
DELASALLE
YOU'RE DOING IT JUST RIGHT!

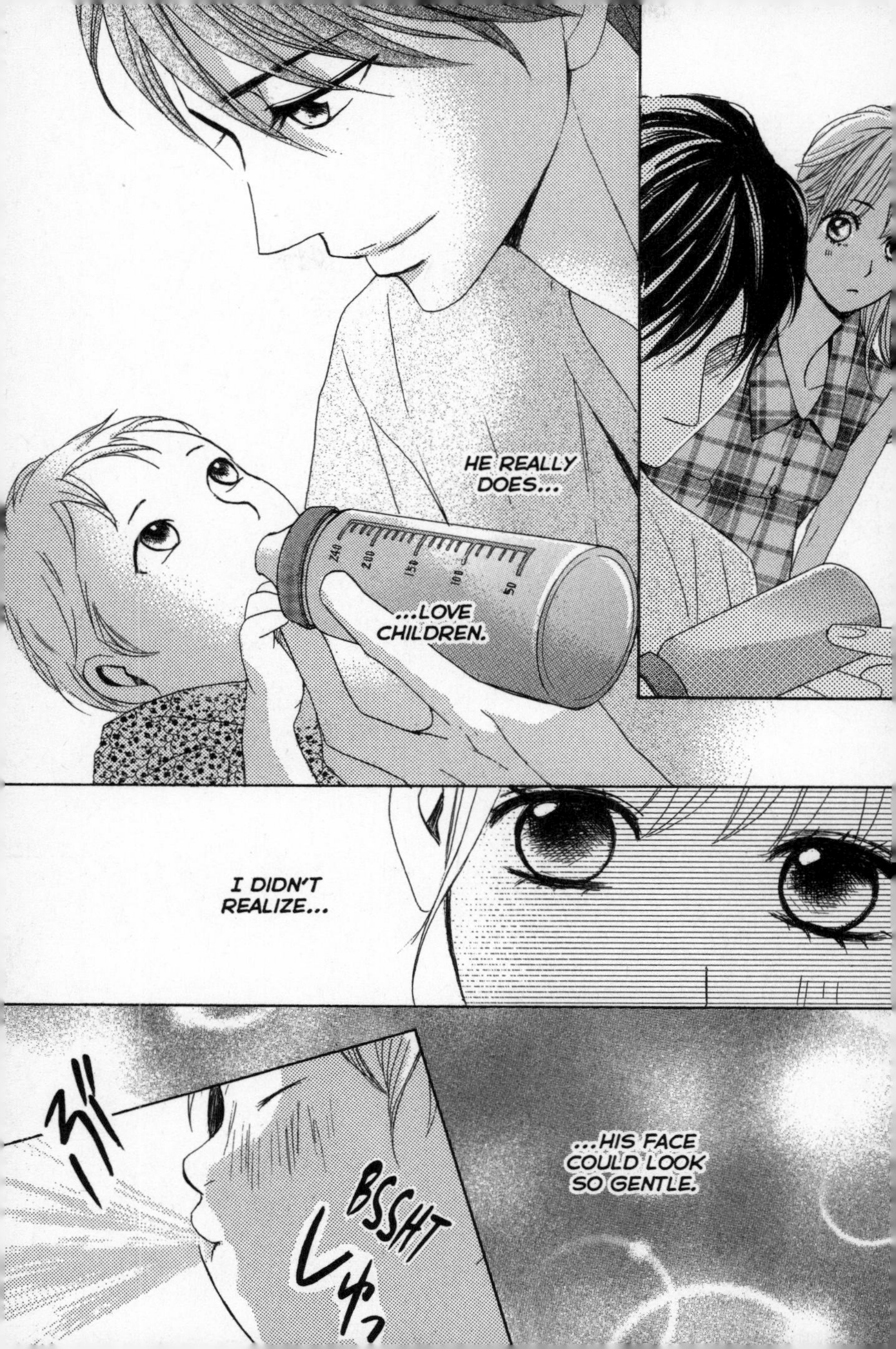
HE REALLY DOES...
...LOVE CHILDREN.
I DIDN'T REALIZE...
...HIS FACE COULD LOOK SO GENTLE.
BSSHT

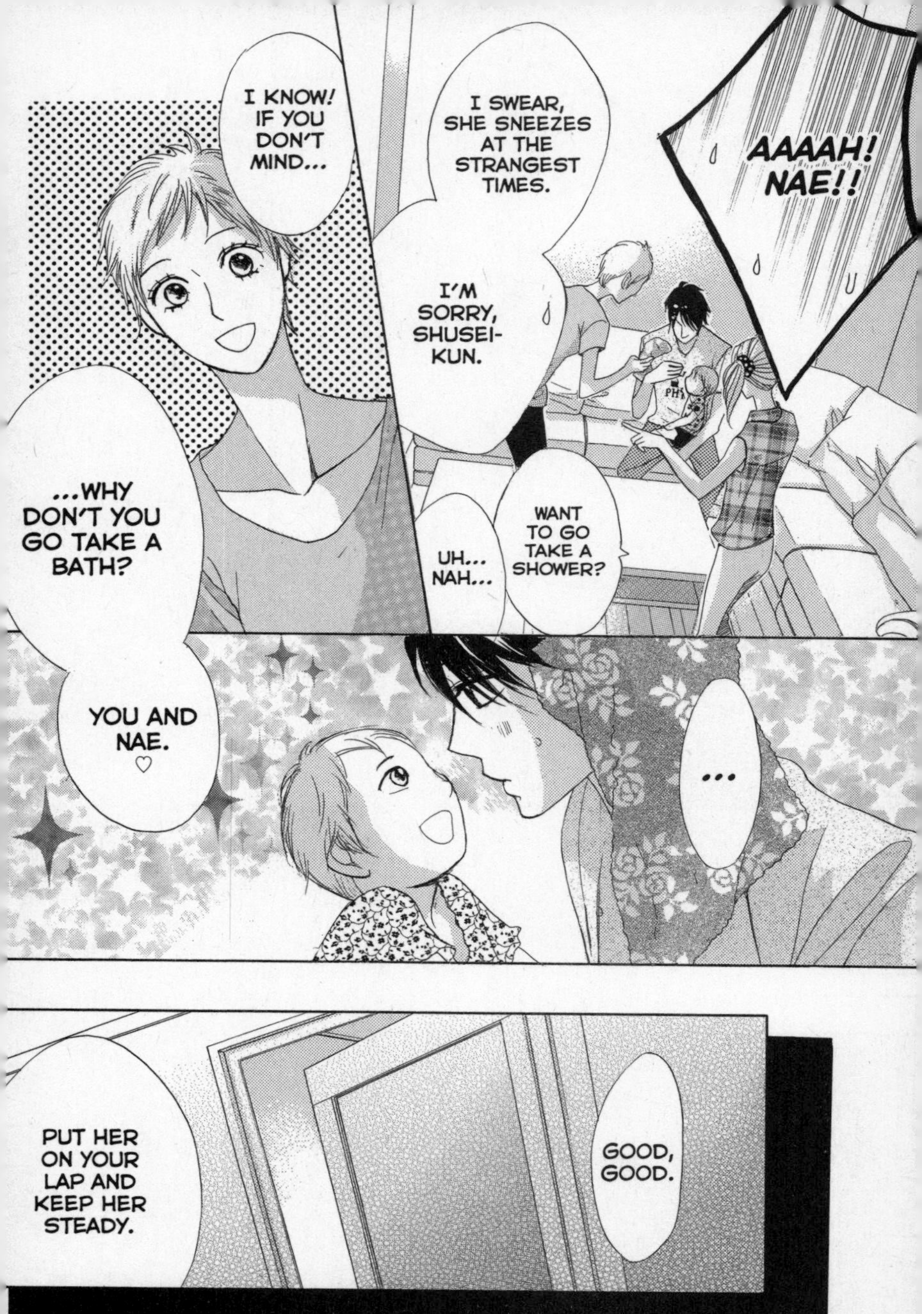

AAAAH! NAE!!
I SWEAR, SHE SNEEZES AT THE STRANGEST TIMES.
I'M SORRY, SHUSEI-KUN.
WANT TO GO TAKE A SHOWER?
UH... NAH...
I KNOW! IF YOU DON'T MIND...
...WHY DON'T YOU GO TAKE A BATH?
YOU AND NAE. ♡
...
GOOD, GOOD.
PUT HER ON YOUR LAP AND KEEP HER STEADY.

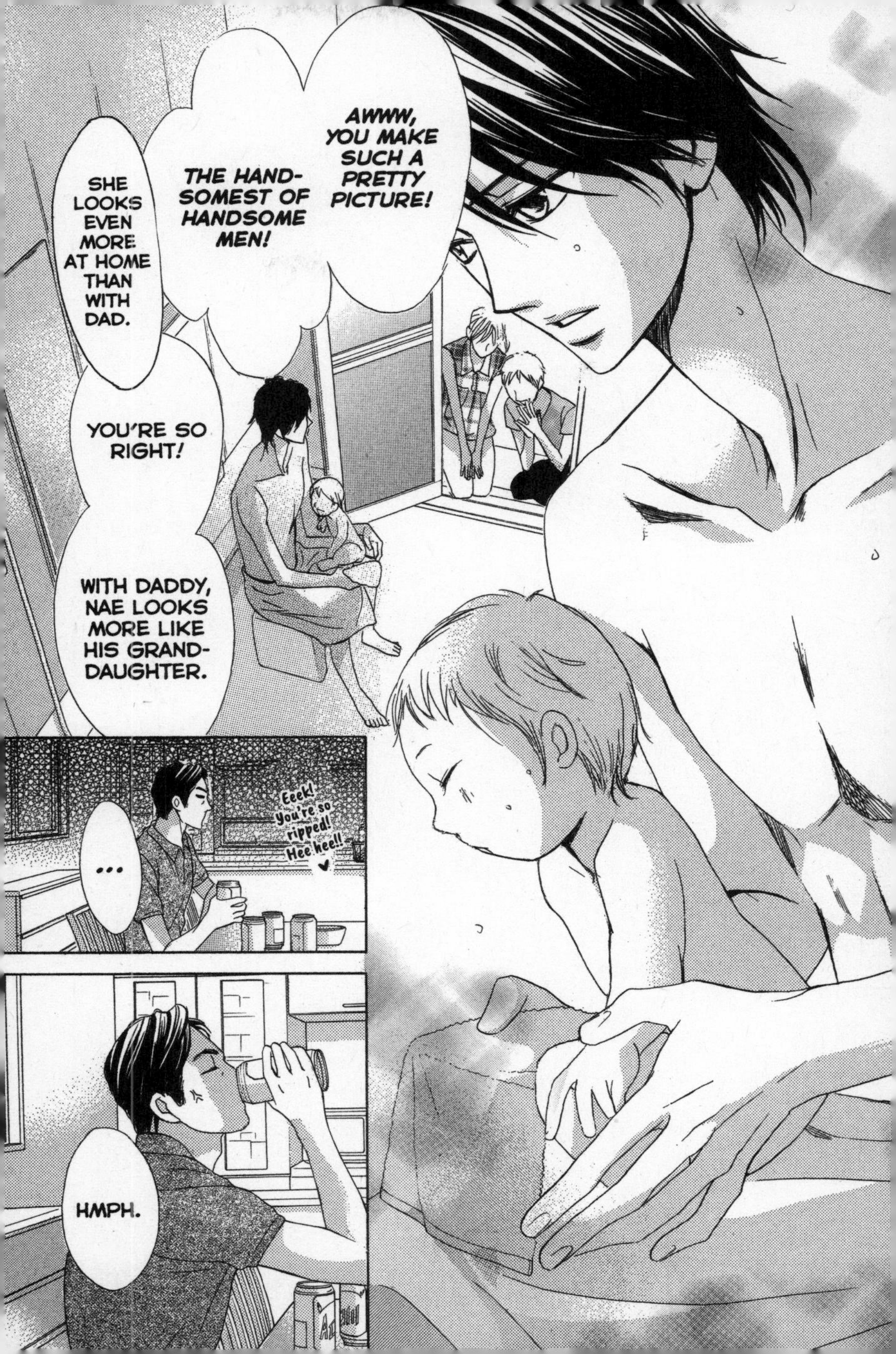
AWWW, YOU MAKE SUCH A PRETTY PICTURE!
THE HAND-SOMEST OF HANDSOME MEN!
SHE LOOKS EVEN MORE AT HOME THAN WITH DAD.
YOU'RE SO RIGHT!
WITH DADDY, NAE LOOKS MORE LIKE HIS GRAND-DAUGHTER.
Eeek! You're so ripped! Hee hee!!
...
HMPH.

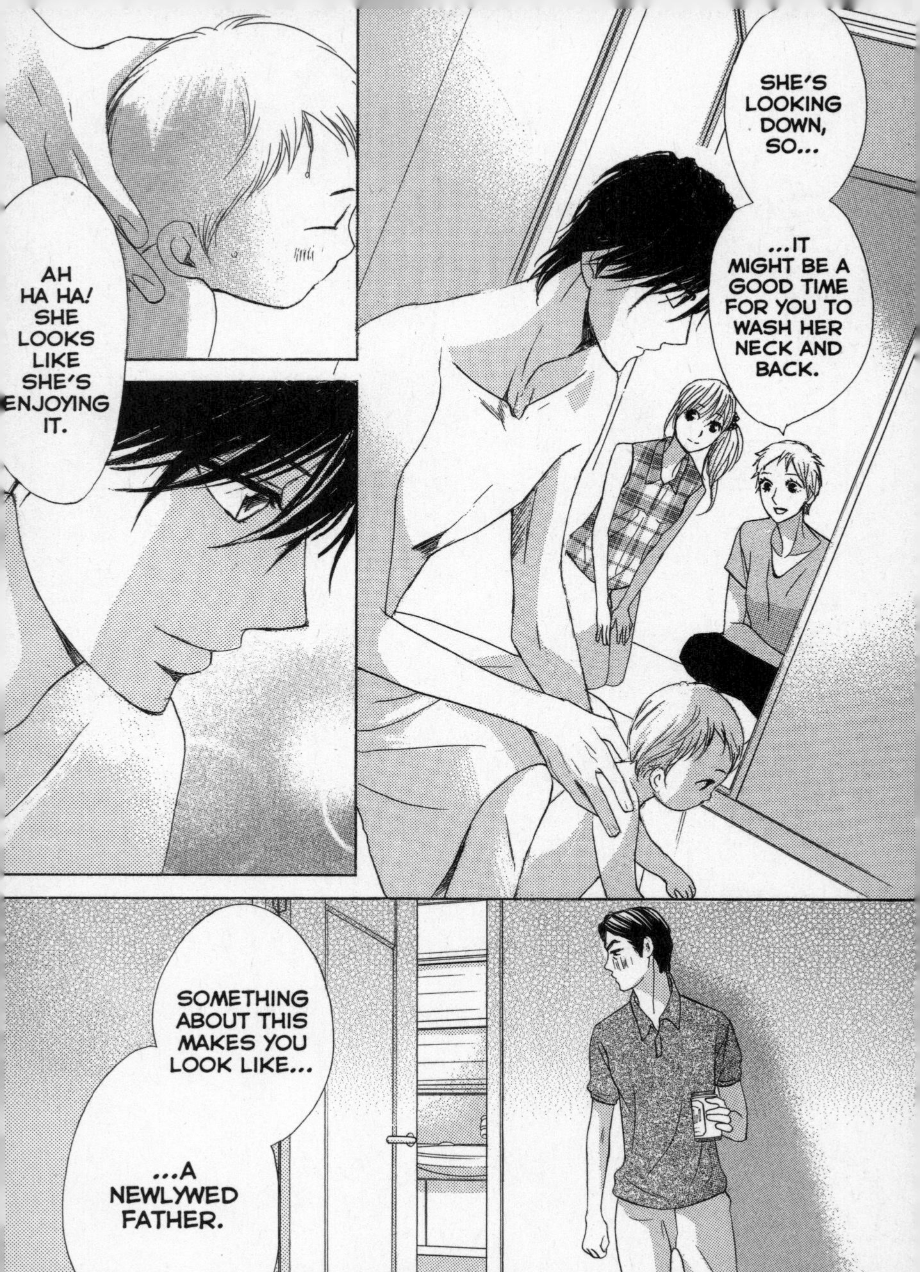
SHE'S LOOKING DOWN, SO...
...IT MIGHT BE A GOOD TIME FOR YOU TO WASH HER NECK AND BACK.
AH HA HA! SHE LOOKS LIKE SHE'S ENJOYING IT.
SOMETHING ABOUT THIS MAKES YOU LOOK LIKE...
...A NEWLYWED FATHER.

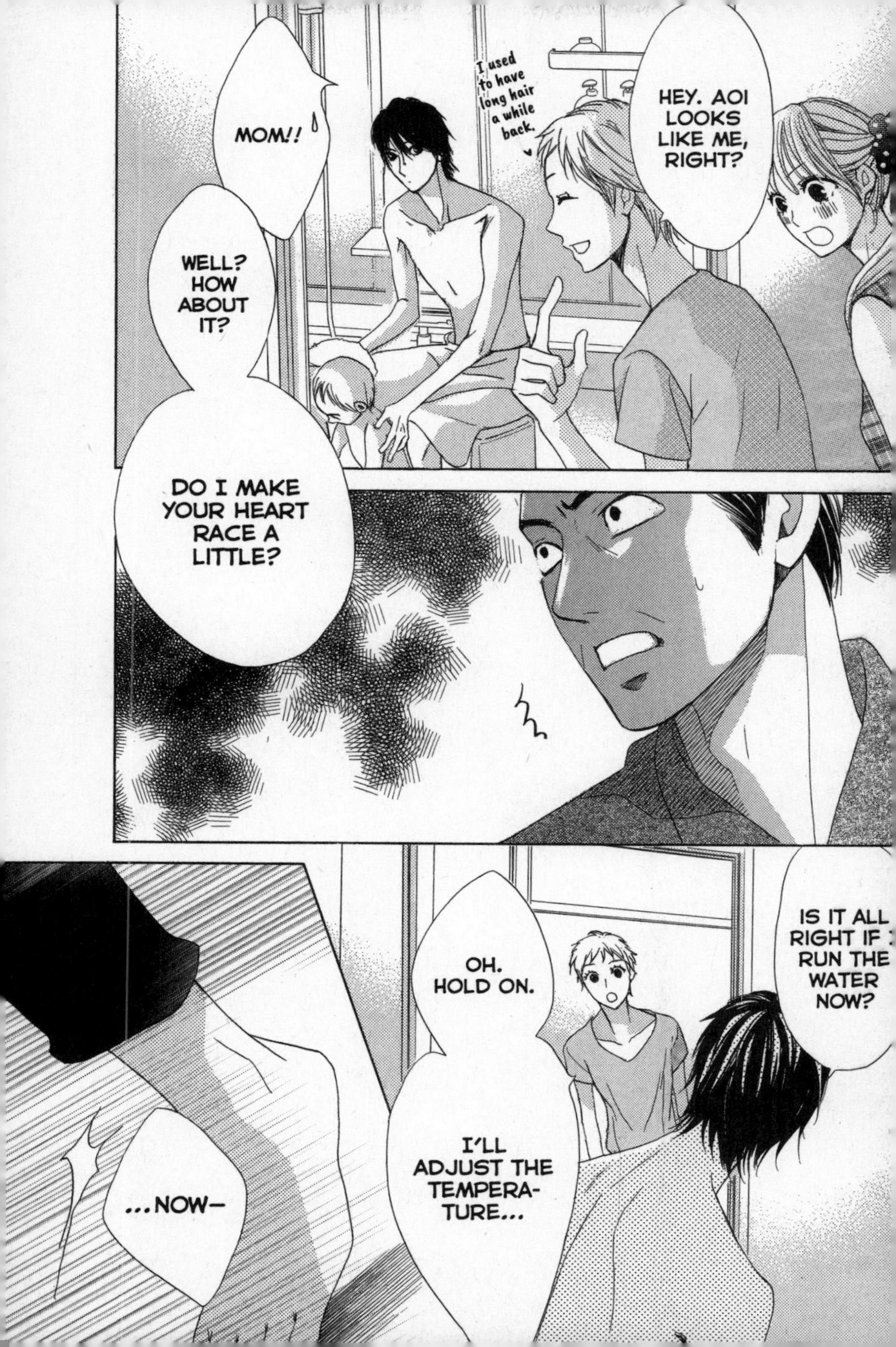
HEY. AOI LOOKS LIKE ME, RIGHT?
I used to have long hair a while back.
MOM!!
WELL? HOW ABOUT IT?
DO I MAKE YOUR HEART RACE A LITTLE?
IS IT ALL RIGHT IF RUN THE WATER NOW?
OH. HOLD ON.
I'LL ADJUST THE TEMPERA-TURE...
...NOW–

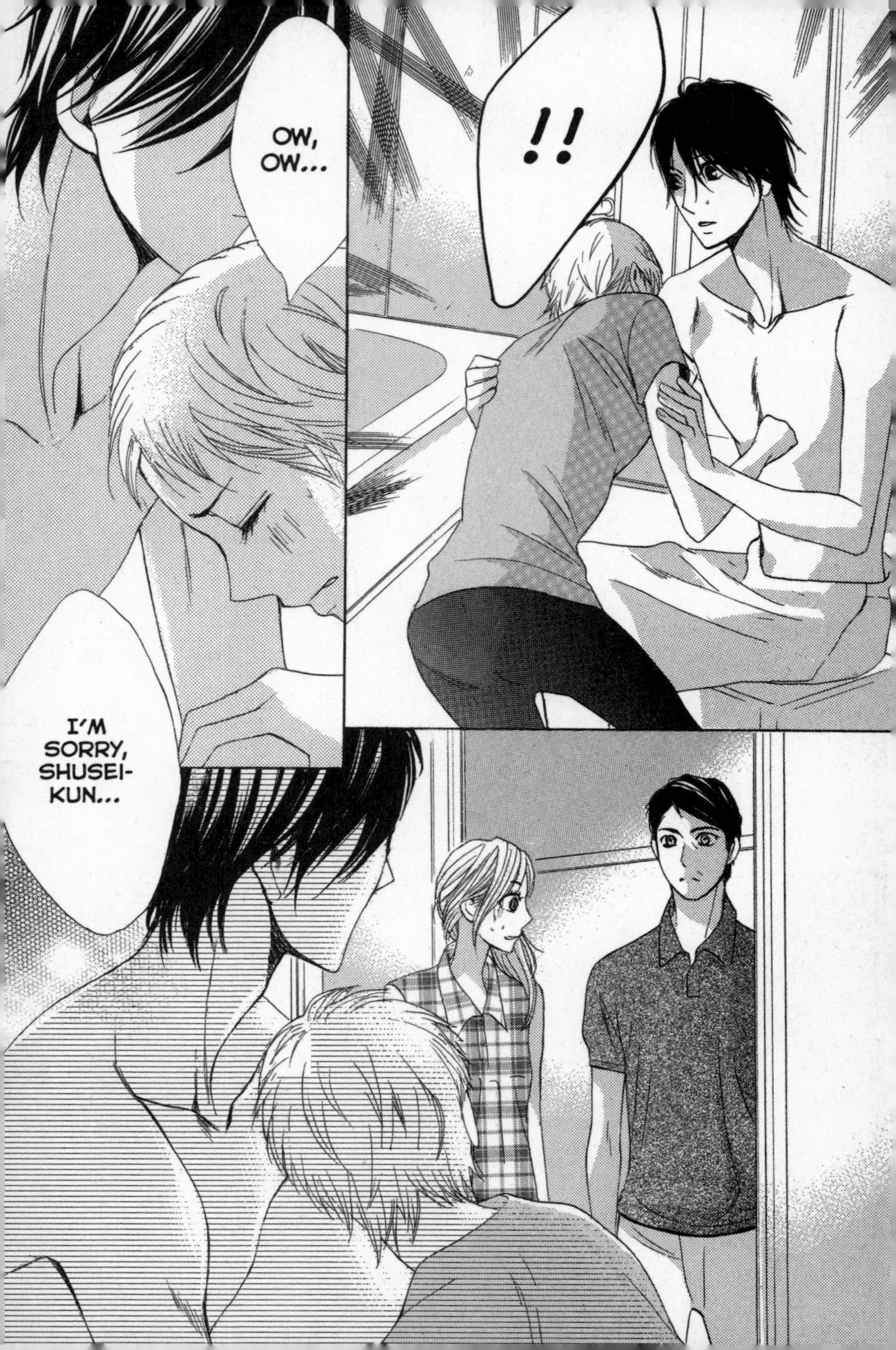
!!
OW, OW...
I'M SORRY, SHUSEI-KUN...

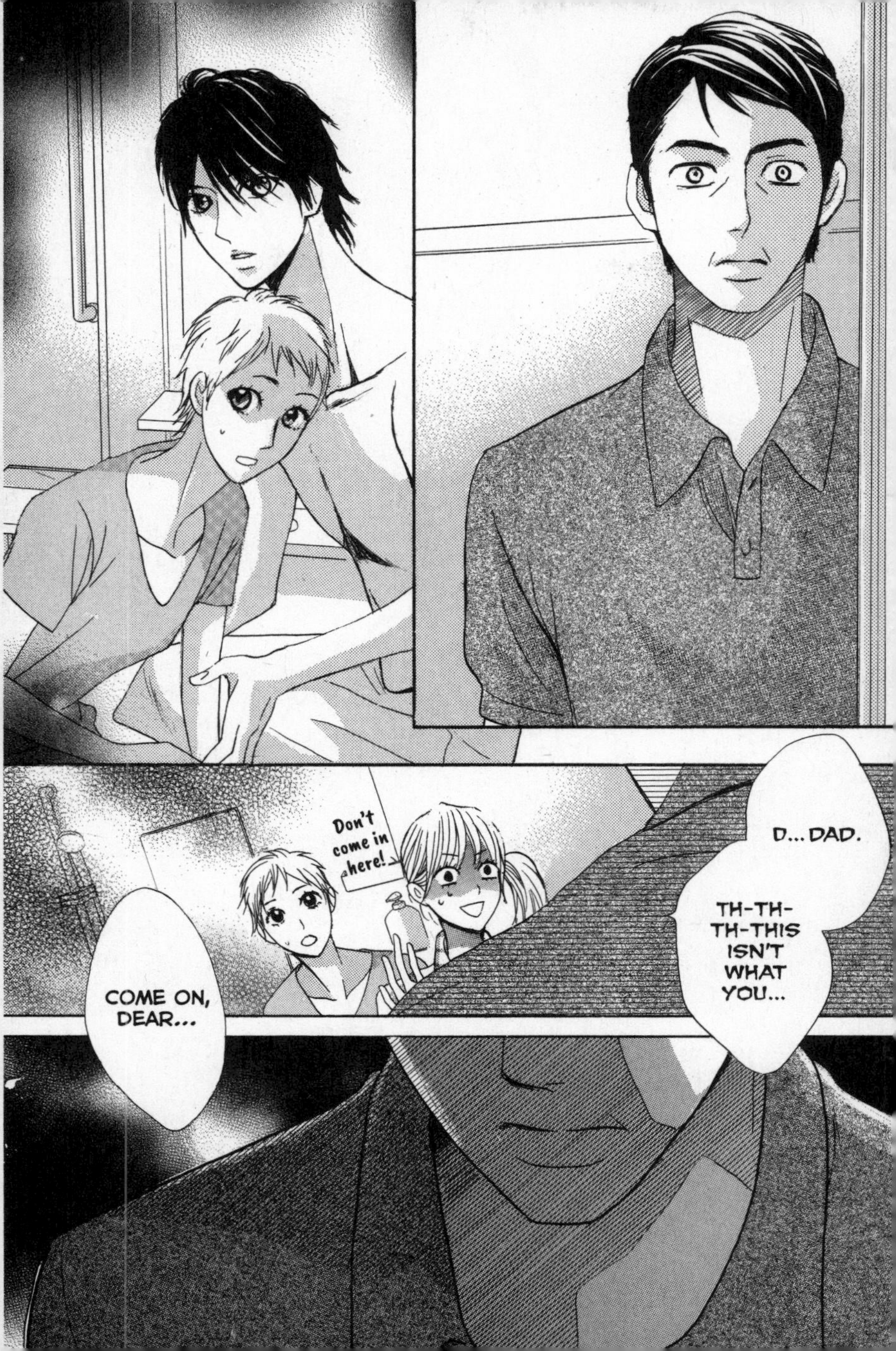
D... DAD.
TH-TH-TH-THIS ISN'T WHAT YOU...
Don't come in here!
COME ON, DEAR...

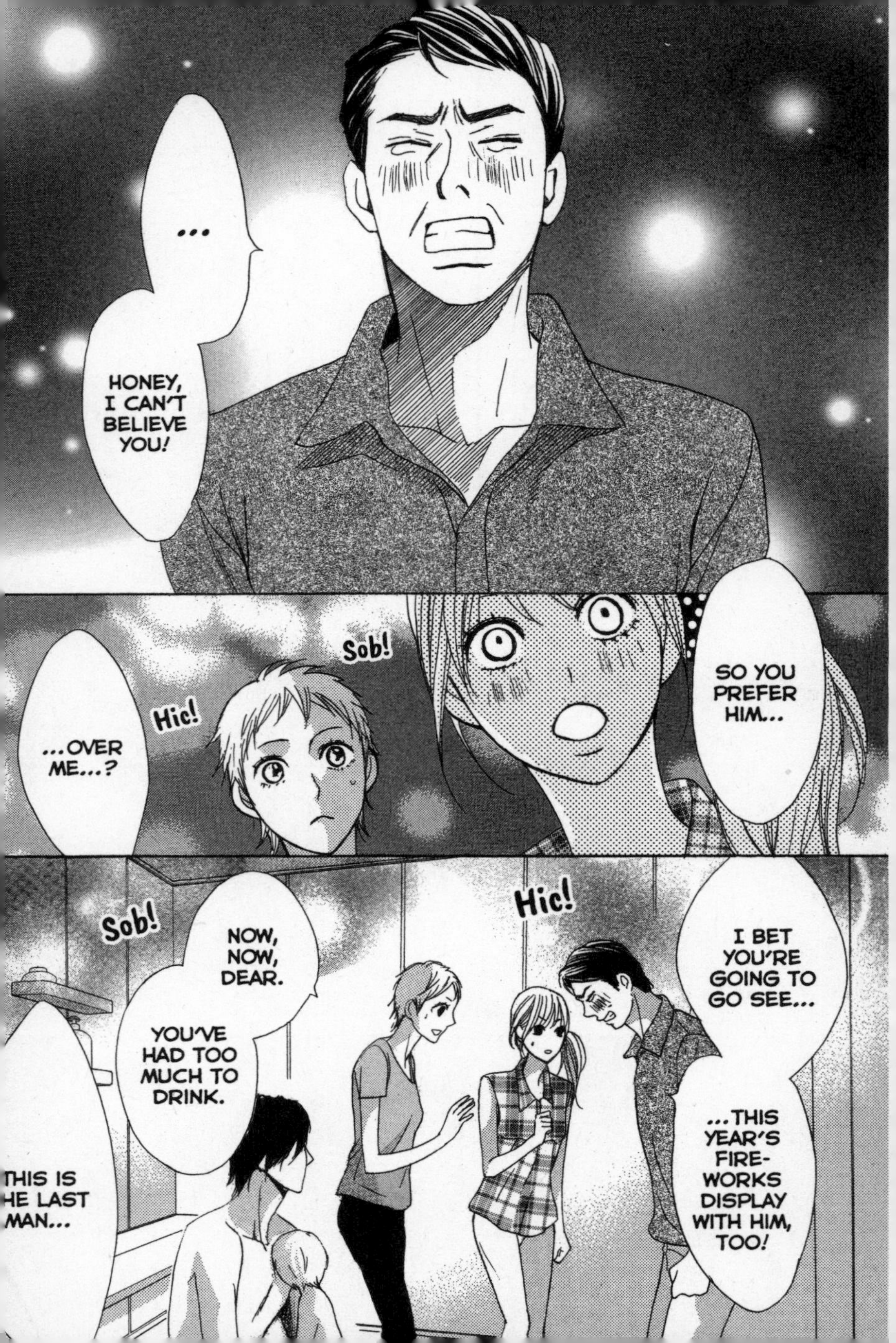
...
HONEY, I CAN'T BELIEVE YOU!
SO YOU PREFER HIM...
Sob!
Hic!
...OVER ME...?
I BET YOU'RE GOING TO GO SEE...
...THIS YEAR'S FIRE-WORKS DISPLAY WITH HIM, TOO!
Hic!
NOW, NOW, DEAR.
YOU'VE HAD TOO MUCH TO DRINK.
Sob!
THIS IS HE LAST MAN...

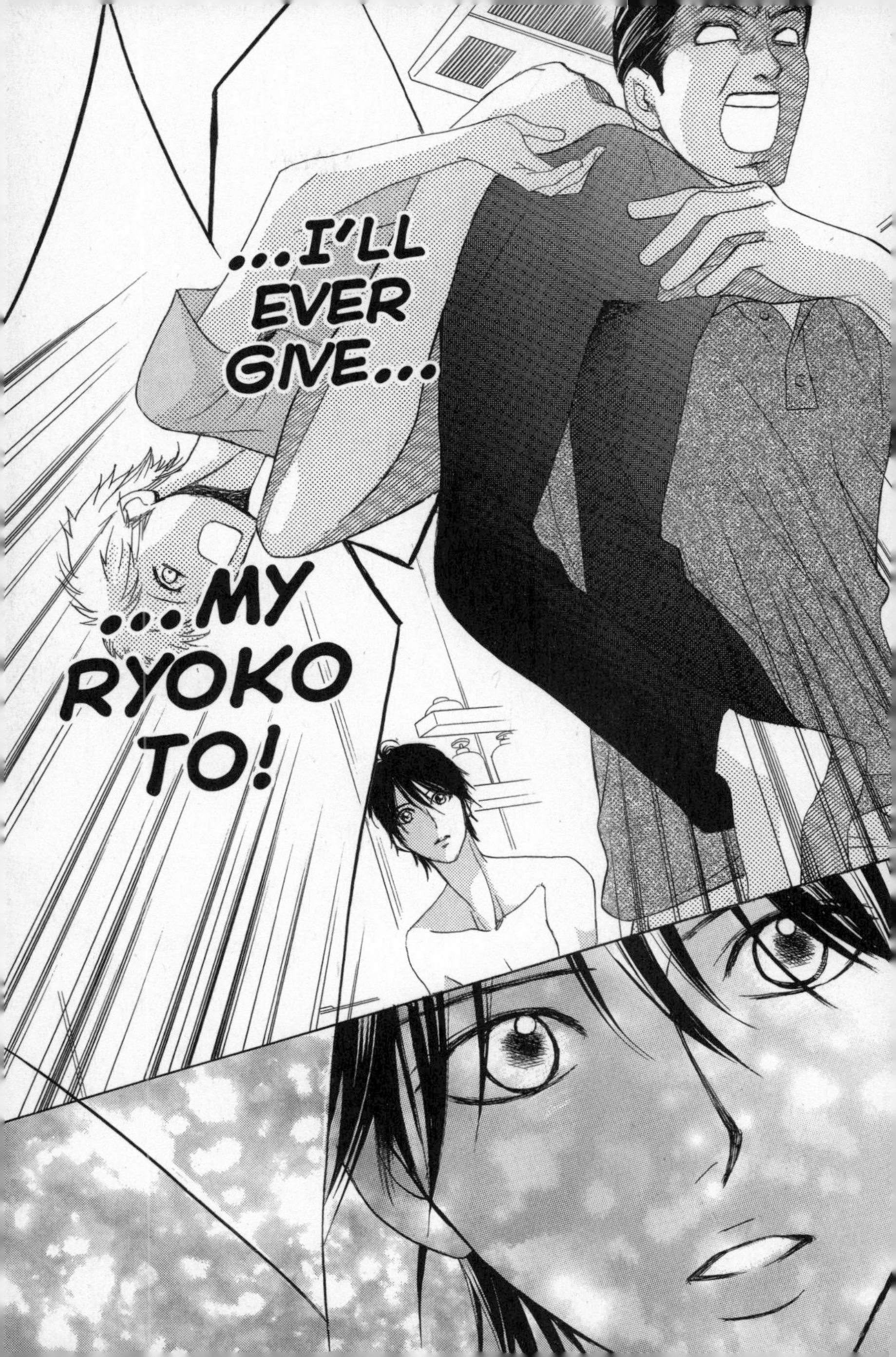
...I'LL EVER GIVE...
...MY RYOKO TO!

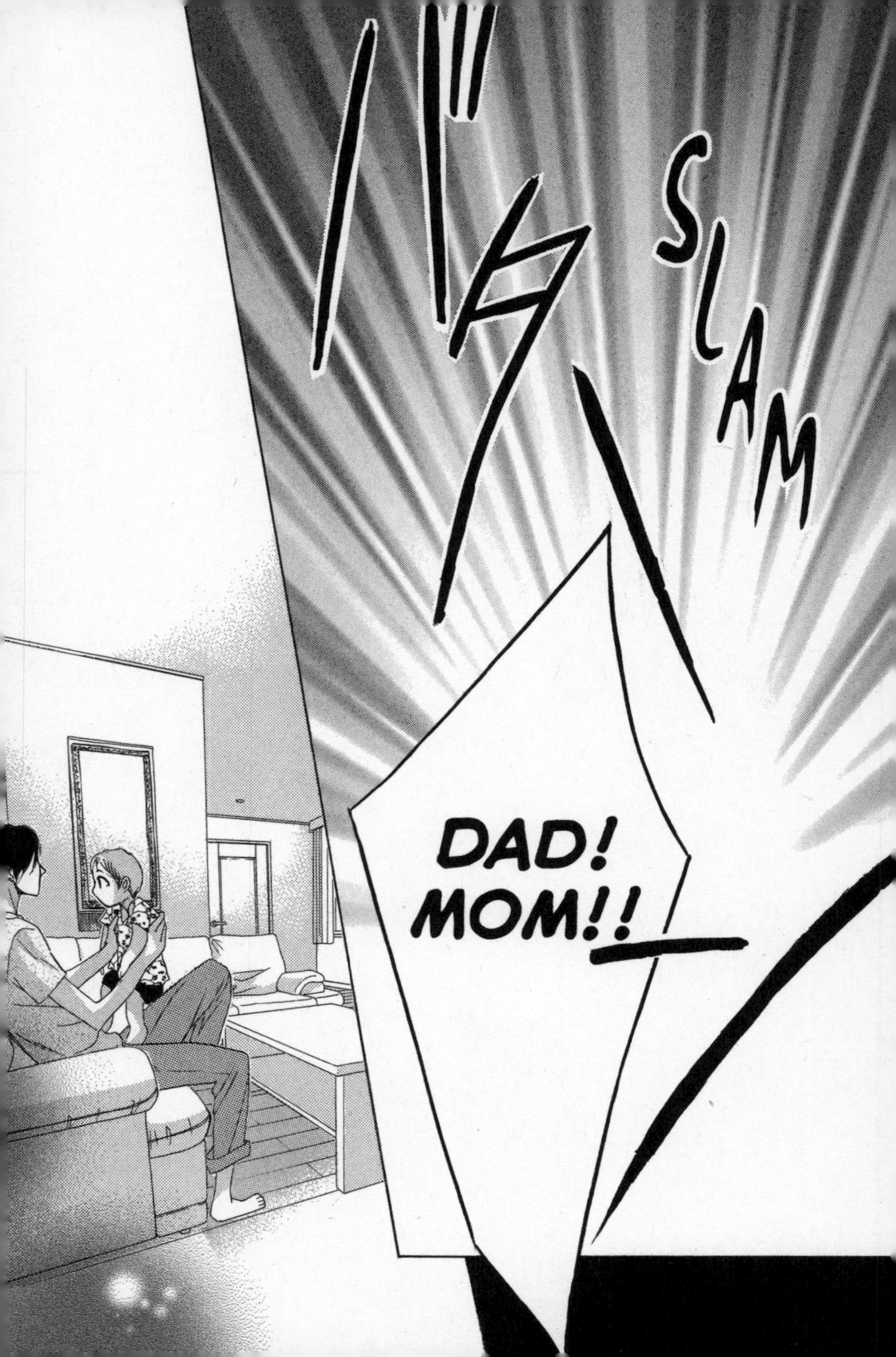
バム
SLAM
DAD!
MOM!!

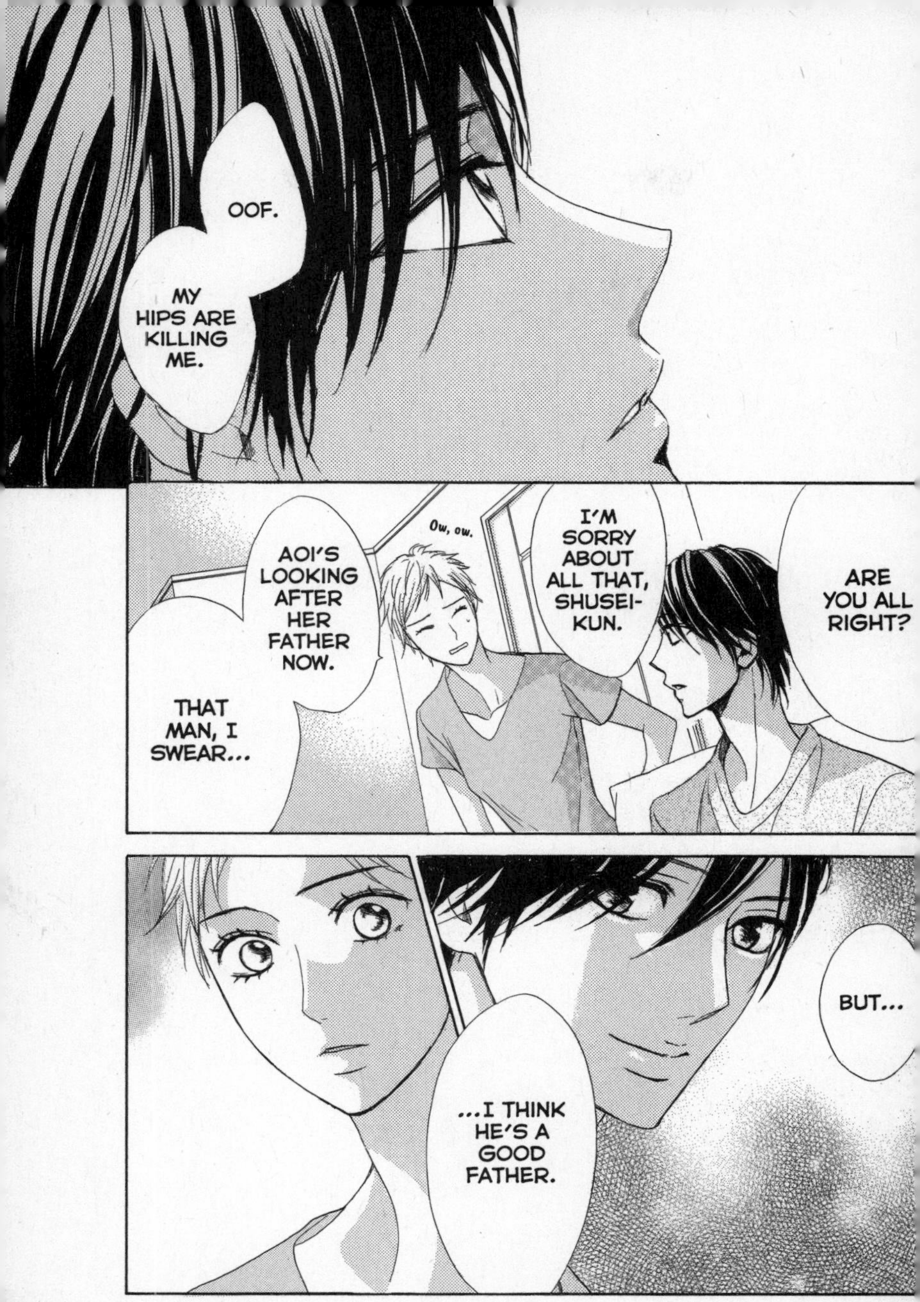
OOF.
MY HIPS ARE KILLING ME.
ARE YOU ALL RIGHT?
I'M SORRY ABOUT ALL THAT, SHUSEI-KUN.
Ow, ow.
AOI'S LOOKING AFTER HER FATHER NOW.
THAT MAN, I SWEAR...
BUT...
...I THINK HE'S A GOOD FATHER.

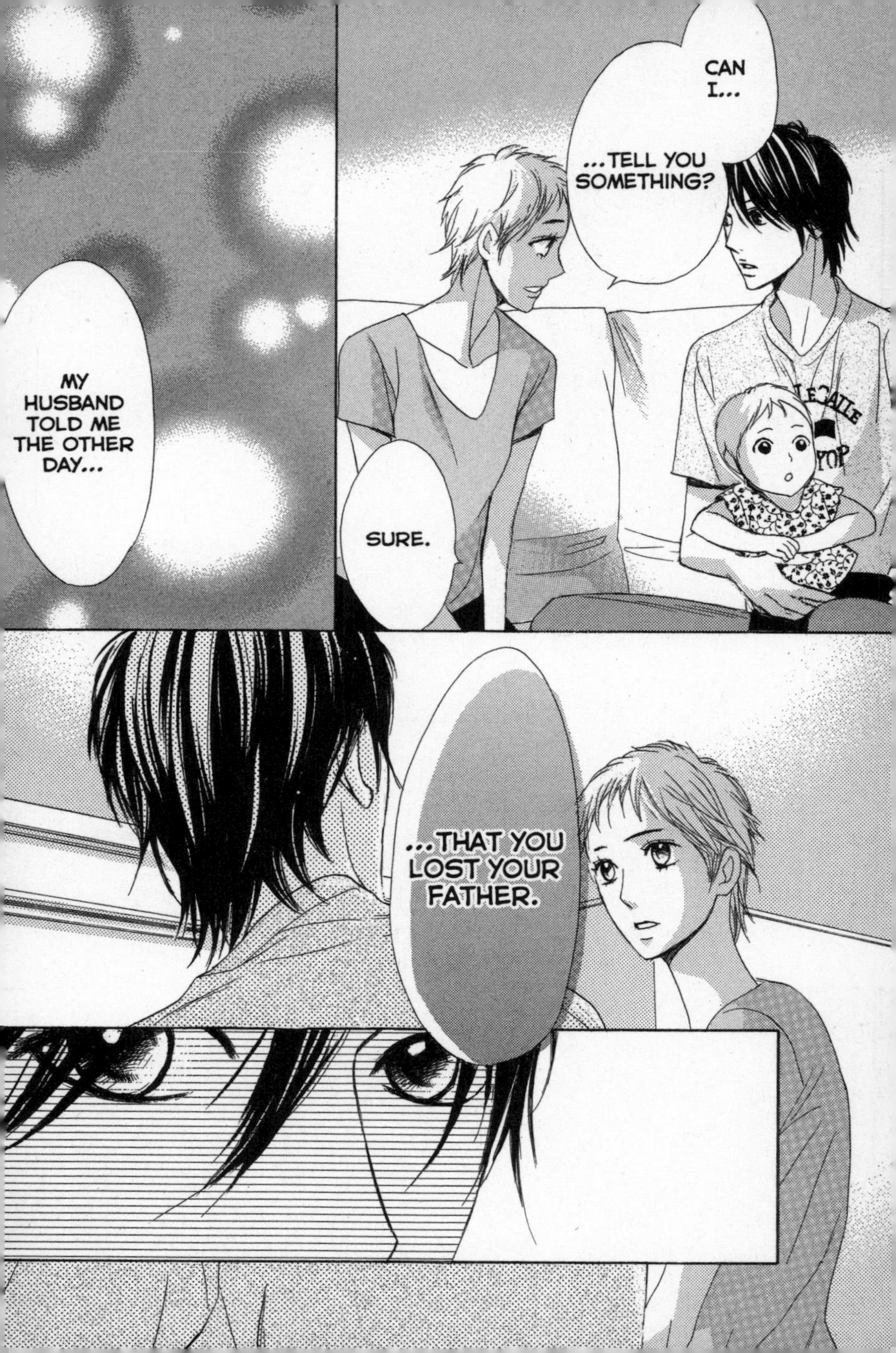
CAN I...
...TELL YOU SOMETHING?
SURE.
MY HUSBAND TOLD ME THE OTHER DAY...
...THAT YOU LOST YOUR FATHER.

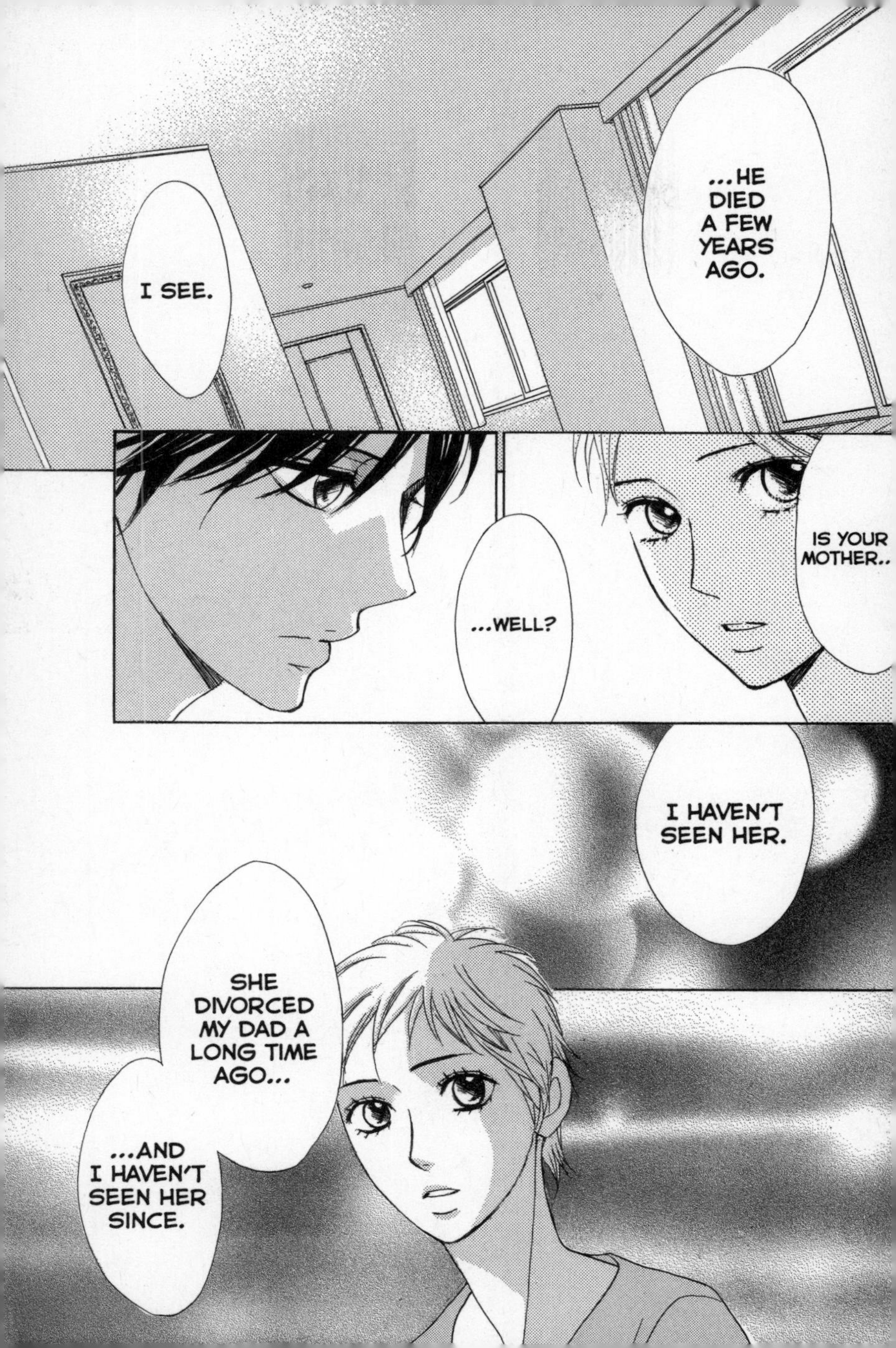
...HE DIED A FEW YEARS AGO.
I SEE.
IS YOUR MOTHER..
...WELL?
I HAVEN'T SEEN HER.
SHE DIVORCED MY DAD A LONG TIME AGO...
...AND I HAVEN'T SEEN HER SINCE.

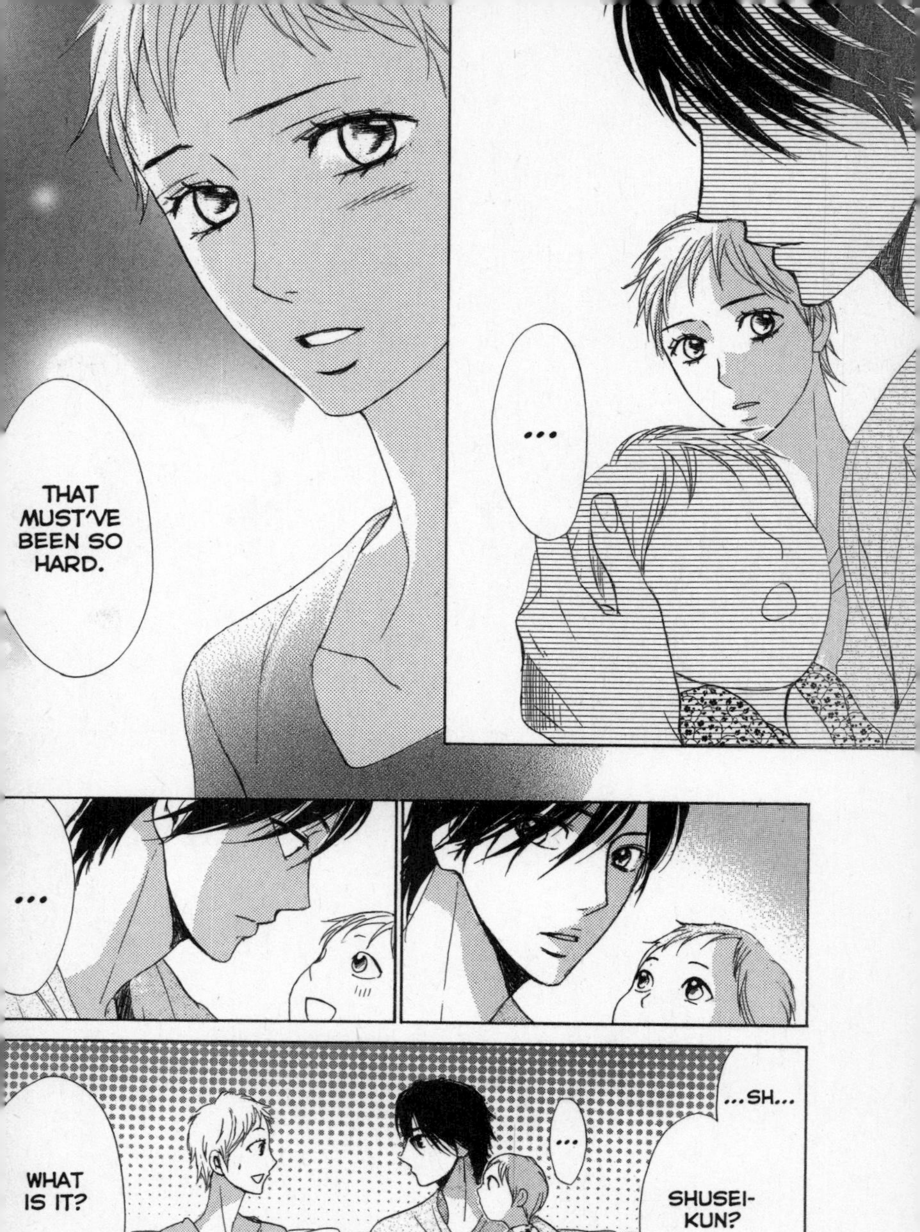
...
THAT MUST'VE BEEN SO HARD.
...
...SH...
SHUSEI-KUN?
...
WHAT IS IT?

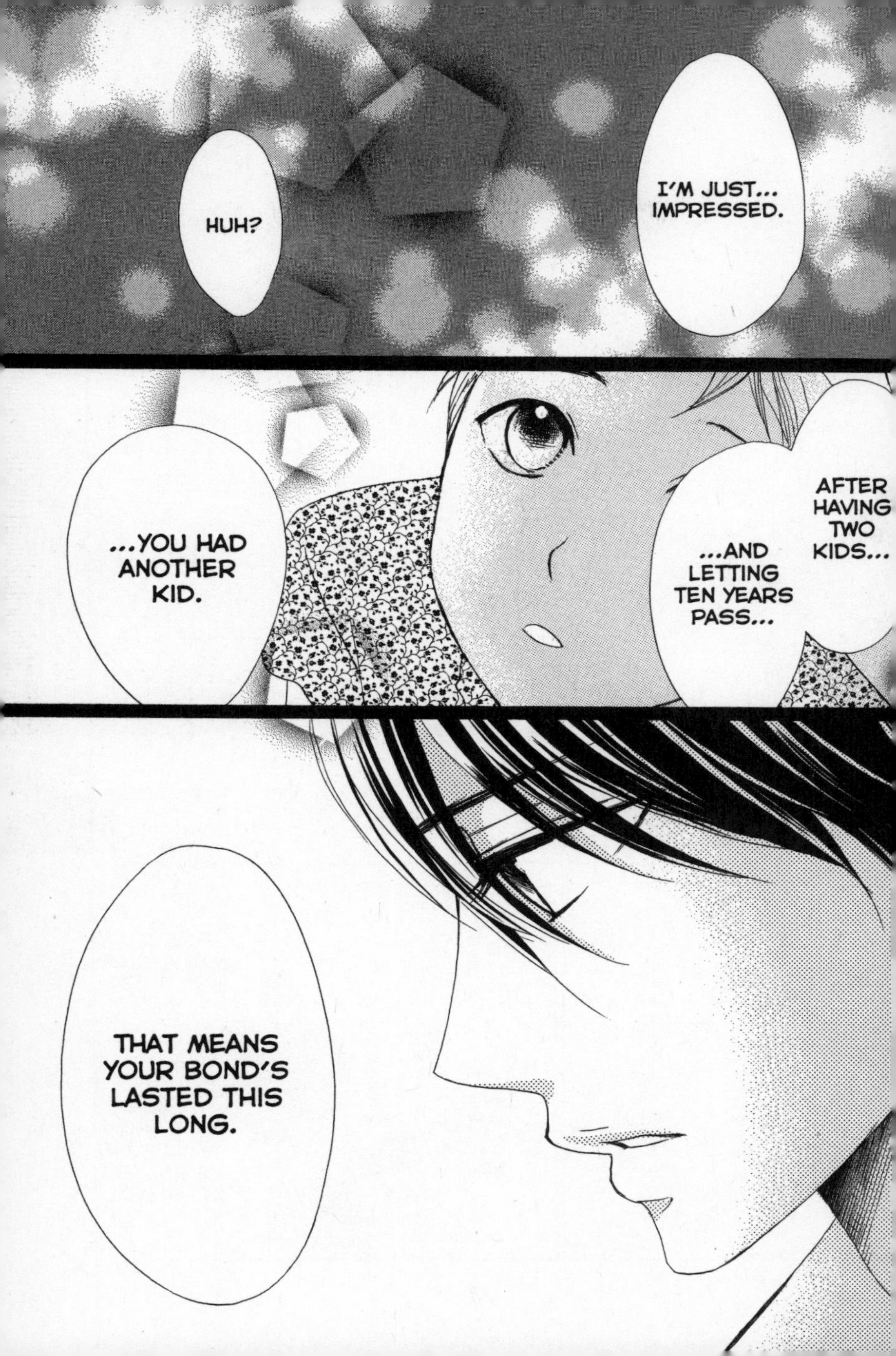
I'M JUST... IMPRESSED.
HUH?
AFTER HAVING TWO KIDS...
...AND LETTING TEN YEARS PASS...
...YOU HAD ANOTHER KID.
THAT MEANS YOUR BOND'S LASTED THIS LONG.

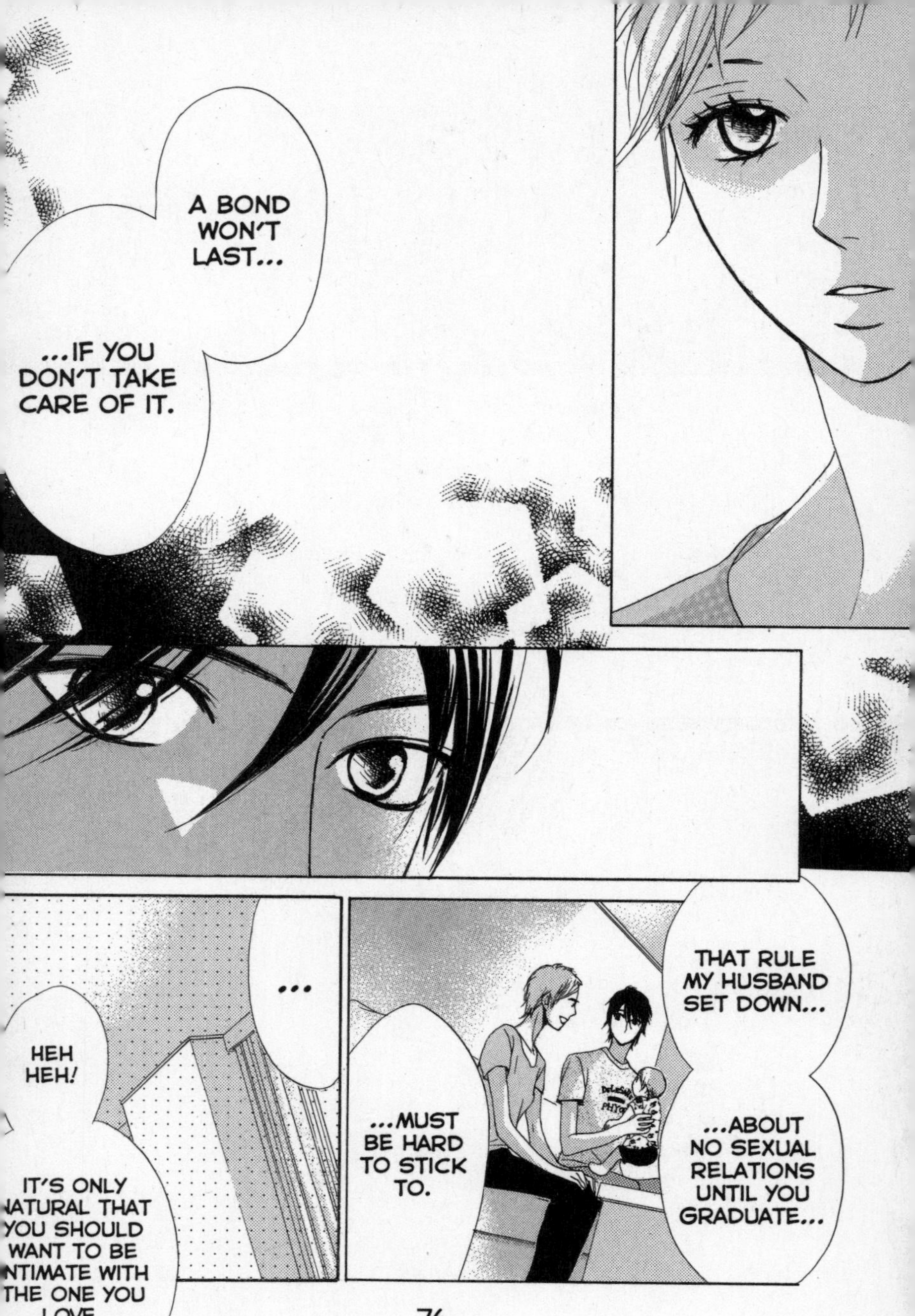
A BOND WON'T LAST...
...IF YOU DON'T TAKE CARE OF IT.
THAT RULE MY HUSBAND SET DOWN...
...ABOUT NO SEXUAL RELATIONS UNTIL YOU GRADUATE...
...MUST BE HARD TO STICK TO.
...
HEH HEH!
IT'S ONLY NATURAL THAT YOU SHOULD WANT TO BE INTIMATE WITH THE ONE YOU LOVE.

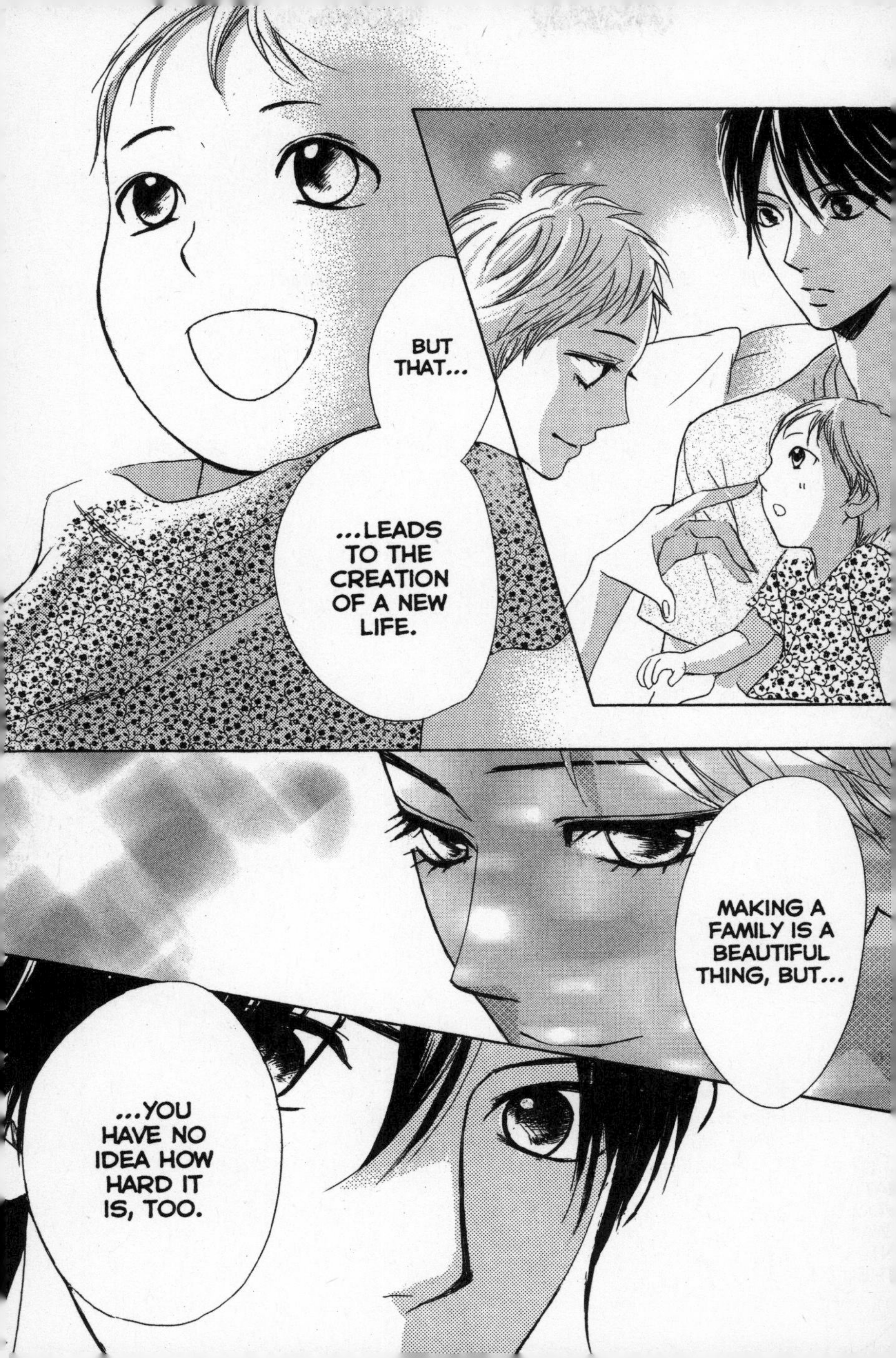
BUT THAT...
...LEADS TO THE CREATION OF A NEW LIFE.
MAKING A FAMILY IS A BEAUTIFUL THING, BUT...
...YOU HAVE NO IDEA HOW HARD IT IS, TOO.

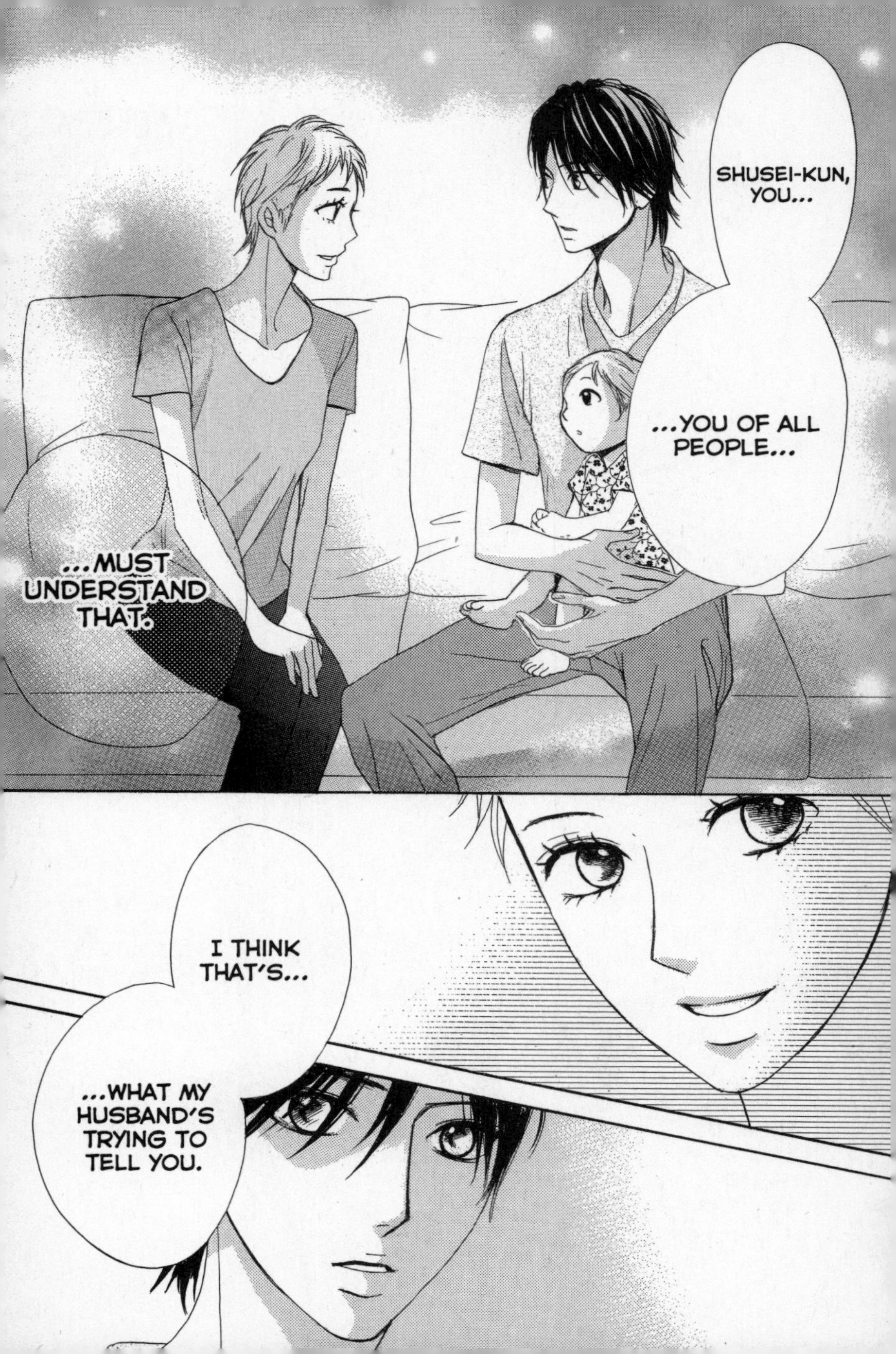
SHUSEI-KUN, YOU...
...YOU OF ALL PEOPLE...
...MUST UNDERSTAND THAT.
I THINK THAT'S...
...WHAT MY HUSBAND'S TRYING TO TELL YOU.

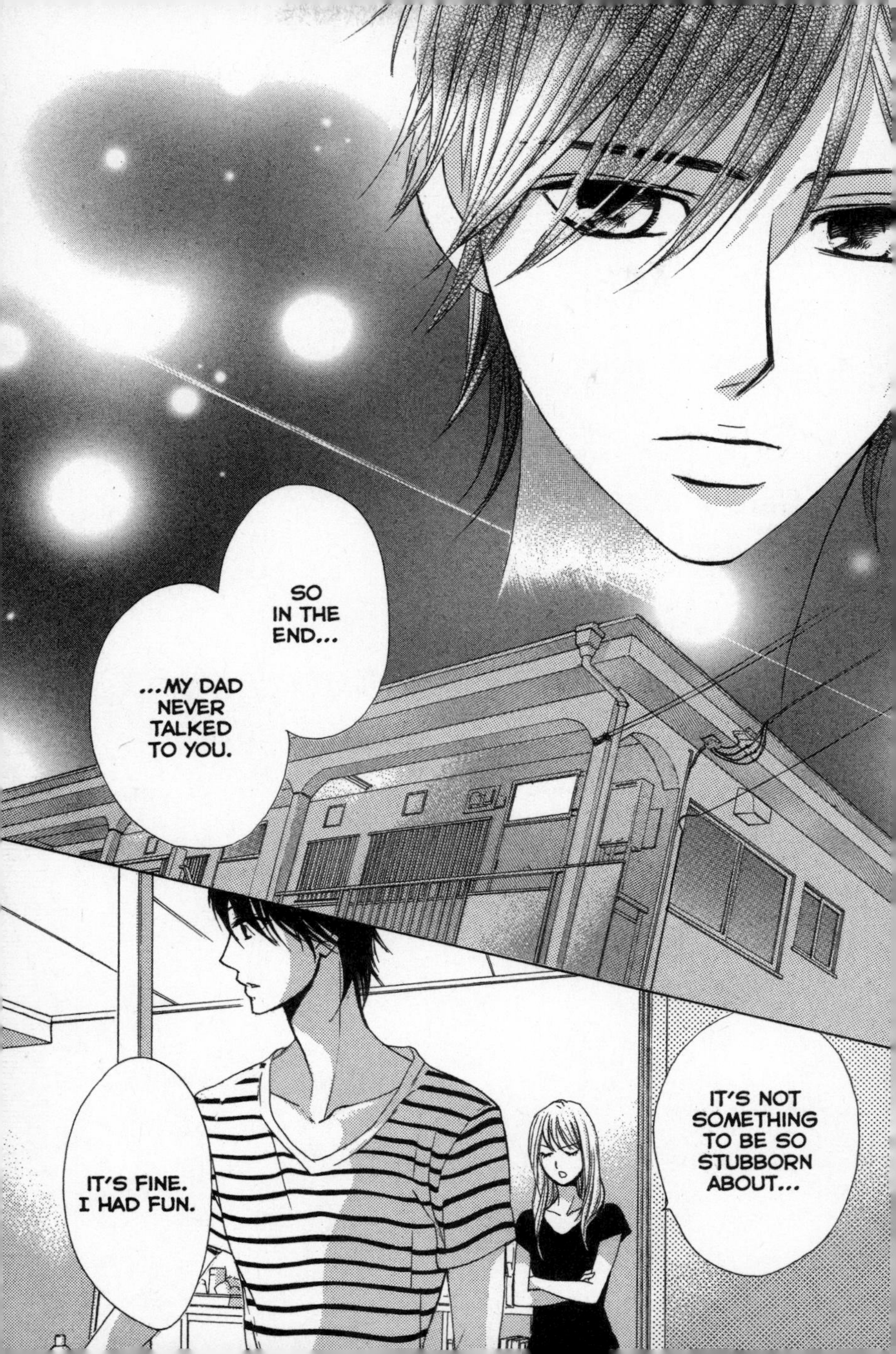
SO IN THE END...
...MY DAD NEVER TALKED TO YOU.
IT'S NOT SOMETHING TO BE SO STUBBORN ABOUT...
IT'S FINE. I HAD FUN.

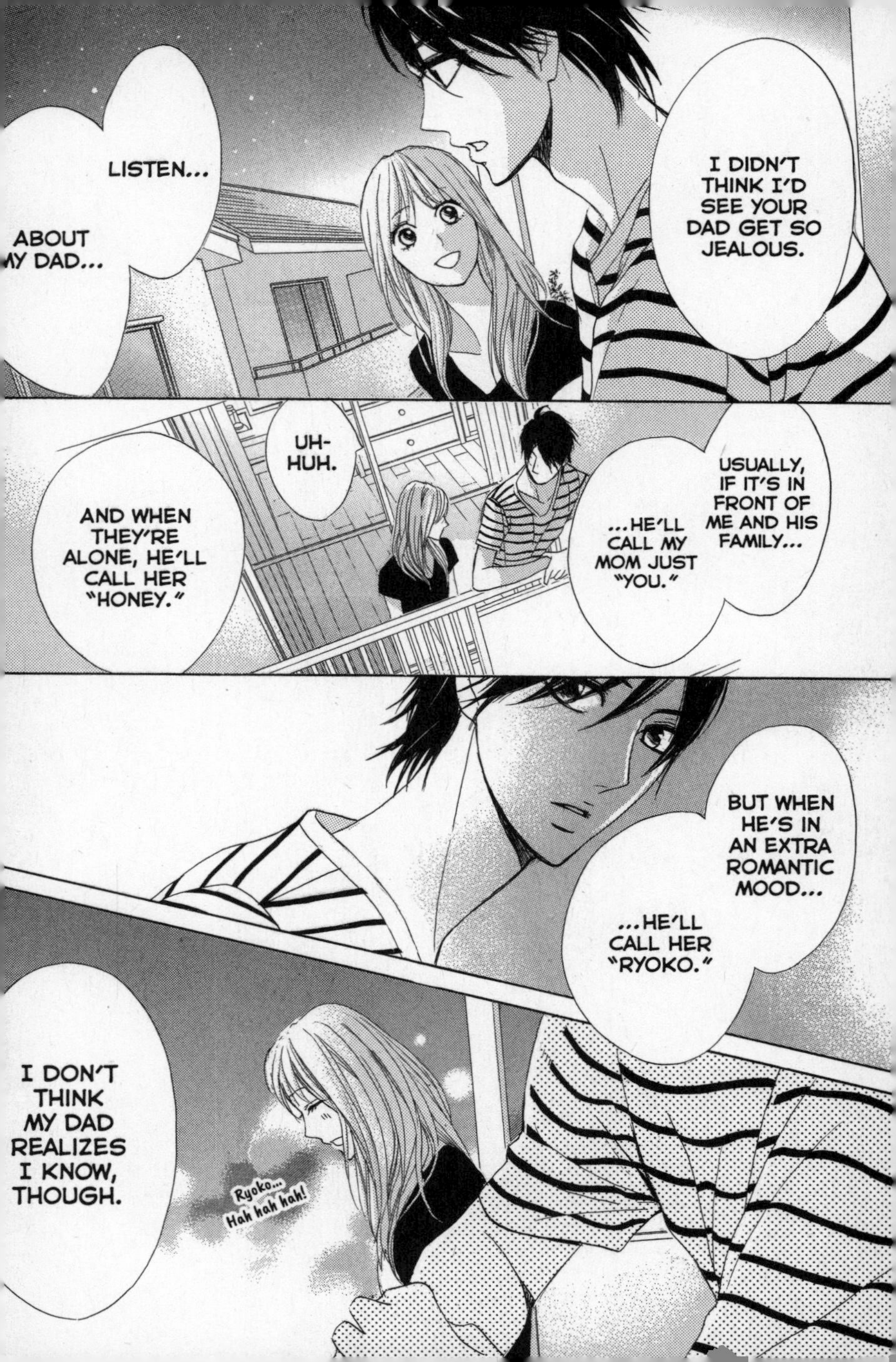
I DIDN'T THINK I'D SEE YOUR DAD GET SO JEALOUS.
LISTEN...
ABOUT MY DAD...
USUALLY, IF IT'S IN FRONT OF ME AND HIS FAMILY...
...HE'LL CALL MY MOM JUST "YOU."
UH-HUH.
AND WHEN THEY'RE ALONE, HE'LL CALL HER "HONEY."
BUT WHEN HE'S IN AN EXTRA ROMANTIC MOOD...
...HE'LL CALL HER "RYOKO."
Ryoko... Hah hah hah!
I DON'T THINK MY DAD REALIZES I KNOW, THOUGH.

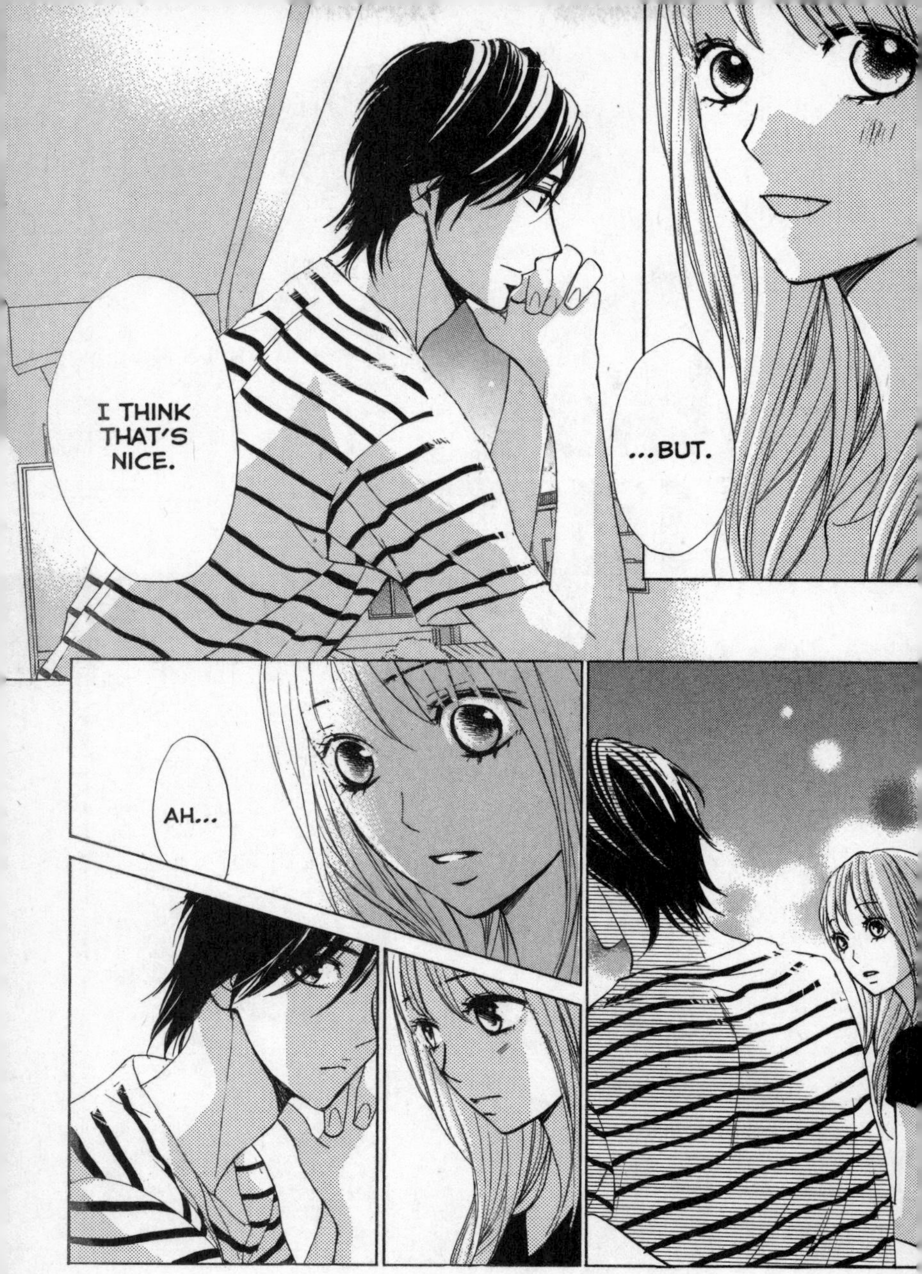
...BUT.
I THINK THAT'S NICE.
AH...

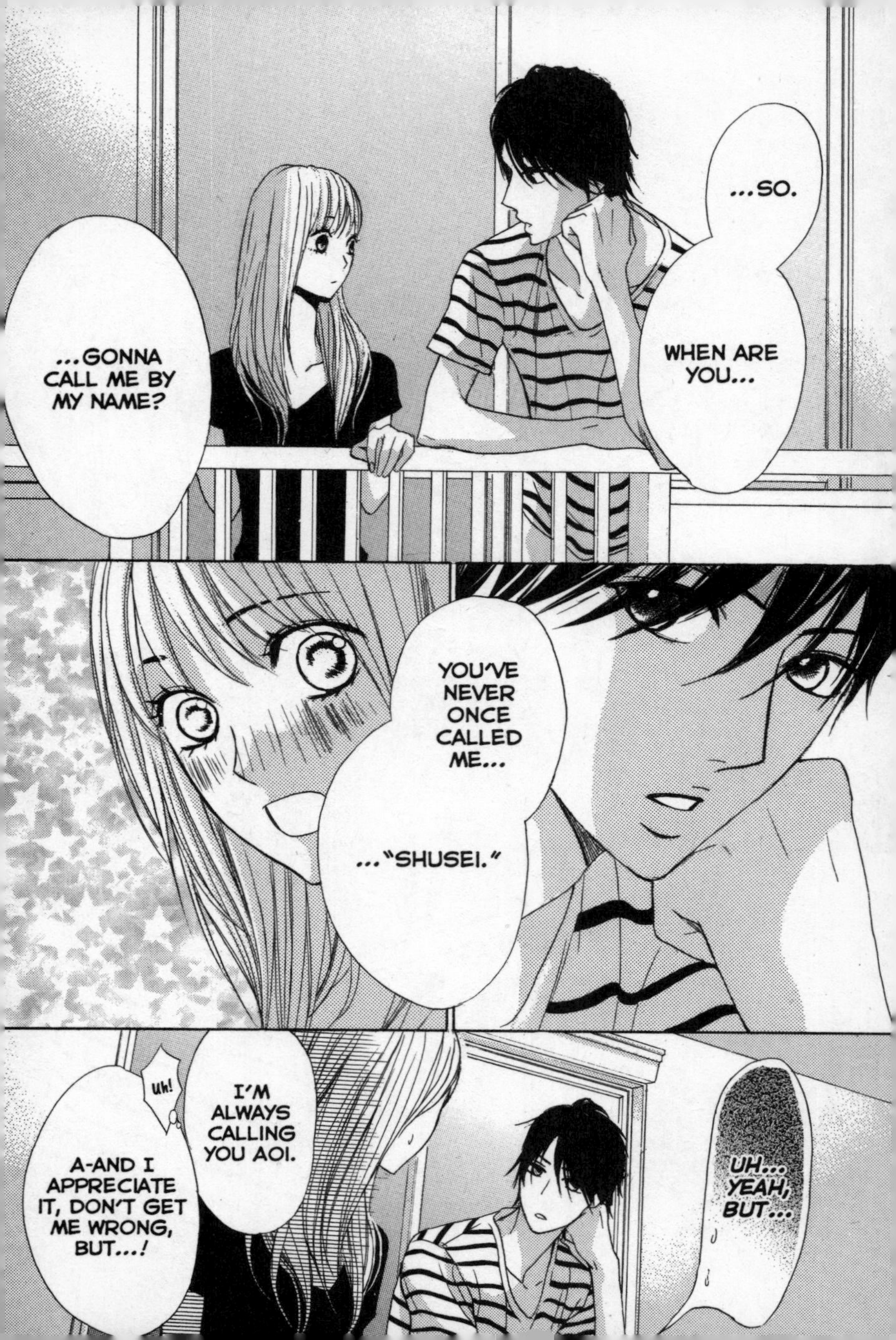
...SO.
WHEN ARE YOU...
...GONNA CALL ME BY MY NAME?
YOU'VE NEVER ONCE CALLED ME...
..."SHUSEI."
UH... YEAH, BUT...
I'M ALWAYS CALLING YOU AOI.
Uh!
A-AND I APPRECIATE IT, DON'T GET ME WRONG, BUT...!

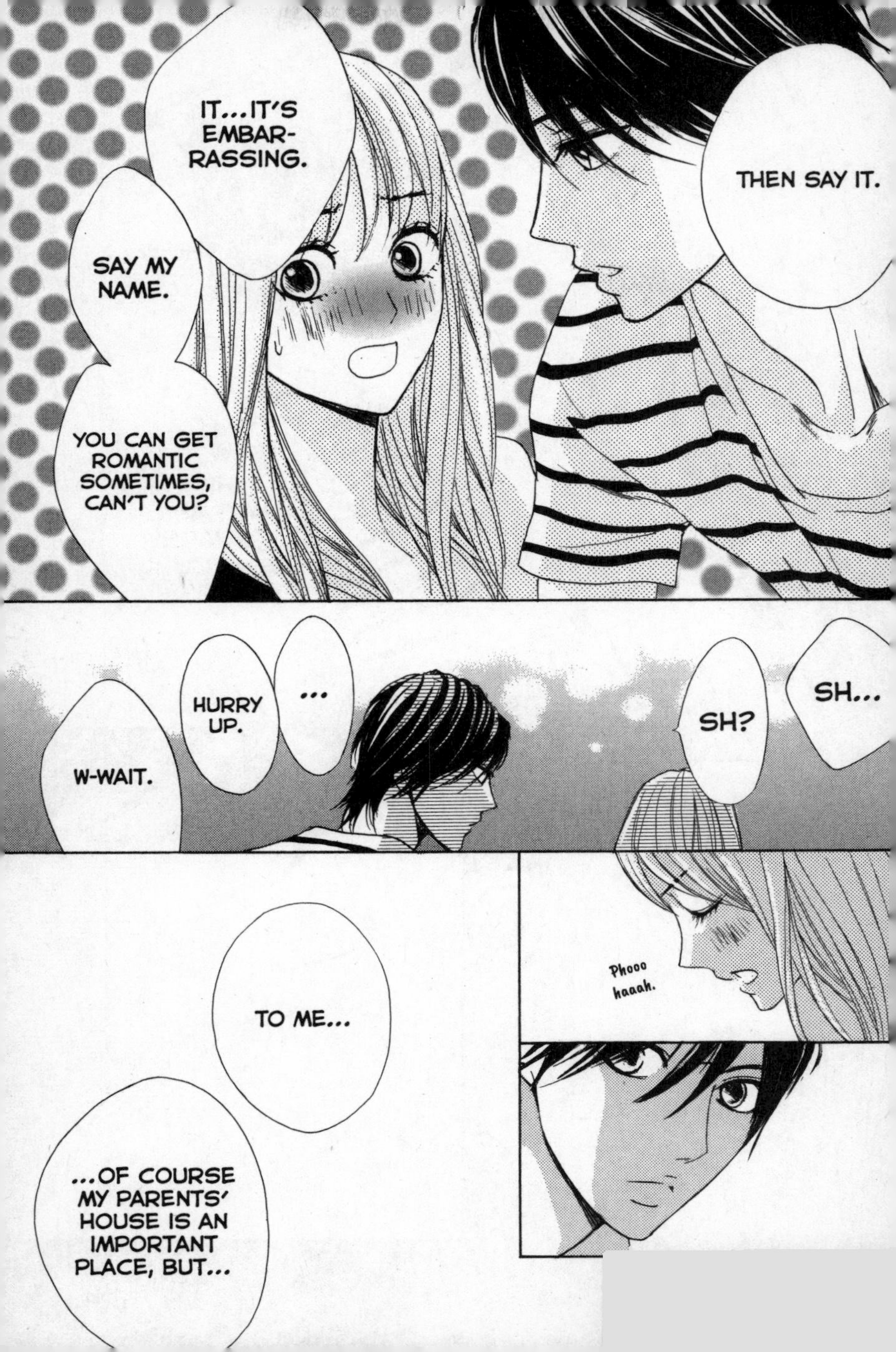
THEN SAY IT.
IT...IT'S EMBAR-RASSING.
SAY MY NAME.
YOU CAN GET ROMANTIC SOMETIMES, CAN'T YOU?
SH...
SH?
...
HURRY UP.
W-WAIT.
Phooo haaah.
TO ME...
...OF COURSE MY PARENTS' HOUSE IS AN IMPORTANT PLACE, BUT...

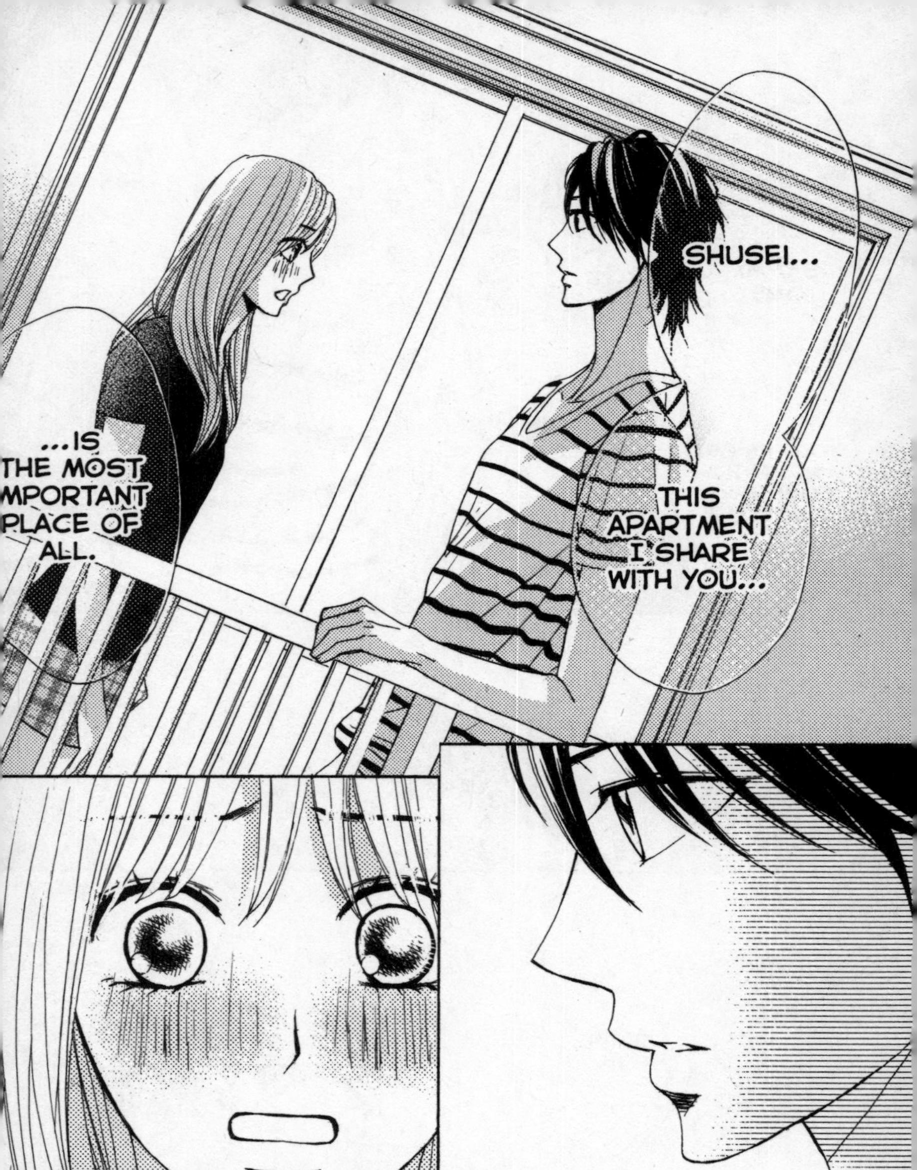
SHUSEI...
THIS APARTMENT I SHARE WITH YOU...
...IS THE MOST MPORTANT PLACE OF ALL.

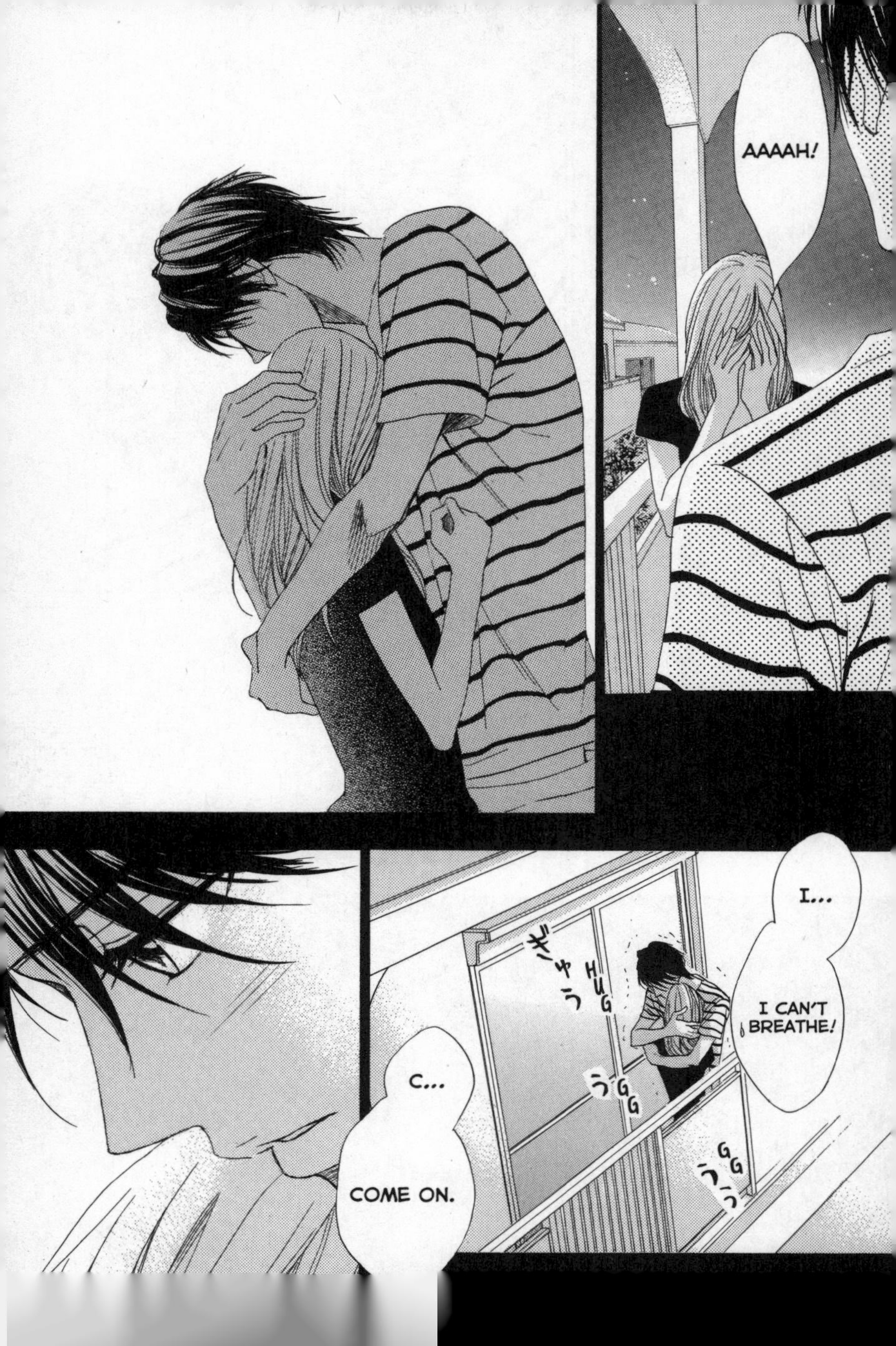
AAAAH!
I...
I CAN'T BREATHE!
ぎゅう
HUG
う
GG
GG
うう
C...
COME ON.

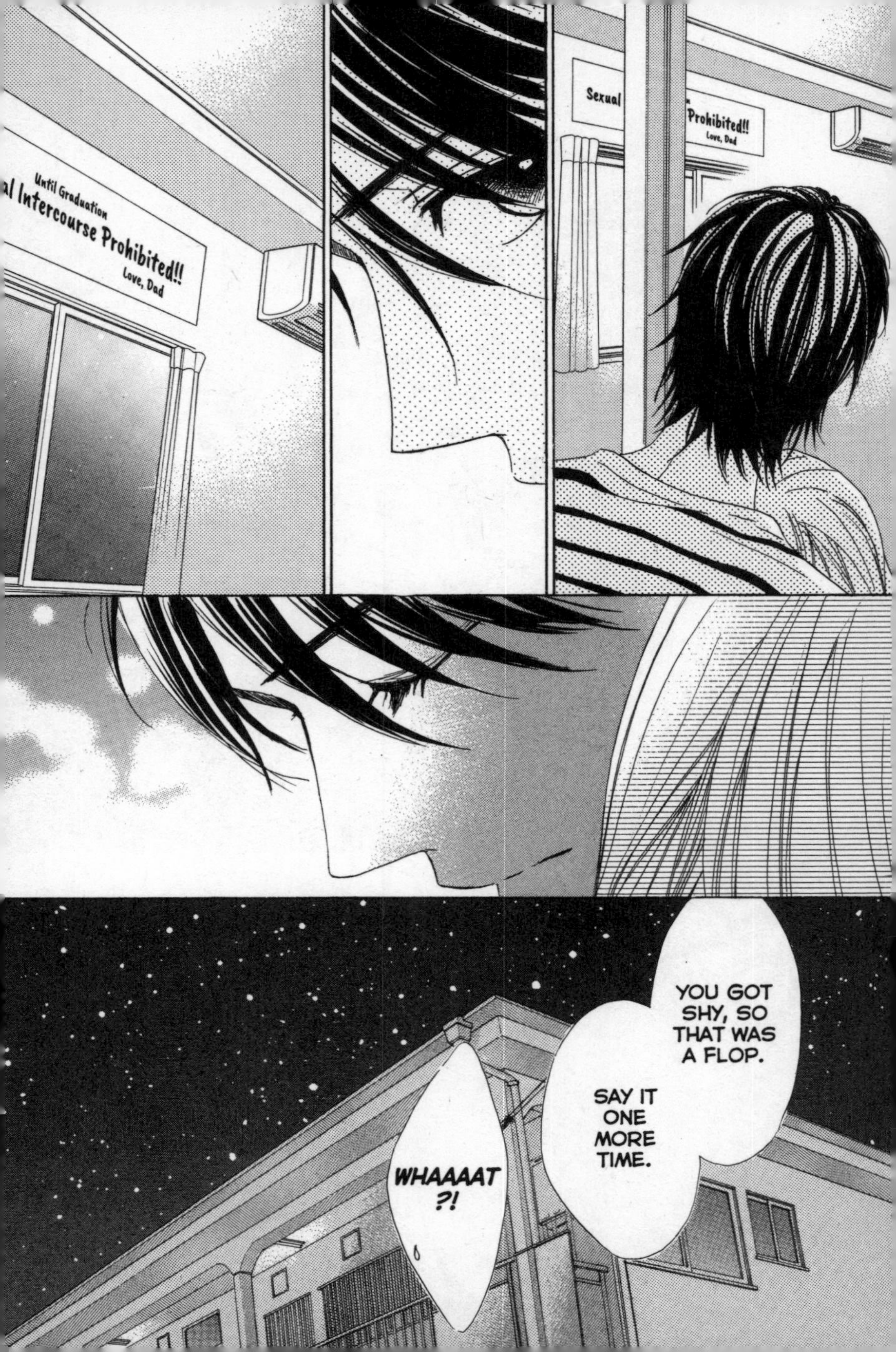
Sexual
Prohibited!!
Love, Dad
Until Graduation
al Intercourse Prohibited!!
Love, Dad
YOU GOT SHY, SO THAT WAS A FLOP.
SAY IT ONE MORE TIME.
WHAAAAT?!

L♥DK

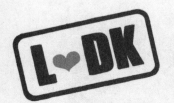

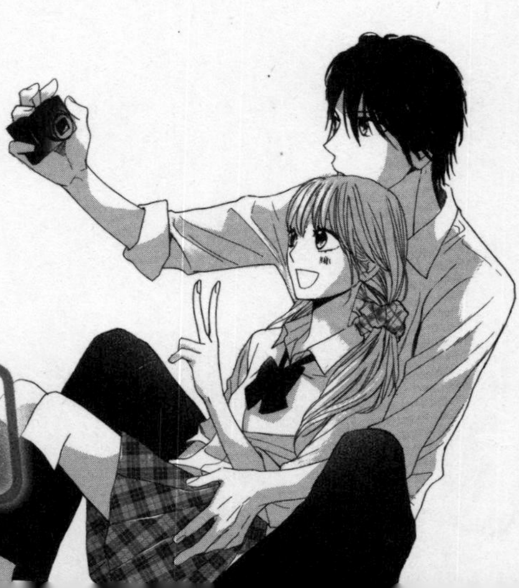

L♥DK

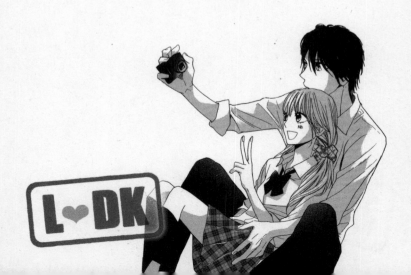

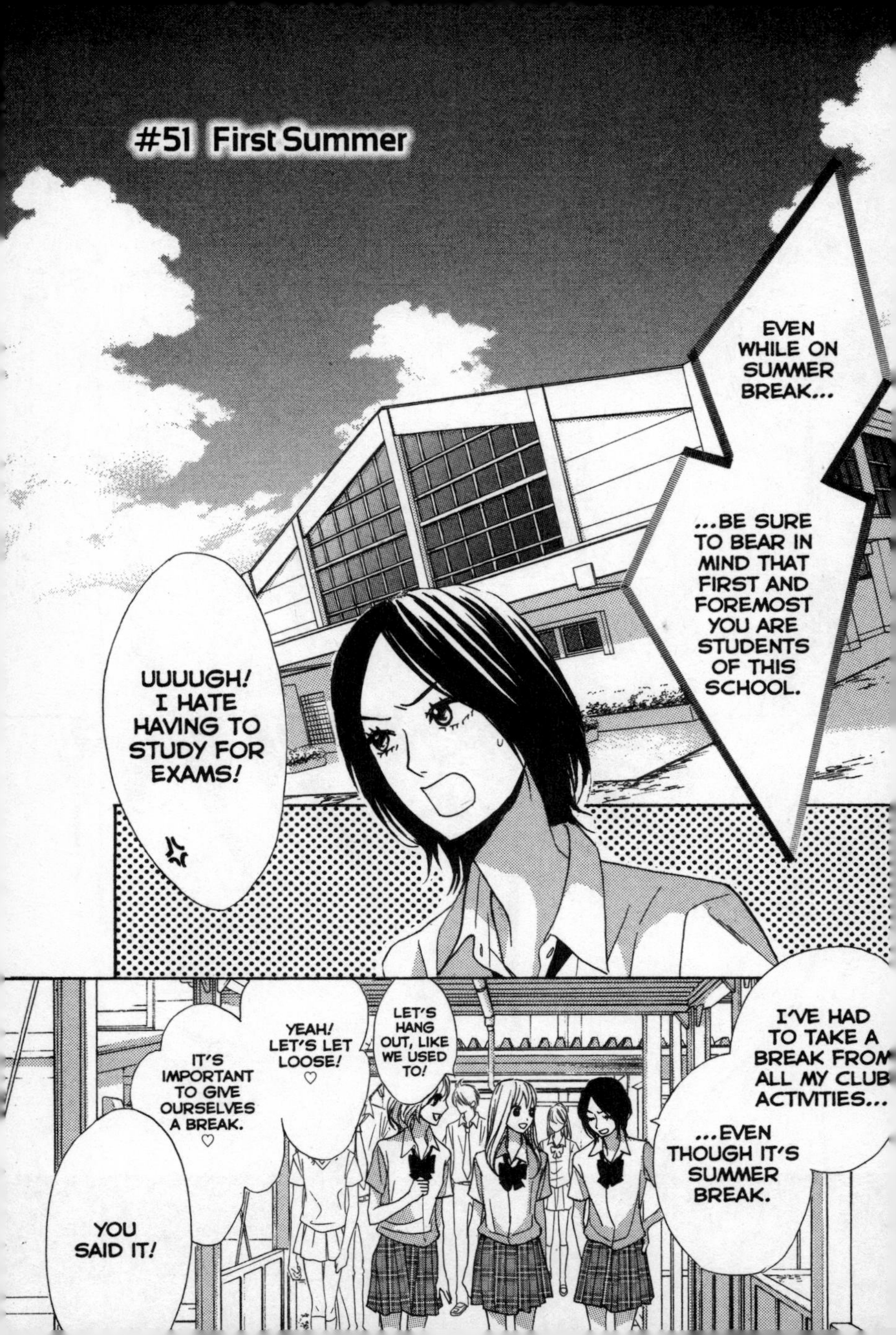
#51 First Summer
EVEN WHILE ON SUMMER BREAK...
...BE SURE TO BEAR IN MIND THAT FIRST AND FOREMOST YOU ARE STUDENTS OF THIS SCHOOL.
UUUUGH! I HATE HAVING TO STUDY FOR EXAMS!
I'VE HAD TO TAKE A BREAK FROM ALL MY CLUB ACTIVITIES...
...EVEN THOUGH IT'S SUMMER BREAK.
LET'S HANG OUT, LIKE WE USED TO!
YEAH! LET'S LET LOOSE! ♡
IT'S IMPORTANT TO GIVE OURSELVES A BREAK. ♡
YOU SAID IT!

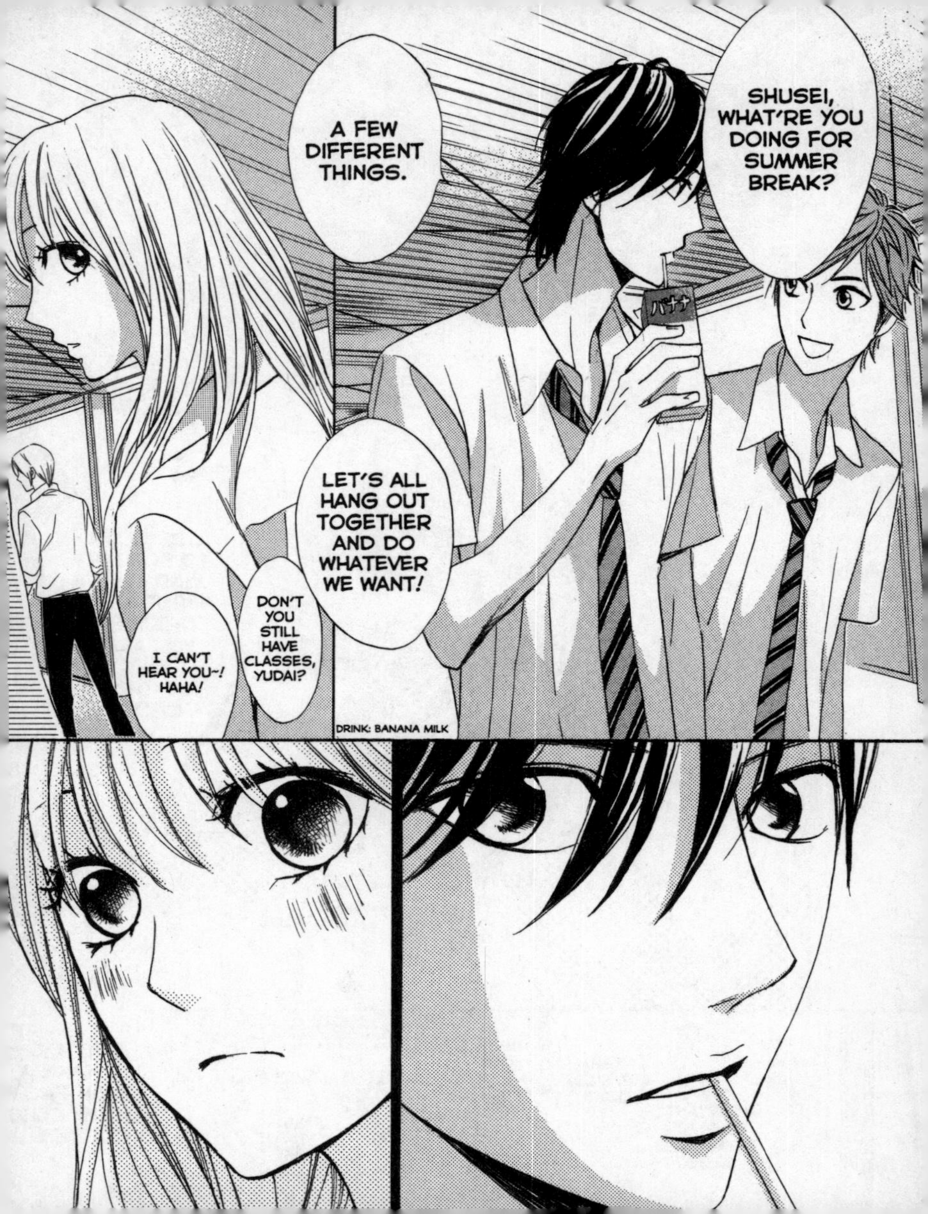
SHUSEI, WHAT'RE YOU DOING FOR SUMMER BREAK?
A FEW DIFFERENT THINGS.
バナナ
LET'S ALL HANG OUT TOGETHER AND DO WHATEVER WE WANT!
DON'T YOU STILL HAVE CLASSES, YUDAI?
I CAN'T HEAR YOU~! HAHA!
DRINK: BANANA MILK

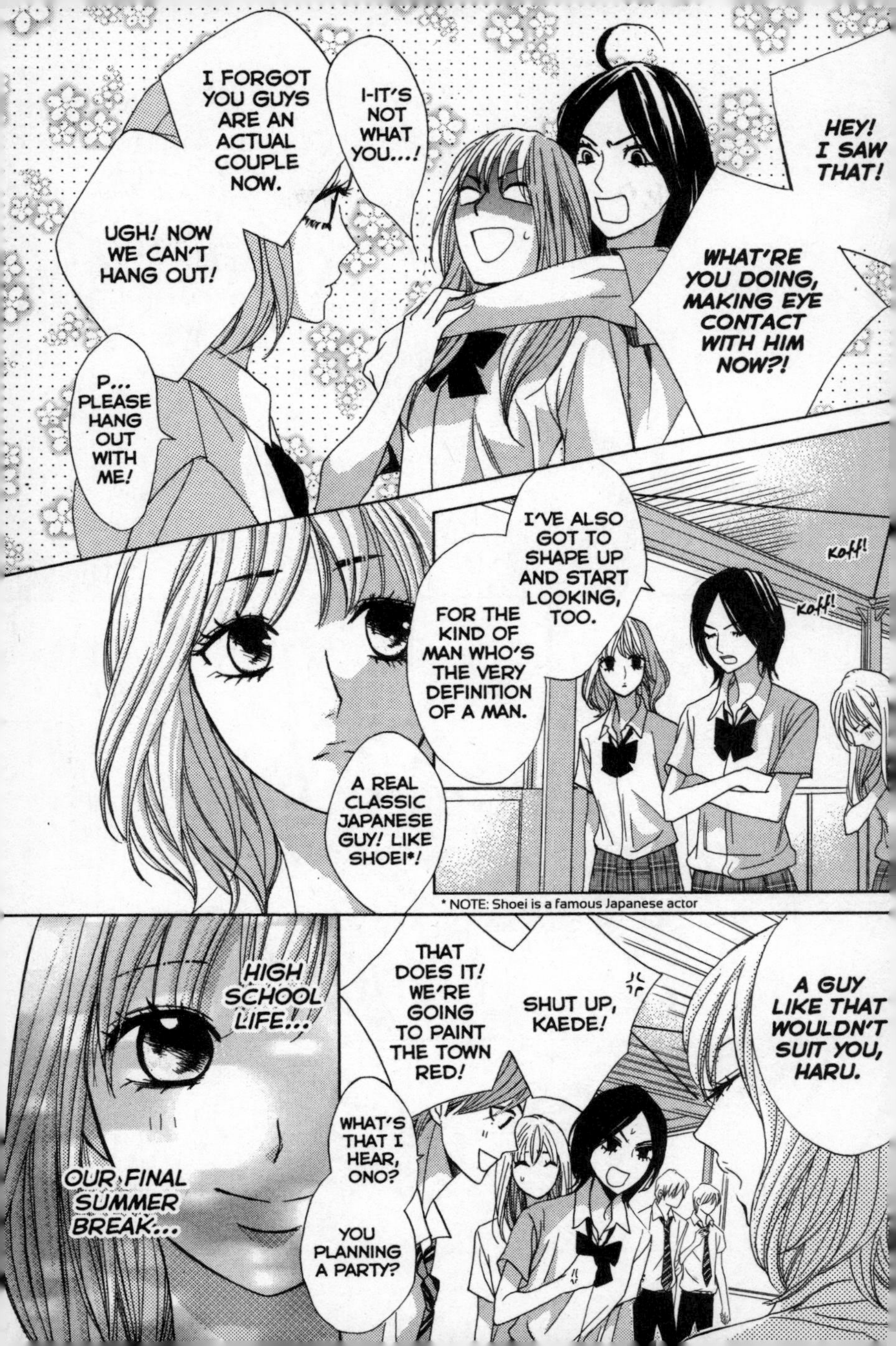
HEY! I SAW THAT!
WHAT'RE YOU DOING, MAKING EYE CONTACT WITH HIM NOW?!
I-IT'S NOT WHAT YOU...!
I FORGOT YOU GUYS ARE AN ACTUAL COUPLE NOW.
UGH! NOW WE CAN'T HANG OUT!
P... PLEASE HANG OUT WITH ME!
Koff!
Koff!
I'VE ALSO GOT TO SHAPE UP AND START LOOKING, TOO.
FOR THE KIND OF MAN WHO'S THE VERY DEFINITION OF A MAN.
A REAL CLASSIC JAPANESE GUY! LIKE SHOEI*!
A GUY LIKE THAT WOULDN'T SUIT YOU, HARU.
SHUT UP, KAEDE!
THAT DOES IT! WE'RE GOING TO PAINT THE TOWN RED!
WHAT'S THAT I HEAR, ONO?
YOU PLANNING A PARTY?
HIGH SCHOOL LIFE...
OUR FINAL SUMMER BREAK...

* NOTE: Shoei is a famous Japanese actor

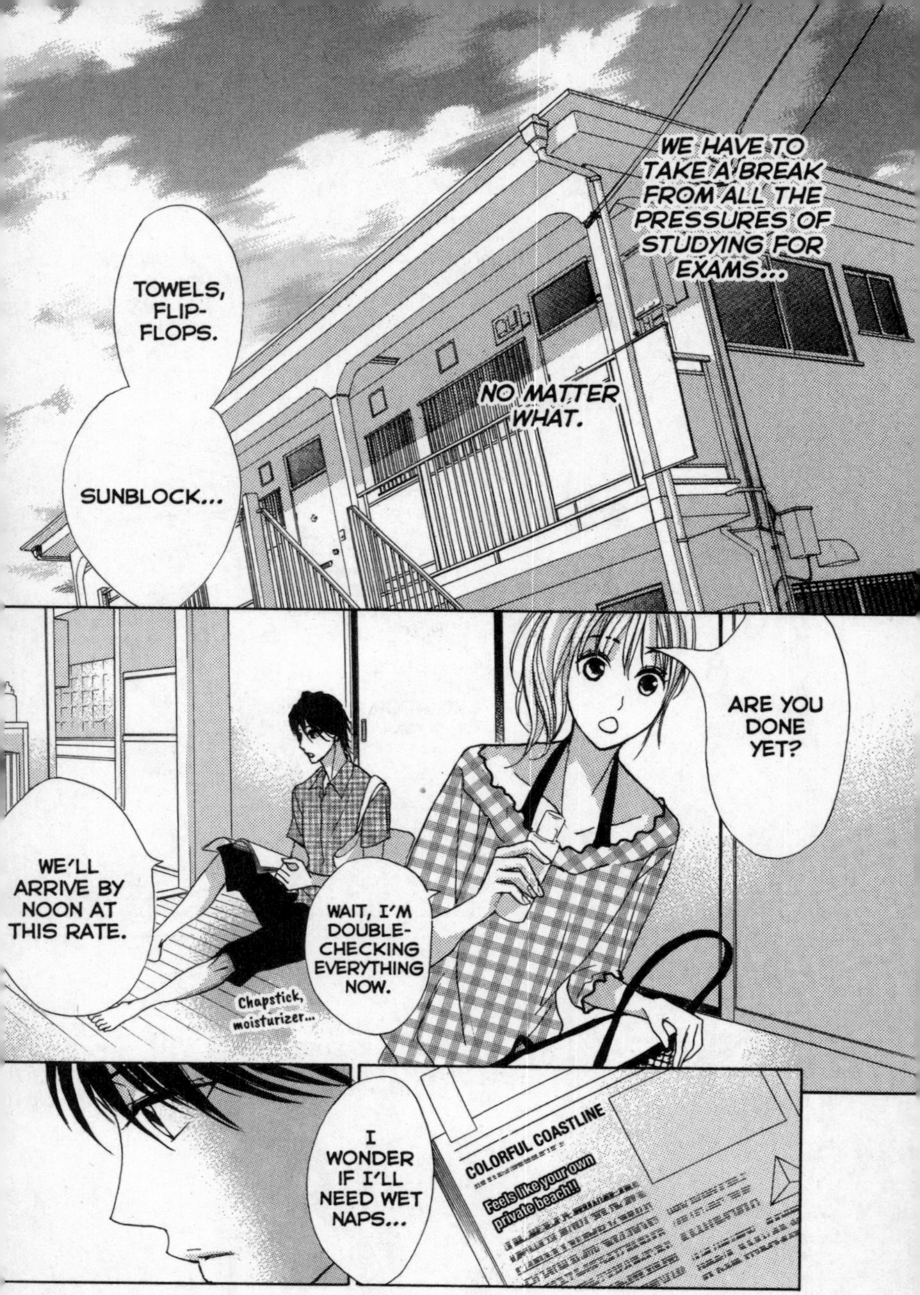
WE HAVE TO TAKE A BREAK FROM ALL THE PRESSURES OF STUDYING FOR EXAMS...
NO MATTER WHAT.
TOWELS, FLIP-FLOPS.
SUNBLOCK...
ARE YOU DONE YET?
WAIT, I'M DOUBLE-CHECKING EVERYTHING NOW.
Chapstick, moisturizer...
WE'LL ARRIVE BY NOON AT THIS RATE.
COLORFUL COASTLINE
Feels like your own private beach!!
I WONDER IF I'LL NEED WET NAPS...

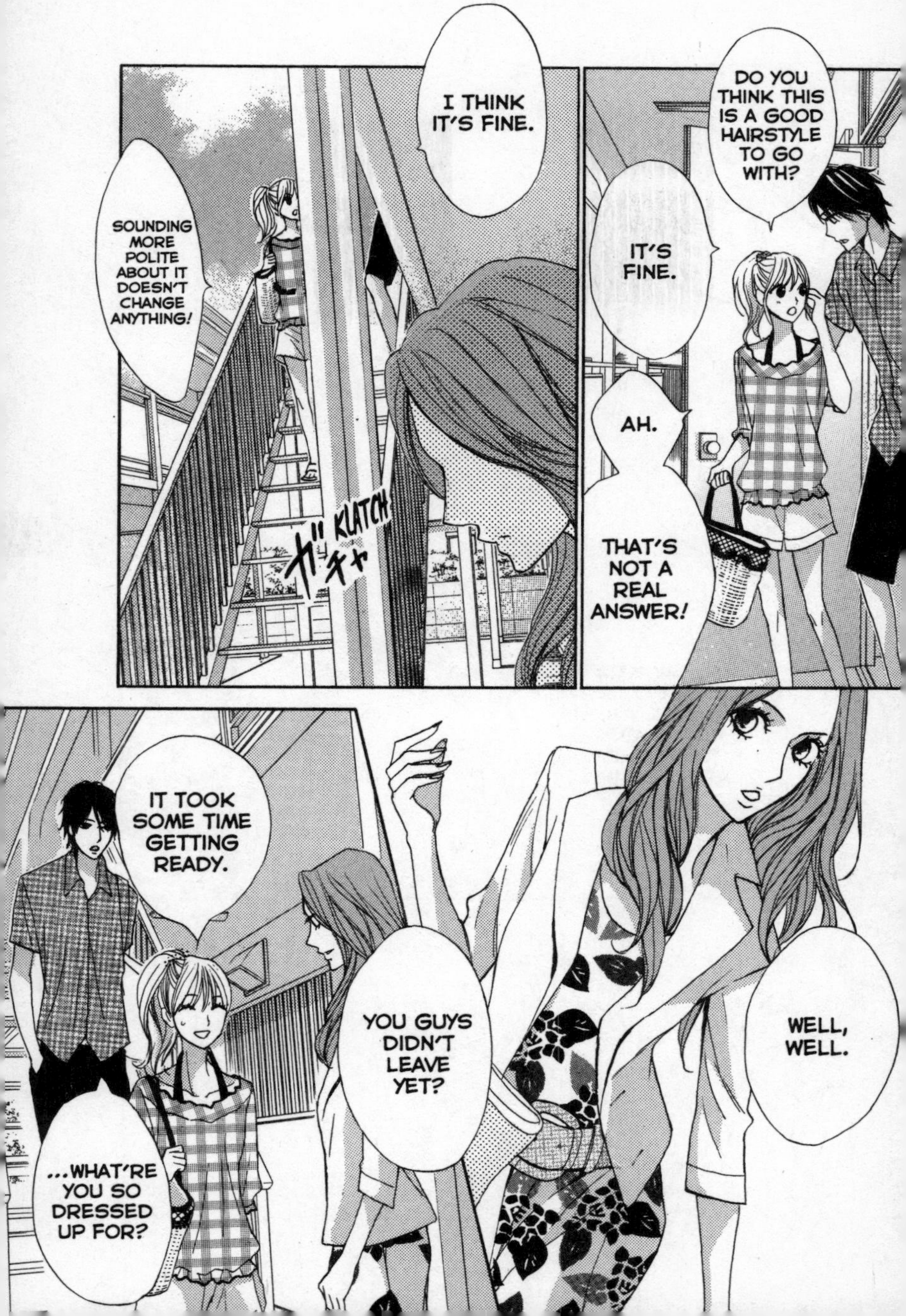
DO YOU THINK THIS IS A GOOD HAIRSTYLE TO GO WITH?
IT'S FINE.
AH.
THAT'S NOT A REAL ANSWER!
I THINK IT'S FINE.
SOUNDING MORE POLITE ABOUT IT DOESN'T CHANGE ANYTHING!
KLATCH
ガチャ
WELL, WELL.
YOU GUYS DIDN'T LEAVE YET?
IT TOOK SOME TIME GETTING READY.
...WHAT'RE YOU SO DRESSED UP FOR?

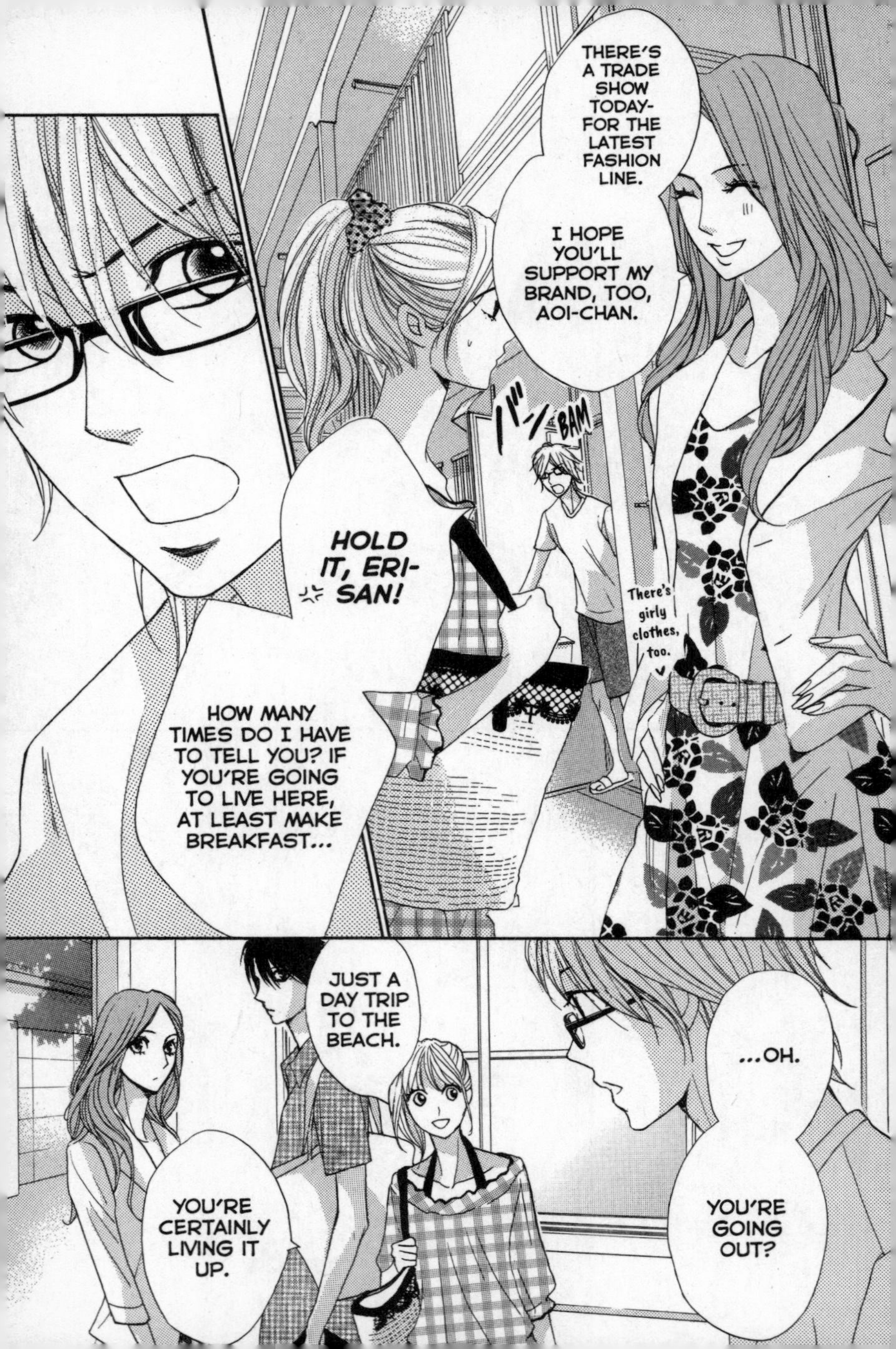
THERE'S A TRADE SHOW TODAY- FOR THE LATEST FASHION LINE.
I HOPE YOU'LL SUPPORT MY BRAND, TOO, AOI-CHAN.
There's girly clothes, too.
BAM
HOLD IT, ERI-SAN!
HOW MANY TIMES DO I HAVE TO TELL YOU? IF YOU'RE GOING TO LIVE HERE, AT LEAST MAKE BREAKFAST...
...OH.
YOU'RE GOING OUT?
JUST A DAY TRIP TO THE BEACH.
YOU'RE CERTAINLY LIVING IT UP.

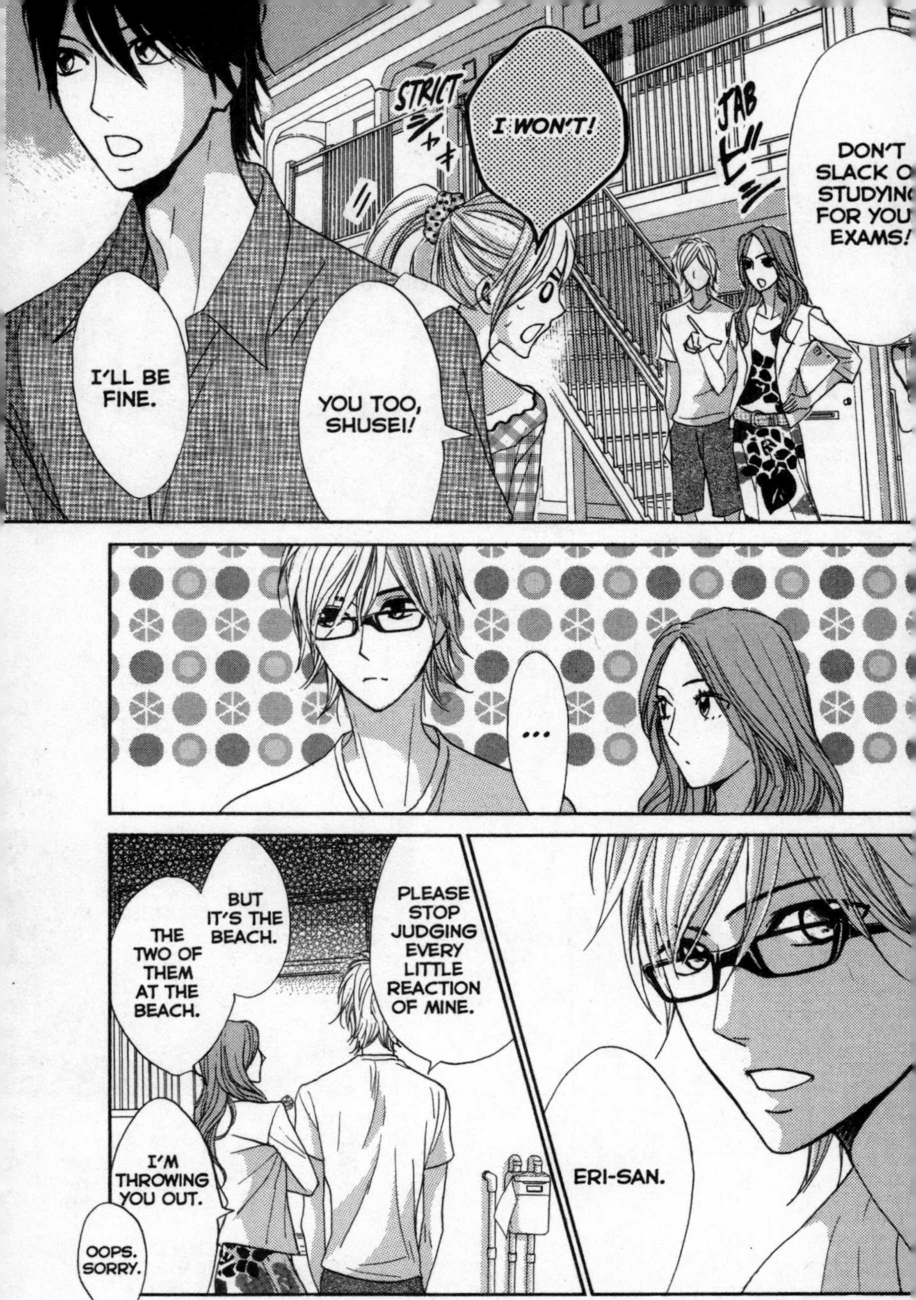
DON'T SLACK O STUDYIN FOR YOU EXAMS!
JAB
I WON'T!
STRICT
YOU TOO, SHUSEI!
I'LL BE FINE.
...
ERI-SAN.
PLEASE STOP JUDGING EVERY LITTLE REACTION OF MINE.
BUT IT'S THE BEACH.
THE TWO OF THEM AT THE BEACH.
I'M THROWING YOU OUT.
OOPS. SORRY.

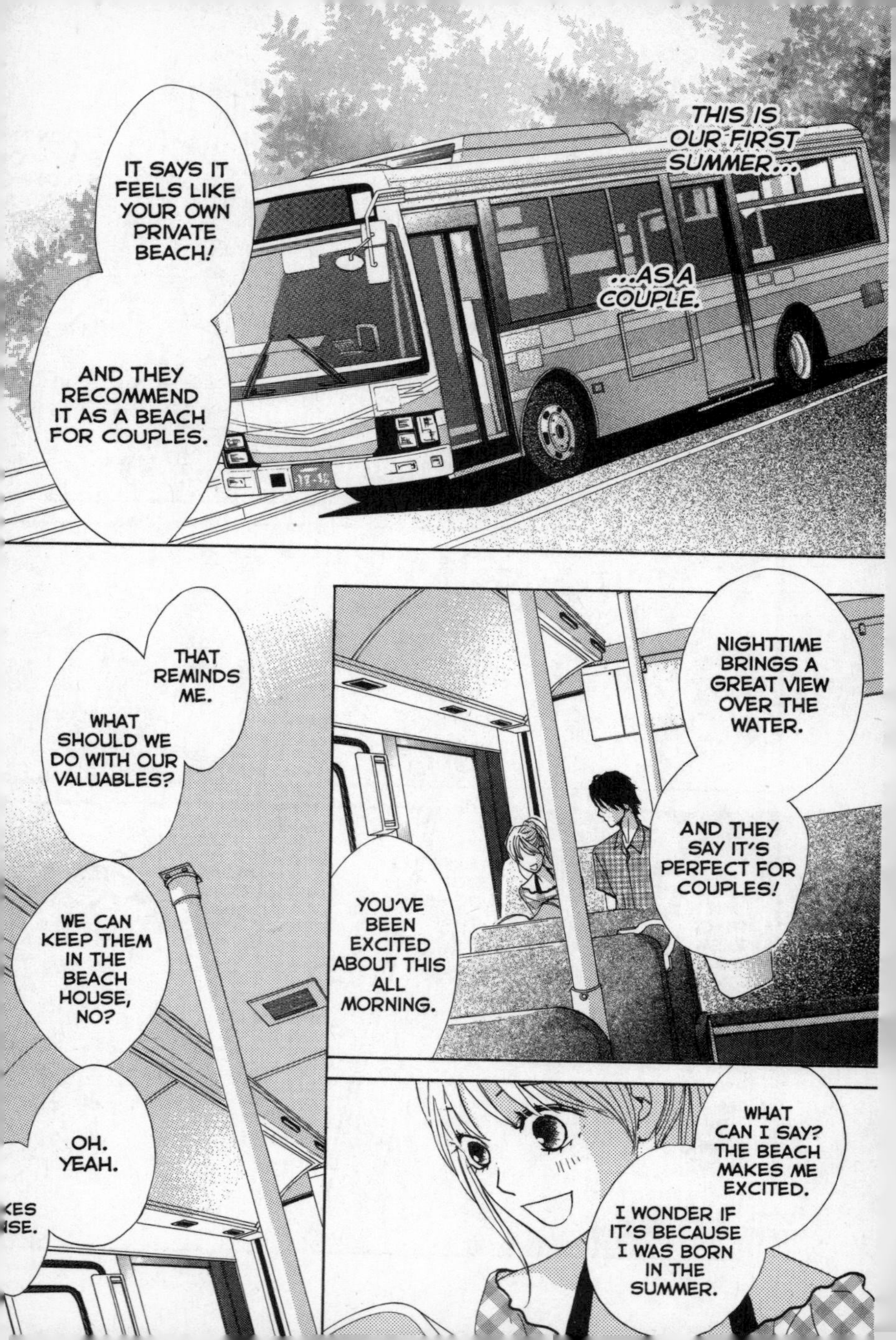
THIS IS OUR FIRST SUMMER...
...AS A COUPLE.
IT SAYS IT FEELS LIKE YOUR OWN PRIVATE BEACH!
AND THEY RECOMMEND IT AS A BEACH FOR COUPLES.
NIGHTTIME BRINGS A GREAT VIEW OVER THE WATER.
AND THEY SAY IT'S PERFECT FOR COUPLES!
YOU'VE BEEN EXCITED ABOUT THIS ALL MORNING.
WHAT CAN I SAY? THE BEACH MAKES ME EXCITED.
I WONDER IF IT'S BECAUSE I WAS BORN IN THE SUMMER.
THAT REMINDS ME.
WHAT SHOULD WE DO WITH OUR VALUABLES?
WE CAN KEEP THEM IN THE BEACH HOUSE, NO?
OH. YEAH.

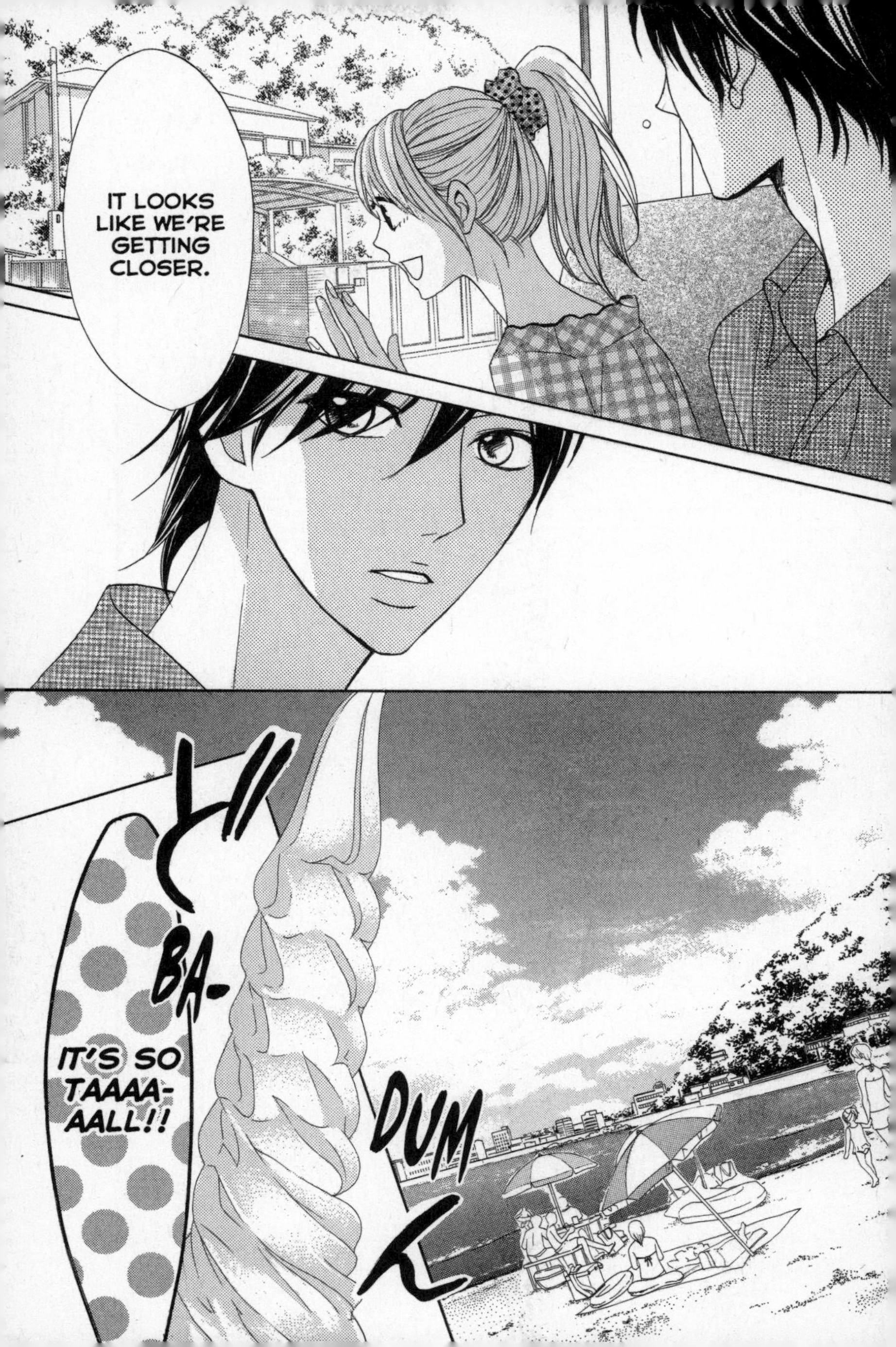
IT LOOKS LIKE WE'RE GETTING CLOSER.
BA-
DUM
IT'S SO TAAAA-AALL!!

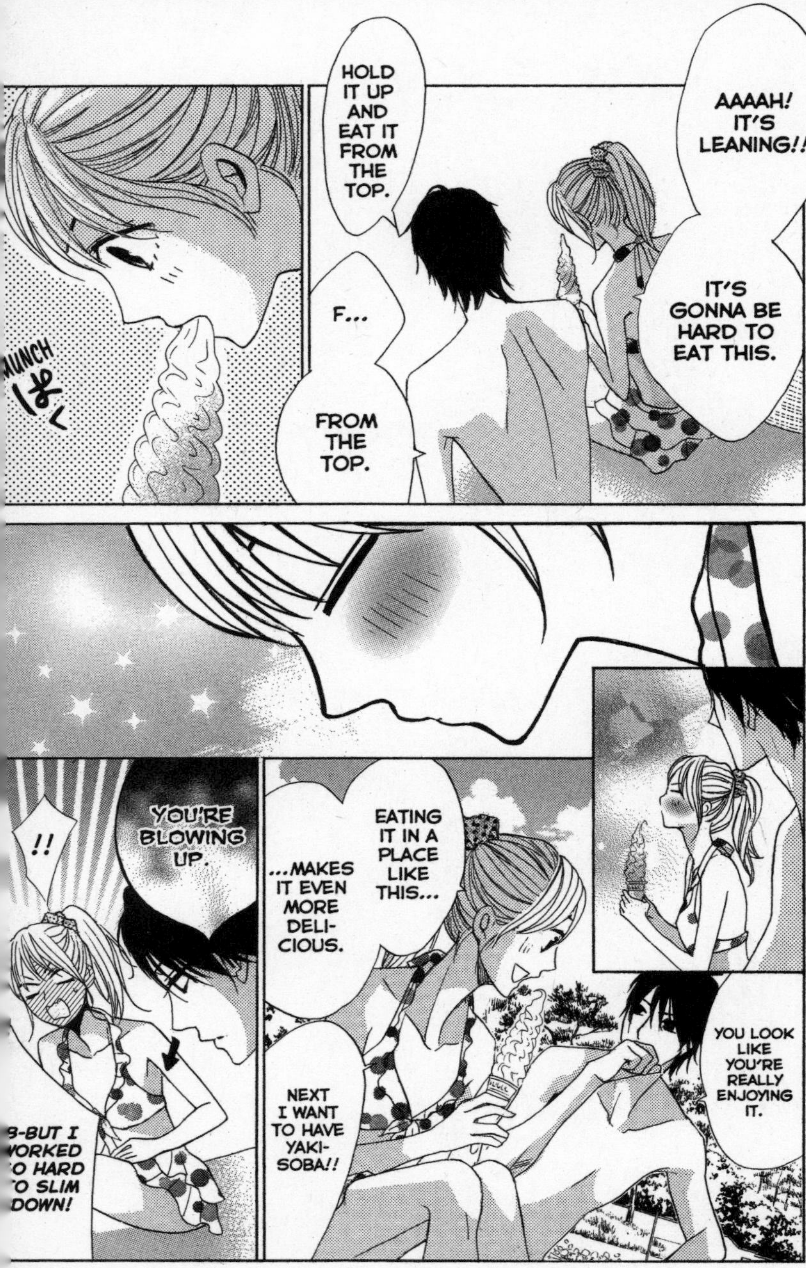
AAAAH! IT'S LEANING!!
IT'S GONNA BE HARD TO EAT THIS.
HOLD IT UP AND EAT IT FROM THE TOP.
F...
FROM THE TOP.
MUNCH
ぱく
EATING IT IN A PLACE LIKE THIS...
...MAKES IT EVEN MORE DELI-CIOUS.
YOU LOOK LIKE YOU'RE REALLY ENJOYING IT.
NEXT I WANT TO HAVE YAKI-SOBA!!
!!
YOU'RE BLOWING UP.
B-BUT I WORKED SO HARD TO SLIM DOWN!

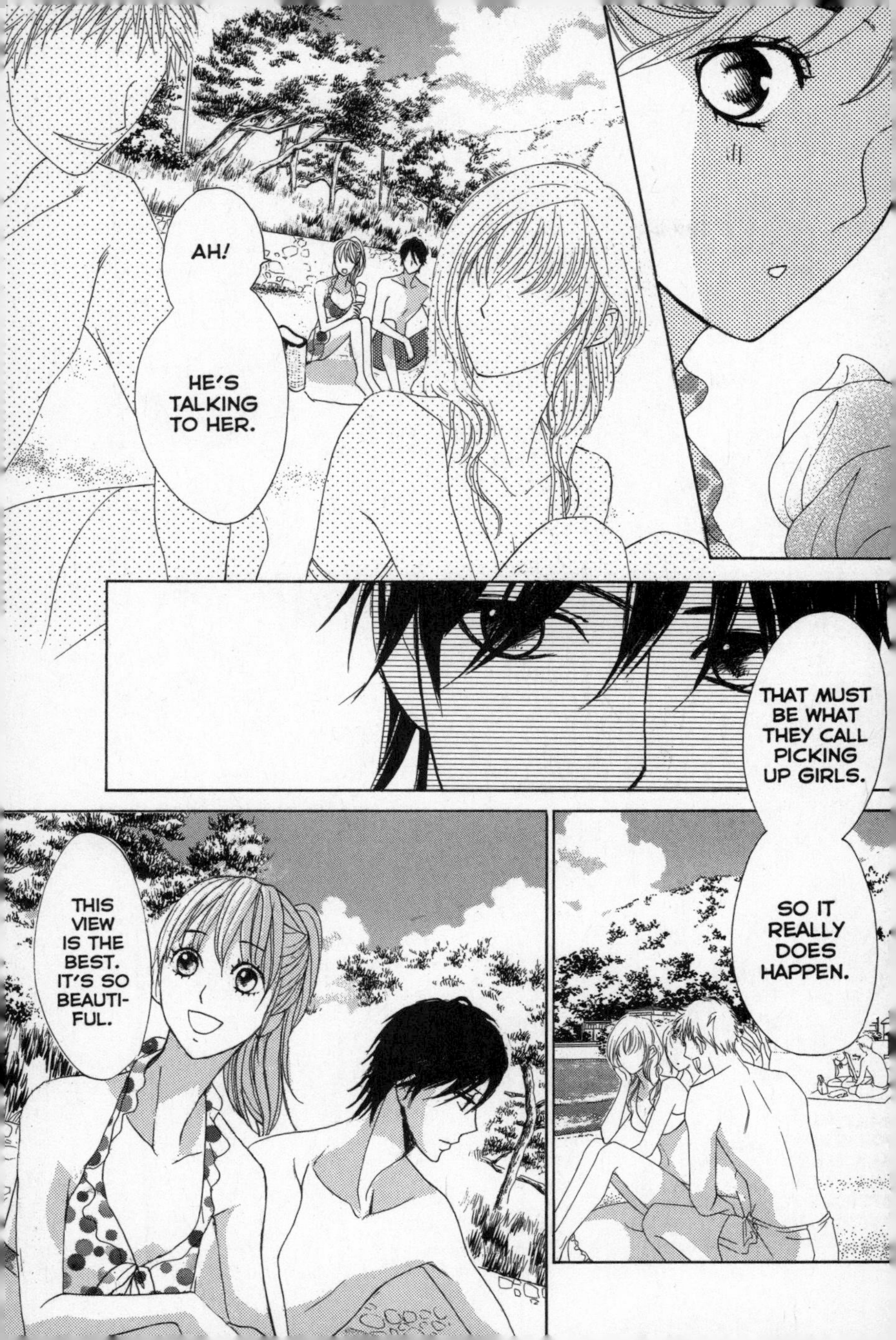
AH!
HE'S TALKING TO HER.
THAT MUST BE WHAT THEY CALL PICKING UP GIRLS.
SO IT REALLY DOES HAPPEN.
THIS VIEW IS THE BEST. IT'S SO BEAUTIFUL.

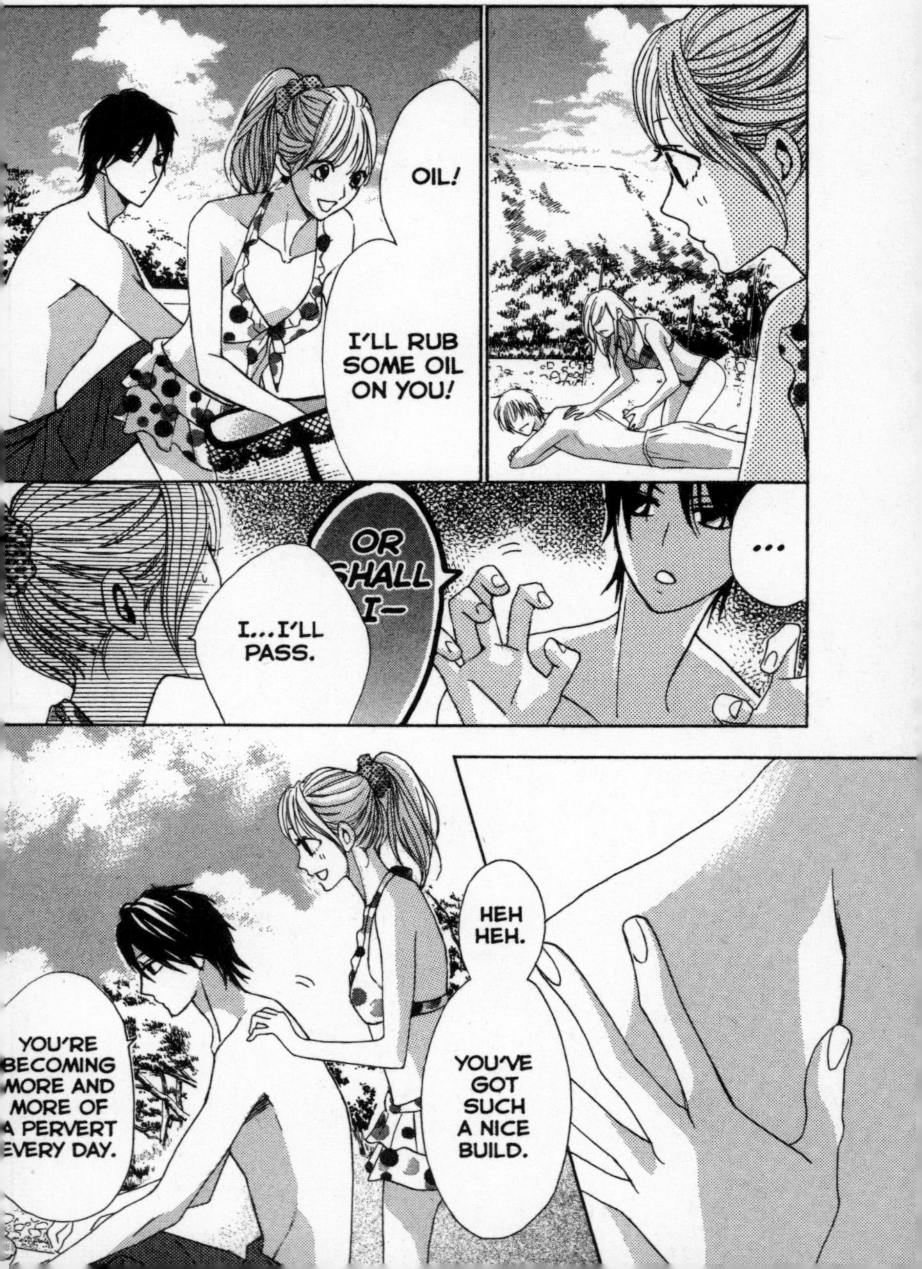
OIL!
I'LL RUB SOME OIL ON YOU!
...
OR SHALL I—
I...I'LL PASS.
HEH HEH.
YOU'VE GOT SUCH A NICE BUILD.
YOU'RE BECOMING MORE AND MORE OF A PERVERT EVERY DAY.

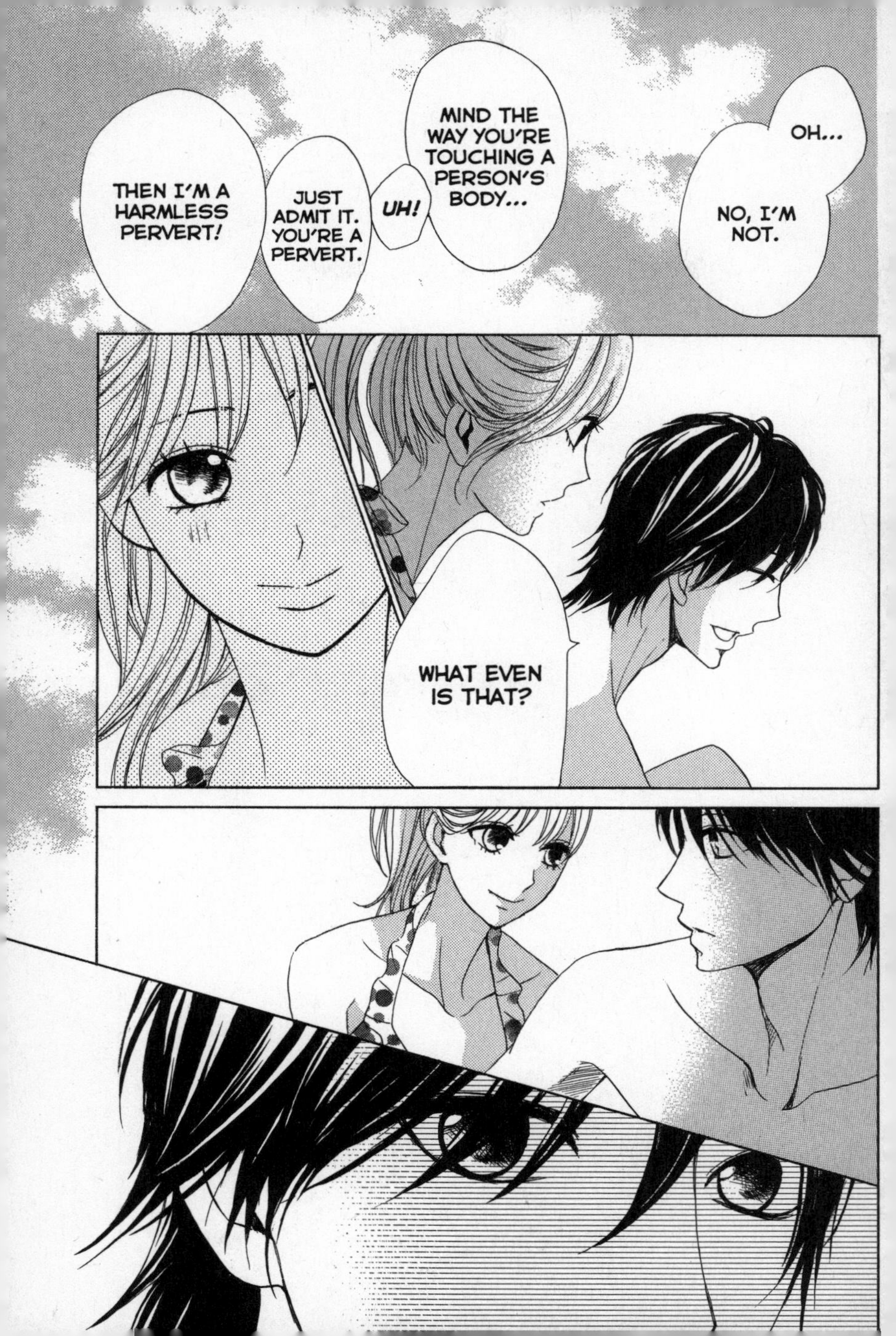
OH...
NO, I'M NOT.
MIND THE WAY YOU'RE TOUCHING A PERSON'S BODY...
UH!
JUST ADMIT IT. YOU'RE A PERVERT.
THEN I'M A HARMLESS PERVERT!
WHAT EVEN IS THAT?

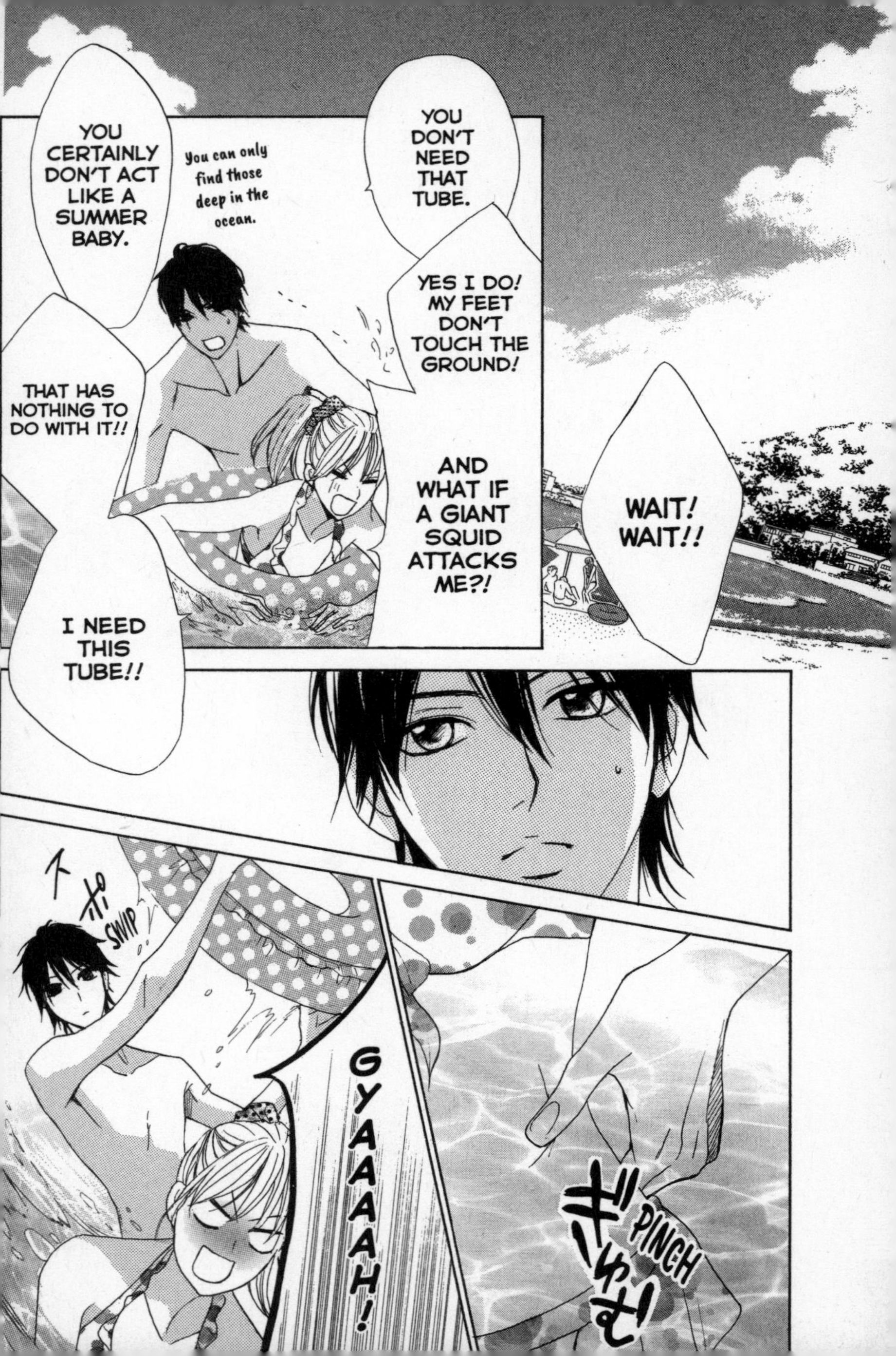

YOU DON'T NEED THAT TUBE.
YES I DO! MY FEET DON'T TOUCH THE GROUND!
AND WHAT IF A GIANT SQUID ATTACKS ME?!
You can only find those deep in the ocean.
YOU CERTAINLY DON'T ACT LIKE A SUMMER BABY.
THAT HAS NOTHING TO DO WITH IT!!
I NEED THIS TUBE!!
WAIT! WAIT!!
ぎゅむ
PINCH
GYAAAAH!
スポ
SWIP

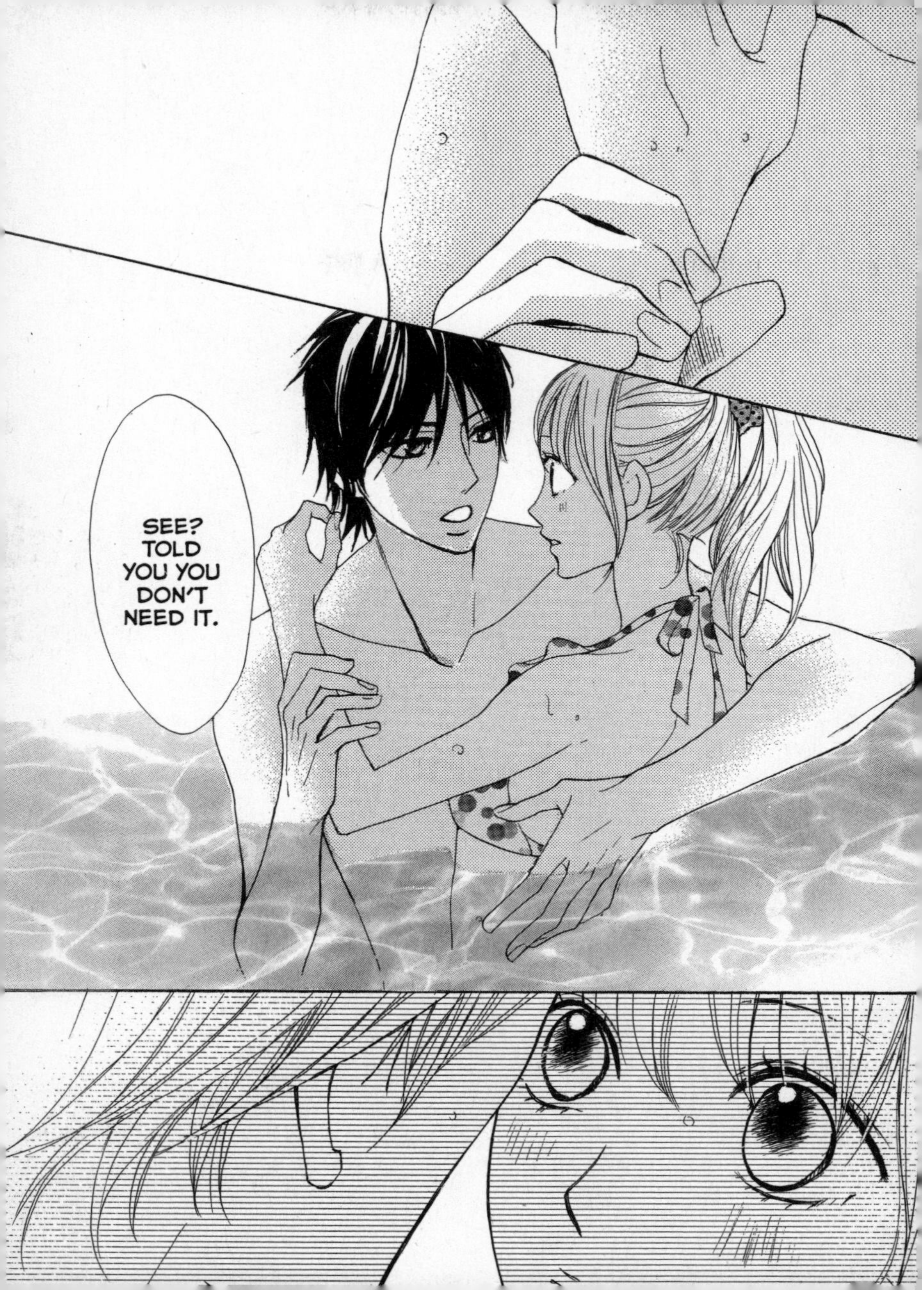
SEE? TOLD YOU YOU DON'T NEED IT.

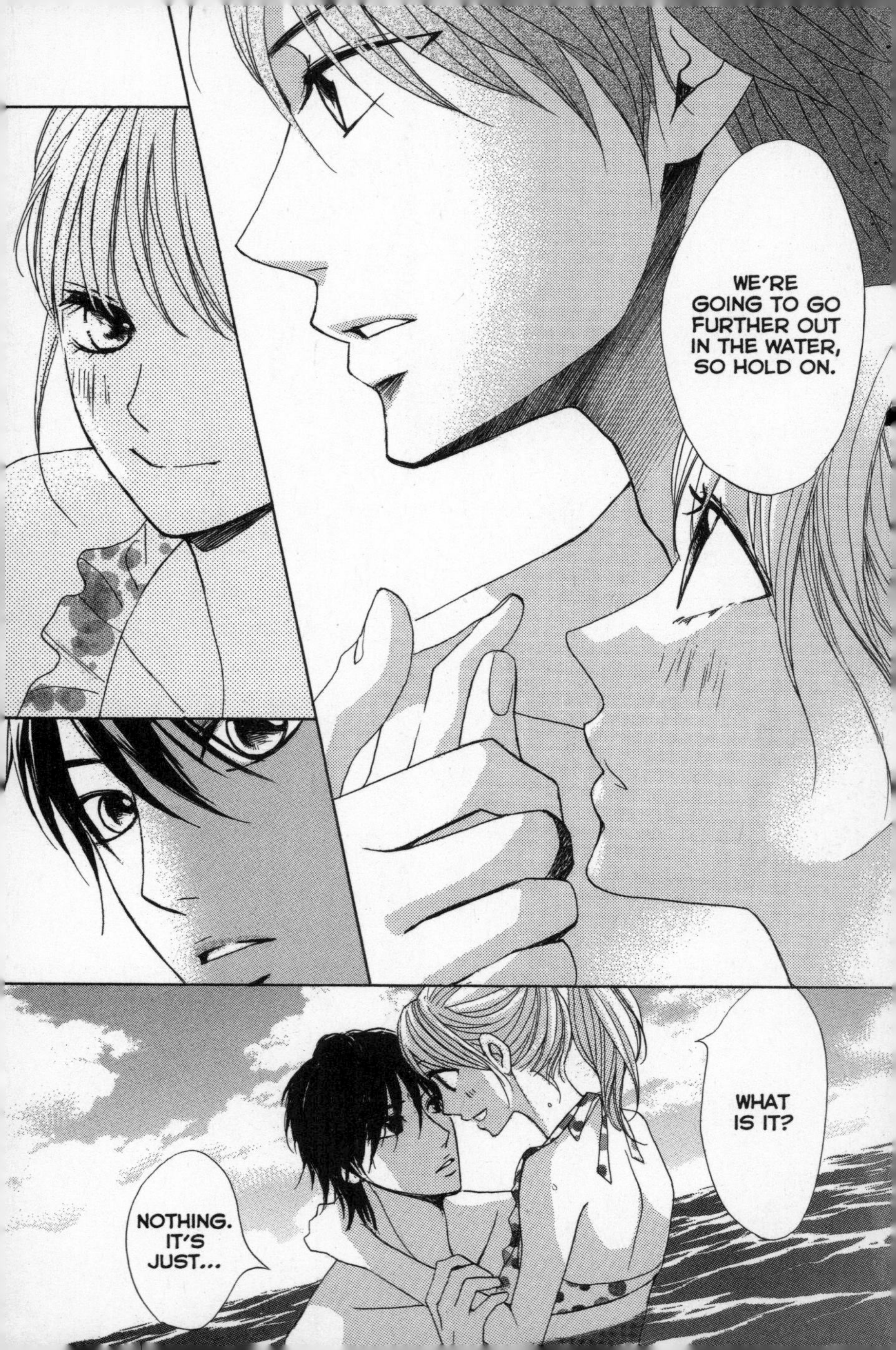
WE'RE GOING TO GO FURTHER OUT IN THE WATER, SO HOLD ON.
WHAT IS IT?
NOTHING. IT'S JUST...

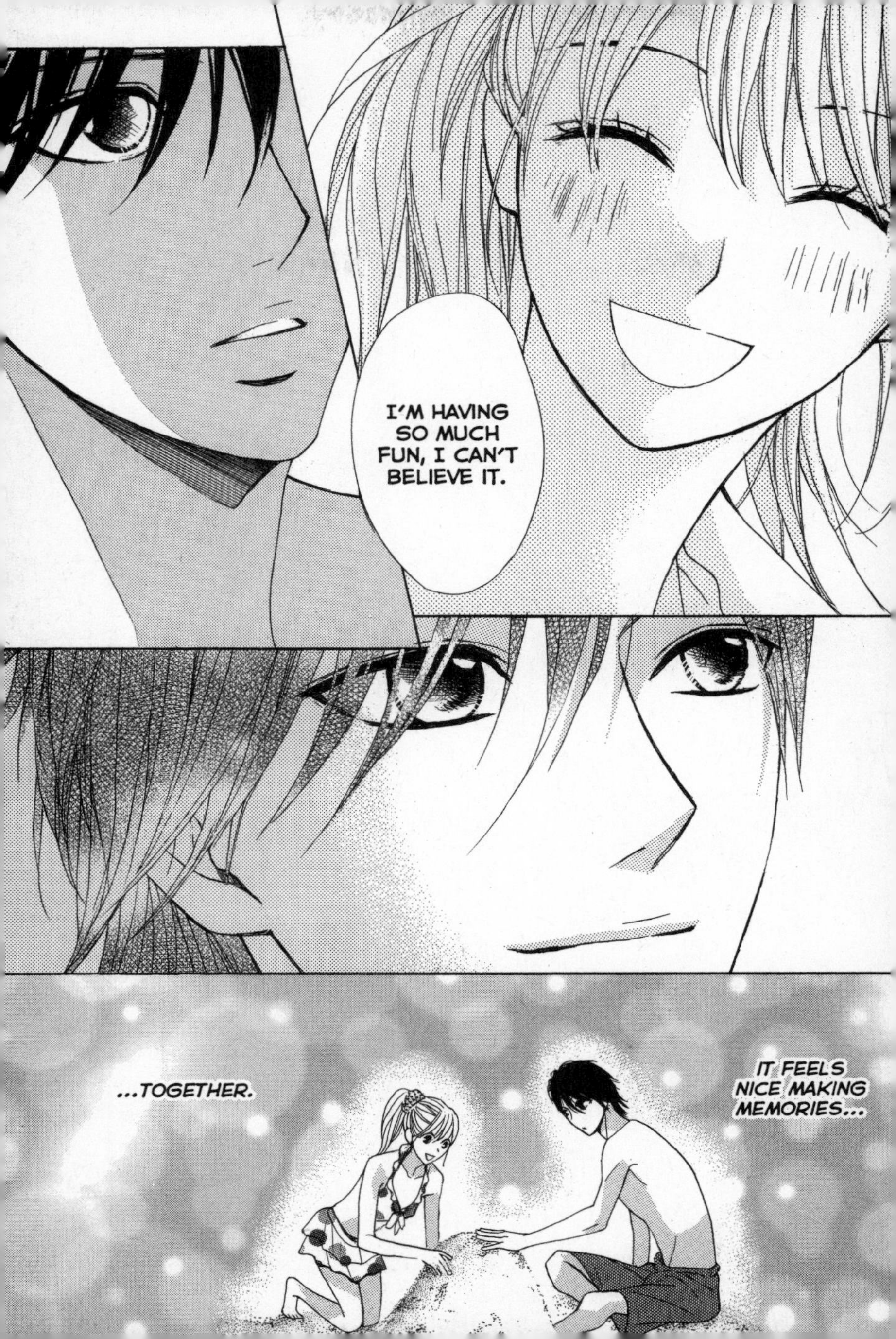
I'M HAVING SO MUCH FUN, I CAN'T BELIEVE IT.
IT FEELS NICE MAKING MEMORIES...
...TOGETHER.

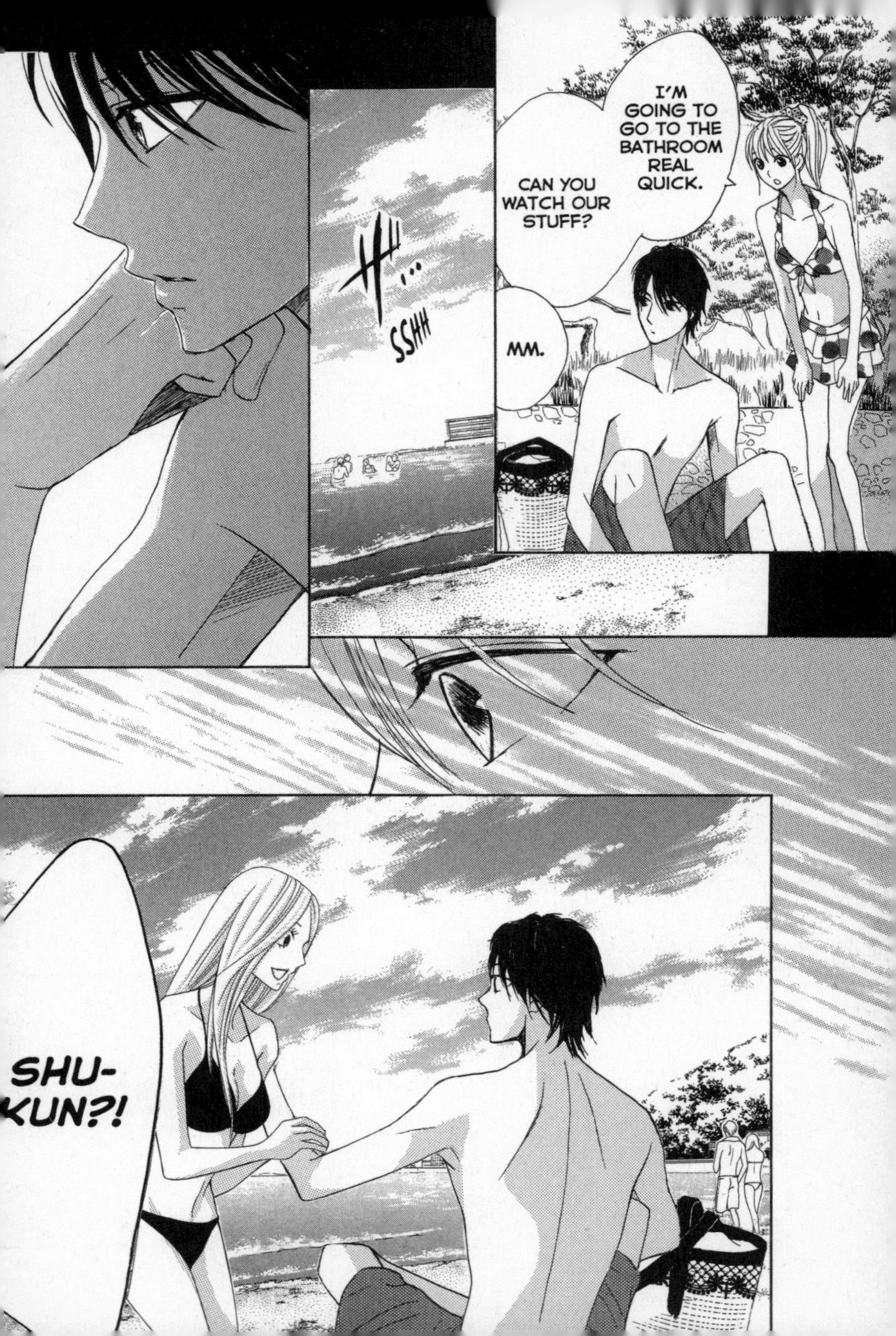
I'M GOING TO GO TO THE BATHROOM REAL QUICK.
CAN YOU WATCH OUR STUFF?
MM.
SSHH
SHU-KUN?!

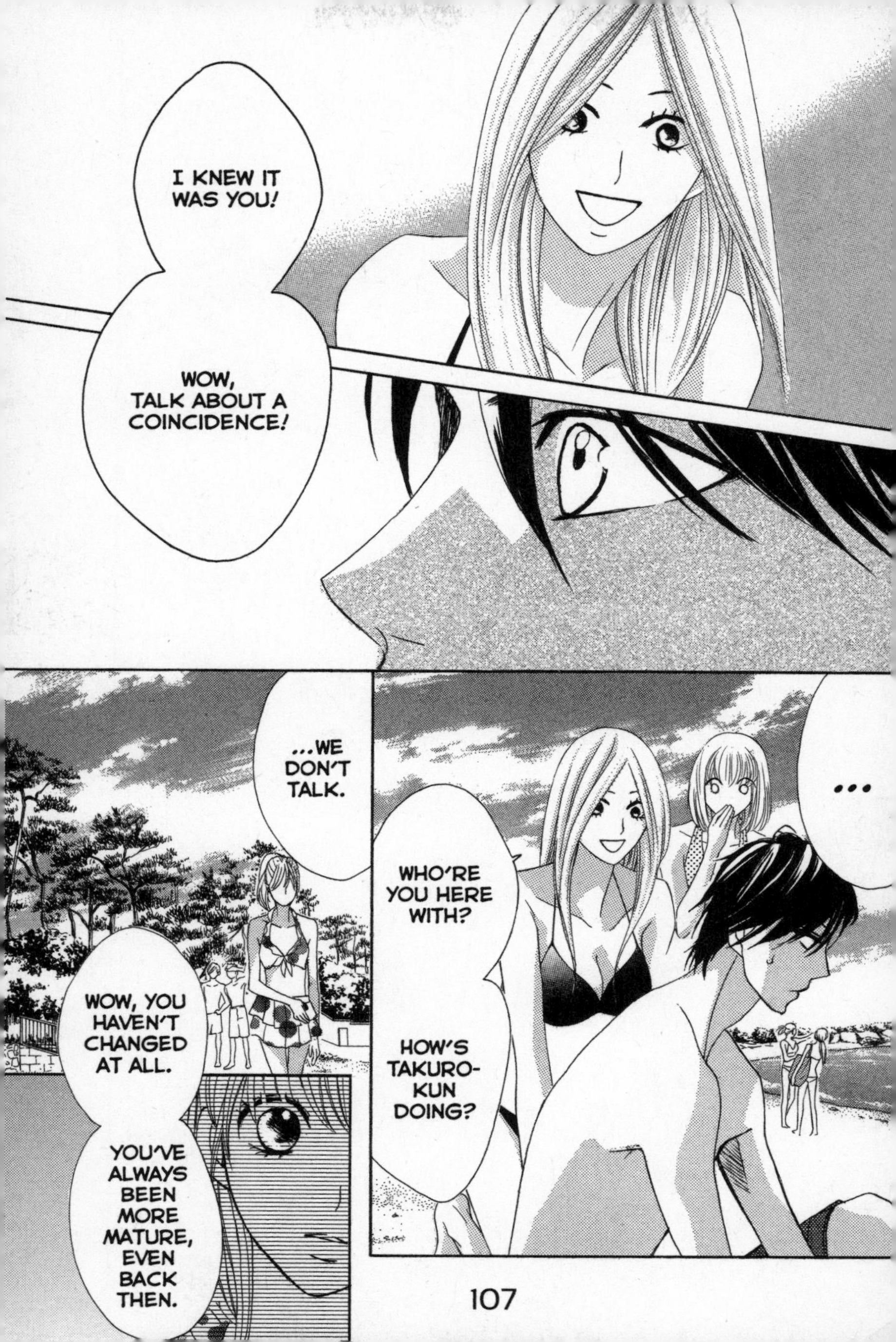
I KNEW IT WAS YOU!
WOW, TALK ABOUT A COINCIDENCE!
...
WHO'RE YOU HERE WITH?
HOW'S TAKURO-KUN DOING?
...WE DON'T TALK.
WOW, YOU HAVEN'T CHANGED AT ALL.
YOU'VE ALWAYS BEEN MORE MATURE, EVEN BACK THEN.

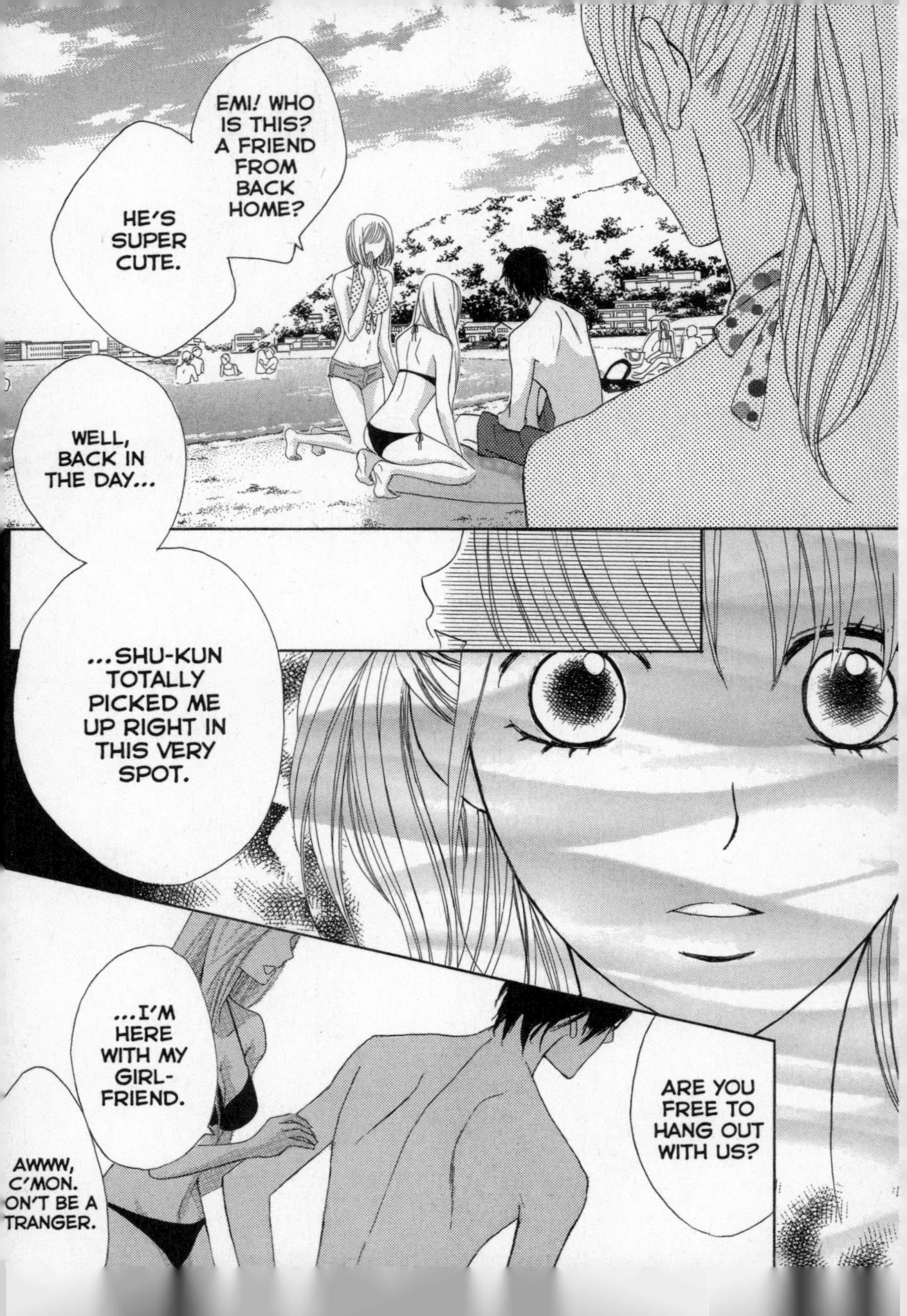
EMI! WHO IS THIS? A FRIEND FROM BACK HOME?
HE'S SUPER CUTE.
WELL, BACK IN THE DAY...
...SHU-KUN TOTALLY PICKED ME UP RIGHT IN THIS VERY SPOT.
ARE YOU FREE TO HANG OUT WITH US?
...I'M HERE WITH MY GIRL-FRIEND.
AWWW, C'MON. ON'T BE A TRANGER.

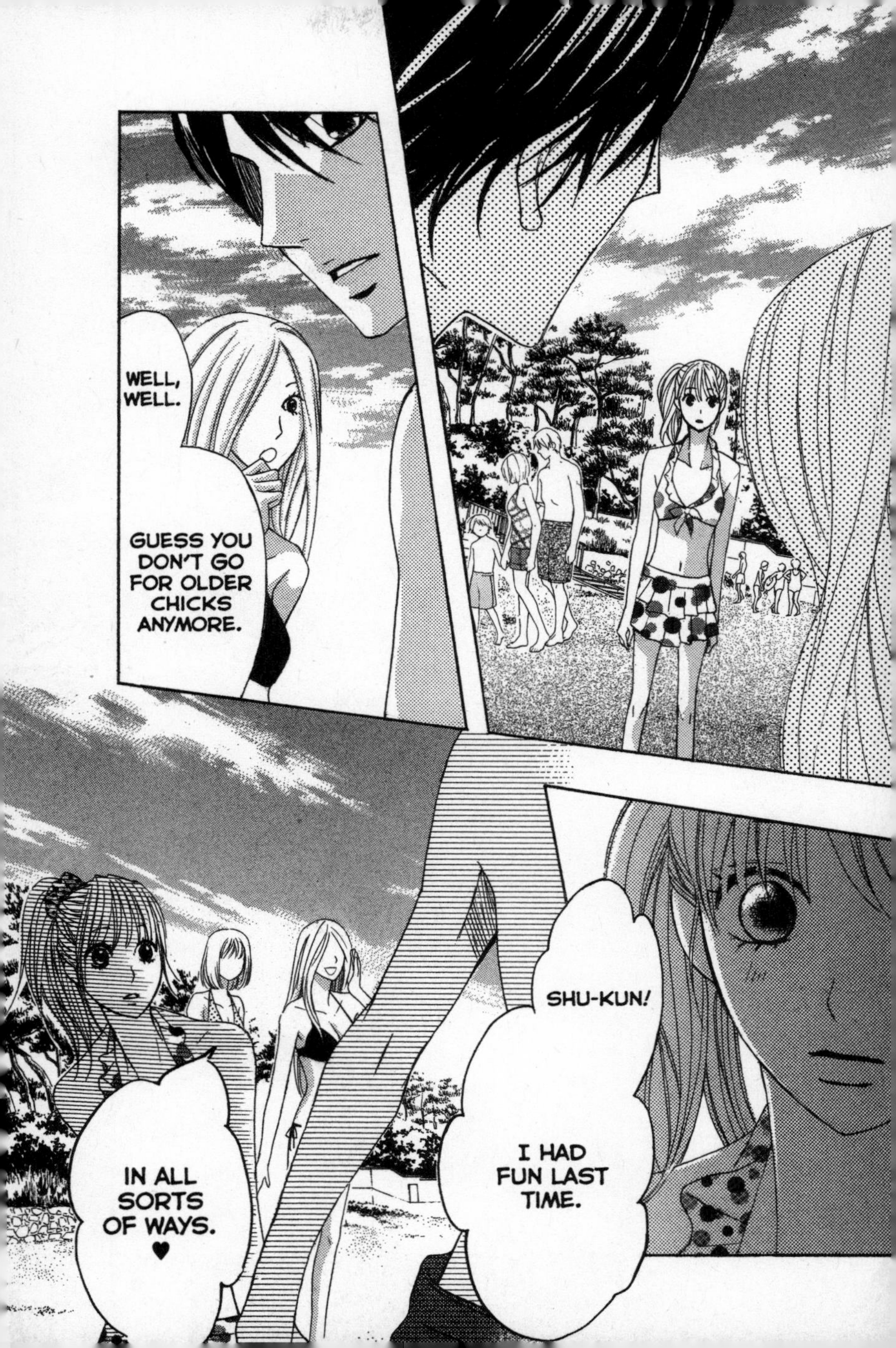
WELL, WELL.
GUESS YOU DON'T GO FOR OLDER CHICKS ANYMORE.
SHU-KUN!
I HAD FUN LAST TIME.
IN ALL SORTS OF WAYS. ♥

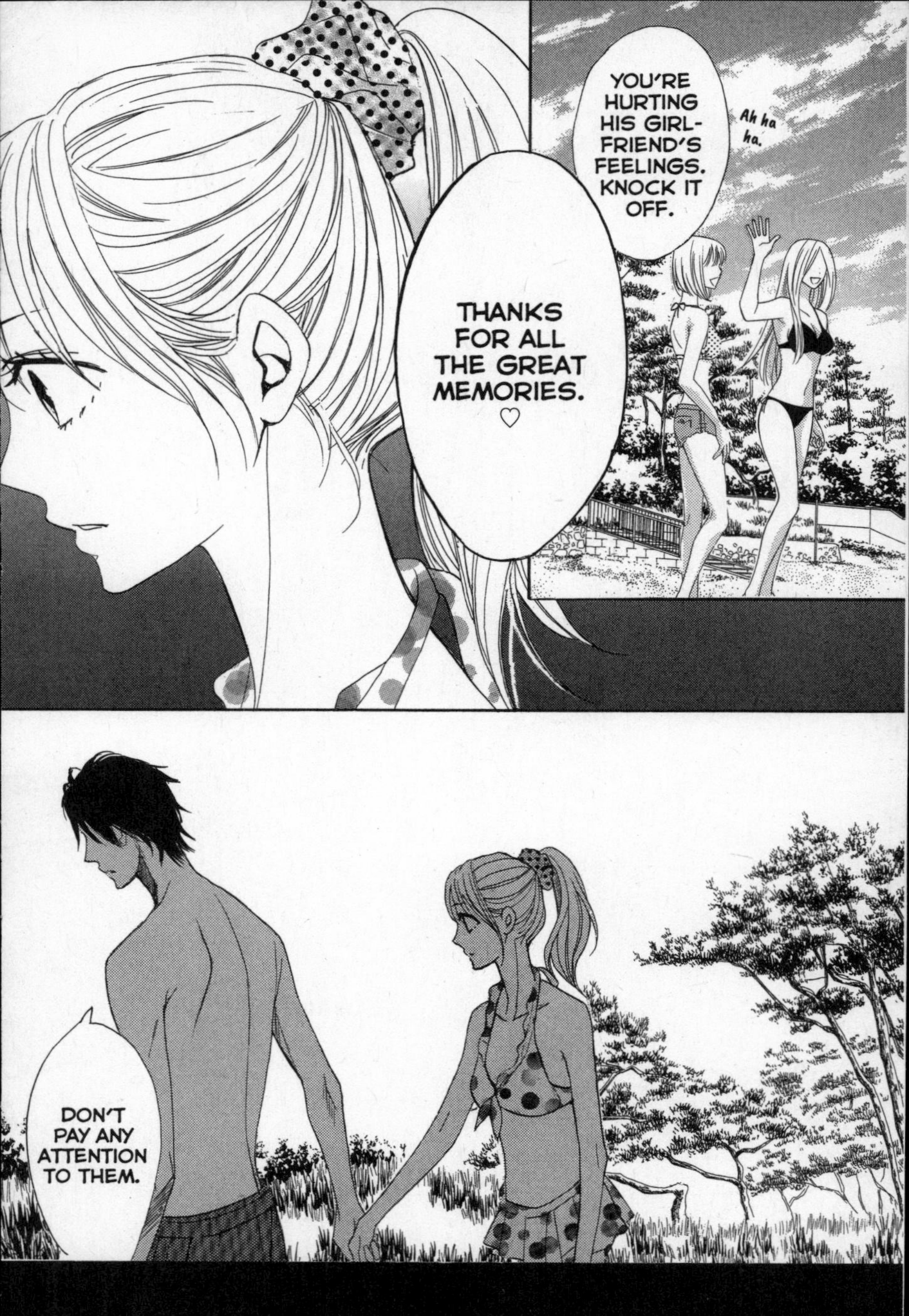
YOU'RE HURTING HIS GIRL-FRIEND'S FEELINGS. KNOCK IT OFF.
Ah ha ha.
THANKS FOR ALL THE GREAT MEMORIES. ♡
DON'T PAY ANY ATTENTION TO THEM.

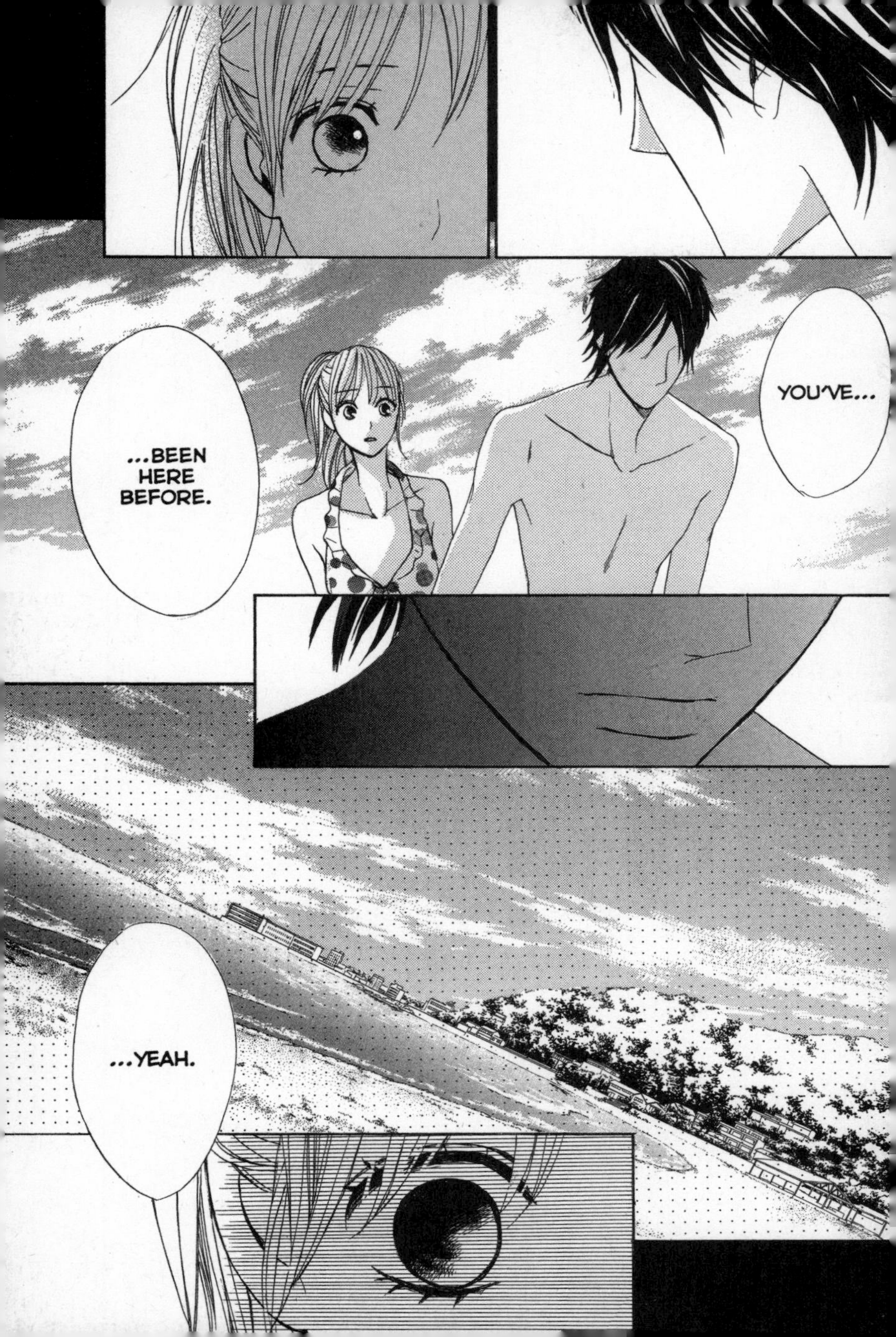
YOU'VE...
...BEEN HERE BEFORE.
...YEAH.

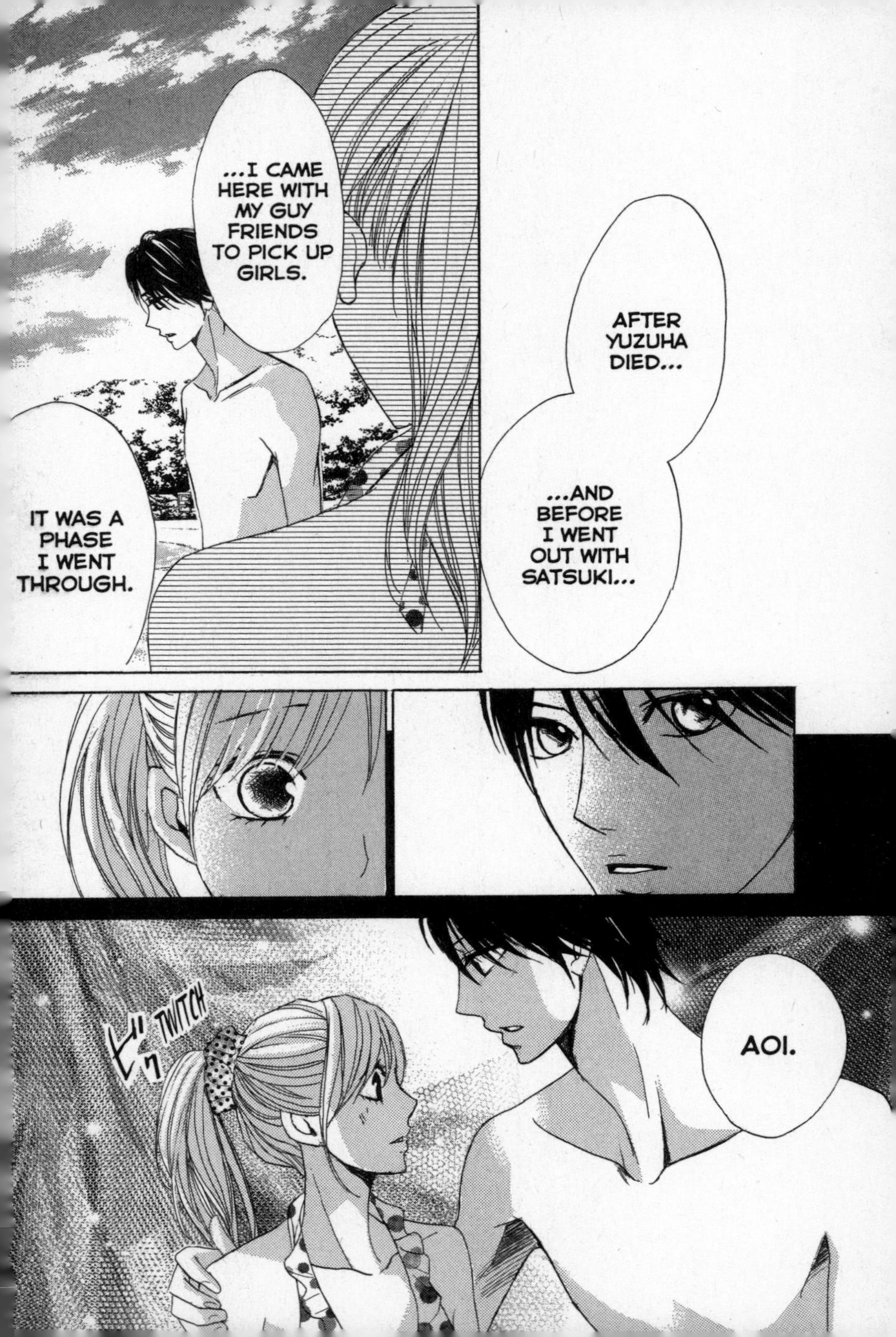
AFTER YUZUHA DIED...
...AND BEFORE I WENT OUT WITH SATSUKI...
...I CAME HERE WITH MY GUY FRIENDS TO PICK UP GIRLS.
IT WAS A PHASE I WENT THROUGH.
AOI.
TWITCH

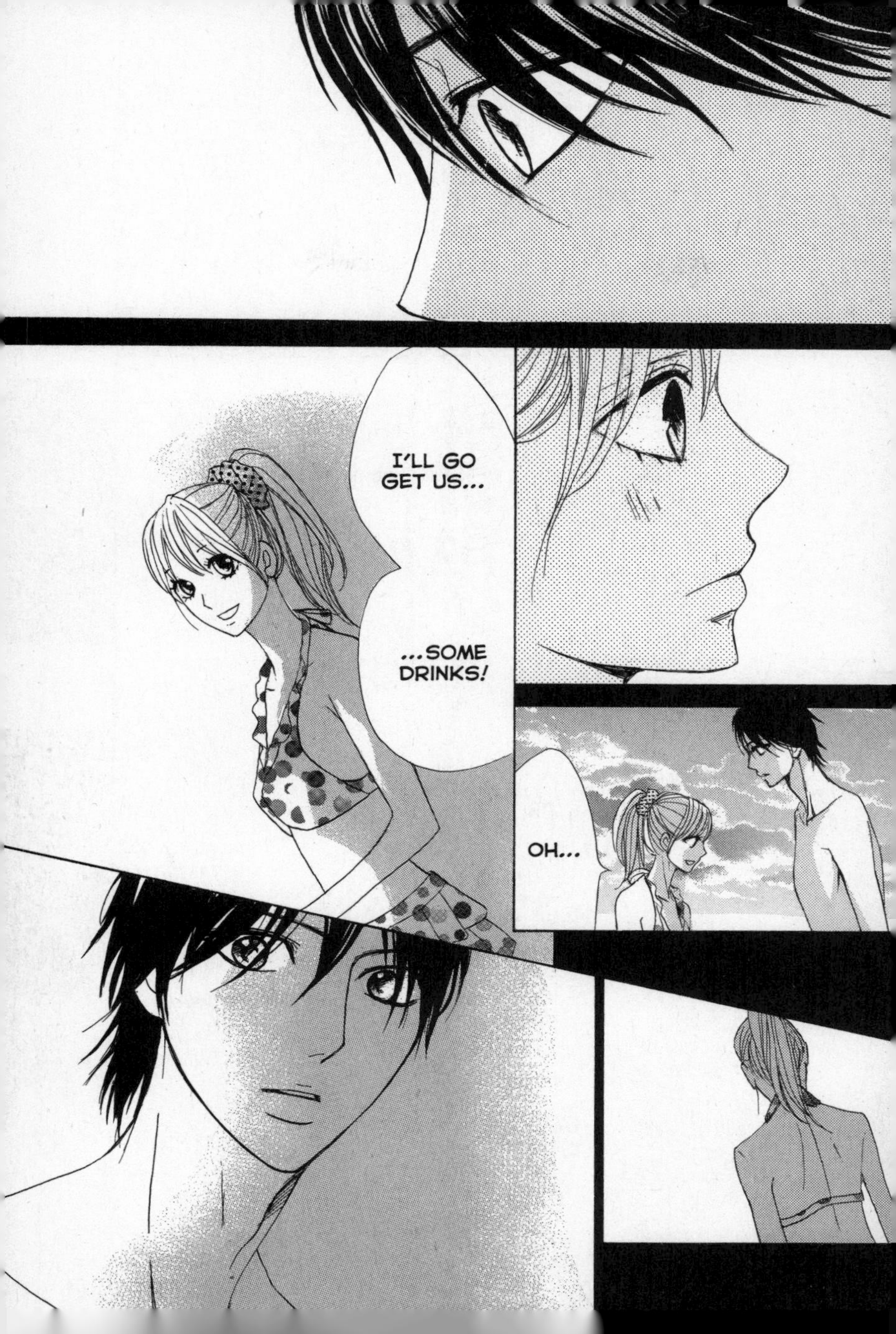
I'LL GO GET US...
...SOME DRINKS!
OH...

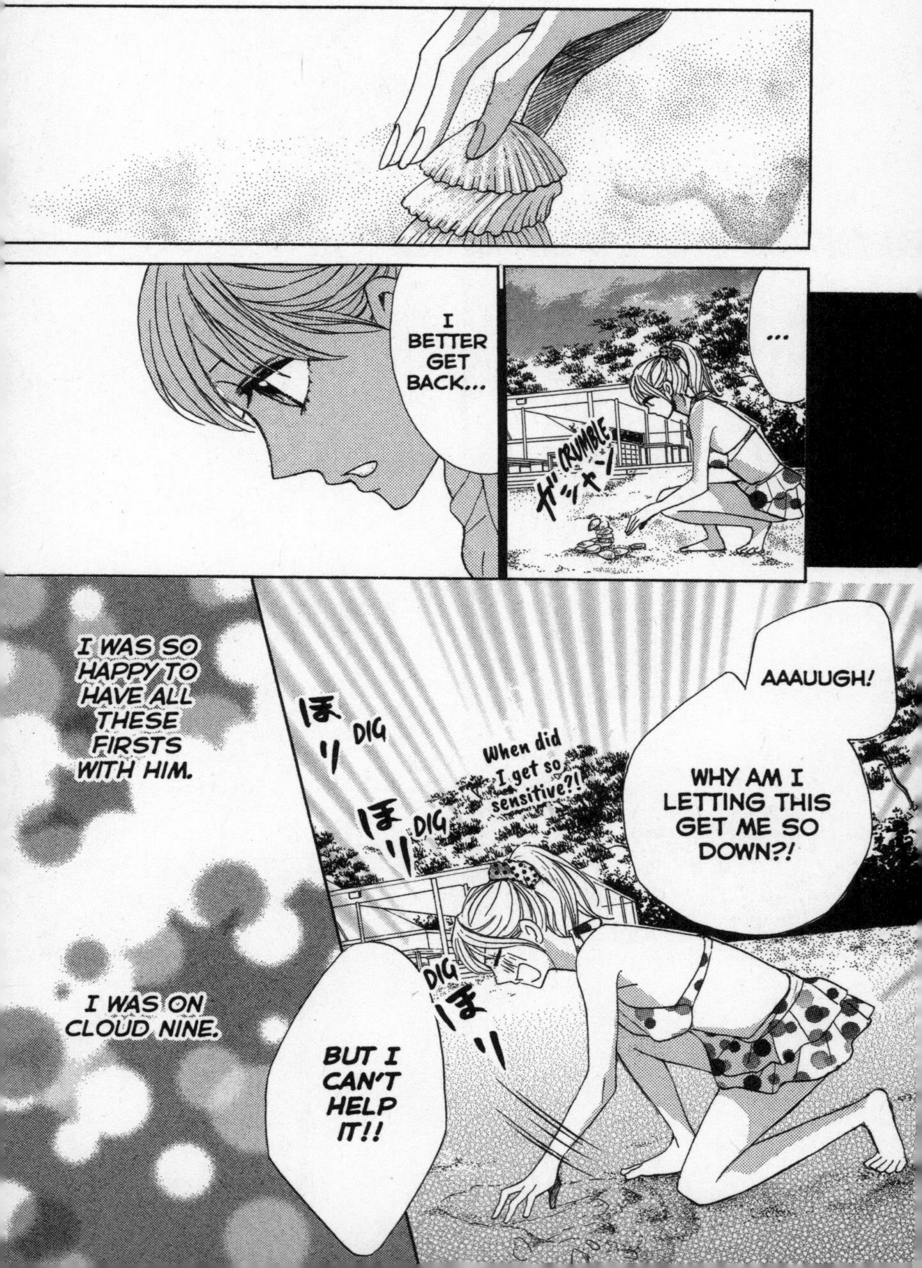
...
CRUMBLE
I BETTER GET BACK...
AAAUUGH!
WHY AM I LETTING THIS GET ME SO DOWN?!
When did I get so sensitive?!
ほり DIG
ほり DIG
I WAS SO HAPPY TO HAVE ALL THESE FIRSTS WITH HIM.
DIG ほり
I WAS ON CLOUD NINE.
BUT I CAN'T HELP IT!!

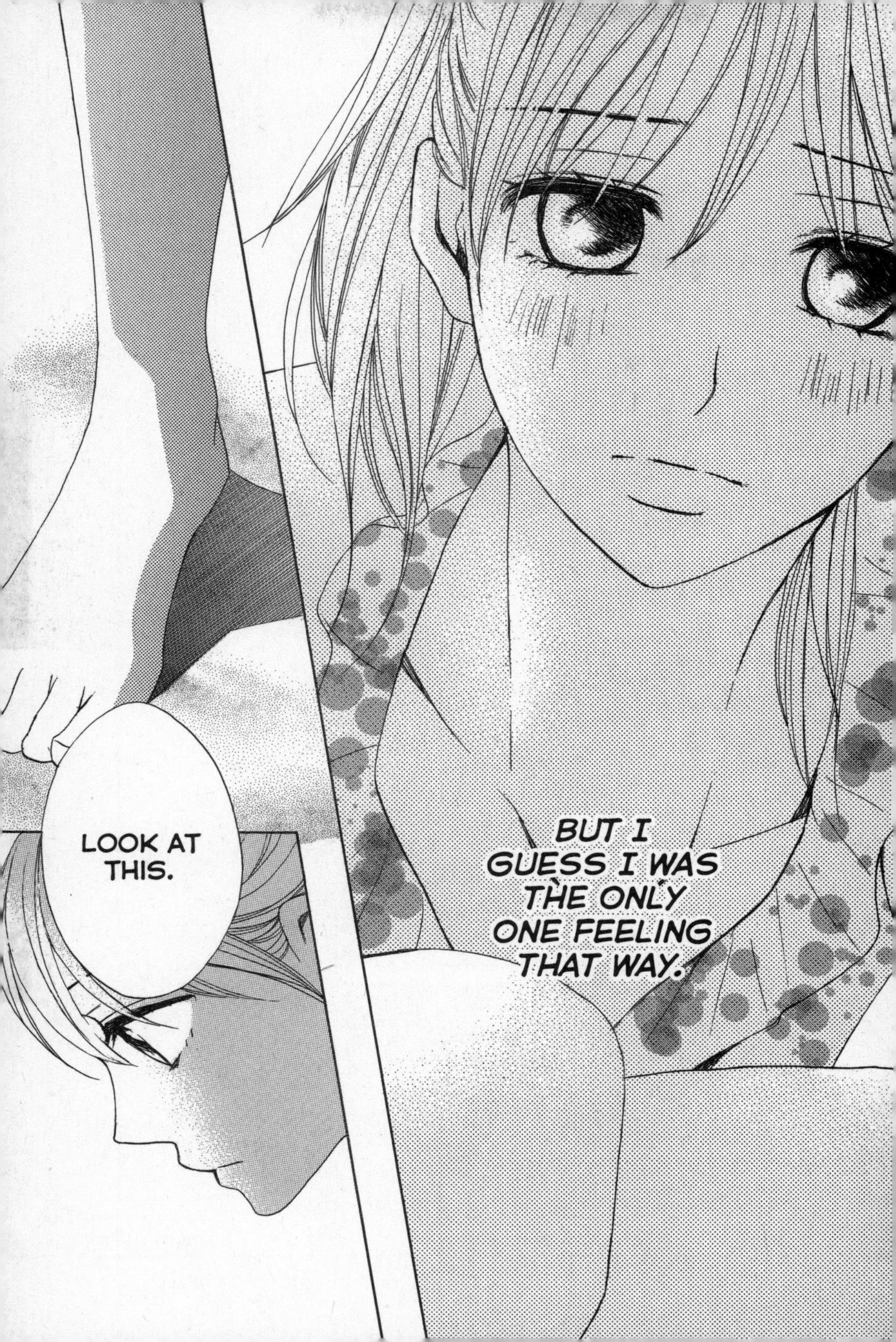
BUT I GUESS I WAS THE ONLY ONE FEELING THAT WAY.
LOOK AT THIS.

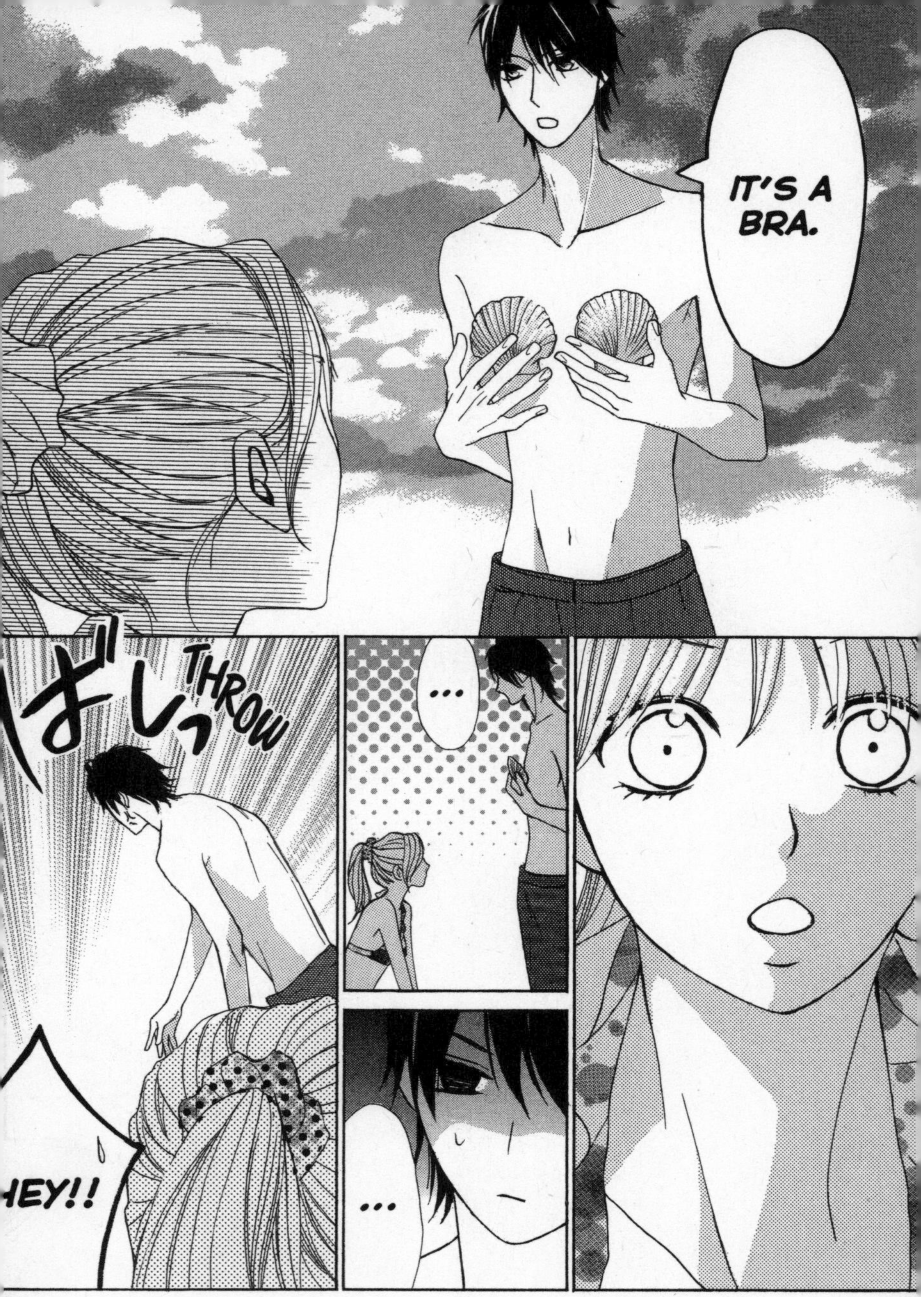
IT'S A BRA.
...
...
おしっ
THROW
HEY!!

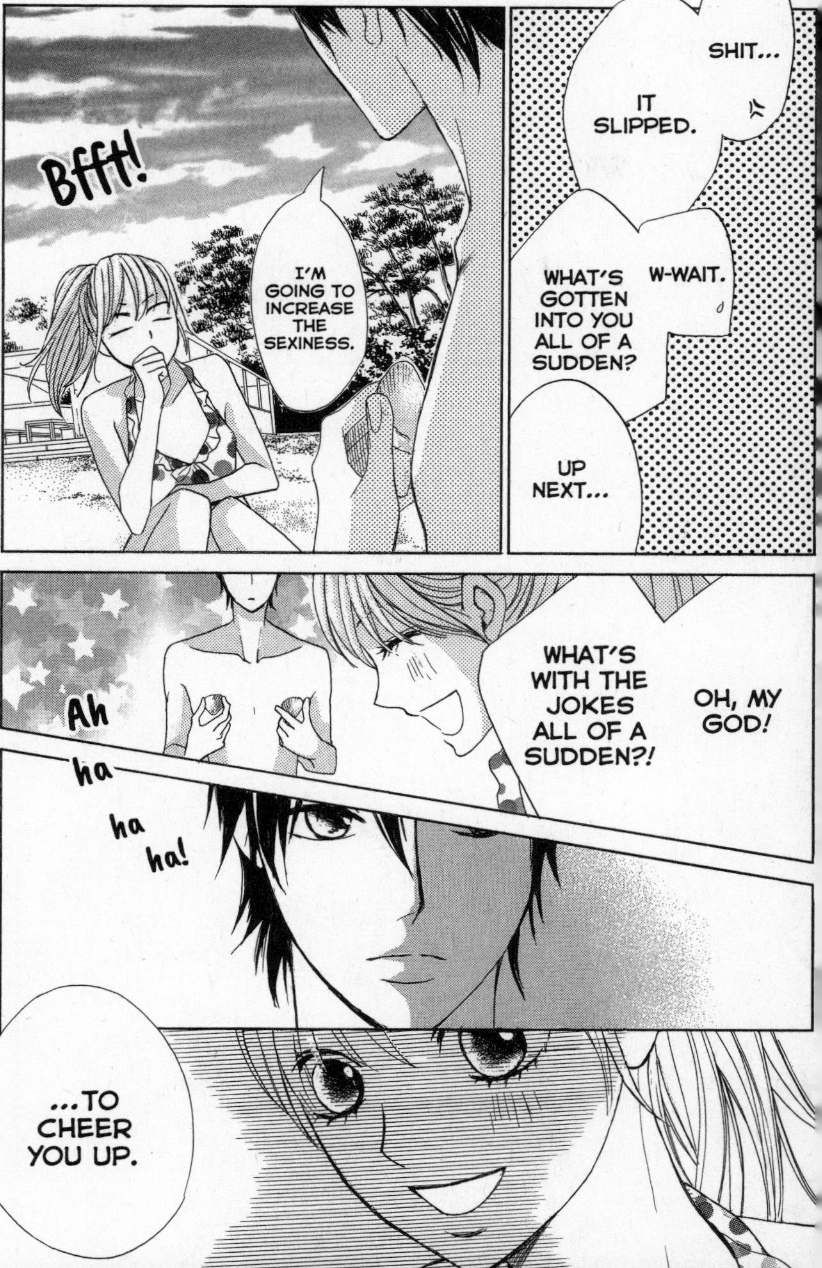
SHIT...
IT SLIPPED.
W-WAIT.
WHAT'S GOTTEN INTO YOU ALL OF A SUDDEN?
UP NEXT...
Bfft!
I'M GOING TO INCREASE THE SEXINESS.
OH, MY GOD!
WHAT'S WITH THE JOKES ALL OF A SUDDEN?!
Ah ha ha ha!
...TO CHEER YOU UP.

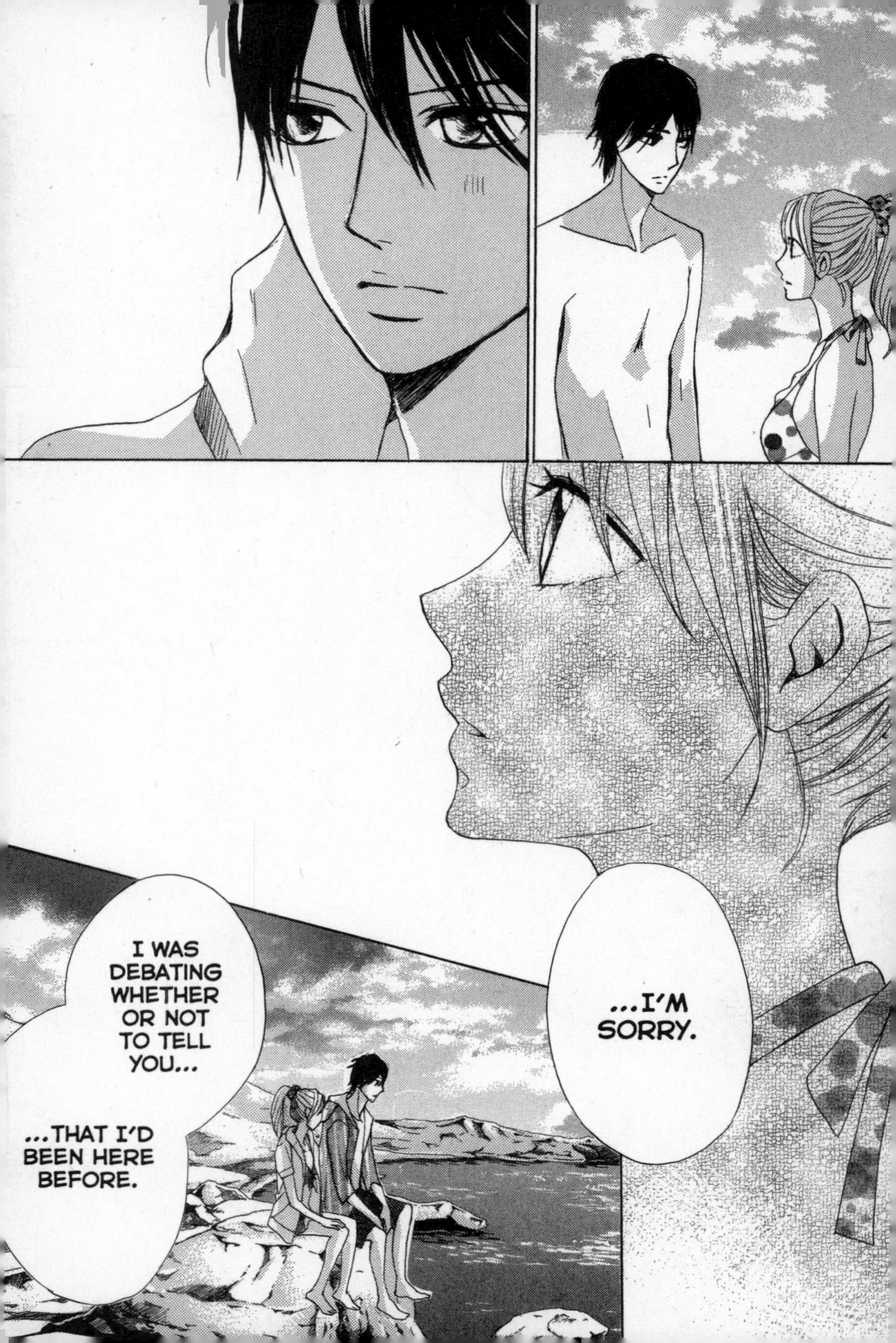
...I'M SORRY.
I WAS DEBATING WHETHER OR NOT TO TELL YOU...
...THAT I'D BEEN HERE BEFORE.

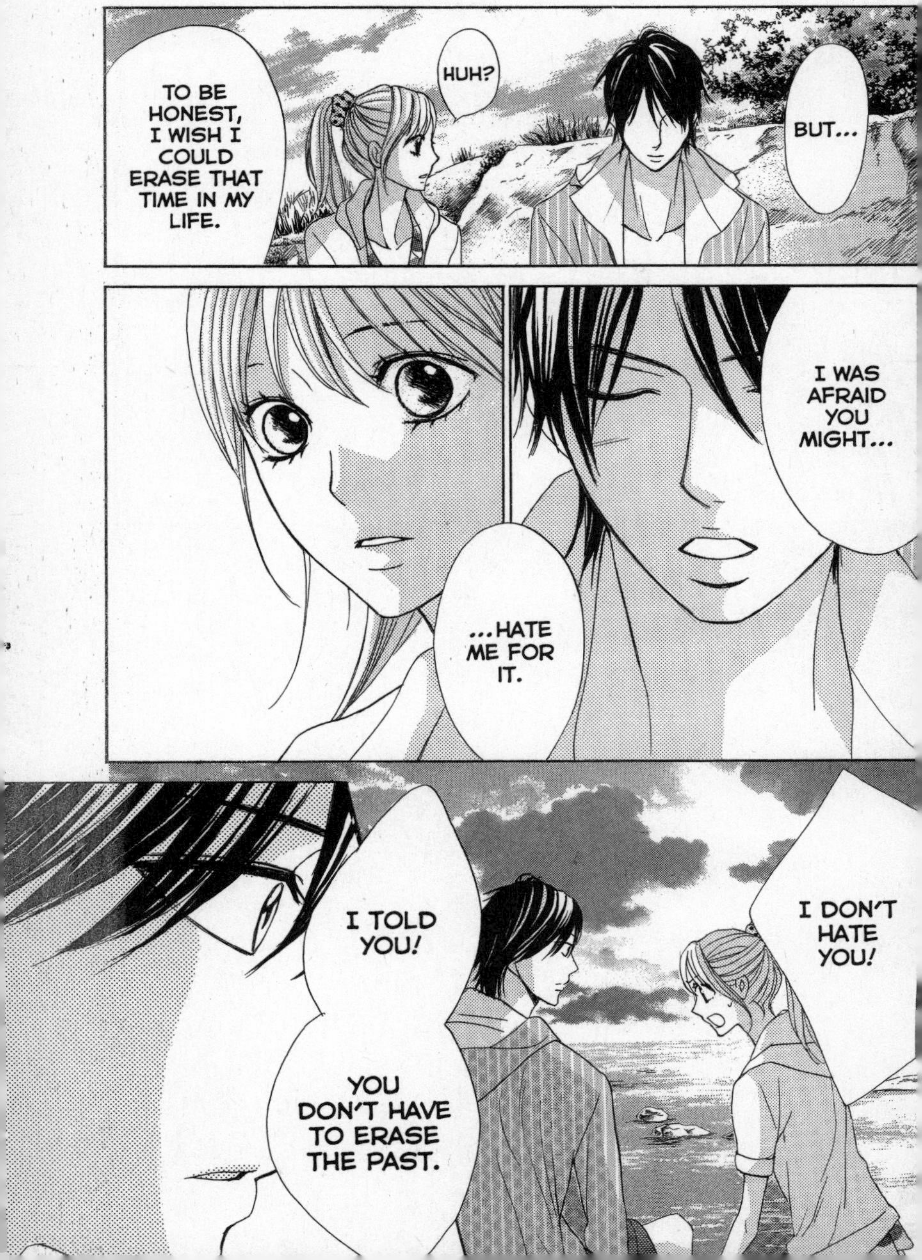
BUT...
HUH?
TO BE HONEST, I WISH I COULD ERASE THAT TIME IN MY LIFE.
I WAS AFRAID YOU MIGHT...
...HATE ME FOR IT.
I DON'T HATE YOU!
I TOLD YOU!
YOU DON'T HAVE TO ERASE THE PAST.

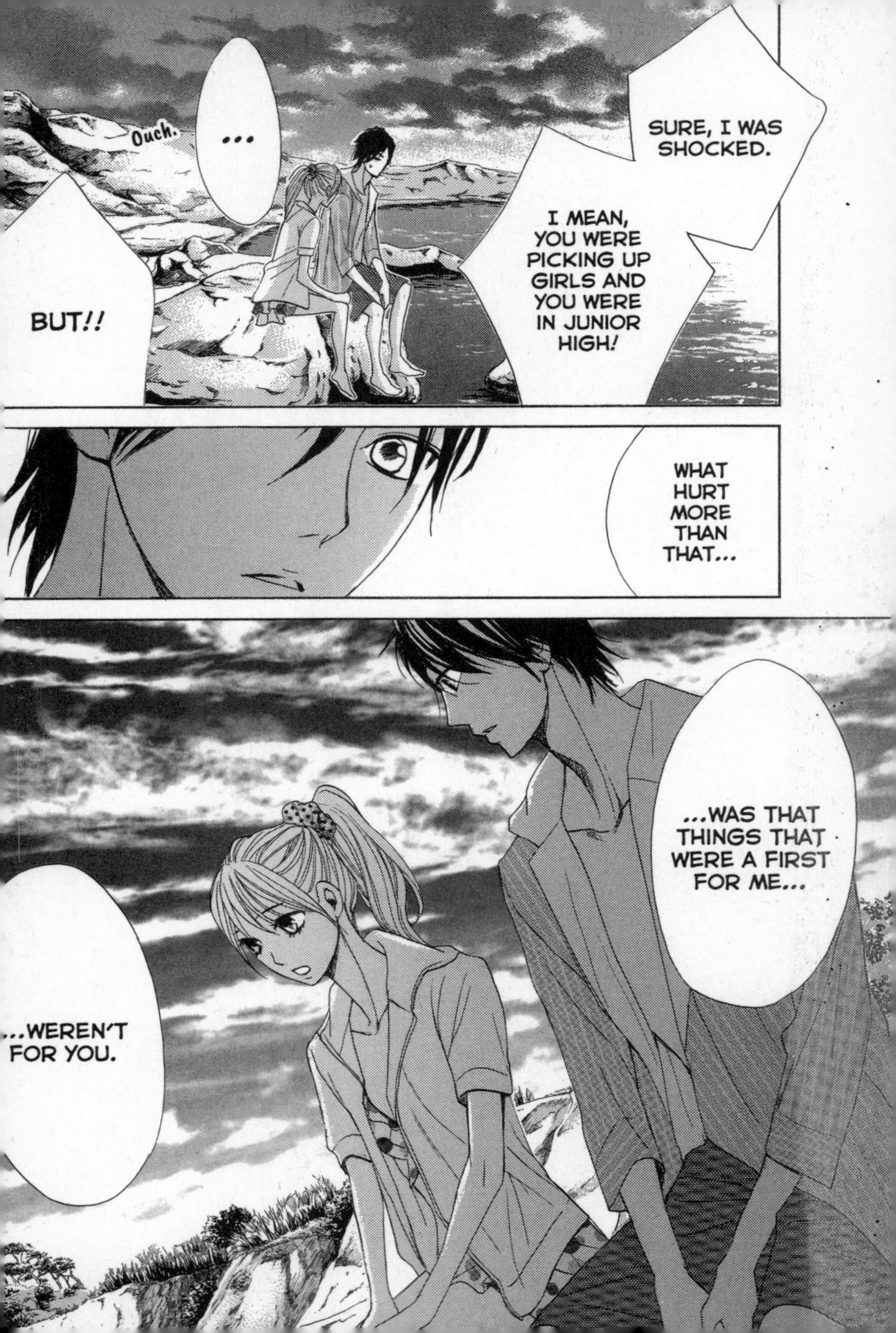
SURE, I WAS SHOCKED.
I MEAN, YOU WERE PICKING UP GIRLS AND YOU WERE IN JUNIOR HIGH!
...
Ouch.
BUT!!
WHAT HURT MORE THAN THAT...
...WAS THAT THINGS THAT WERE A FIRST FOR ME...
...WEREN'T FOR YOU.

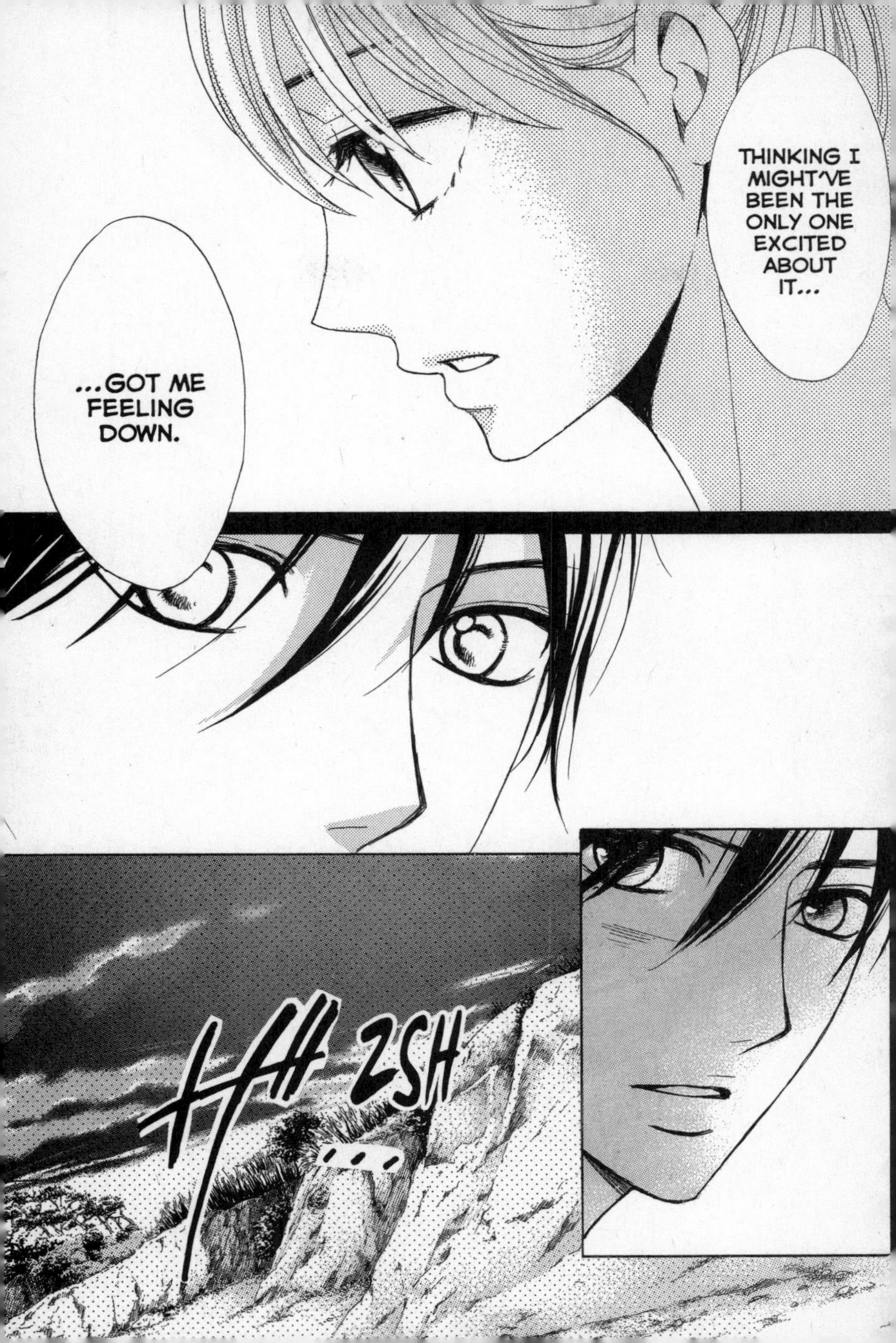
THINKING I MIGHT'VE BEEN THE ONLY ONE EXCITED ABOUT IT...
...GOT ME FEELING DOWN.
ZSH
...

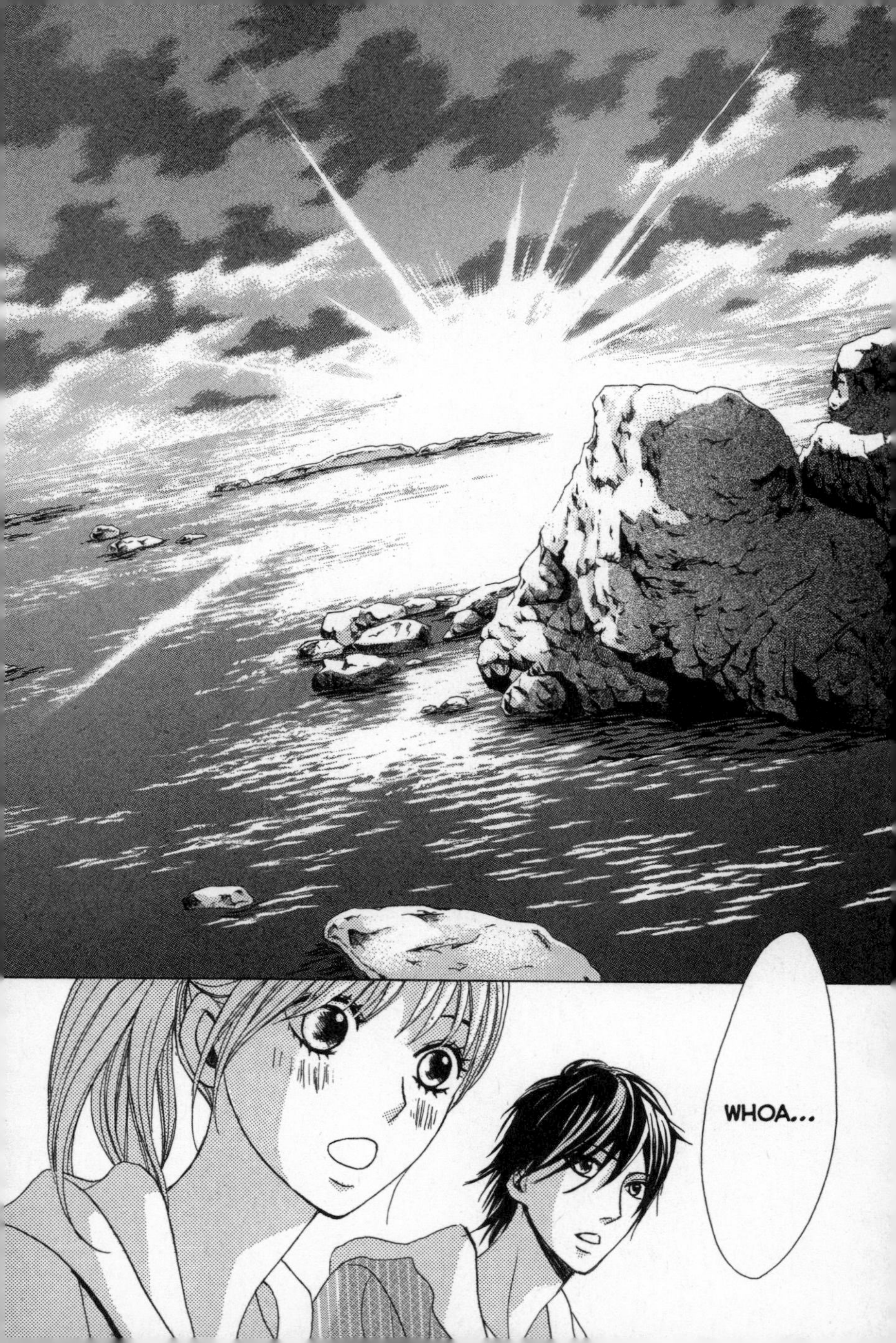
WHOA...

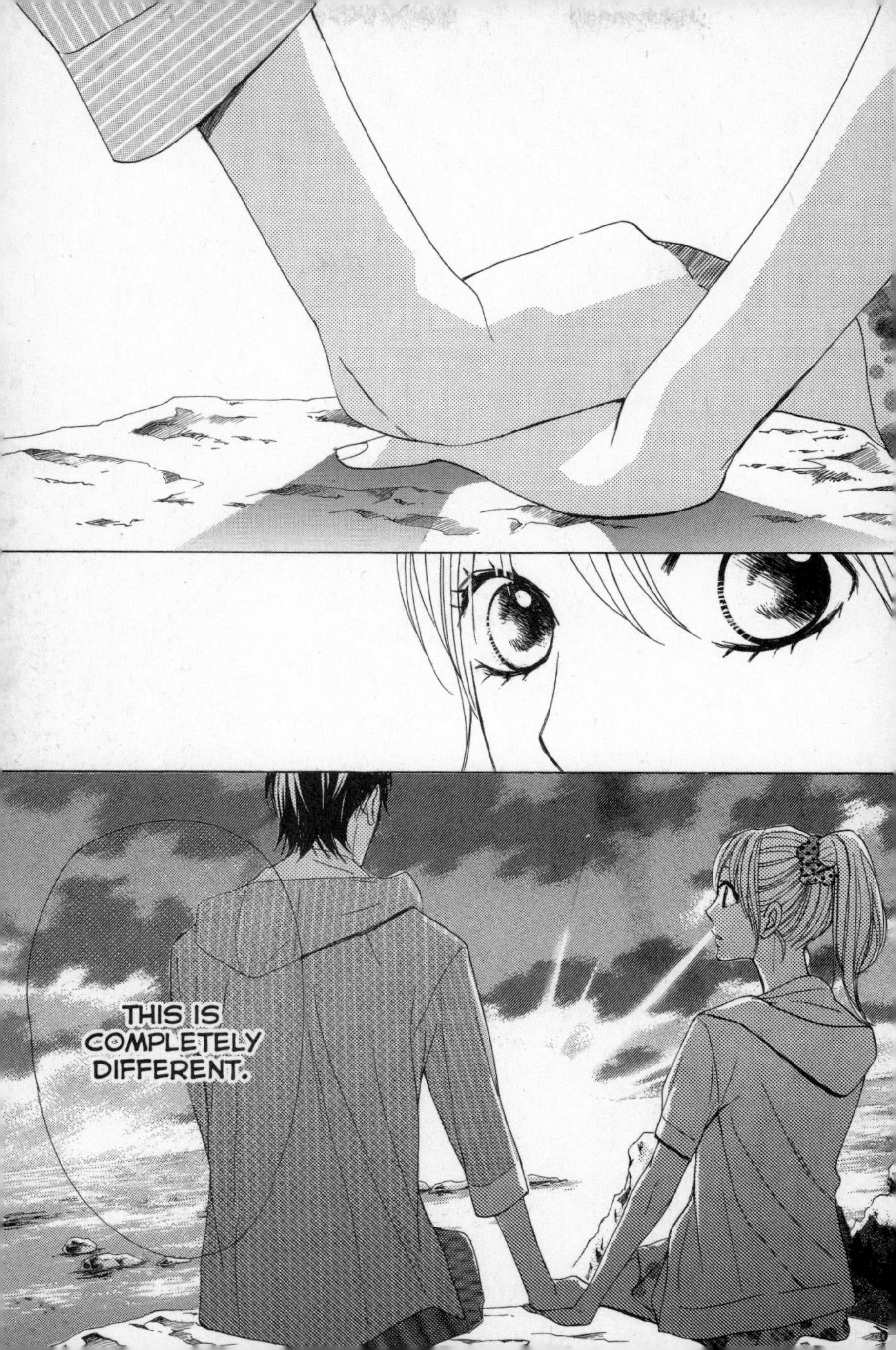
THIS IS COMPLETELY DIFFERENT.

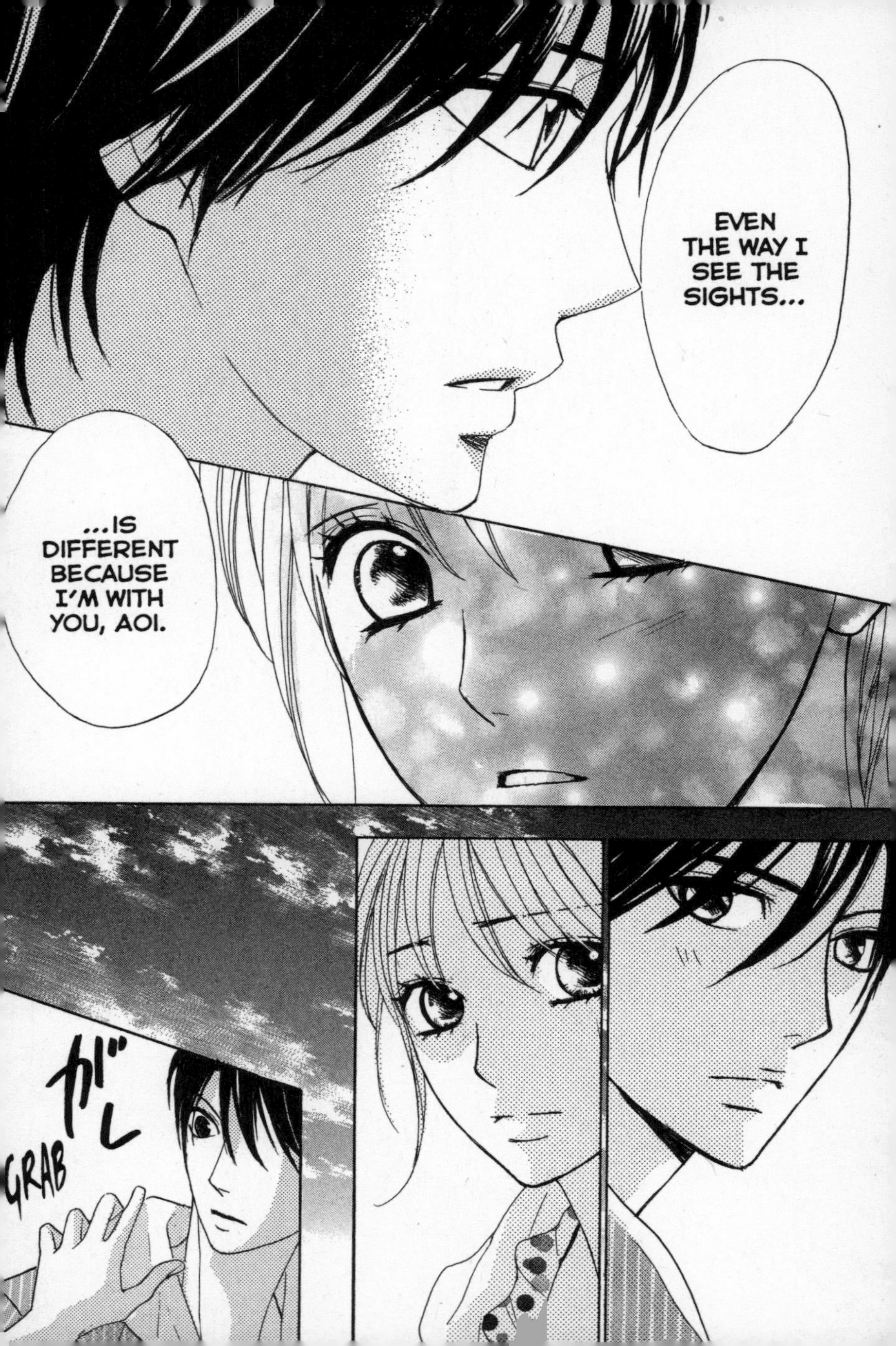
EVEN THE WAY I SEE THE SIGHTS...
...IS DIFFERENT BECAUSE I'M WITH YOU, AOI.
GRAB

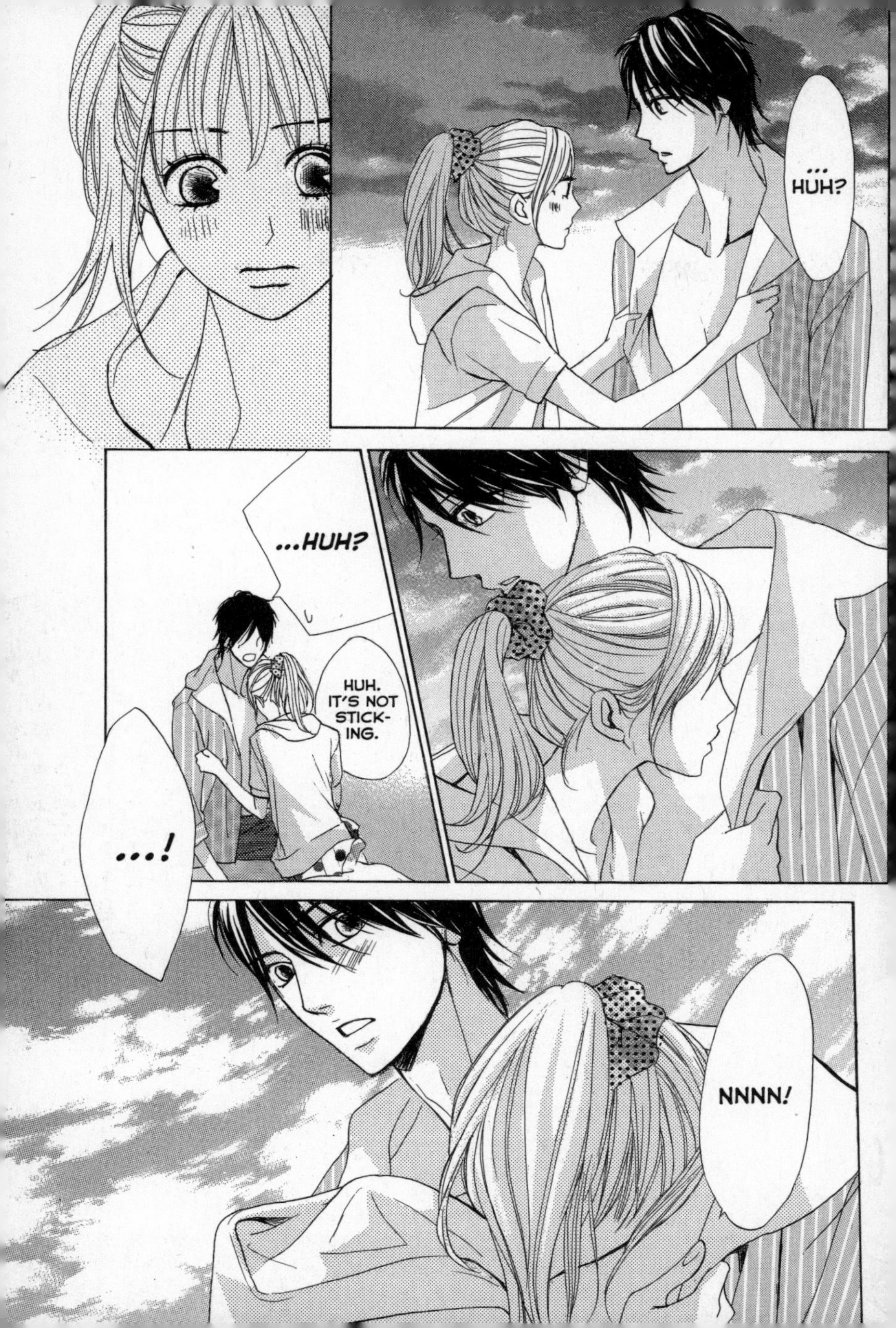
...HUH?
...HUH?
HUH. IT'S NOT STICKING.
...!
NNNN!

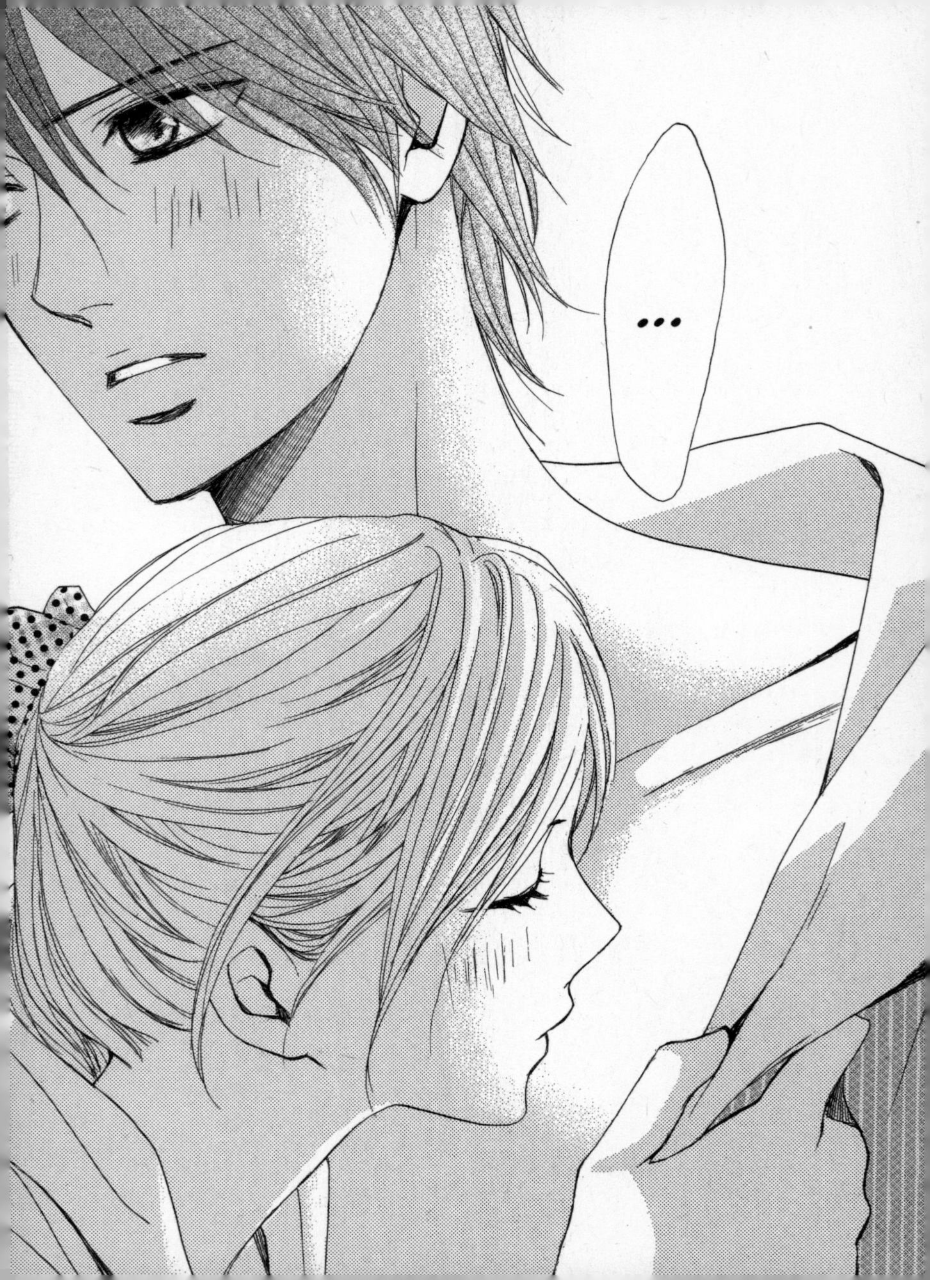
...

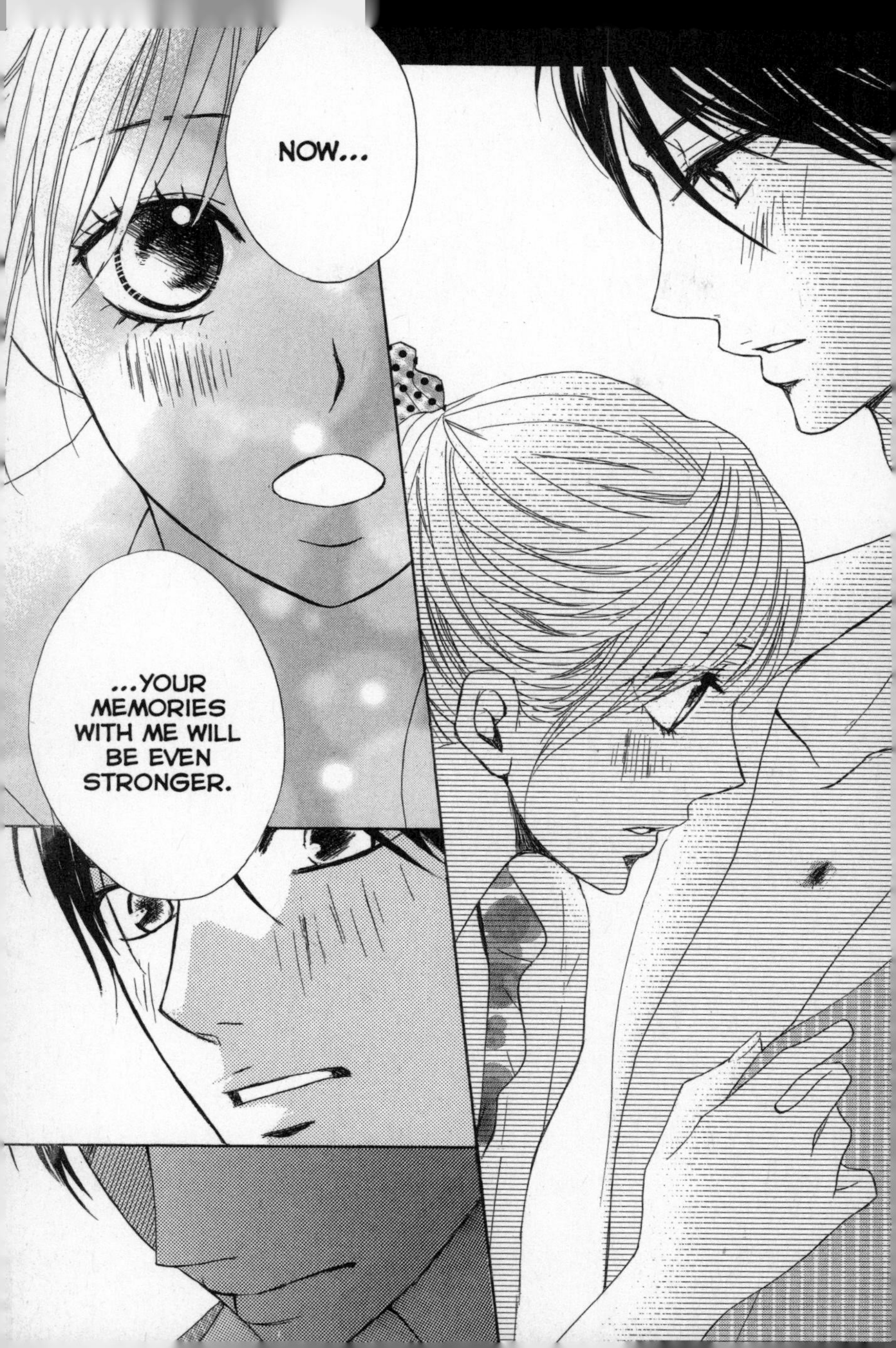
NOW...
...YOUR MEMORIES WITH ME WILL BE EVEN STRONGER.

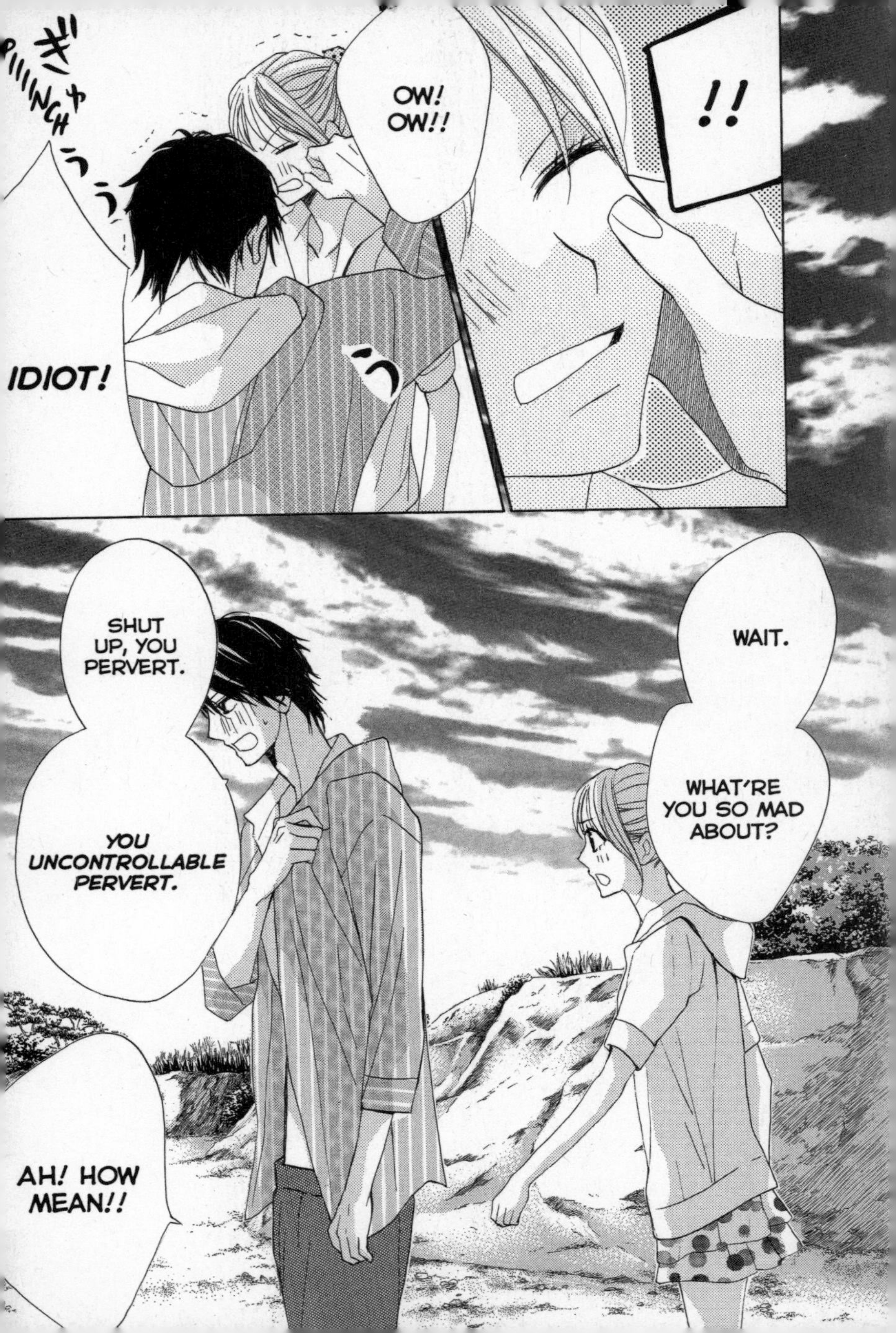

!!
OW! OW!!
ぎゅう
PIIIINCH
IDIOT!
WAIT.
WHAT'RE YOU SO MAD ABOUT?
SHUT UP, YOU PERVERT.
YOU UNCONTROLLABLE PERVERT.
AH! HOW MEAN!!

#52 Big Bro

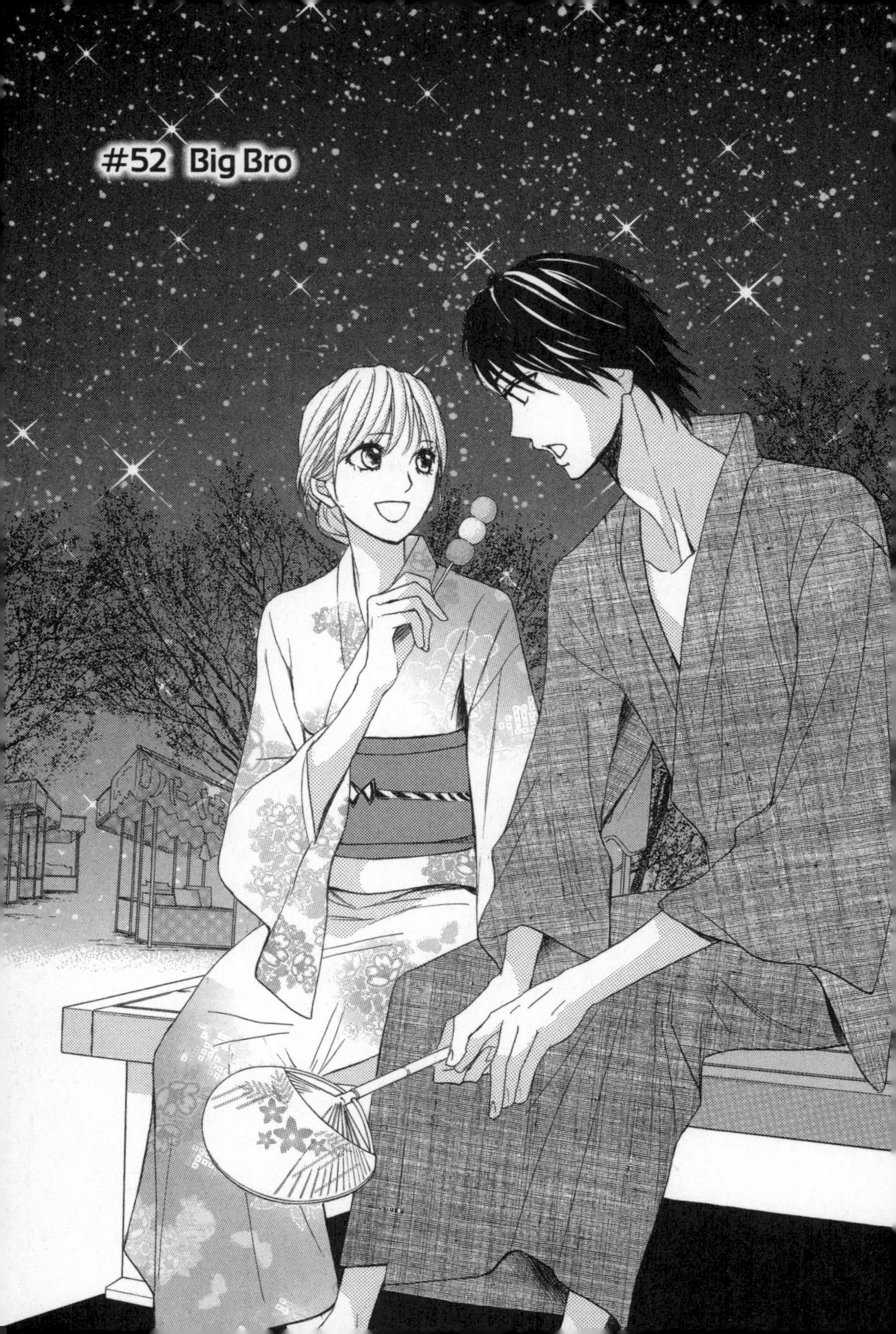

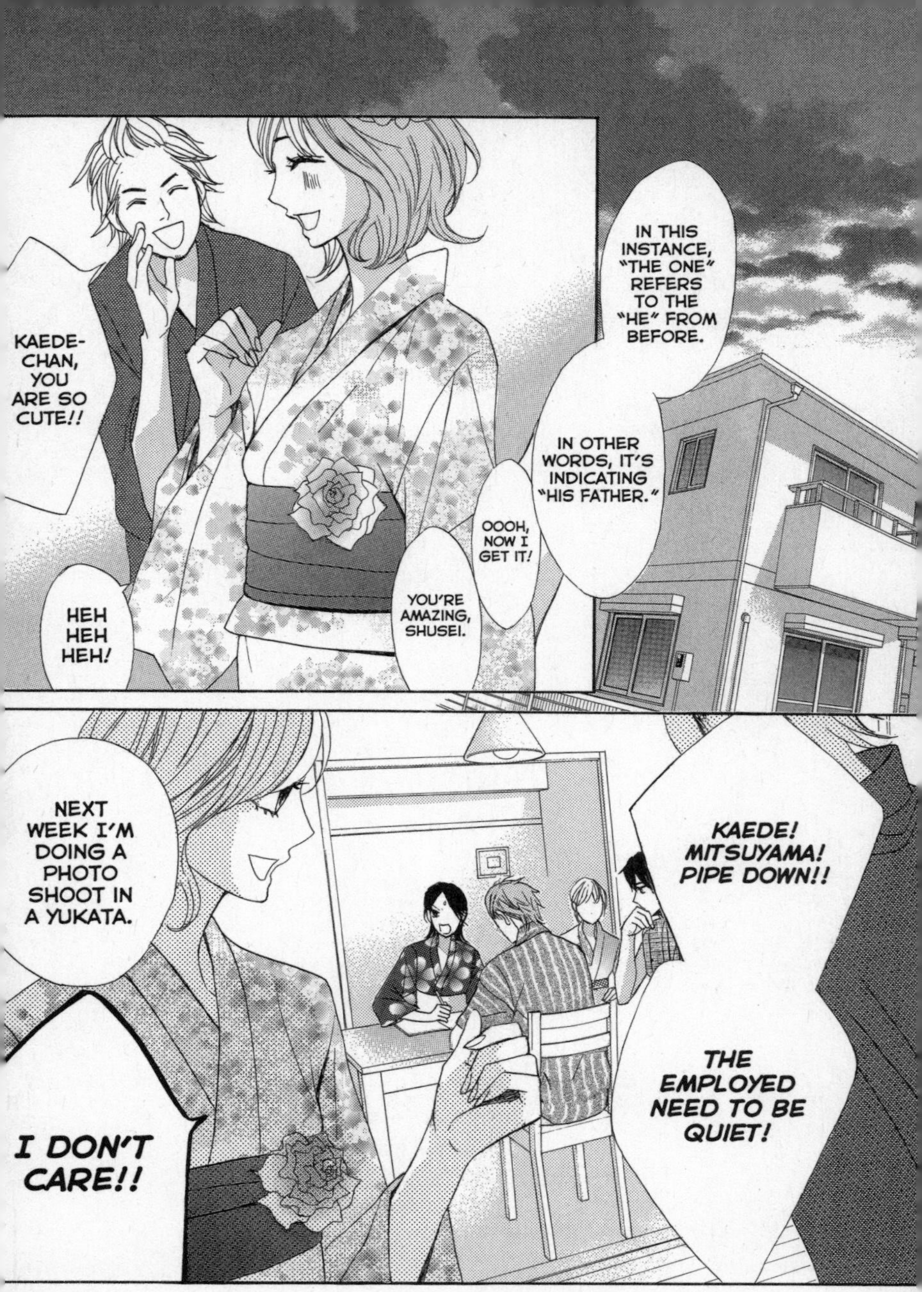
IN THIS INSTANCE, "THE ONE" REFERS TO THE "HE" FROM BEFORE.
IN OTHER WORDS, IT'S INDICATING "HIS FATHER."
OOOH, NOW I GET IT!
YOU'RE AMAZING, SHUSEI.
KAEDE-CHAN, YOU ARE SO CUTE!!
HEH HEH HEH!
KAEDE! MITSUYAMA! PIPE DOWN!!
THE EMPLOYED NEED TO BE QUIET!
NEXT WEEK I'M DOING A PHOTO SHOOT IN A YUKATA.
I DON'T CARE!!

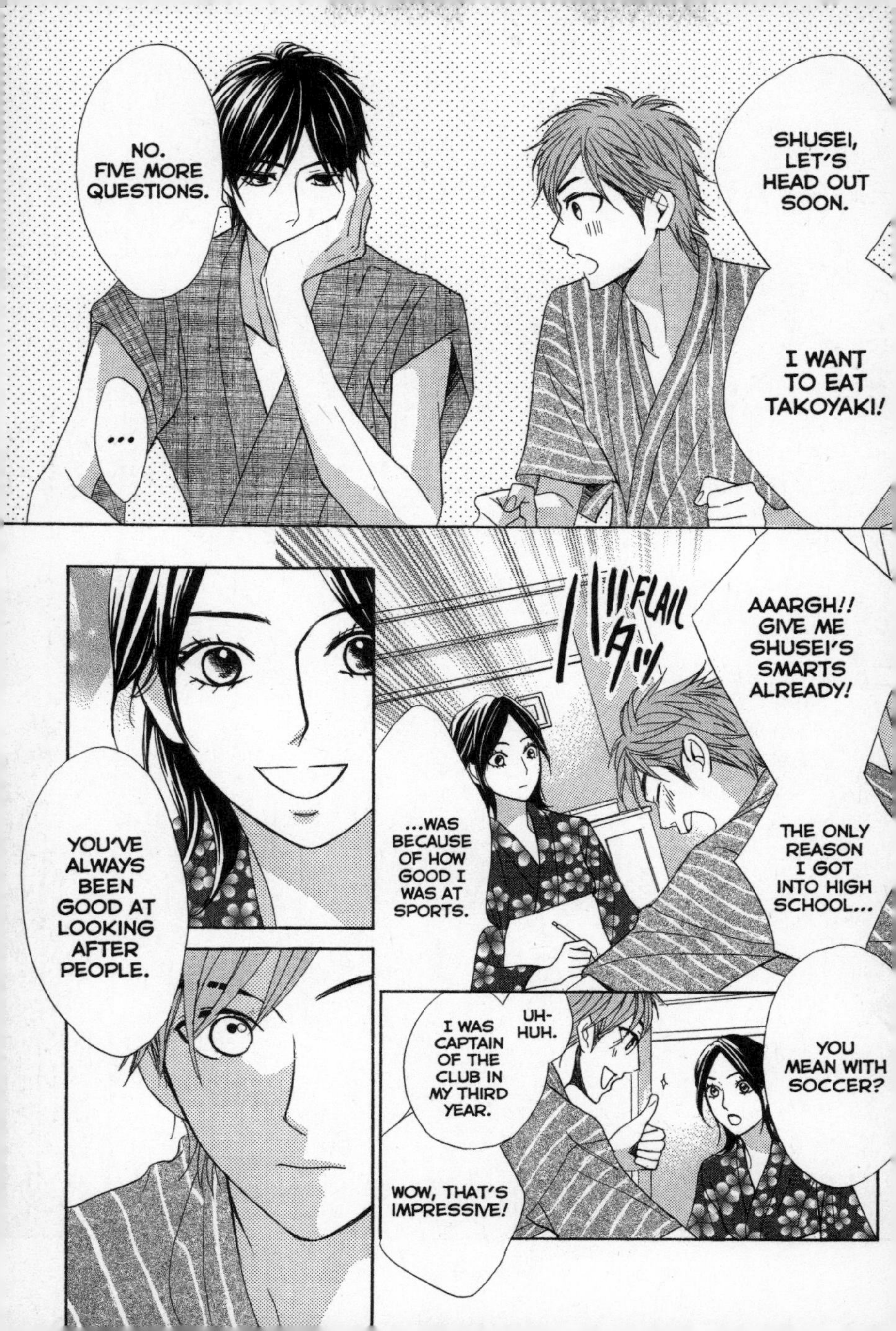

SHUSEI, LET'S HEAD OUT SOON.
I WANT TO EAT TAKOYAKI!
NO. FIVE MORE QUESTIONS.
...
バタッ FLAIL
AAARGH!! GIVE ME SHUSEI'S SMARTS ALREADY!
THE ONLY REASON I GOT INTO HIGH SCHOOL...
...WAS BECAUSE OF HOW GOOD I WAS AT SPORTS.
YOU MEAN WITH SOCCER?
UH-HUH.
I WAS CAPTAIN OF THE CLUB IN MY THIRD YEAR.
WOW, THAT'S IMPRESSIVE!
YOU'VE ALWAYS BEEN GOOD AT LOOKING AFTER PEOPLE.

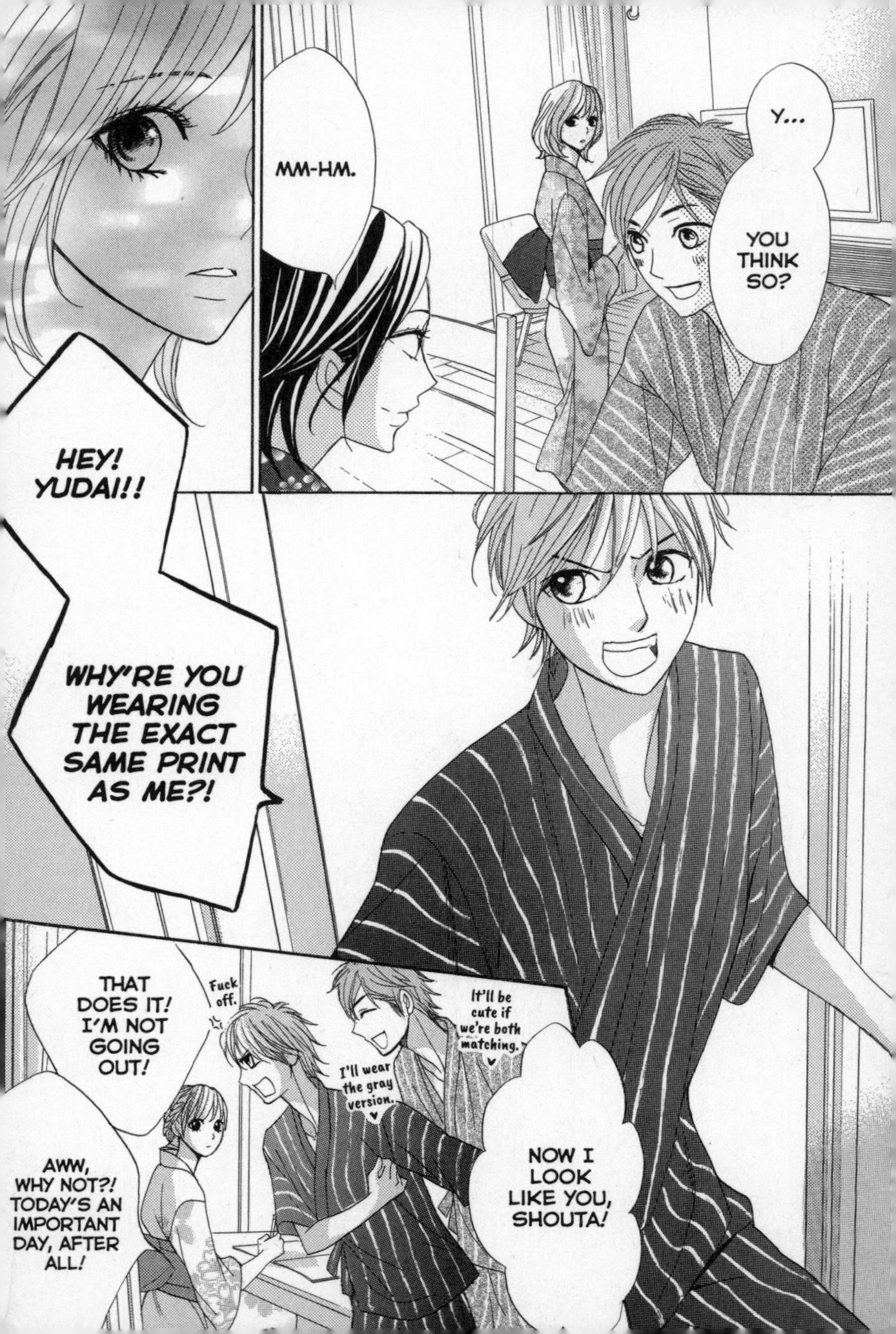
Y...
YOU THINK SO?
MM-HM.
HEY! YUDAI!!
WHY'RE YOU WEARING THE EXACT SAME PRINT AS ME?!
NOW I LOOK LIKE YOU, SHOUTA!
It'll be cute if we're both matching. ♥
I'll wear the gray version. ♥
Fuck off.
THAT DOES IT! I'M NOT GOING OUT!
AWW, WHY NOT?! TODAY'S AN IMPORTANT DAY, AFTER ALL!

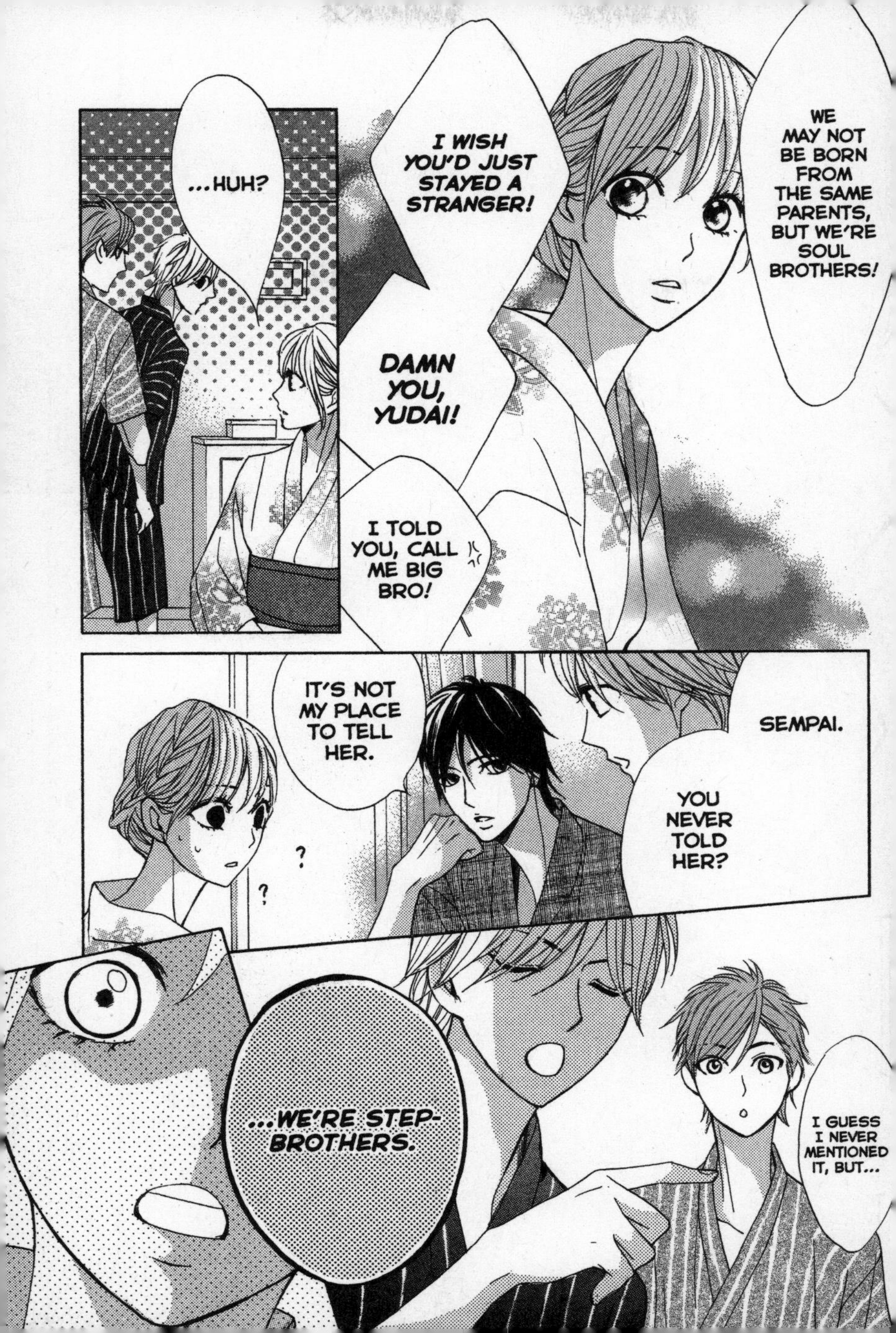
WE MAY NOT BE BORN FROM THE SAME PARENTS, BUT WE'RE SOUL BROTHERS!
I WISH YOU'D JUST STAYED A STRANGER!
DAMN YOU, YUDAI!
I TOLD YOU, CALL ME BIG BRO!
...HUH?
SEMPAI.
YOU NEVER TOLD HER?
IT'S NOT MY PLACE TO TELL HER.
?
?
I GUESS I NEVER MENTIONED IT, BUT...
...WE'RE STEP-BROTHERS.

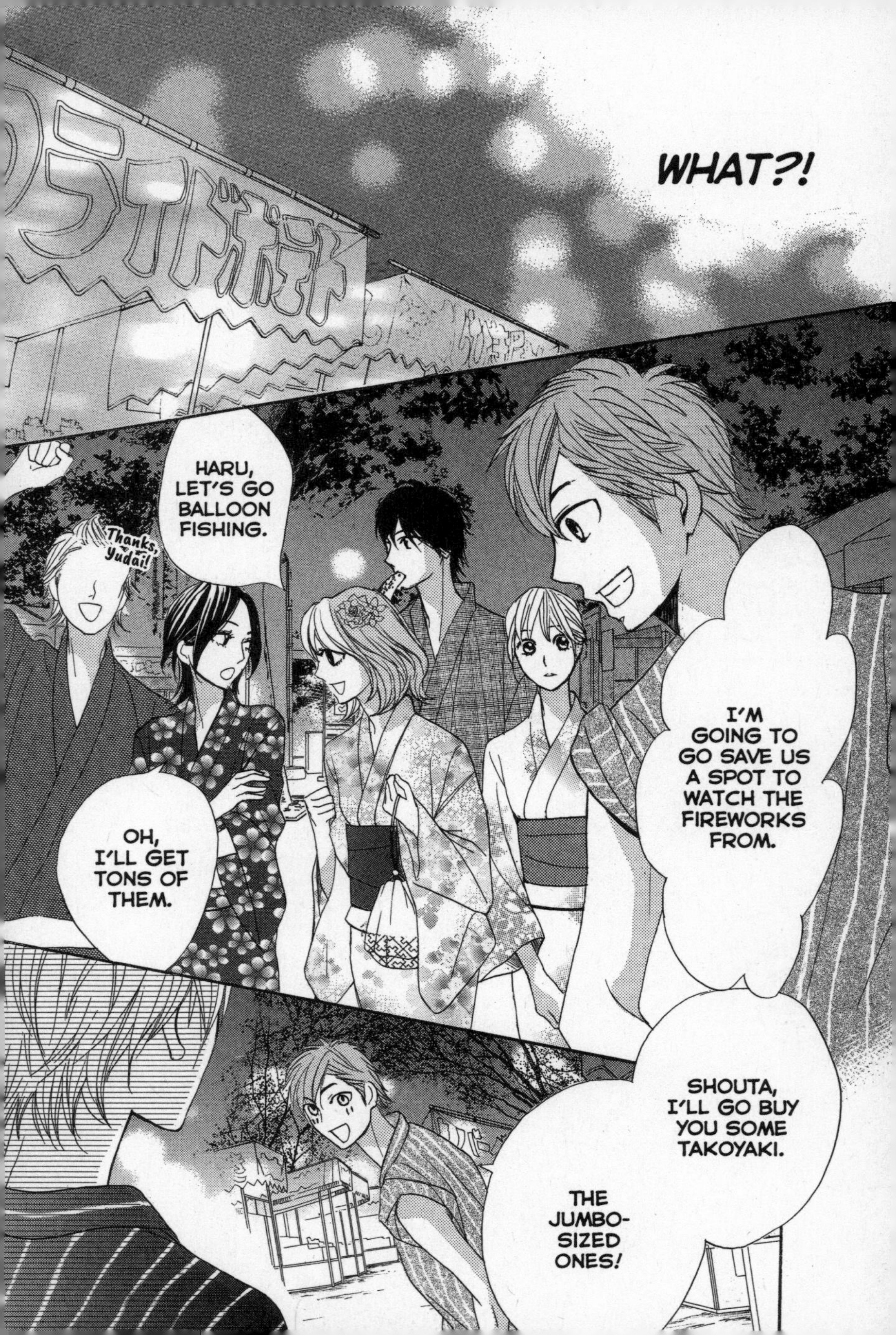

WHAT?!
I'M GOING TO GO SAVE US A SPOT TO WATCH THE FIREWORKS FROM.
HARU, LET'S GO BALLOON FISHING.
Thanks, Yudai!
OH, I'LL GET TONS OF THEM.
SHOUTA, I'LL GO BUY YOU SOME TAKOYAKI.
THE JUMBO-SIZED ONES!

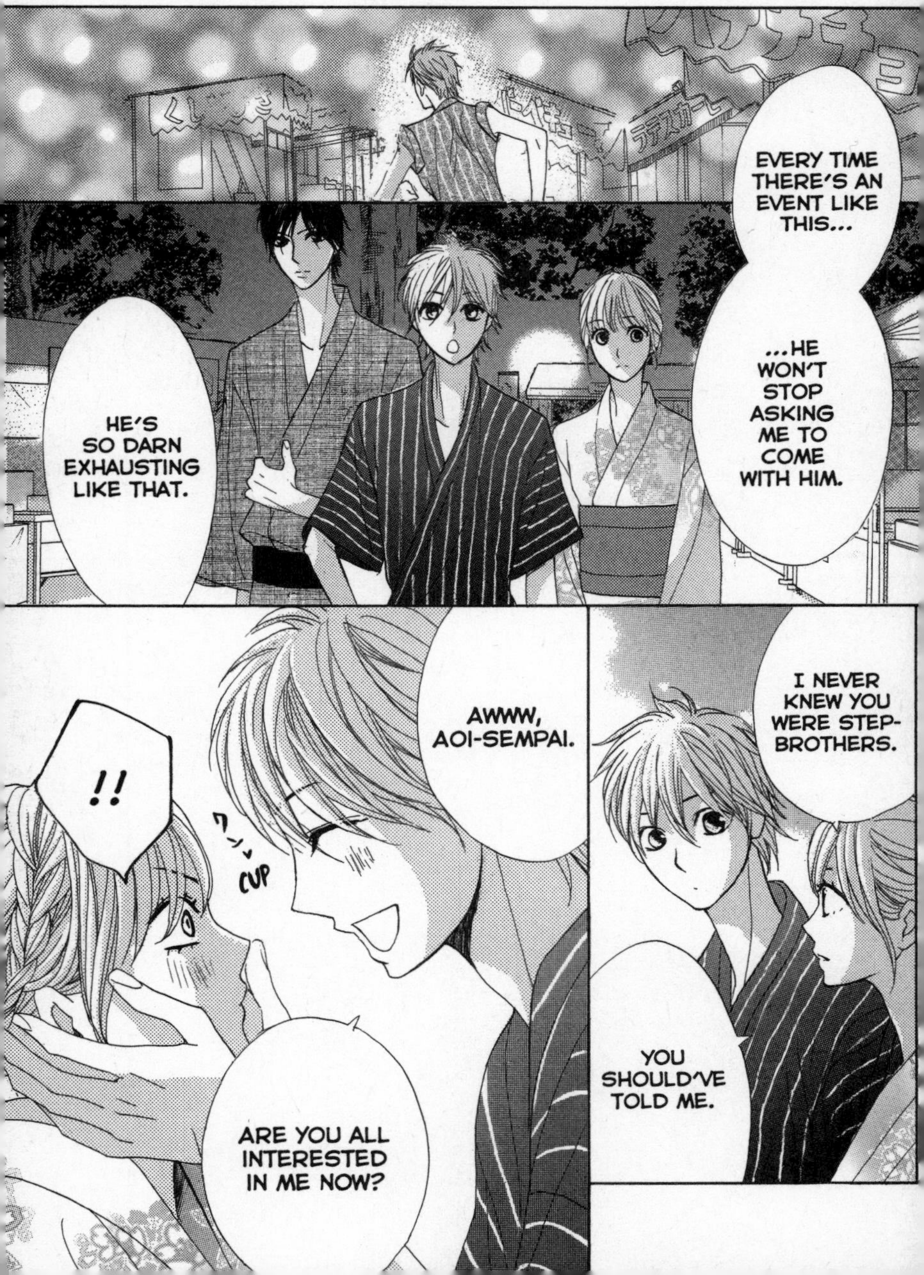
EVERY TIME THERE'S AN EVENT LIKE THIS...
...HE WON'T STOP ASKING ME TO COME WITH HIM.
HE'S SO DARN EXHAUSTING LIKE THAT.
I NEVER KNEW YOU WERE STEP-BROTHERS.
YOU SHOULD'VE TOLD ME.
AWWW, AOI-SEMPAI.
!!
CUP
ARE YOU ALL INTERESTED IN ME NOW?

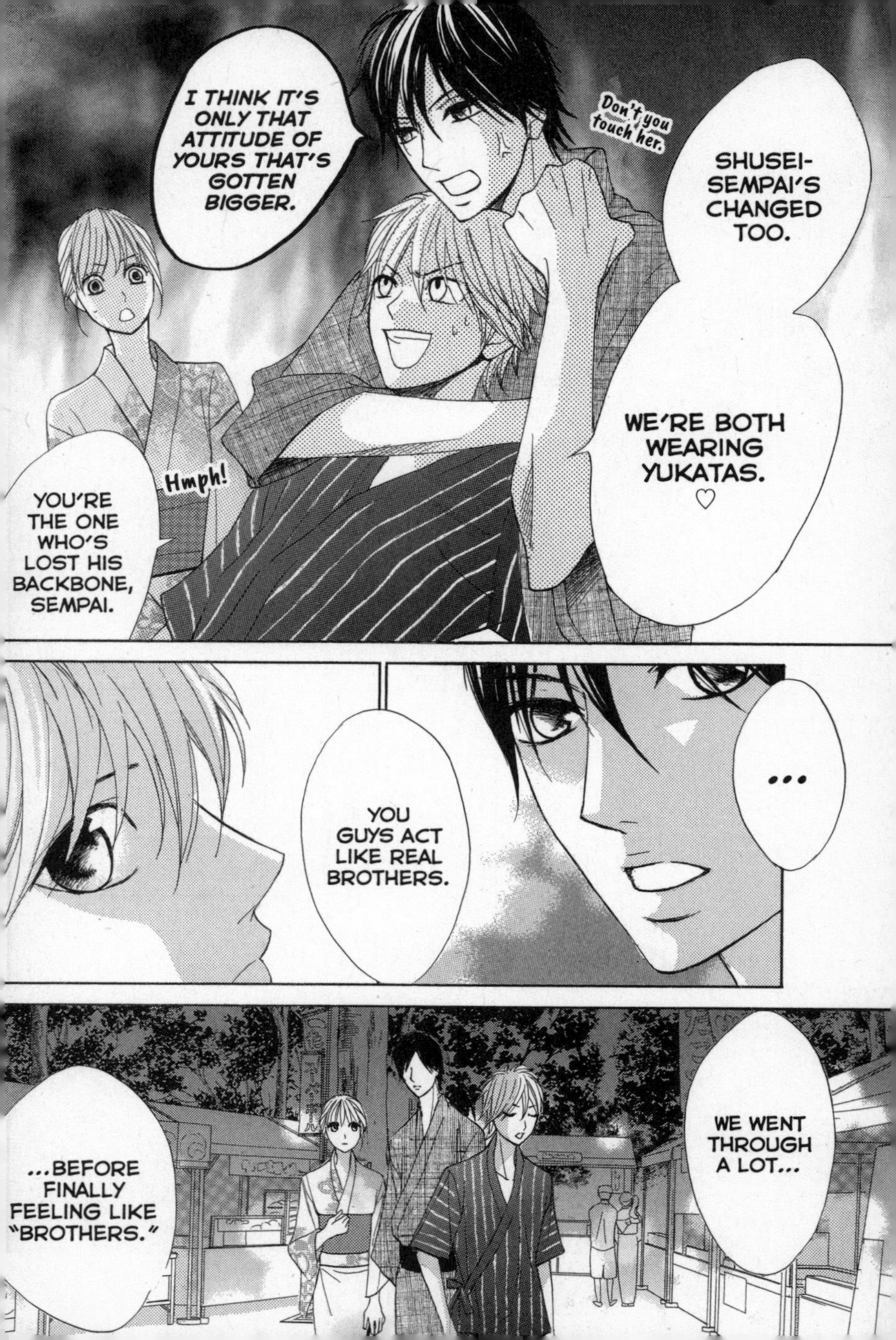
SHUSEI-SEMPAI'S CHANGED TOO.
WE'RE BOTH WEARING YUKATAS. ♡
Don't you touch her.
I THINK IT'S ONLY THAT ATTITUDE OF YOURS THAT'S GOTTEN BIGGER.
Hmph!
YOU'RE THE ONE WHO'S LOST HIS BACKBONE, SEMPAI.
...
YOU GUYS ACT LIKE REAL BROTHERS.
WE WENT THROUGH A LOT...
...BEFORE FINALLY FEELING LIKE "BROTHERS."

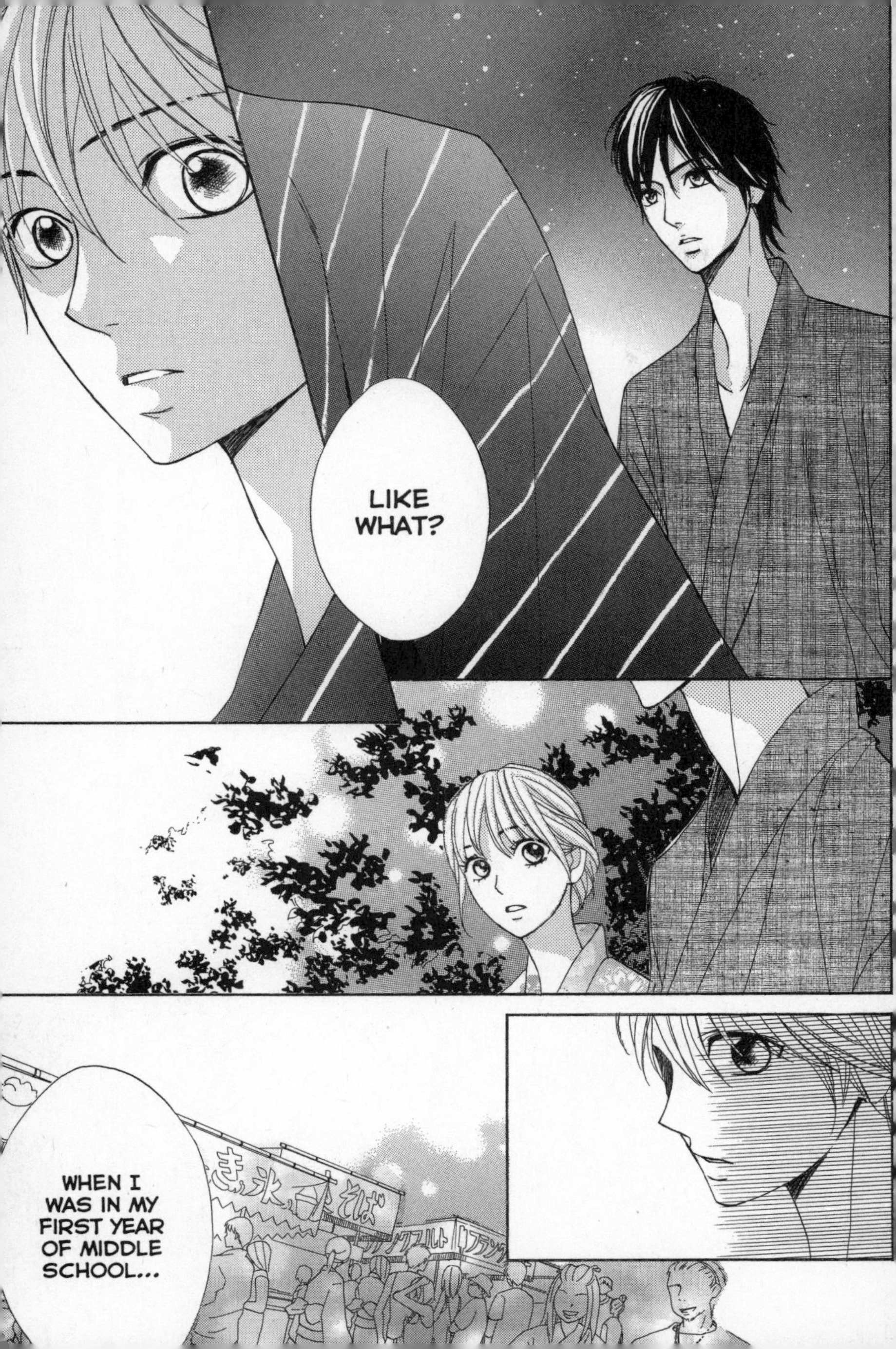
LIKE WHAT?
WHEN I WAS IN MY FIRST YEAR OF MIDDLE SCHOOL...

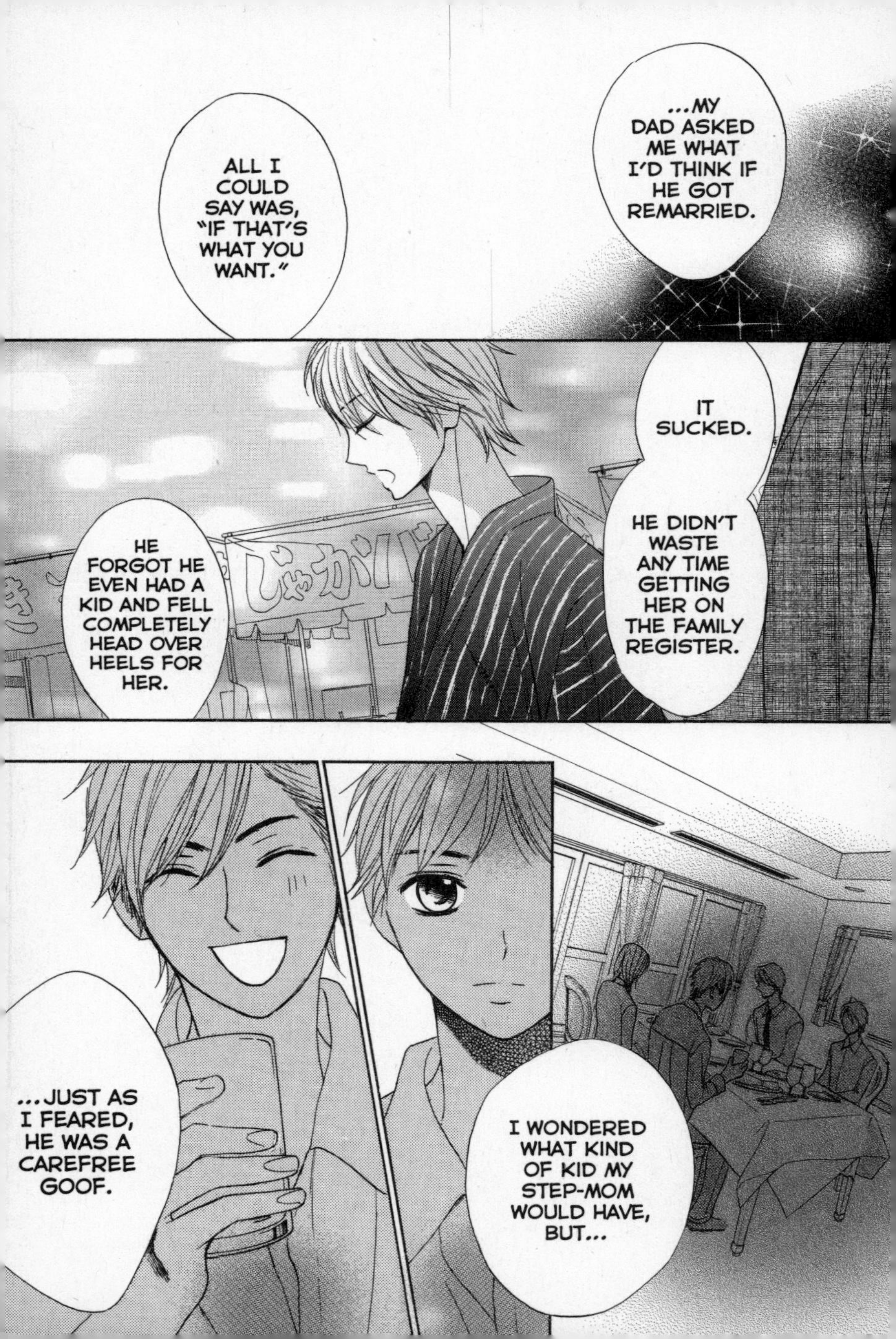

...MY DAD ASKED ME WHAT I'D THINK IF HE GOT REMARRIED.
ALL I COULD SAY WAS, "IF THAT'S WHAT YOU WANT."
IT SUCKED.
HE DIDN'T WASTE ANY TIME GETTING HER ON THE FAMILY REGISTER.
HE FORGOT HE EVEN HAD A KID AND FELL COMPLETELY HEAD OVER HEELS FOR HER.
I WONDERED WHAT KIND OF KID MY STEP-MOM WOULD HAVE, BUT...
...JUST AS I FEARED, HE WAS A CAREFREE GOOF.

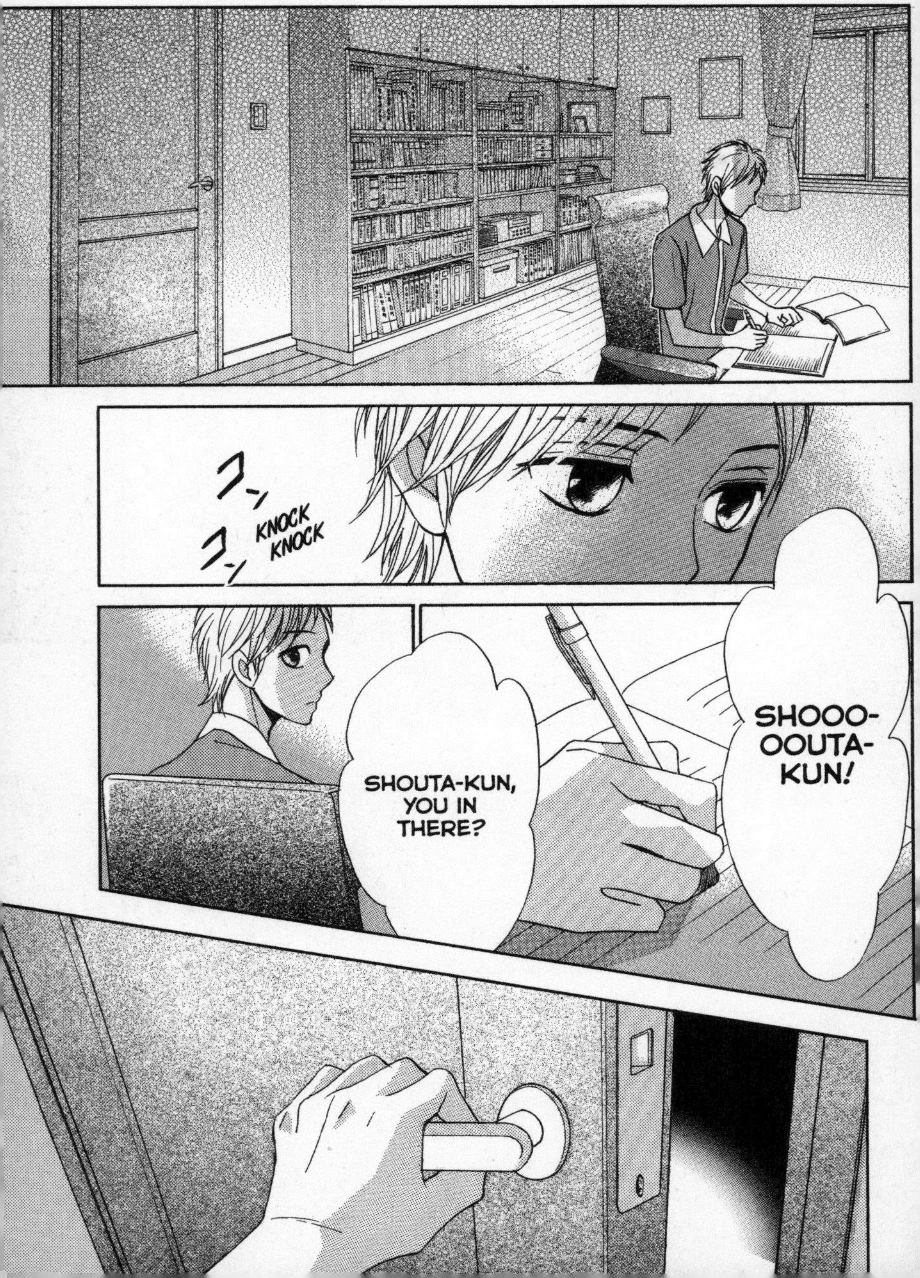
コン
コン
KNOCK KNOCK
SHOOOO-OOUTA-KUN!
SHOUTA-KUN, YOU IN THERE?

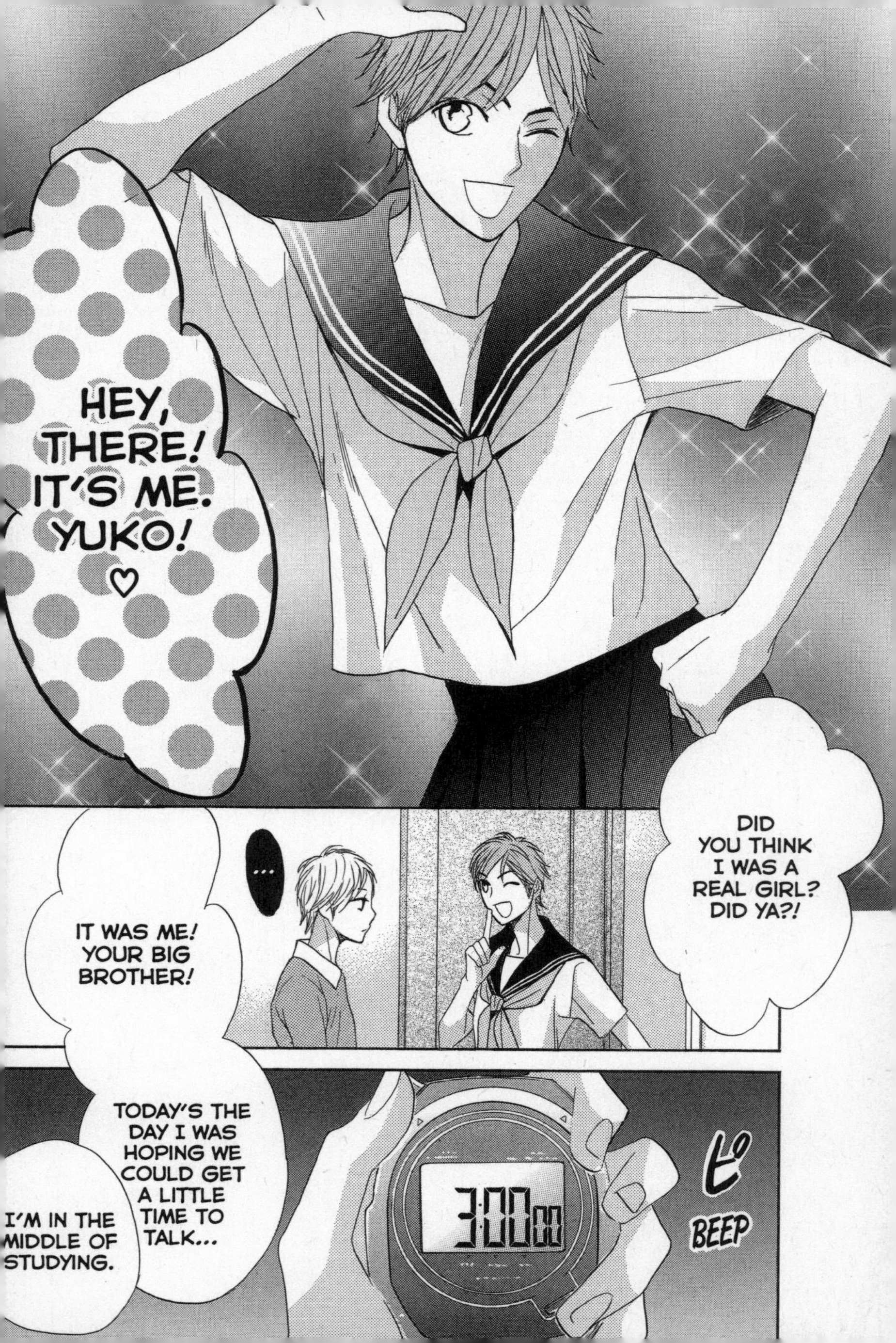
HEY, THERE! IT'S ME. YUKO! ♡
DID YOU THINK I WAS A REAL GIRL? DID YA?!
...
IT WAS ME! YOUR BIG BROTHER!
ピ
BEEP
3:00 00
TODAY'S THE DAY I WAS HOPING WE COULD GET A LITTLE TIME TO TALK...
I'M IN THE MIDDLE OF STUDYING.

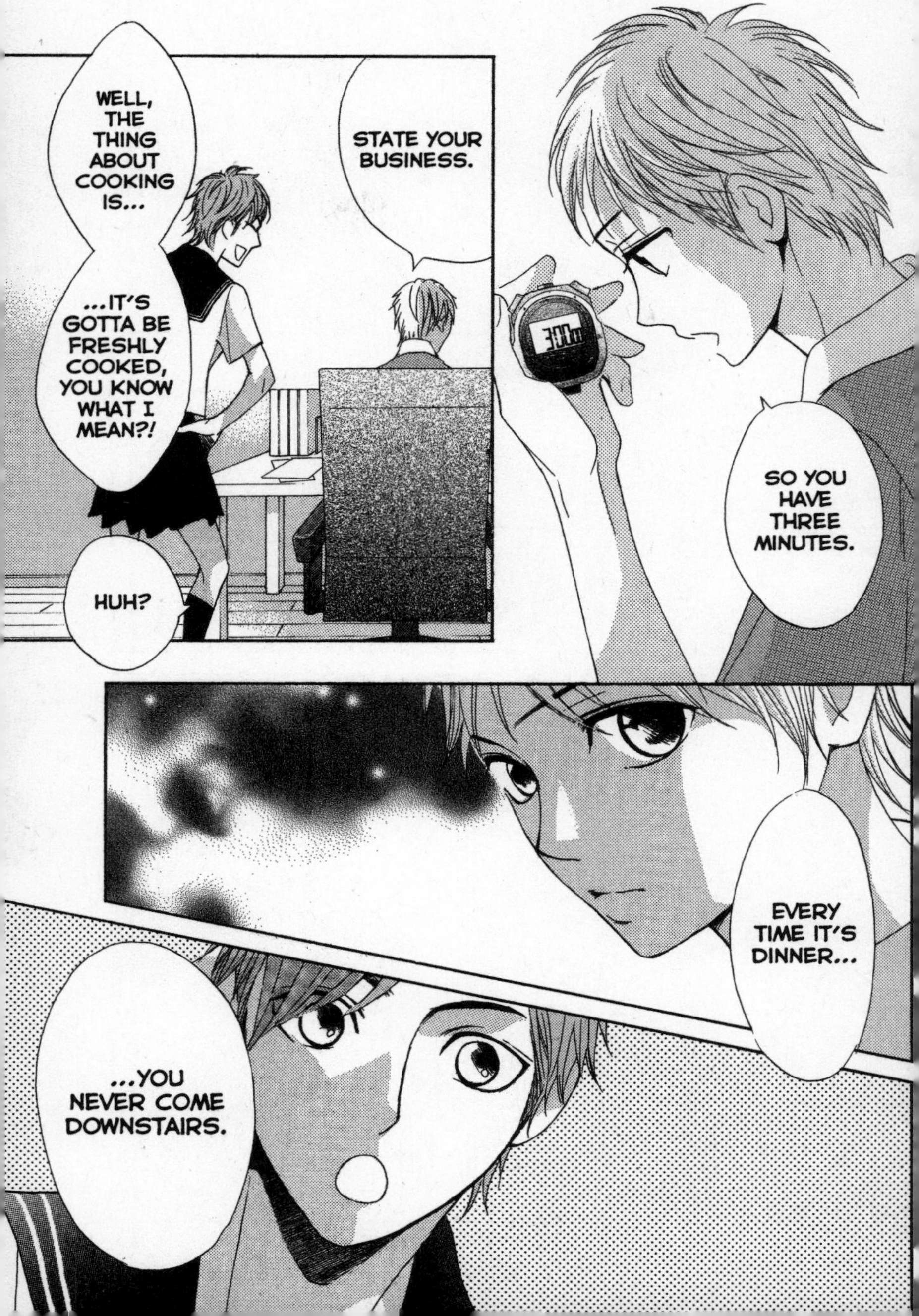
SO YOU HAVE THREE MINUTES.
STATE YOUR BUSINESS.
WELL, THE THING ABOUT COOKING IS...
...IT'S GOTTA BE FRESHLY COOKED, YOU KNOW WHAT I MEAN?!
HUH?
EVERY TIME IT'S DINNER...
...YOU NEVER COME DOWNSTAIRS.

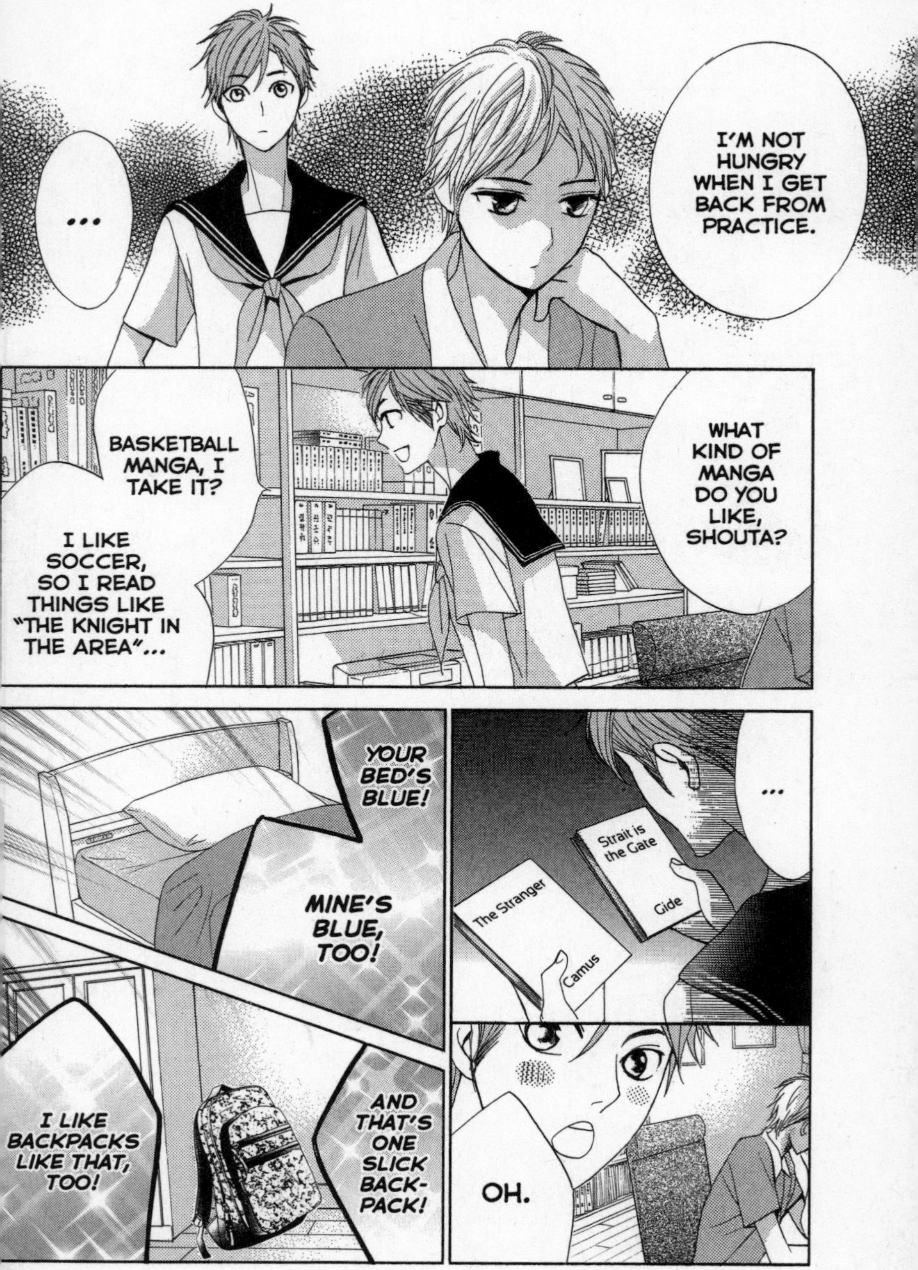
I'M NOT HUNGRY WHEN I GET BACK FROM PRACTICE.
...
WHAT KIND OF MANGA DO YOU LIKE, SHOUTA?
BASKETBALL MANGA, I TAKE IT?
I LIKE SOCCER, SO I READ THINGS LIKE "THE KNIGHT IN THE AREA"...
...
Strait is the Gate
Gide
The Stranger
Camus
OH.
YOUR BED'S BLUE!
MINE'S BLUE, TOO!
AND THAT'S ONE SLICK BACK-PACK!
I LIKE BACKPACKS LIKE THAT, TOO!

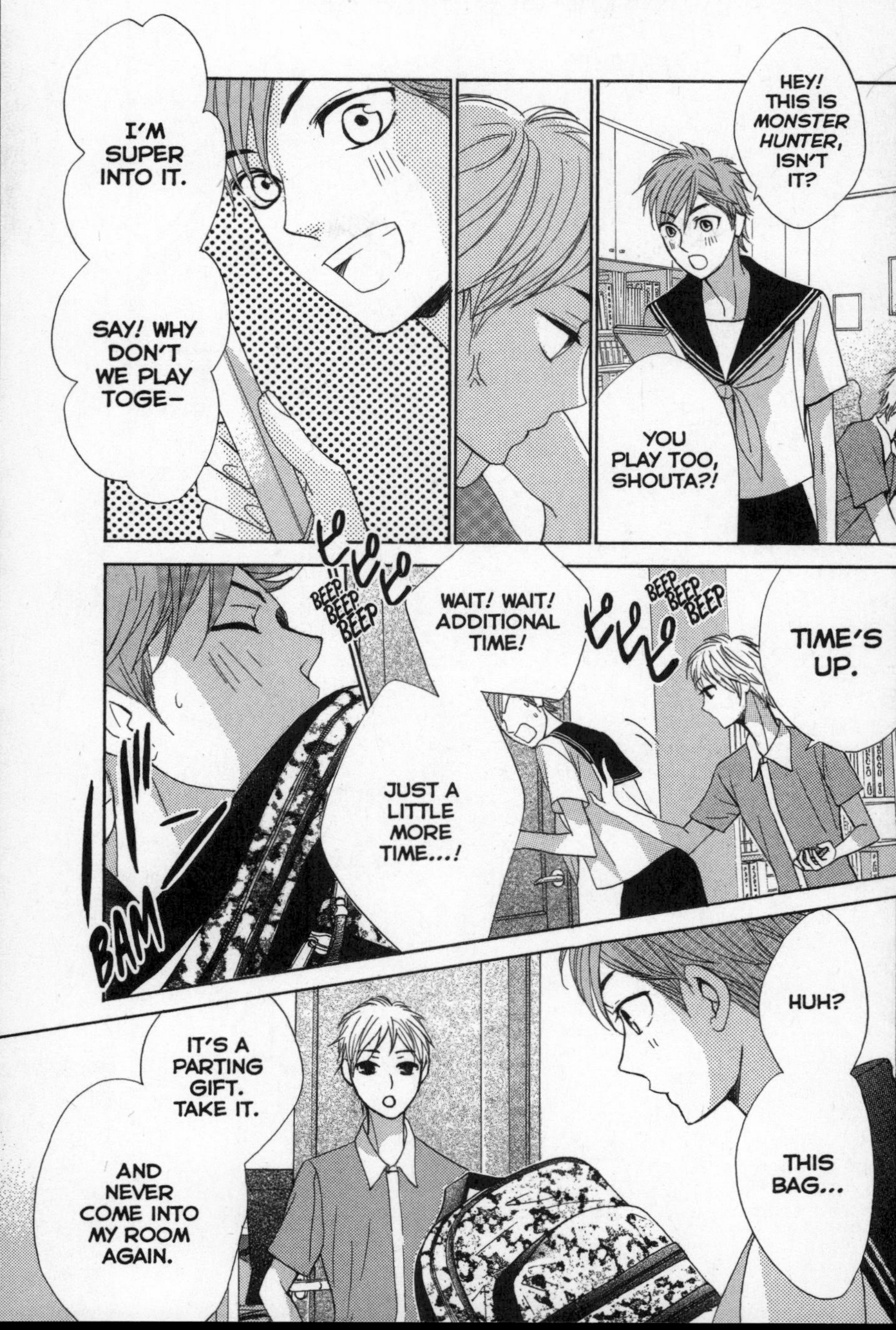
HEY! THIS IS MONSTER HUNTER, ISN'T IT?
YOU PLAY TOO, SHOUTA?!
I'M SUPER INTO IT.
SAY! WHY DON'T WE PLAY TOGE–
TIME'S UP.
ピピピ
BEEP BEEP BEEP
WAIT! WAIT! ADDITIONAL TIME!
JUST A LITTLE MORE TIME...!
ピピピ
BEEP BEEP BEEP
BAM
HUH?
THIS BAG...
IT'S A PARTING GIFT. TAKE IT.
AND NEVER COME INTO MY ROOM AGAIN.

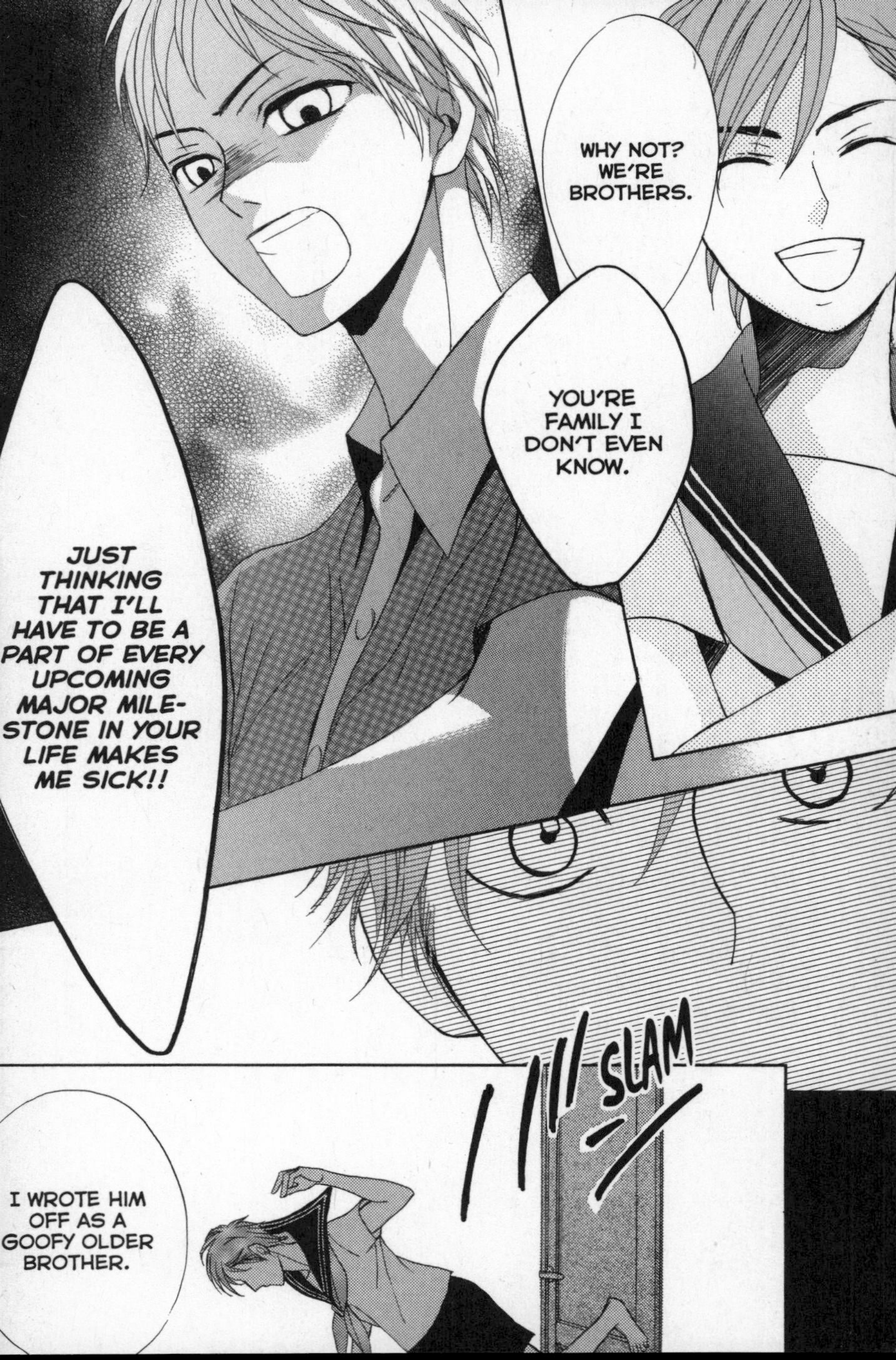
WHY NOT? WE'RE BROTHERS.
YOU'RE FAMILY I DON'T EVEN KNOW.
JUST THINKING THAT I'LL HAVE TO BE A PART OF EVERY UPCOMING MAJOR MILE-STONE IN YOUR LIFE MAKES ME SICK!!
SLAM
I WROTE HIM OFF AS A GOOFY OLDER BROTHER.

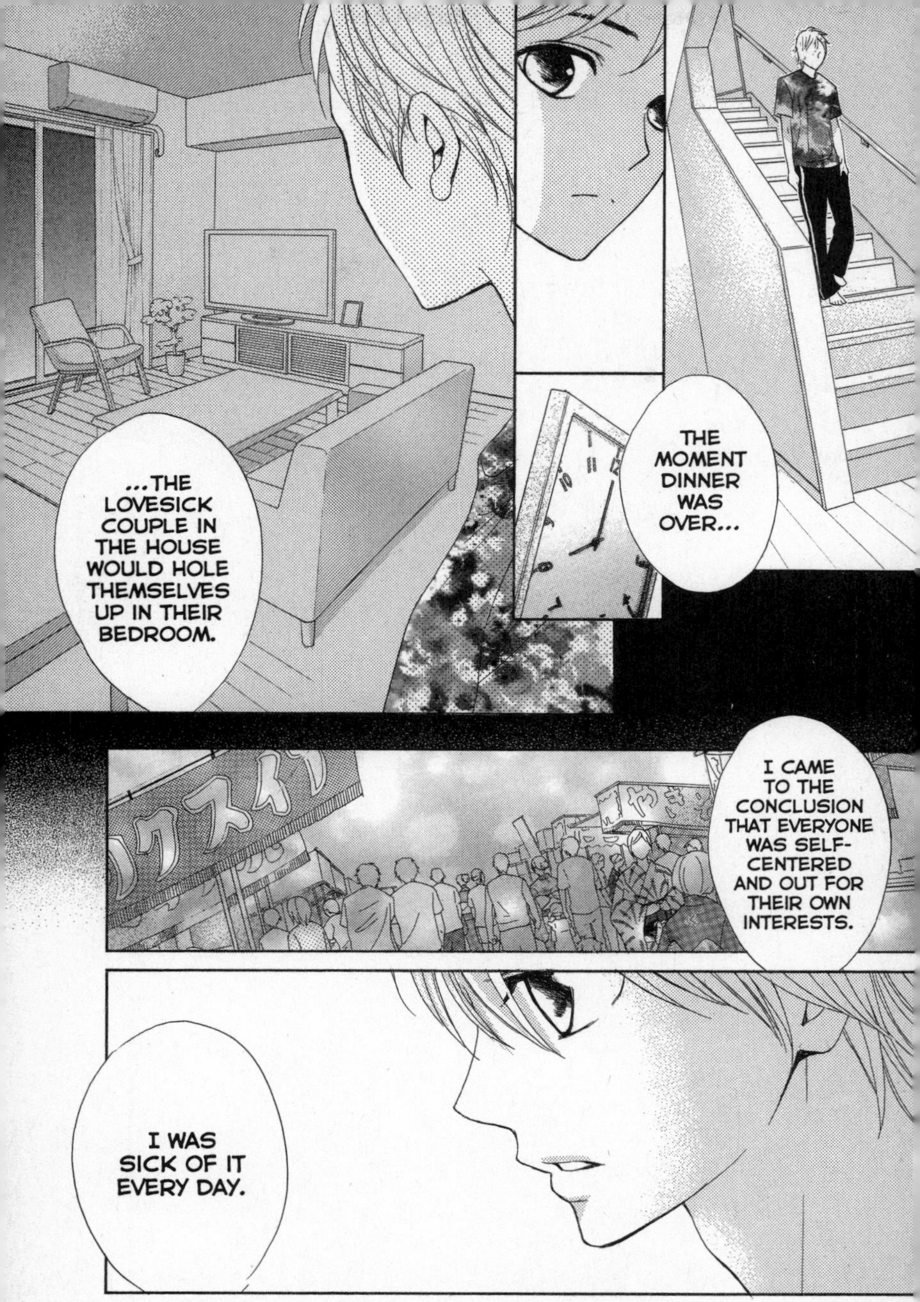
THE MOMENT DINNER WAS OVER...
...THE LOVESICK COUPLE IN THE HOUSE WOULD HOLE THEMSELVES UP IN THEIR BEDROOM.
I CAME TO THE CONCLUSION THAT EVERYONE WAS SELF-CENTERED AND OUT FOR THEIR OWN INTERESTS.
I WAS SICK OF IT EVERY DAY.

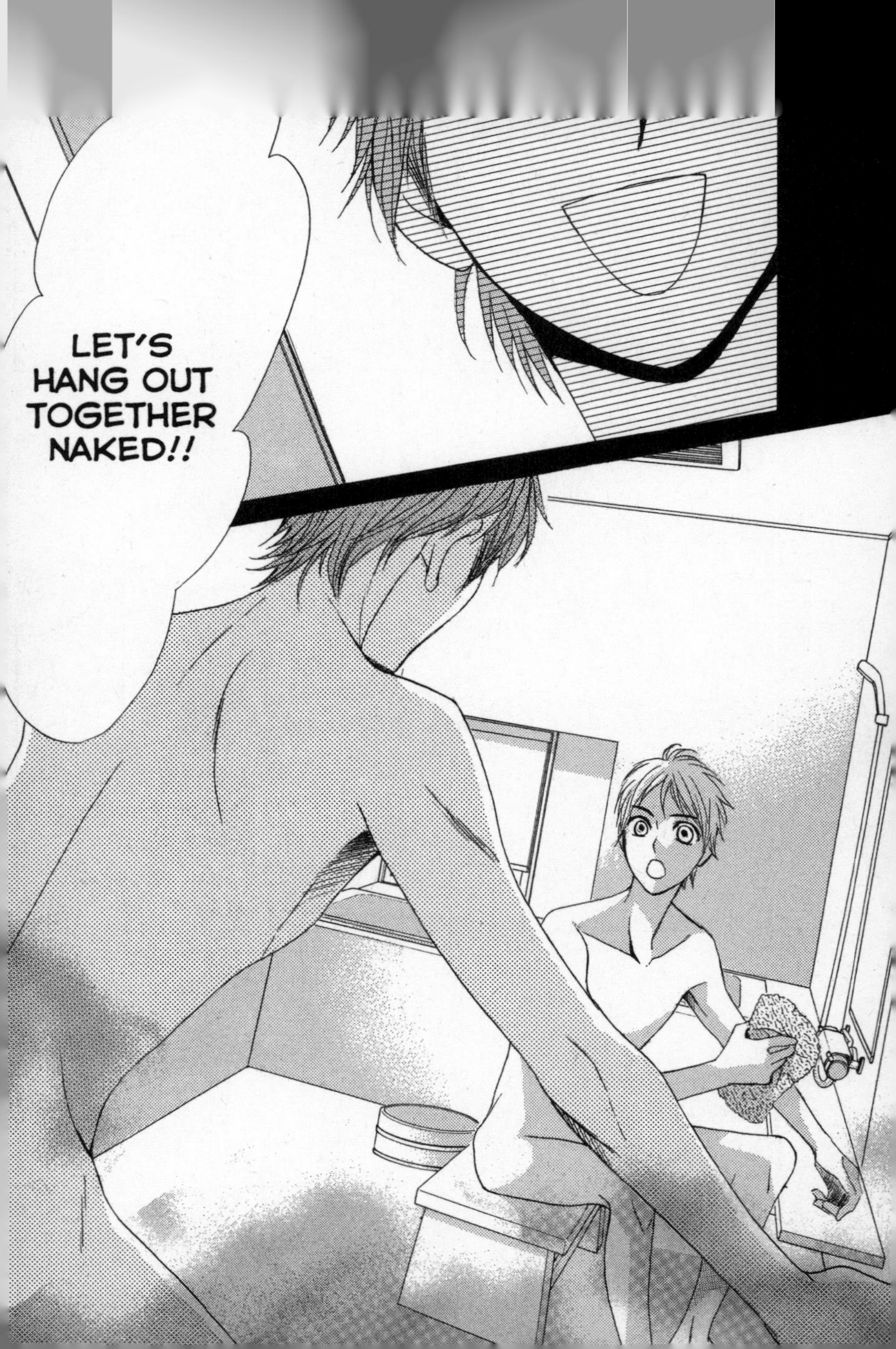
LET'S HANG OUT TOGETHER NAKED!!

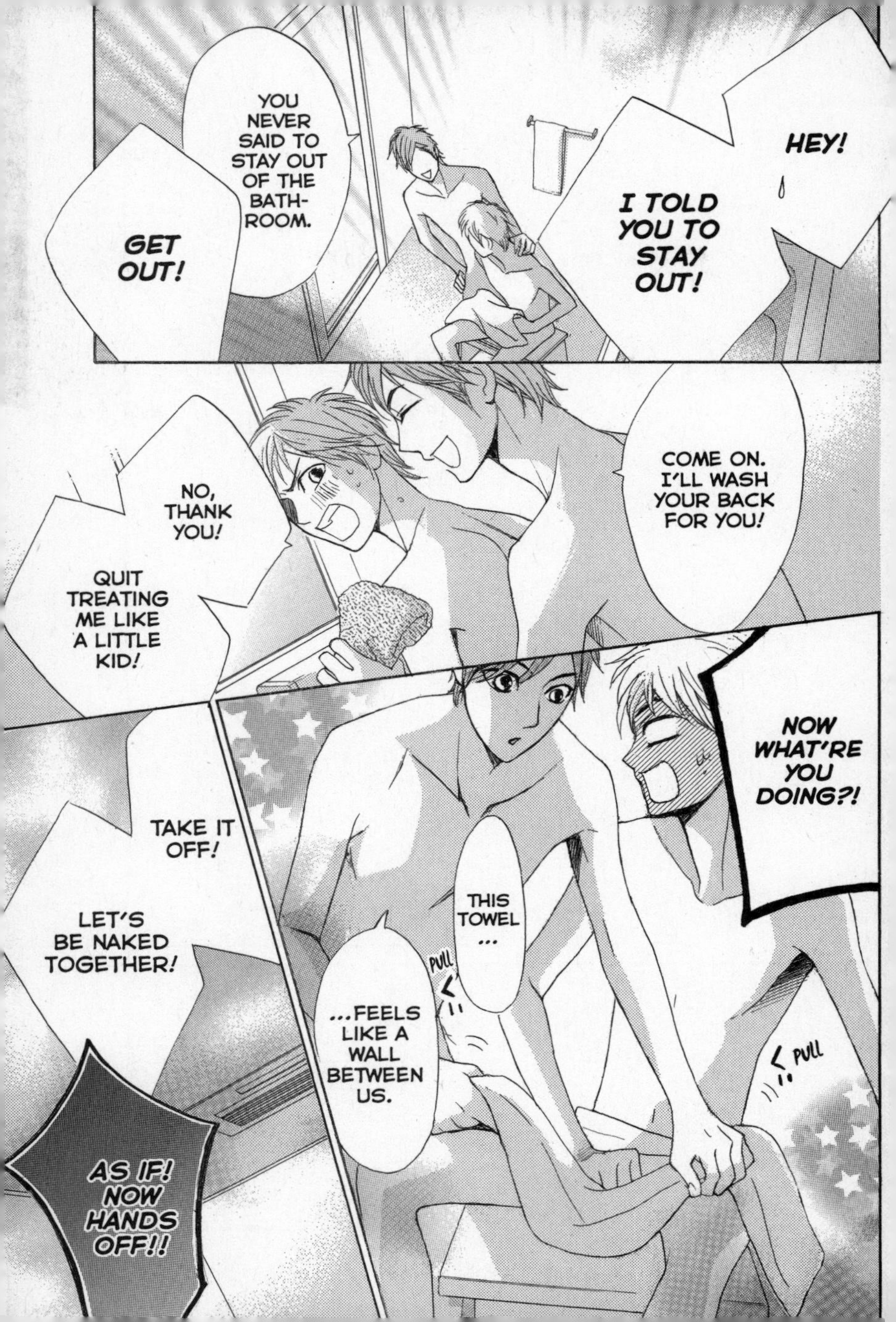
HEY!
I TOLD YOU TO STAY OUT!
YOU NEVER SAID TO STAY OUT OF THE BATH-ROOM.
GET OUT!
COME ON. I'LL WASH YOUR BACK FOR YOU!
NO, THANK YOU!
QUIT TREATING ME LIKE A LITTLE KID!
NOW WHAT'RE YOU DOING?!
PULL
THIS TOWEL...
PULL
...FEELS LIKE A WALL BETWEEN US.
TAKE IT OFF!
LET'S BE NAKED TOGETHER!
AS IF! NOW HANDS OFF!!

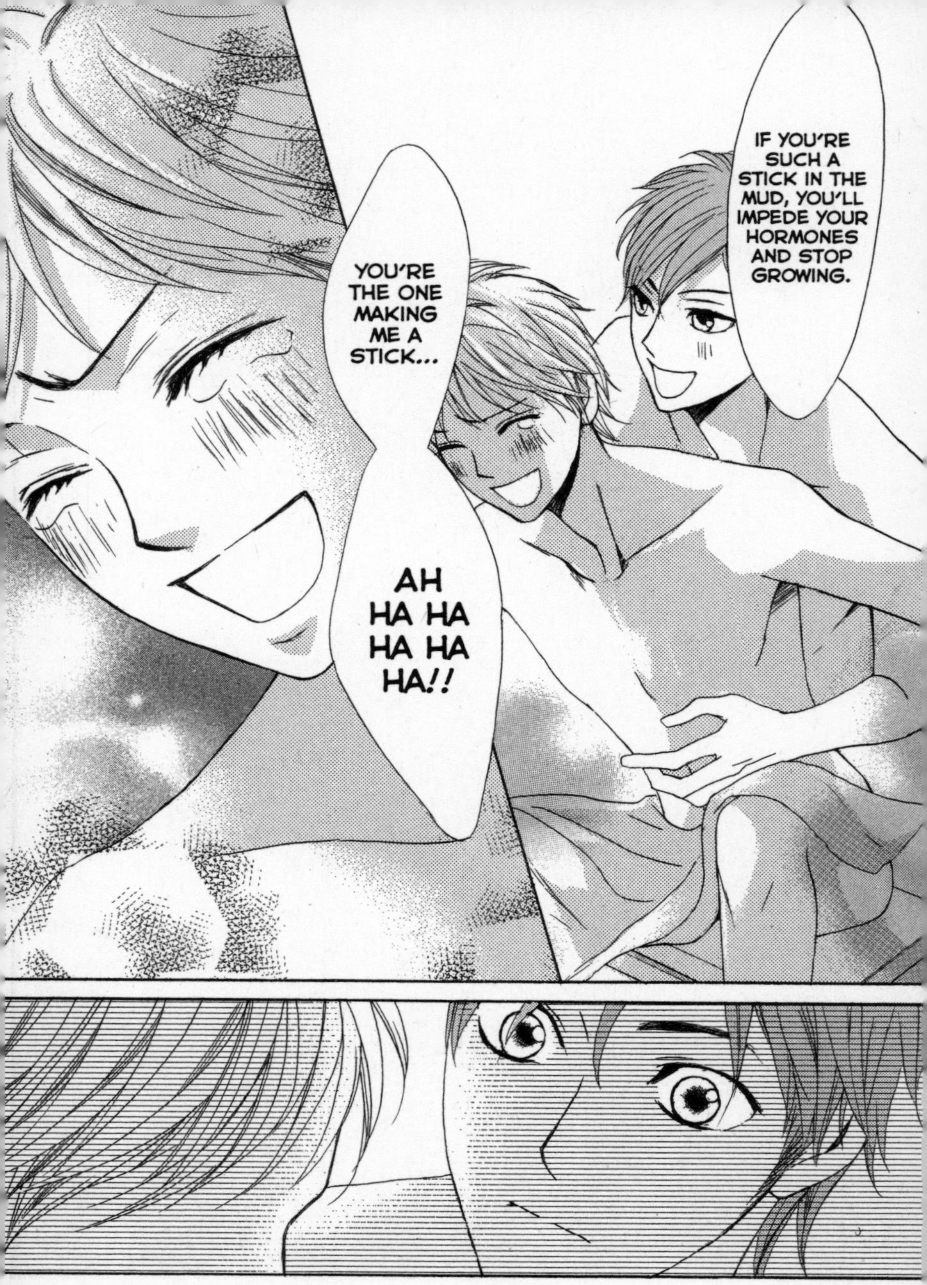
IF YOU'RE SUCH A STICK IN THE MUD, YOU'LL IMPEDE YOUR HORMONES AND STOP GROWING.
YOU'RE THE ONE MAKING ME A STICK...
AH HA HA HA HA HA!!

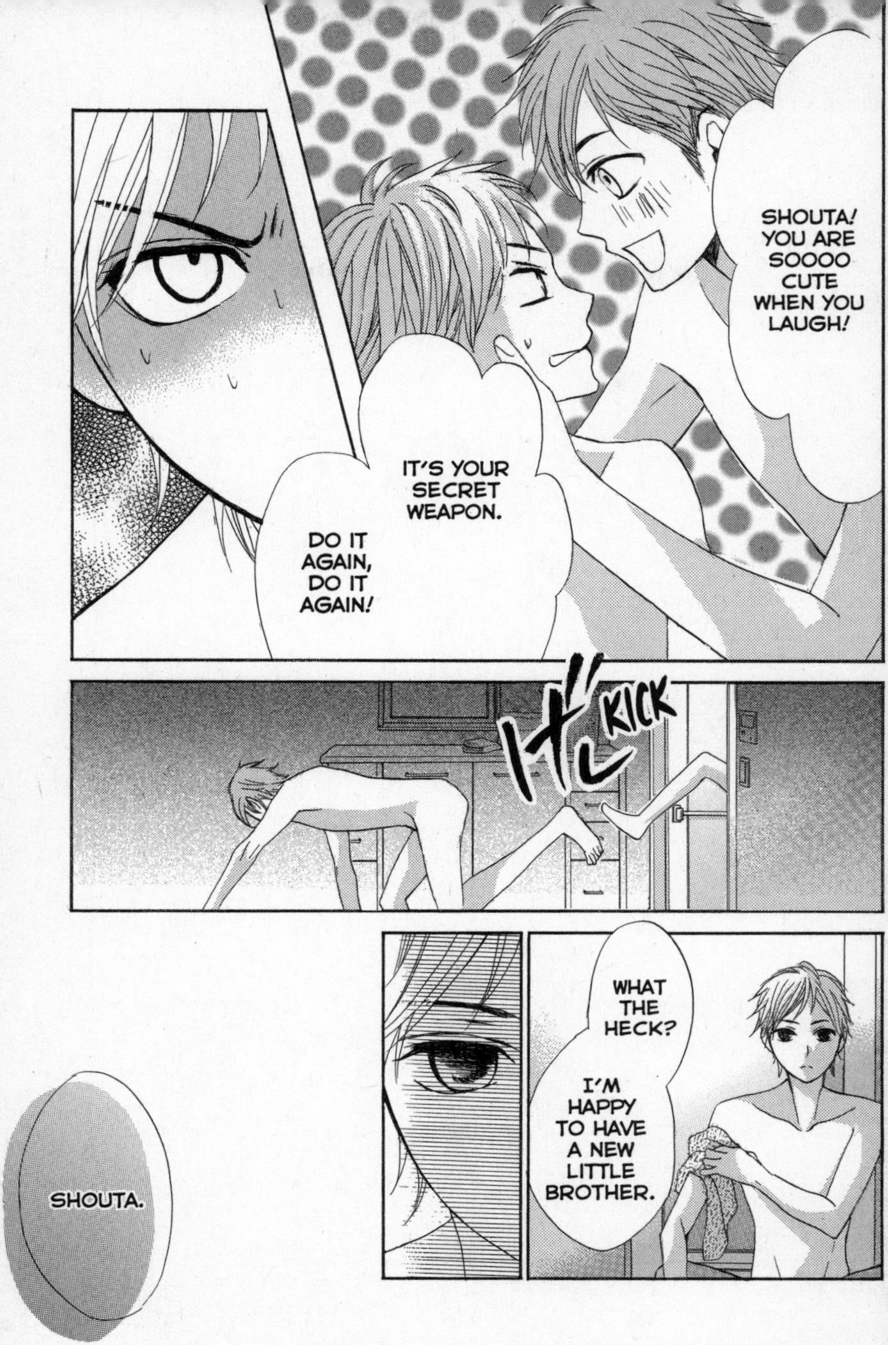
SHOUTA! YOU ARE SOOOO CUTE WHEN YOU LAUGH!
IT'S YOUR SECRET WEAPON.
DO IT AGAIN, DO IT AGAIN!
KICK
WHAT THE HECK?
I'M HAPPY TO HAVE A NEW LITTLE BROTHER.
SHOUTA.

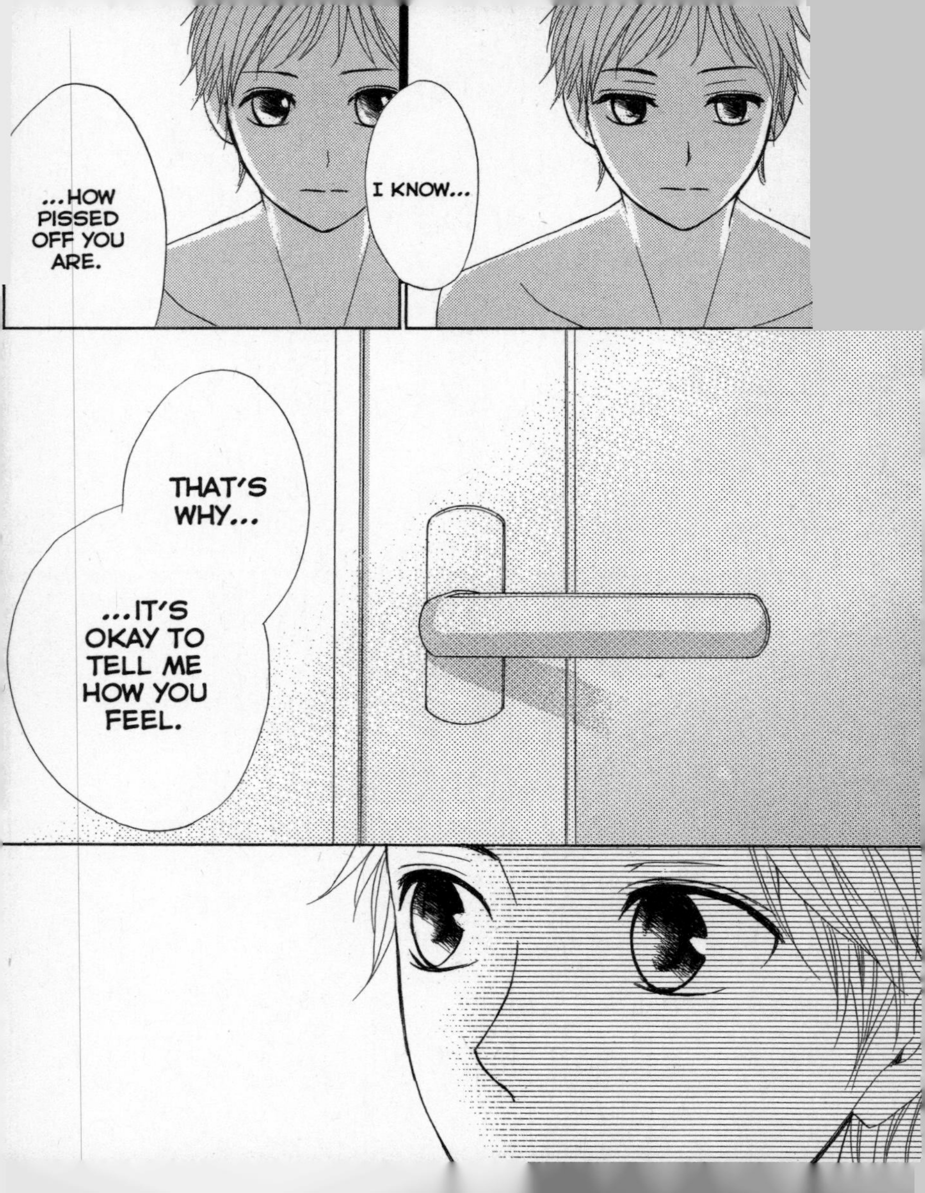
I KNOW...
...HOW PISSED OFF YOU ARE.
THAT'S WHY...
...IT'S OKAY TO TELL ME HOW YOU FEEL.

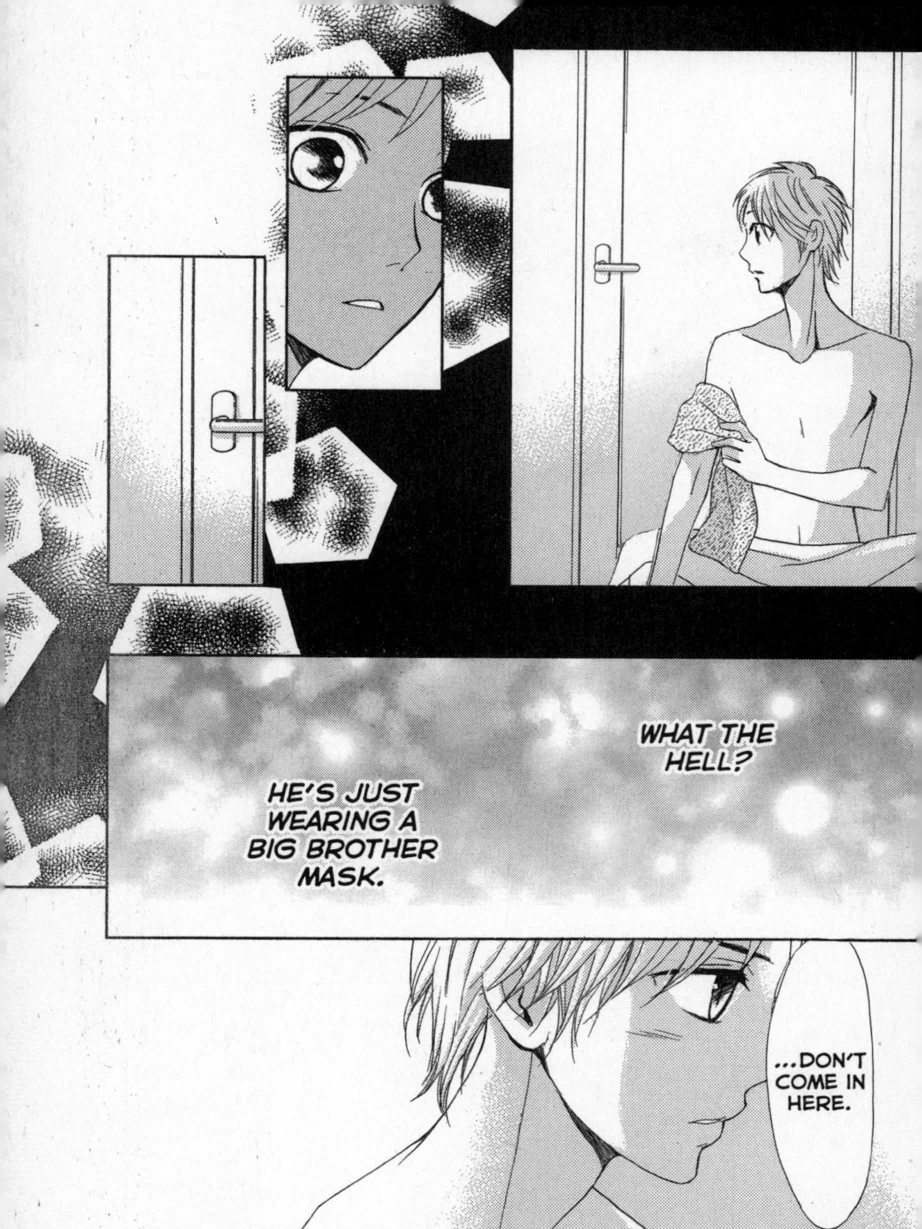
WHAT THE HELL?
HE'S JUST WEARING A BIG BROTHER MASK.
...DON'T COME IN HERE.

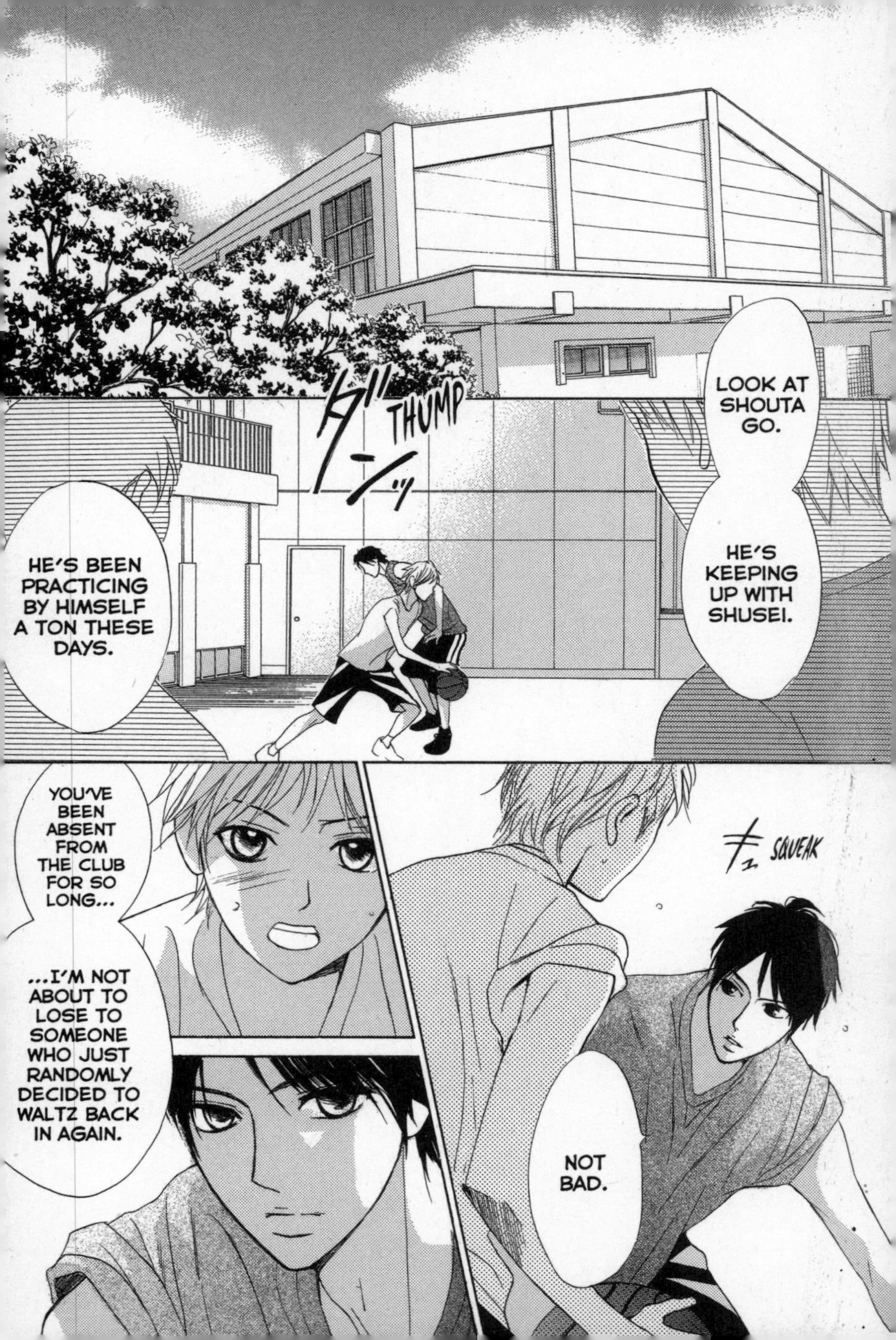
ダーンッ THUMP
LOOK AT SHOUTA GO.
HE'S KEEPING UP WITH SHUSEI.
HE'S BEEN PRACTICING BY HIMSELF A TON THESE DAYS.
キュ SQUEAK
NOT BAD.
YOU'VE BEEN ABSENT FROM THE CLUB FOR SO LONG...
...I'M NOT ABOUT TO LOSE TO SOMEONE WHO JUST RANDOMLY DECIDED TO WALTZ BACK IN AGAIN.

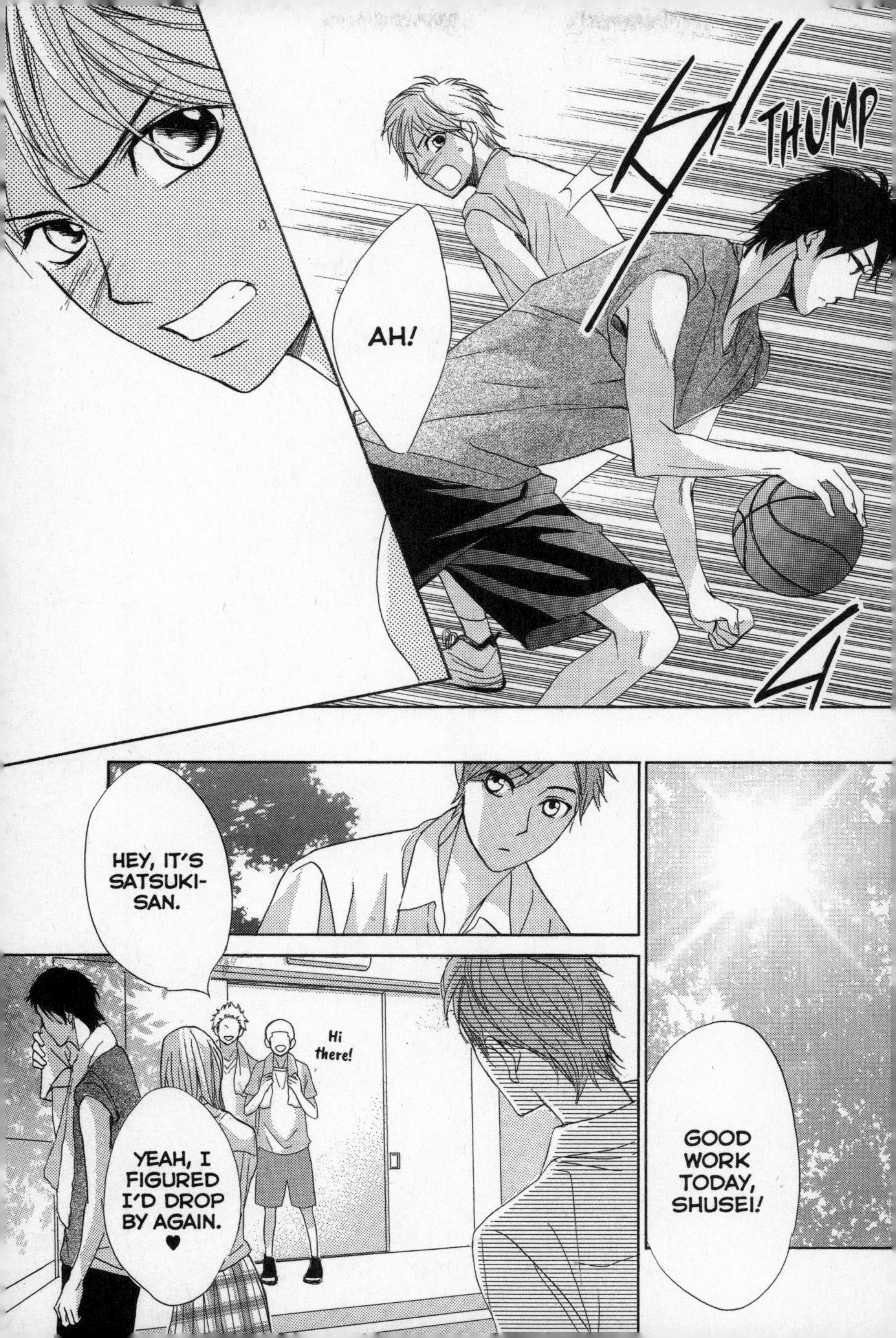
THUMP
AH!
GOOD WORK TODAY, SHUSEI!
HEY, IT'S SATSUKI-SAN.
Hi there!
YEAH, I FIGURED I'D DROP BY AGAIN. ♥

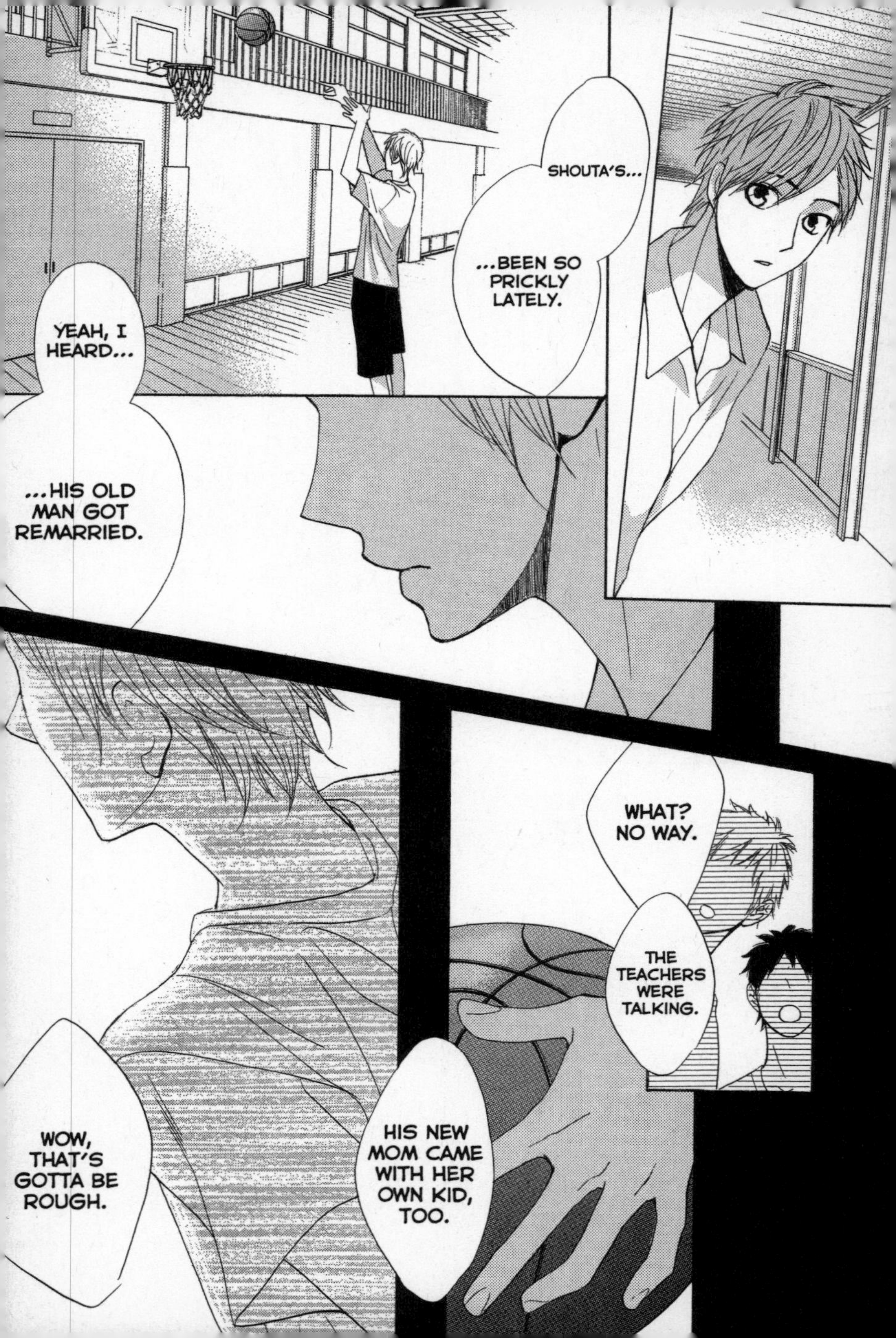
SHOUTA'S...
...BEEN SO PRICKLY LATELY.
YEAH, I HEARD...
...HIS OLD MAN GOT REMARRIED.
WHAT? NO WAY.
THE TEACHERS WERE TALKING.
HIS NEW MOM CAME WITH HER OWN KID, TOO.
WOW, THAT'S GOTTA BE ROUGH.

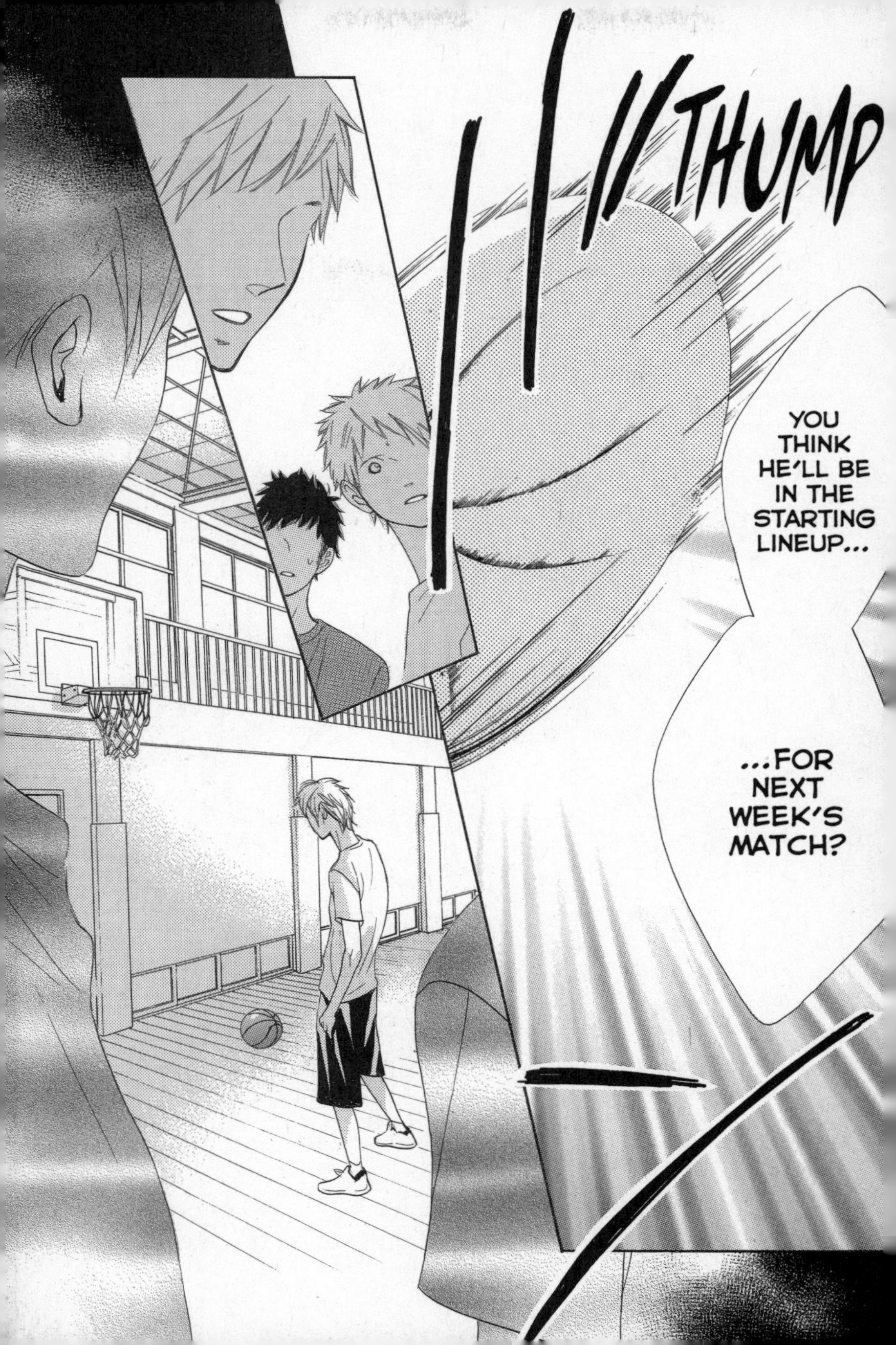
THUMP
YOU THINK HE'LL BE IN THE STARTING LINEUP...
...FOR NEXT WEEK'S MATCH?

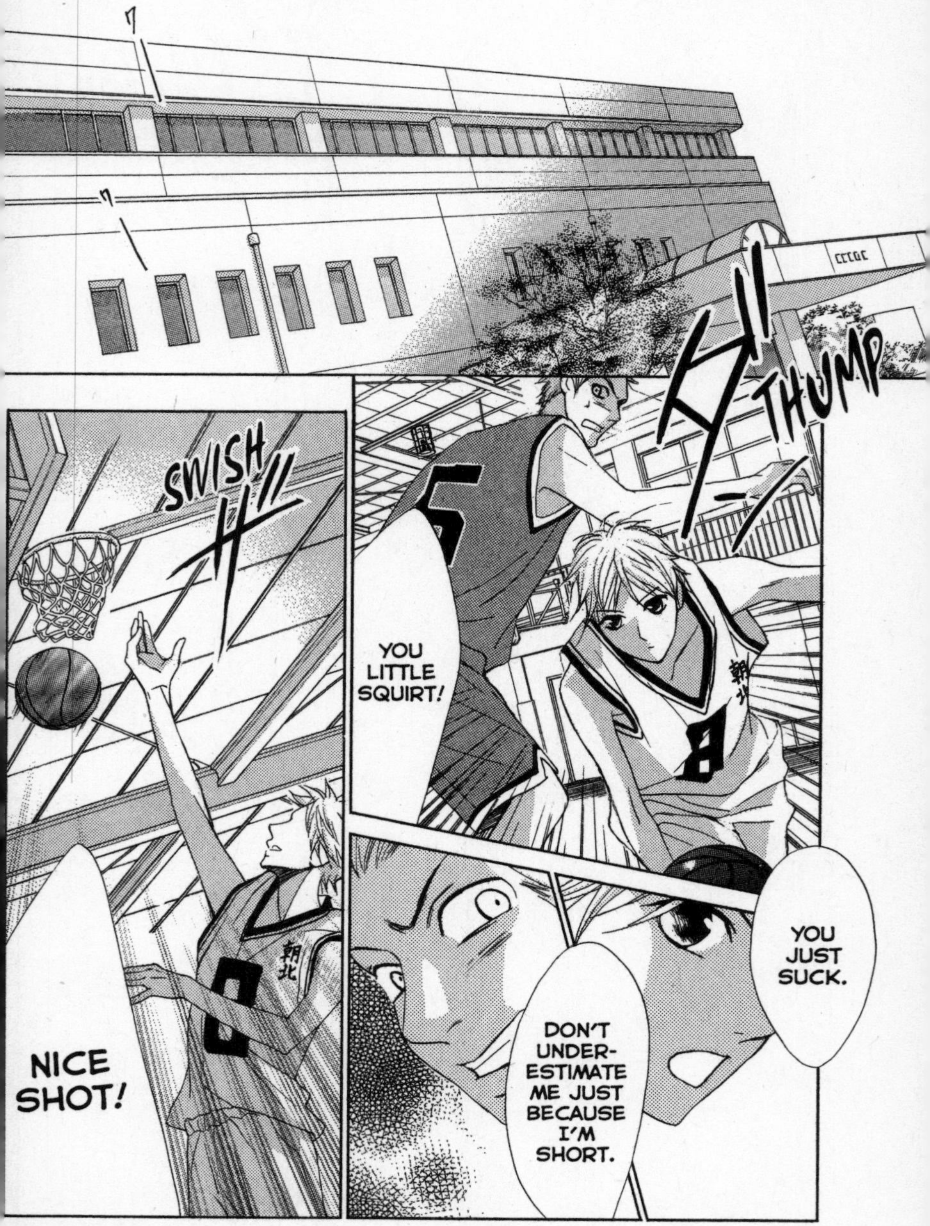
THUMP
YOU LITTLE SQUIRT!
YOU JUST SUCK.
DON'T UNDER-ESTIMATE ME JUST BECAUSE I'M SHORT.
SWISH
NICE SHOT!

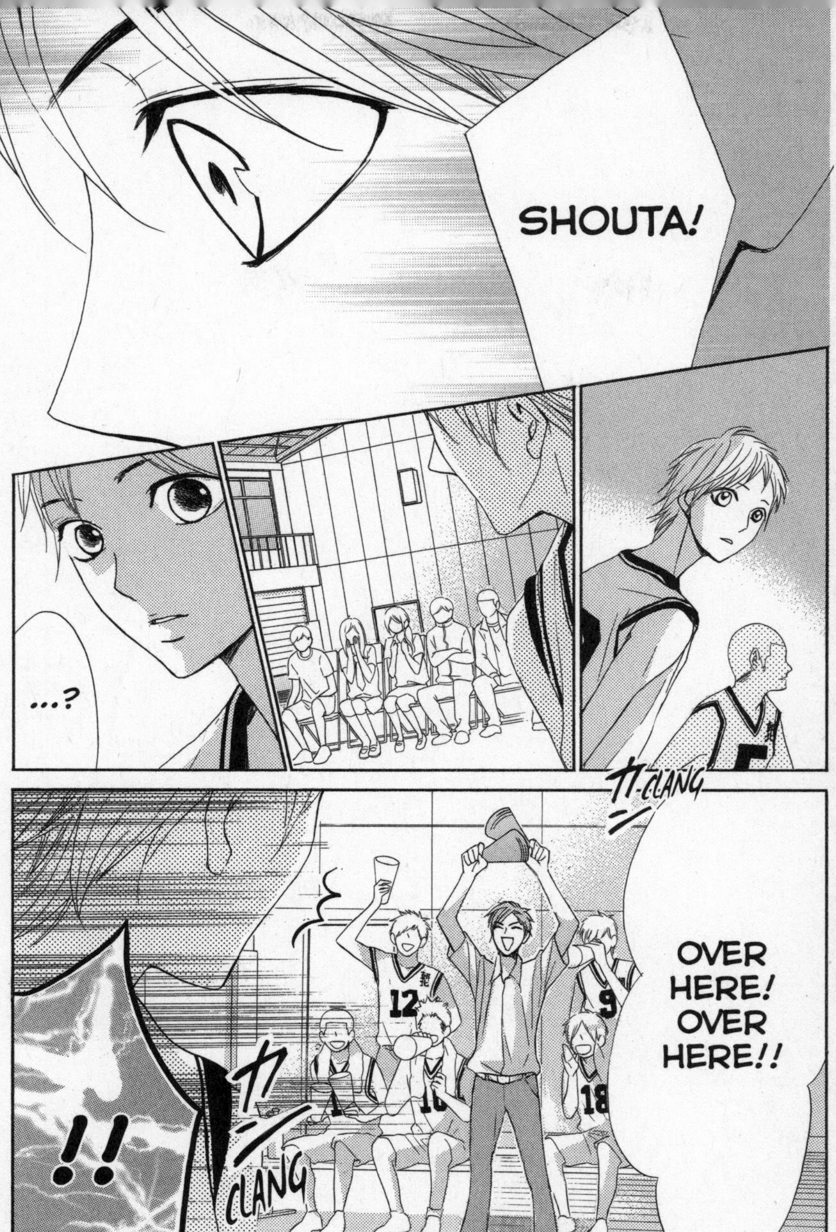
SHOUTA!
...?
CLANG
OVER HERE! OVER HERE!!
!!
CLANG

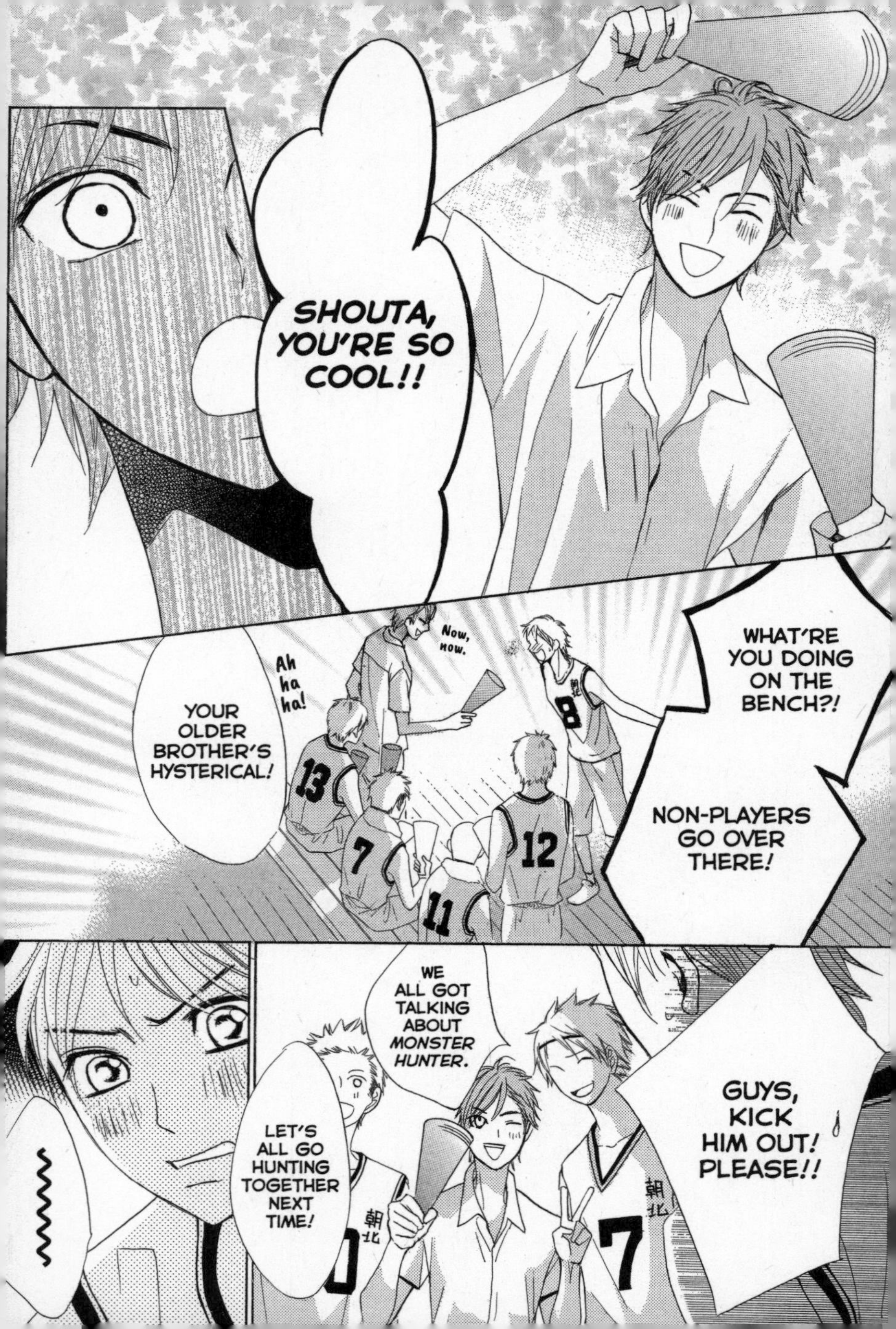
SHOUTA, YOU'RE SO COOL!!
WHAT'RE YOU DOING ON THE BENCH?!
NON-PLAYERS GO OVER THERE!
Now, now.
Ah ha ha!
YOUR OLDER BROTHER'S HYSTERICAL!
GUYS, KICK HIM OUT! PLEASE!!
WE ALL GOT TALKING ABOUT MONSTER HUNTER.
LET'S ALL GO HUNTING TOGETHER NEXT TIME!

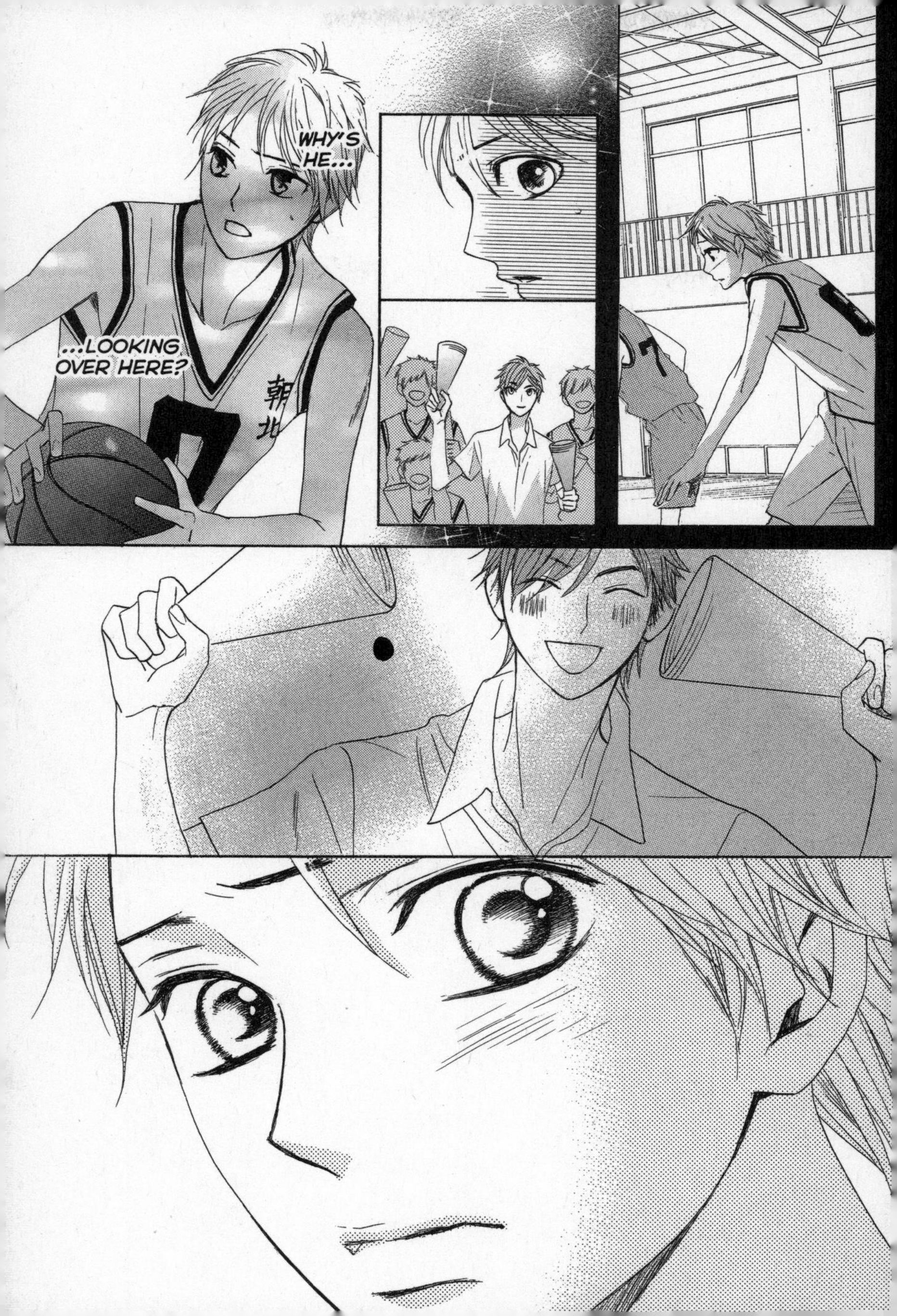
WHY'S HE...
...LOOKING OVER HERE?

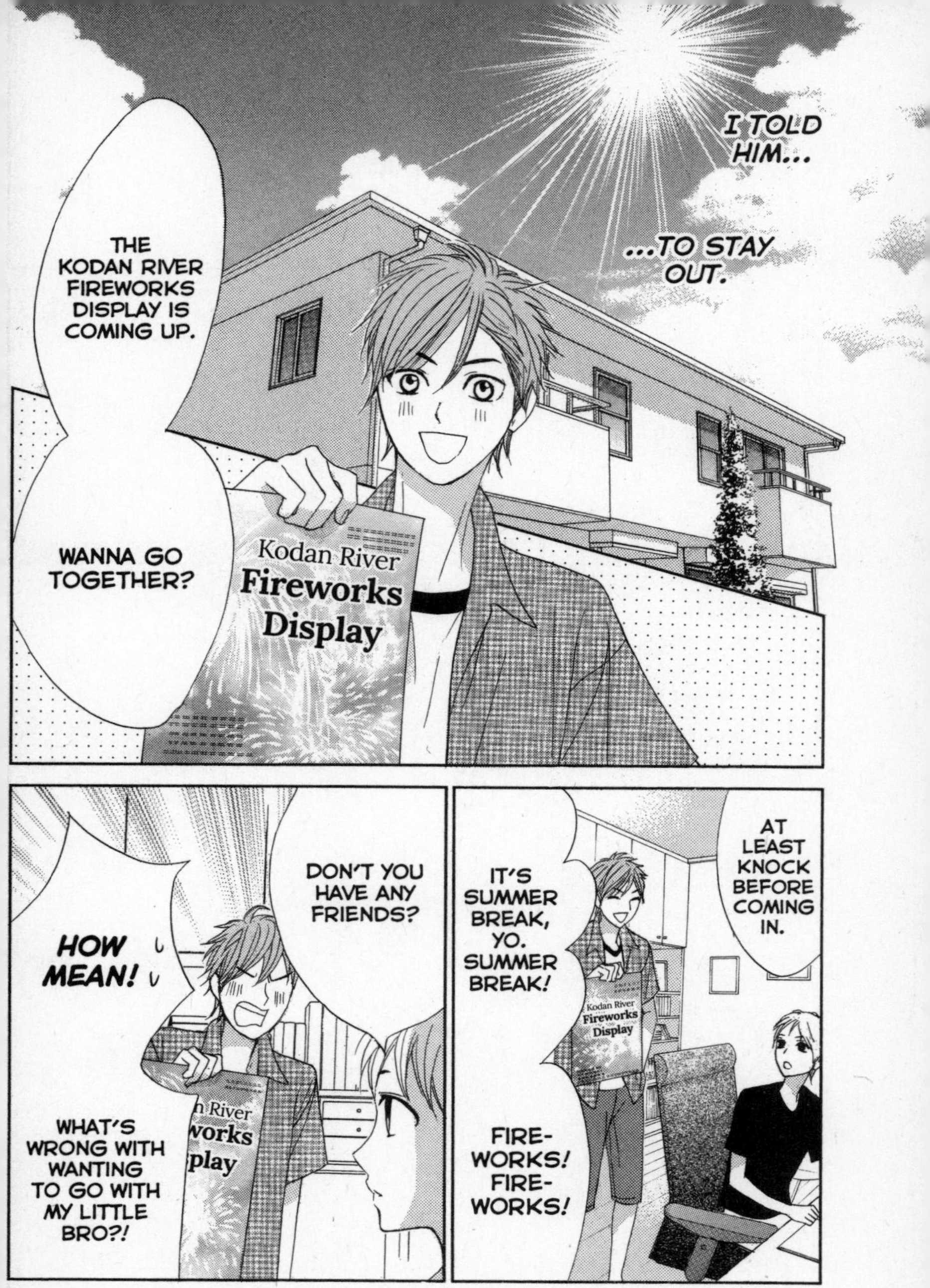

I TOLD HIM...
...TO STAY OUT.
THE KODAN RIVER FIREWORKS DISPLAY IS COMING UP.
WANNA GO TOGETHER?
Kodan River Fireworks Display
AT LEAST KNOCK BEFORE COMING IN.
IT'S SUMMER BREAK, YO. SUMMER BREAK!
Kodan River Fireworks Display
FIRE-WORKS! FIRE-WORKS!
DON'T YOU HAVE ANY FRIENDS?
HOW MEAN!
WHAT'S WRONG WITH WANTING TO GO WITH MY LITTLE BRO?!

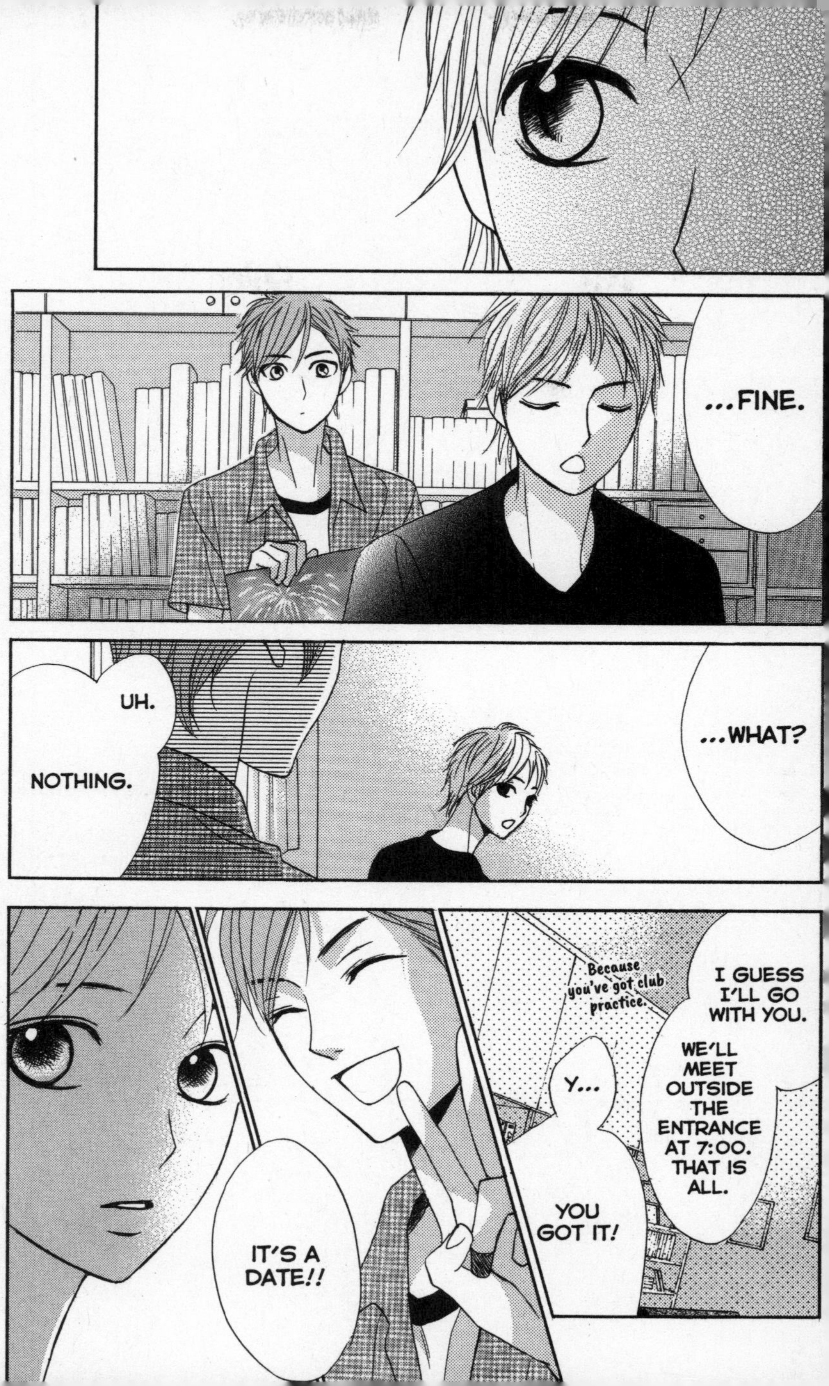
...FINE.
...WHAT?
UH.
NOTHING.
I GUESS I'LL GO WITH YOU.
WE'LL MEET OUTSIDE THE ENTRANCE AT 7:00. THAT IS ALL.
Because you've got club practice.
Y...
YOU GOT IT!
IT'S A DATE!!

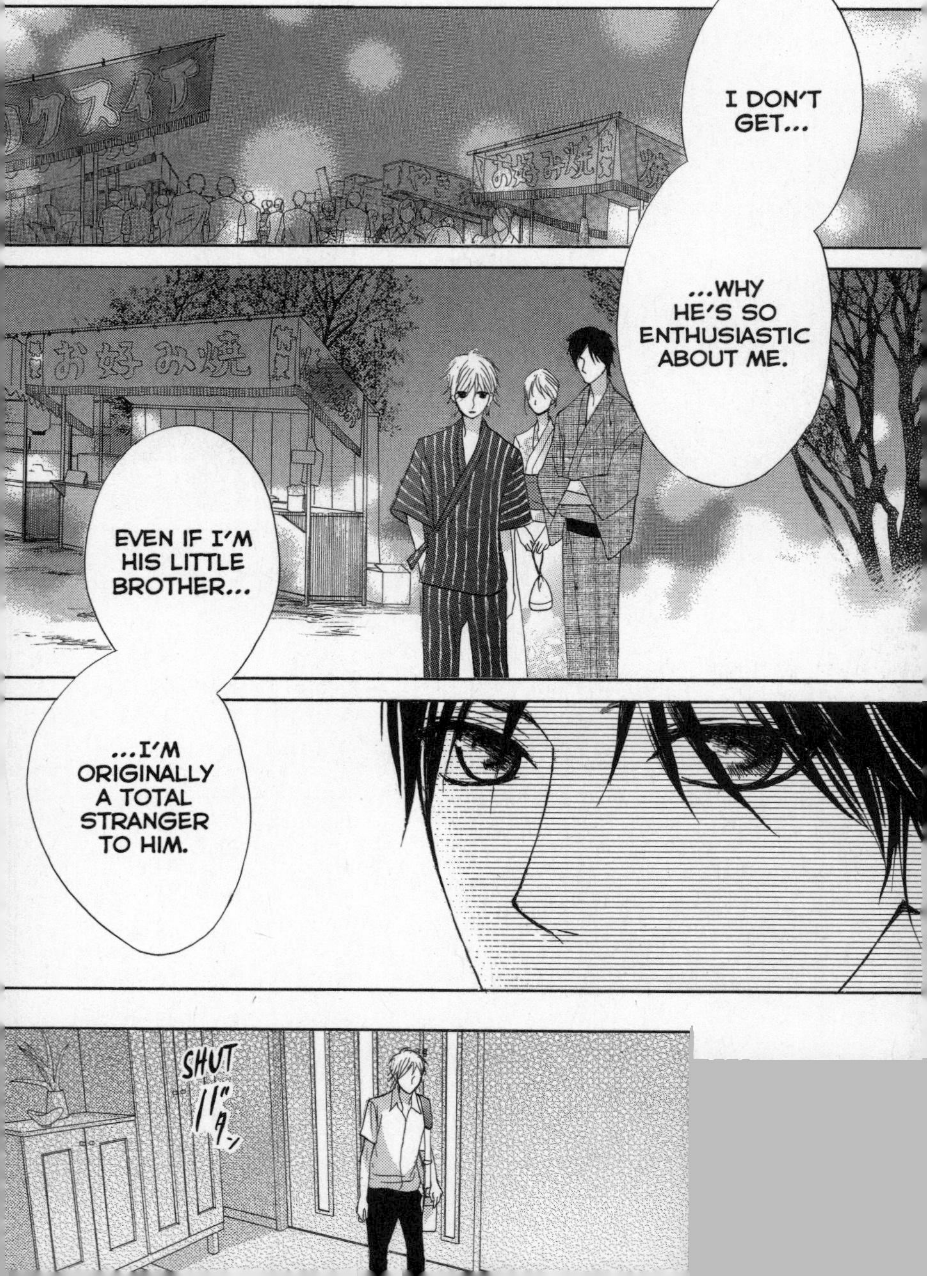
I DON'T GET...
...WHY HE'S SO ENTHUSIASTIC ABOUT ME.
お好み焼
EVEN IF I'M HIS LITTLE BROTHER...
...I'M ORIGINALLY A TOTAL STRANGER TO HIM.
SHUT
バタン

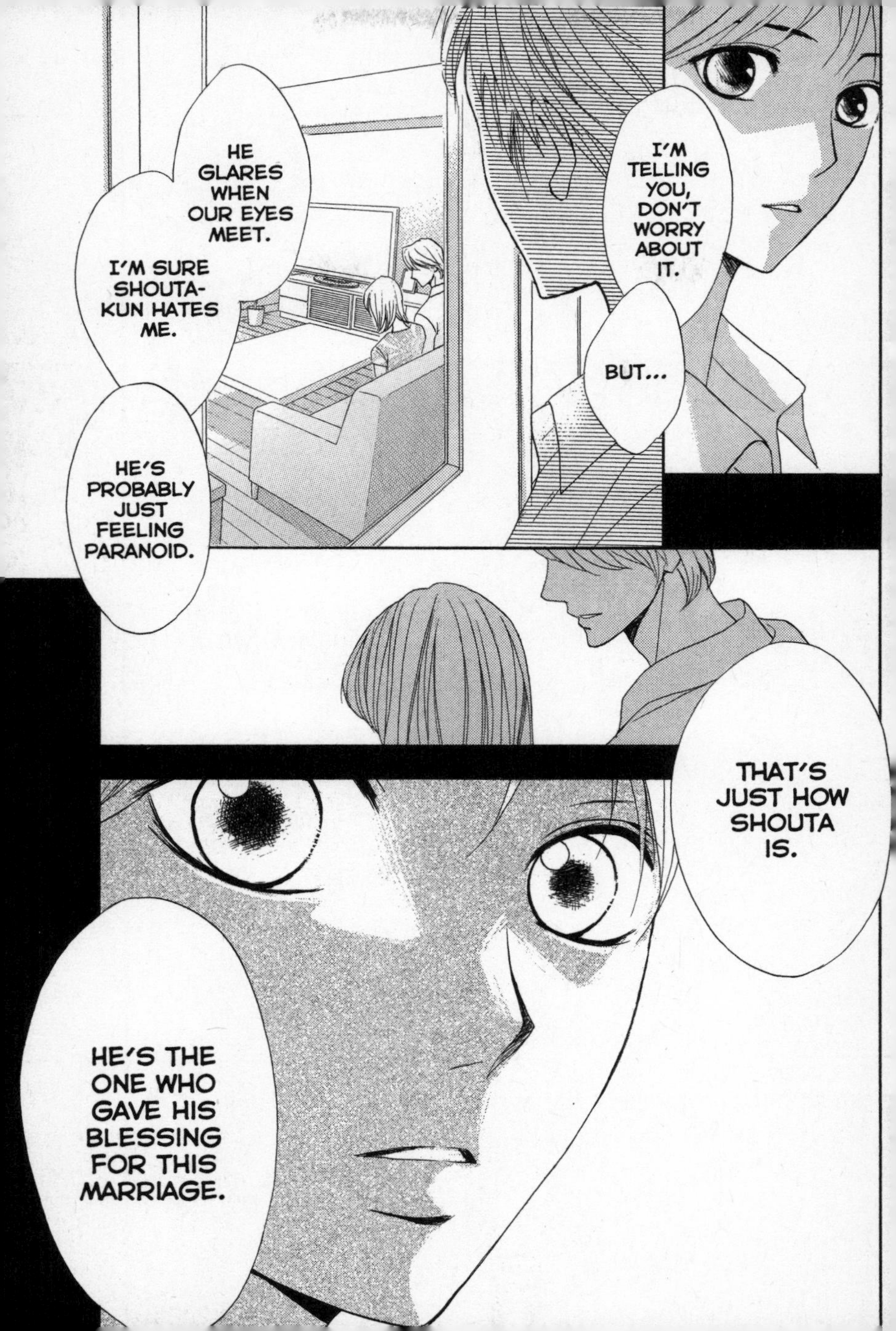
I'M TELLING YOU, DON'T WORRY ABOUT IT.
BUT...
HE GLARES WHEN OUR EYES MEET.
I'M SURE SHOUTA-KUN HATES ME.
HE'S PROBABLY JUST FEELING PARANOID.
THAT'S JUST HOW SHOUTA IS.
HE'S THE ONE WHO GAVE HIS BLESSING FOR THIS MARRIAGE.

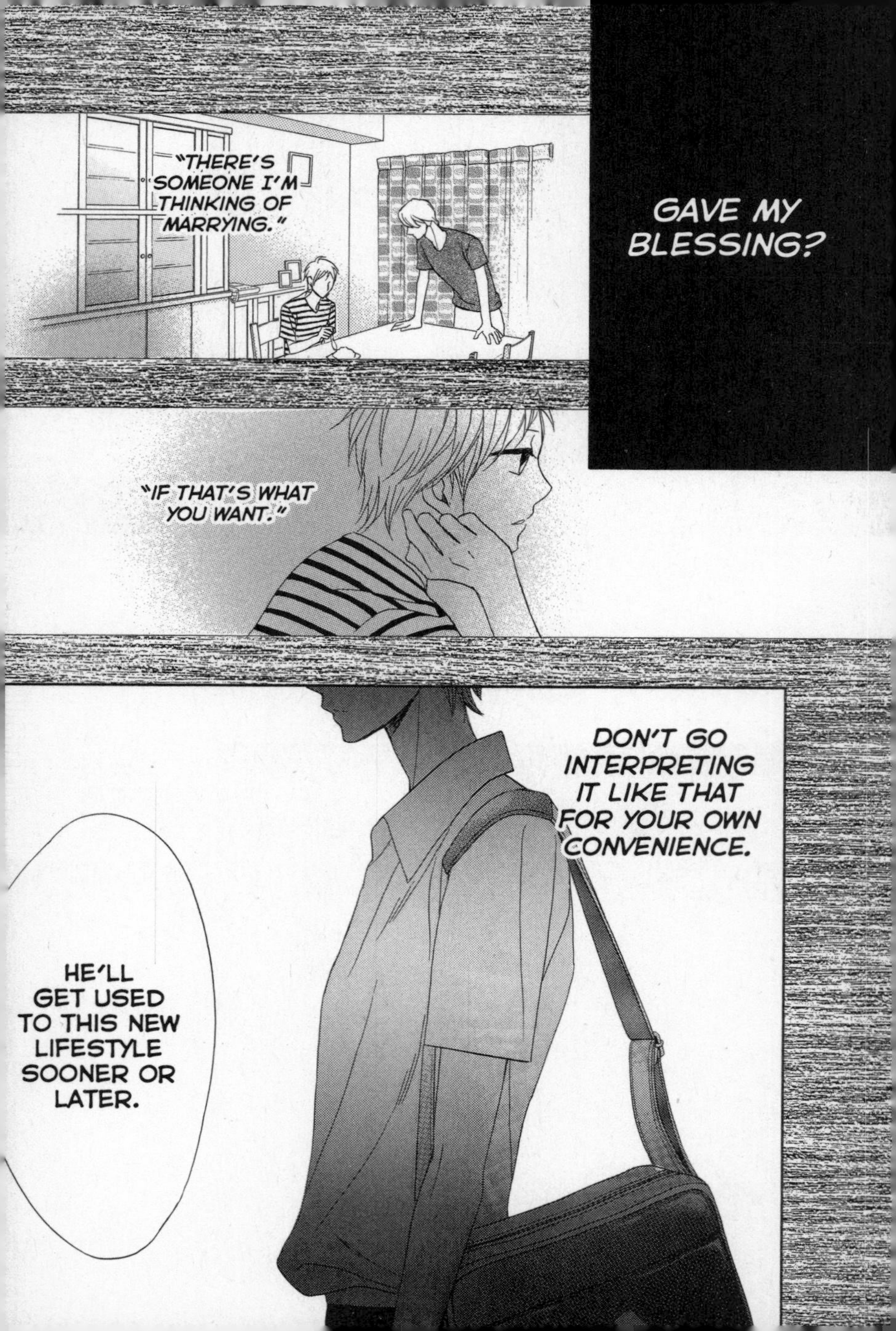
GAVE MY BLESSING?
"THERE'S SOMEONE I'M THINKING OF MARRYING."
"IF THAT'S WHAT YOU WANT."
DON'T GO INTERPRETING IT LIKE THAT FOR YOUR OWN CONVENIENCE.
HE'LL GET USED TO THIS NEW LIFESTYLE SOONER OR LATER.

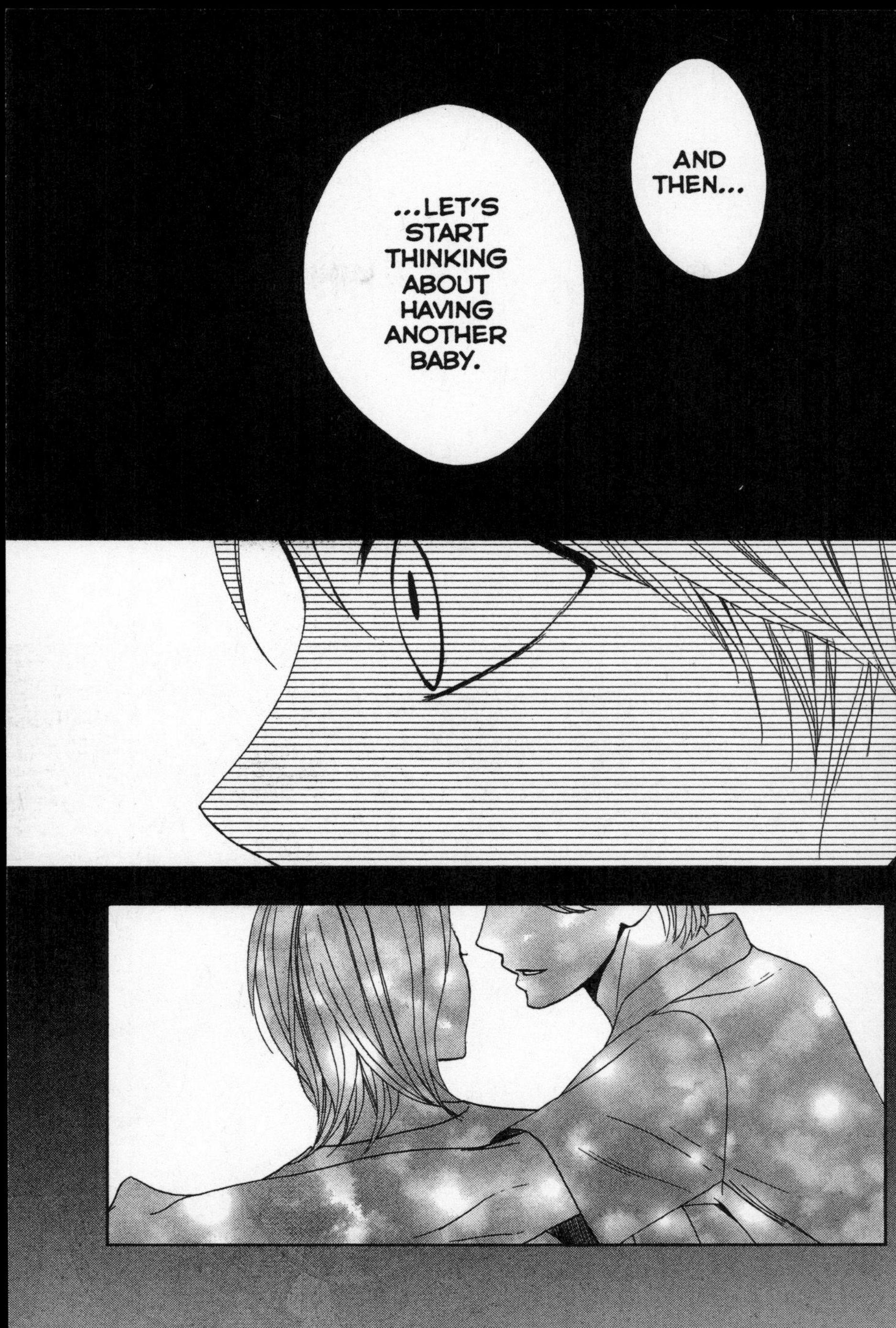
AND THEN...
...LET'S START THINKING ABOUT HAVING ANOTHER BABY.

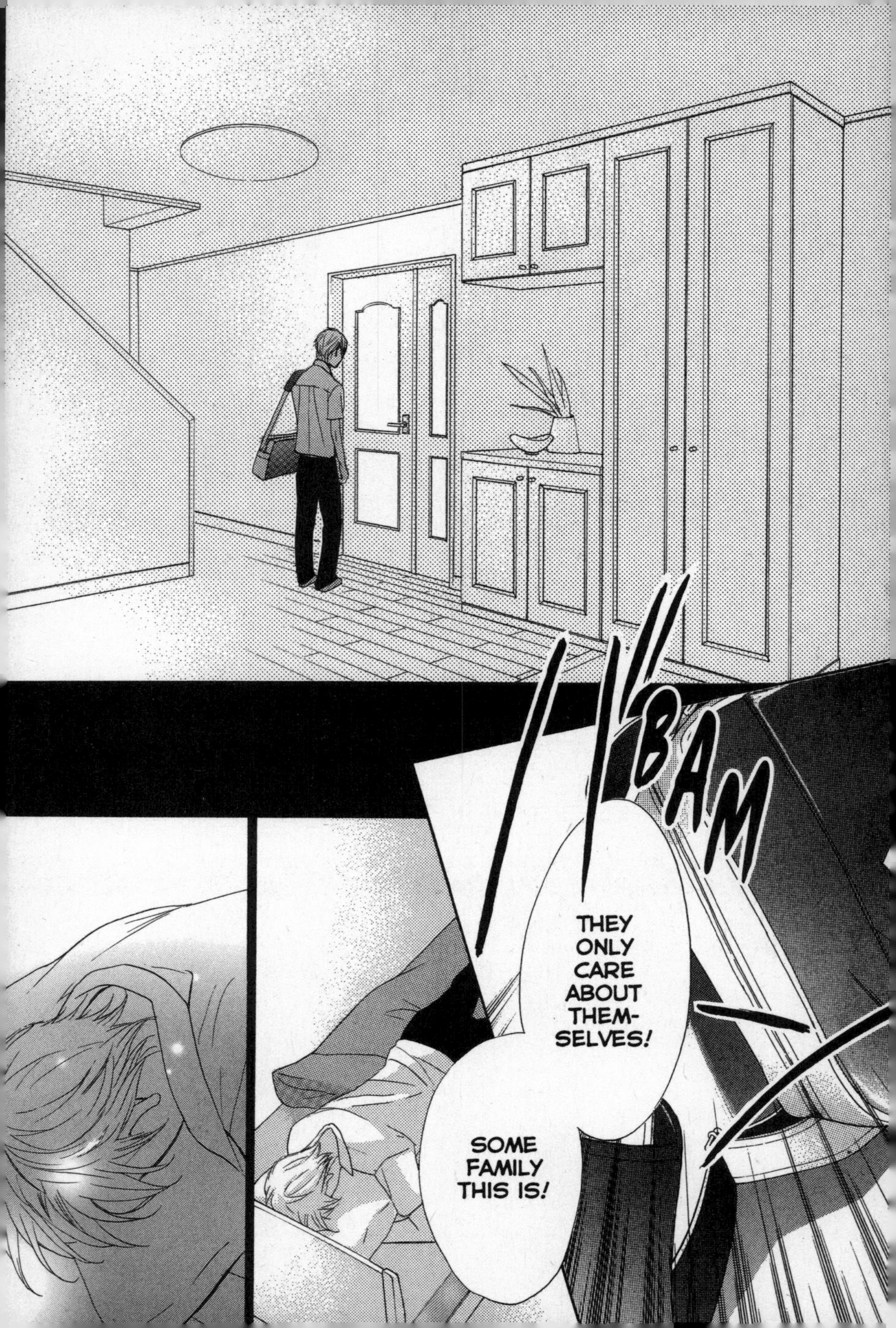
BAM
THEY ONLY CARE ABOUT THEM-SELVES!
SOME FAMILY THIS IS!

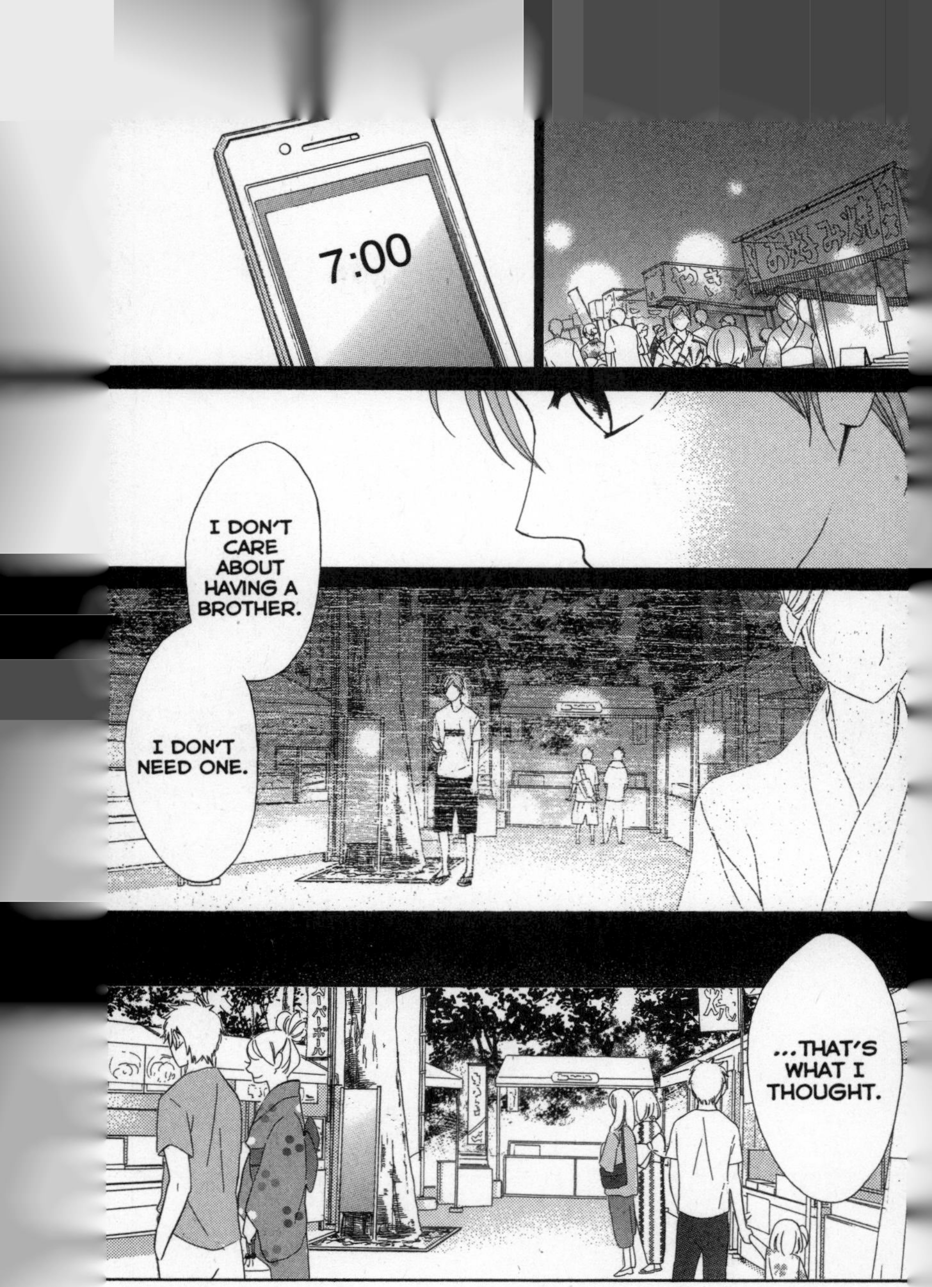
7:00
I DON'T CARE ABOUT HAVING A BROTHER.
I DON'T NEED ONE.
...THAT'S WHAT I THOUGHT.
スーパーボール

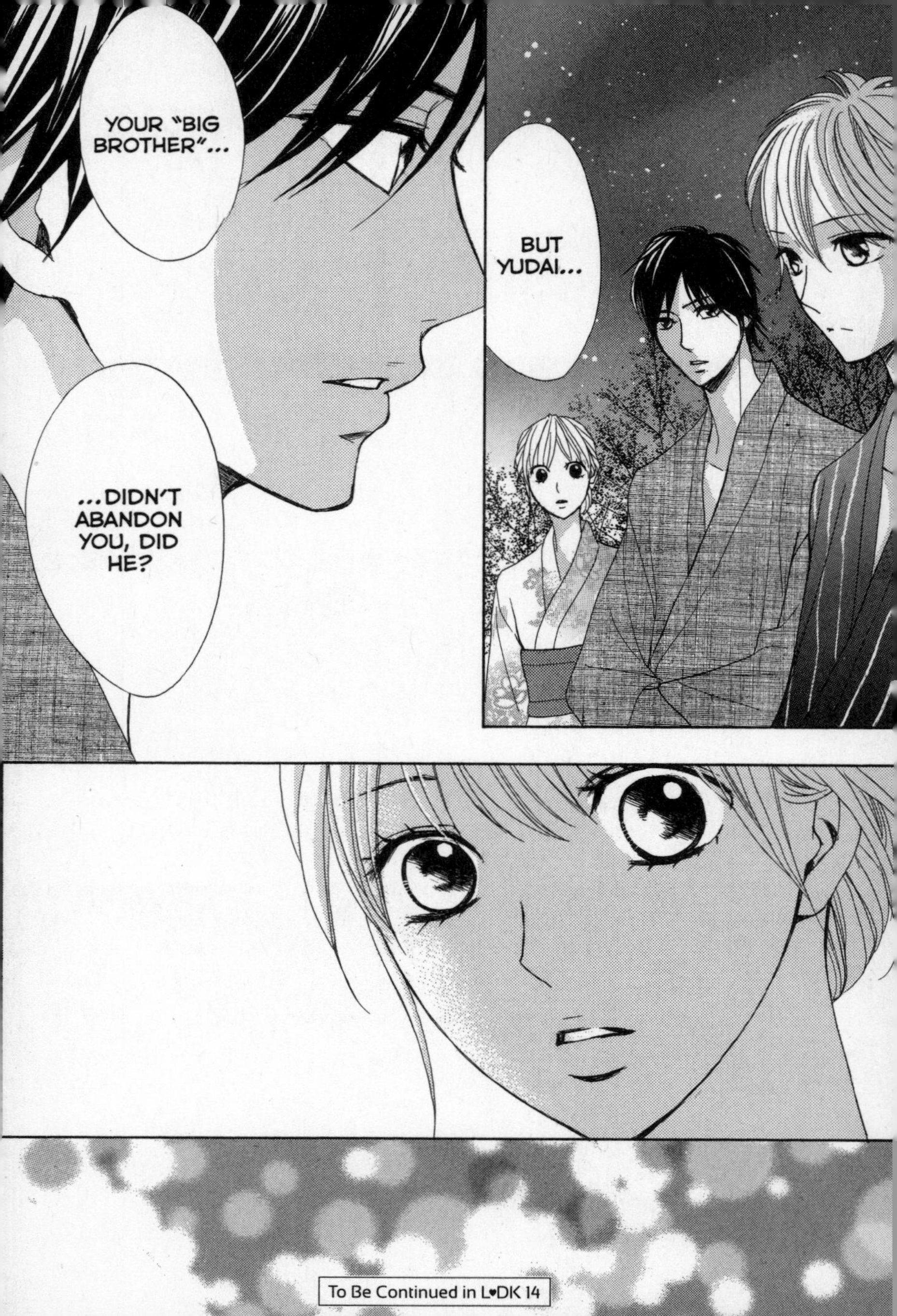
BUT YUDAI...
YOUR "BIG BROTHER"...
...DIDN'T ABANDON YOU, DID HE?
To Be Continued in L♥DK 14

L♥DK

Character File (3)

Wataru Sanjo

- Height, Weight: 176cm, 65kg
- Blood Type: A
- Birthday: April 21, Taurus
- Favorite Animal: Lion
- Favorite Color: Pale Blue, reddish orange
- Strong Point: Patient, early riser
- Special Skills: Cooking (especially Italian), can pop a wheelie on a motorcycle
- Likes: Cleaning, the smell of fabric softener, the night sky, reusable tumblers
- Dislikes: The smell of ginkgo, egotistical people
- Catchphrase: "You serious?"

Character File (4)

Eri Kugayama
(Shusei's older sister)

- Height, Weight: 166cm, 48kg
- Blood Type: B
- Birthday: September 13, Virgo
- Favorite Animal: Bull,
  cat (Chinchilla)
- Favorite Color: Purple, pink, black
- Strong Point: Free thinker, goes at
  her own pace
- Special Skills: Modeling, diving,
  licensed aromatherapist
- Likes: Traveling, black coffee,
  hot yoga, impulse purchases,
  brand clothing from her
  company
- Dislikes: Stubborn people, bugs,
  green peas
- Catchphrase: "I'll kick you."

AFTERWORD

Hello, everyone! This is Ayu Watanabe. Thank you for picking up volume 13 of L♡DK! I am currently partaking in Billy's Boot Camp. Memories (LOL). Anyway, I have some good news to share!!

The cinematic adaptation of L♡DK is coming out next spring!!!

Unbelievable!!! Shocking!!!

The *obi* around this volume shows a shot of both Ayame Goriki-chan, who plays Aoi, and Kento Yamazaki-kun, who plays Shusei!! I'd made a colored illustration for a previous announcement for it (you can see it on the inside flap of the front cover of this volume ♡), and they went and used the pose from there for the promotional shot! I was so moved. When this photo was taken, they still hadn't started filming yet, and would you believe it was the first time these two met?! Though nervous and shy with each other, they started shooting, and you'd never know they weren't anything but on the most intimate of terms. The way they were able to take cues from the cameraman so on point showed that they really are actors. Now, as I sit here writing this afterword, the movie is being filmed with all the best of reviews, and a manga that's reporting on it is scheduled to be released in a whole separate volume. Goriki-chan is bubbly and full of life, and Yamazaki-kun is brimming (?) with phero-mones. I was able to capture some great moments on paper, such as when the two of them were working together to learn their parts and some inside scoops during filming on set, so please look out for those. There were a lot of of candid shots taken in this movie, so please visit the official L♡DK Twitter account (@loveldk) to see them. You won't wanna miss it!

Editor's Note: Japanese manga often include paper *obi*, or paper belt advertisements, wrapped around the lower half of the cover. These often advertise when a manga is being made into an anime, a drama CD, or, in L♡DK's case, is getting a cinematic release.

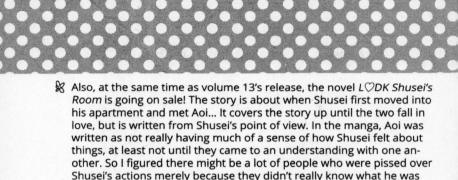

✿ Also, at the same time as volume 13's release, the novel *L♡DK Shusei's Room* is going on sale! The story is about when Shusei first moved into his apartment and met Aoi... It covers the story up until the two fall in love, but is written from Shusei's point of view. In the manga, Aoi was written as not really having much of a sense of how Shusei felt about things, at least not until they came to an understanding with one another. So I figured there might be a lot of people who were pissed over Shusei's actions merely because they didn't really know what he was thinking... (LOL) I can't very well explain to the readers with words his feelings in each and every scene, and I am lacking as a storyteller, so I was looking forward to this coming out, too.

In the novel version, all of Shusei's deepest thoughts are exposed in all their glory. Ran Satomi-san's writing is so wonderful; she did a very accurate job portraying Shusei's emotions. You're not going to want to miss Shusei feeling embarrassed and conflicted over his love. ♡

And with that, I hope I get to see you again in volume 14 so you can see what becomes of their lovey-dovey ♡ living situation.

special thanks

K. Hamano
N. Imai
Y. Negishi
S. Mitsuhashi
M. Nagata

Mosuko
A. Hioki
S. Naka
U. Ishizawa

my family
my friends

M. Morita
Y. Ikumi
M. Horiuchi

AND YOU

Ayu Watanabe
Aug. 2013

Everyday Essentials, Item 13
Tea Set

It's tough on the body to only drink healthy drinks, so I drink a variety of flavored teas. Nothing beats feeling refreshed. But if I take too long of a break, I don't want to return to my desk, so I must exercise caution (LOL).

L♥DK

LDK volume 13 is a work of fiction. Names, characters, places, and incidents are the products of the author's imagination or are used fictitiously. Any resemblance to actual events, locales, or persons, living or dead, is entirely coincidental.

A Kodansha Comics Trade Paperback Original.

Published in the United States by Kodansha Comics, an imprint of Kodansha USA Publishing, LLC, New York.

Publication rights for this English edition arranged through Kodansha Ltd., Tokyo.

First published in Japan in 2013 by Kodansha Ltd., Tokyo, as *L♡DK*, volume 13.

ISBN 978-1-63236-166-0

Printed in the United States of America.

www.kodanshacomics.com

9 8 7 6 5 4 3 2 1

Translation: Christine Dashiell
Lettering: Sara Linsley
Editing: Tiff Ferentini
Kodansha Comics Edition Cover Design: Phil Balsman